THE MAKING OF UNITED STATES INTERNATIONAL ECONOMIC POLICY

D1502979

THE MAKING OF UNITED STATES INTERNATIONAL ECONOMIC POLICY

Principles, Problems, and Proposals for Reform

STEPHEN D. COHEN

Foreword by Paul Volcker

Fifth Edition

Westport, Connecticut
London

Library of Congress Cataloging-in-Publication Data

Cohen, Stephen D.
    The making of United States international economic policy :
principles, problems, and proposals for reform / Stephen D. Cohen ;
foreword by Paul Volcker.—5th ed.
        p.   cm.
    Includes bibliographical references and index.
        ISBN 0–275–96503–1 (alk. paper).—ISBN 0–275–96504–X (pbk. :
alk. paper)
        1. United States—Foreign economic relations.   I. Title.
    II. Title: United States international economic policy.
    HF1455.C576   2000
    337.73—dc21   99–34427

British Library Cataloguing in Publication Data is available.

Library of Congress Catalog Card Number: 99–34427
ISBN: 0–275–96503–1
        0–275–96504–X (pbk.)

First published in 2000

Praeger Publishers, 88 Post Road West, Westport, CT 06881
An imprint of Greenwood Publishing Group, Inc.
www.praeger.com

Printed in the United States of America

The paper used in this book complies with the
Permanent Paper Standard issued by the National
Information Standards Organization (Z39.48–1984).

10 9 8 7 6 5 4 3 2 1

To Linda, Sondra, and Marc

Contents

Foreword by Paul Volcker

It has become a happy tradition for me to write a few words to introduce successive editions of Professor Steve Cohen's text on international economic policy. The substantive challenges seem never-ending, with the speed of globalization and the epidemic of financial crises in recent years underscoring the point. And it all puts pressure on the organizational arrangements that Professor Cohen deals with in this book so extensively, drawing on his long experience as participant and observer.

The words I wrote years ago in introducing the third edition remain relevant:

Questions of international trade and finance are particularly difficult to deal with responsibly as part of the political process. Even more than in most areas of economics, the apparent direct and visible implications or particular actions—such as trade restrictions—on specific firms or industries may be quite different from the ultimate implications for trade, for economic activity, and for employment. The convenient assumption in analyzing an economic policy measure that "all else is held equal" is a particularly thin reed to rely upon in an area where political decisions beget political responses at home or abroad. The sheer complexity and pace of change of international economic life make even technical judgments more difficult. At the other end of the spectrum, questions of foreign policy and national security compete with economic considerations in shaping decisions.

All of that makes more pointed Professor Cohen's long-standing concerns about the policy process and the organization of the federal government for international economic policy. Over the years, intense battles have been endemic within and among the departments of government on precisely those issues. While congressional interest has waxed and waned with changing perceptions of the nation's international economic performance, the sense of policy frustration is clearly rising, and with it the possibility of fresh organizational initiatives.

The battle lines are complicated and vigorously defended not just because bureaucratic turf is involved, as it obviously is, but because of the impression—also obviously correct—that process and organization can affect the broad substantive direction of policy as well as the "efficiency" and coherence with which policy decisions are reached.

What strikes me now, as I write in early 1999, is the renewed importance of international monetary and exchange rate issues, matters that in my judgment have been too long neglected.

The role of both the International Monetary Fund and the World Bank have come into question. The enormous growth in highly liquid funds available for international investment poses new issues, particularly for small open economies. The volatility of their exchange rates is extreme, an important factor disrupting their economic progress. With the new European common currency, new issues in the monetary area will arise among the major economic powers.

In concept, open markets and globalization should bring enormous economic benefits. In practice, achieving that result can't be left to markets alone. Political leadership, most of all from the United States, is essential. But leadership can't be effective in a vacuum. Organization and experience still count. And this book amplifies those issues with skill and understanding.

Introduction and Acknowledgments

International economic policy straddles the two highest priorities of the modern nation-state: economic prosperity and national security. It is simultaneously the external dimension of domestic economic policy and the economic component of foreign policy. This strategic positioning presents a dilemma for international economic policy: its unique characteristics are seldom studied and analyzed as a separate and distinct phenomenon. For too long, it has been viewed either as a low-level subordinate by foreign policy officials or as a foreign cousin by domestic economic policy practitioners. The failure of most U.S. policymakers to respect international economic policy as a distinct entity has been a critical factor in shaping the substance of that policy. Caught between the domestic economic and foreign policy machines, this policy has often been inconsistent, inappropriate, or tepid.

As a consequence, the importance of international economic policy continues to outpace the quality of its content and the efficiency of its conduct. The spiraling dynamic of global interdependence suggests that a second- or third-best U.S. international economic policy already is a costly burden for all major participants in the world economy. The international economic challenges of the twenty-first century are sure to intensify. The United States and its trading partners will be better off if decision-makers and the public at large possess a better understanding of international economic policy. It is also to everyone's advantage if the United States has the best possible organization and procedures to formulate and implement that policy. As used in this book, the policymaking process encompasses a number of different activities: planning, data collection and assessment, identification of problems, articulation of options, making specific decisions, implementation of those decisions, and evaluation of existing policies and programs.[1]

I initiated this study and am updating it because of three assumptions made about the organizational process by which the international economic policy of the United States is planned, decided, and implemented:

- It frequently is an important factor in shaping substance: organizational issues in international economic policy are mainly struggles for power, that is, the ability to convert specific values and priorities into policy. Organization is not merely an ornament in the U.S. international economic policy equation. Procedural control has long been a prize coveted by rival bureaucratic factions living together in uncertain harmony.

- A unique organizational process is, in a sense, the thing that makes international economic policy a distinct field and not simply a subordinate of broader policy areas. The inherently multifaceted nature of the subject requires delicate trade-offs among its four basic elements: domestic and foreign aspects of both economic and political considerations. It is due to the inherent nature of the subject, not an accident of organization, that conflicting priorities must be reconciled so frequently.

- The shortcomings of the process can and should be remedied. Improvements would reduce some of the obstacles to achieving better and more responsive policy substance.

When classified as a comprehensive study aimed specifically at the entire U.S. international economic policymaking organization and written without any use of government funding, this book is still unique. Why should such a vacuum exist? There are several reasons. One is the two-cultures syndrome, whereby economists are uninterested in organizational dynamics, while most political scientists are baffled by the complexity and breadth of economic policy. For illustration, one need only look to published case studies of the bureaucratic politics paradigm, where, typically, one will find nothing beyond analyses of traditional national security issues. Second, the subject matter has not yet caught the public's fancy. Most Americans have only recently (if at all) come to realize that the spiraling importance of international economic policy to their economic well-being justifies their paying closer attention to it. A third reason that this book is unique is that academic political economists writing in this field tend to over-concentrate on the political dynamics of import policy in their effort to produce a unified model of decision-making. This overly narrow focus ignores both the importance of export policy and the fact that while trade policy is an important part of international economic policy, it is not synonymous with this all-inclusive term.

The basic premise of this study is that there are three prerequisites for a more constructive, effective, clear, and consistent U.S. international economic policy. The first is a thorough understanding of the distinctive characteristics of this policy phenomenon. The second is that policymakers have access to objective, up-to-date information about all of the major economic and political factors that they must weigh in the course of reconciling competing domestic and foreign priorities. The last prerequisite is the need for organizational reforms to improve the policymaking process.

The number one objective of this book is to provide the concepts, facts, and proposals needed to satisfy these three prerequisites. I have sought to achieve this objective by means of a scholarly, iconoclastic examination of the international economic policymaking process conducted by an informed nonparticipant "looking in from the outside." A totally dispassionate view toward the merits of any individual bureaucratic perspective or special interest viewpoint is, hopefully, maintained throughout. The hoped-for objectivity of an outsider has been molded to extensive research involving primary source material and interviews with past and present decision-makers. No other non-governmental study exists of organizational arrangements covering the entire range of international economic relations. It continues to be my hope that this book will not only increase understanding of these policies but also stir thinking in the short term about organizational shortcomings and bring about actual change in the medium term.

The first of this study's five parts presents an analysis of the content and context of international economic policy. The emphasis here is on an explanation of how the fusion between political and economic forces has created a separate policy phenomenon with a considerable and growing impact on both domestic economic policy management and world politics.

Part II provides an empirical review of the identities, responsibilities, attitudes, and actions of the major players: the executive branch, the Congress, and special interest groups in the private sector.

Part III utilizes decision-making theory and case studies to explain why and how the U.S. international economic policymaking process functions within the departments, White House offices, and agencies of the executive branch. The notion that there is some single, all-pervasive determinant of, or pattern to, U.S. international economic policymaking is rejected in favor of the thesis that a number of decision-making models must be employed to explain actions by government officials who are not operating by a single set of rules or a single behavioral pattern. A large number of case studies are offered to demonstrate how each of eight intra–executive branch decision-making models has produced specific policies. Additional decisions are described to suggest ample numbers of sui generis actions that do not conform to any one of the principal models. The oft-used gambit of selectively choosing a limited number of examples to support a preordained master theory of how the system works has not been used here.

In Part IV, I demonstrate how U.S. international economic policymaking since the 1980s has been dominated by the inter-branch model in which Congress acting unilaterally or in concert with the administration has charted the broad directions of that policy. Following a chapter on the dynamics of the model, three chapters are each devoted to a major case study illustrating the diverse forms of executive-legislative efforts to craft policy guidelines suitable to their divergent philosophies and needs.

The final section of this study begins with a critique of existing organization and an outline of the requirements for an optimal U.S. decision-making process. This exposition sets the stage for the last chapter's recommendations for improving the U.S. international economic policymaking process. The proposals for improving the existing system are based on a number of criteria, such as not favoring any single constituency or cause. Another important criterion utilized is that the proposals for reform reflect an appreciation of the unique, distinctive nature of international economic policy as a conglomeration of domestic and external political and economic goals.

All in all, this study is more a beginning than a definitive statement. The quantity and quality of the international economic policy literature still fail to do justice to the importance and distinctiveness of this subject. Most foreign policy scholars are still lacking in their understanding of both economic forces in general and the growing impact of external economic forces on the domestic economy. Similarly, domestic economists need to become more aware that history and culture are sufficiently different among countries that all market economies do not necessarily function the same and that national economic institutions are not universally identical in their design and operation. The gap between political science and economics must be bridged when the subject is international economic policy.

Reasonable people may disagree with my concept of international economic policy. They may also disagree with the recommendations. Second only to actual acceptance of most of the recommended reforms, the success of this study will be measured by its ability to provoke thought and thereby engender a lengthy and provocative debate about the making of this policy in the United States.

Several people have provided me with important assistance in the preparation of the fifth edition of this book. First and foremost, I want to express deep appreciation to my graduate assistants, Kristina Medic, Alina Eldred, Erin J. Leonard, and Emily Hemstreet, for their extensive and excellent assistance both in the research phase and the editing process. I extend a collective thank-you to the numerous government officials and business lobbyists who generously gave of their time to speak to me on a not-for-attribution basis. Their firsthand knowledge of how things work in Washington was invaluable to me in analyzing the inner workings of the international economic policy process. Of course, I take full responsibility for all factual mistakes, opinions, and recommendations for change. On a personal note, I wish to again extend special appreciation to my wife, Linda, and my children, Sondra and Marc, for their encouragement in writing this book.

NOTE

1. This study views the totality of the U.S. international economic policymaking process in the same way that William Wallace viewed the British foreign policy process: the system is less one of a series of separately identifiable decisions than of "a continuous flow of policy, in which successive messages received about the international environ-

ment, the interpretation given to the information received, the preconceptions of those responsible for policy, their assessment of possible alternatives, . . . and the organizational context within which they make policy, all combine to shape the direction of that flow'' William Wallace, *The Foreign Policy Process in Britain* (London: Royal Institute of International Affairs, 1975), pp. 5–6.

Acronyms

AID	Agency for International Development
ATP	Advanced Technology Program
CBO	Congressional Budget Office
CCC	Commodity Credit Corporation (Agriculture Department)
CEA	Council of Economic Advisers
CEP	Council on Economic Policy
CFEP	Council on Foreign Economic Policy
CIA	Central Intelligence Agency
CIEC	Conference on International Economic Cooperation
CIEP	Council on International Economic Policy
CRS	Congressional Research Service
DARPA	Defense Advanced Research Projects Agency
DCC	Development Coordination Committee
DICP	Department of International Commercial Policy (as proposed in this book)
DIT	Department of Industry and Technology (as proposed in this book)
E/B	Bureau of Economic and Business Affairs (State Department)
EC	European Community
EEC	European Economic Community
EMS	European Monetary System
EPA	Environmental Protection Agency
EPB	Economic Policy Board
EPC	Economic Policy Council

EPG	Economic Policy Group
ESF	Economic Support Fund
EU	European Union (formerly known as the EEC and EC)
Ex-Im	Export-Import Bank
FAS	Foreign Agricultural Service
FCC	Federal Communications Commission
FCCSET	Federal Coordinating Council for Science, Engineering, and Technology
FDA	Food and Drug Administration
Fed	Board of Governors of the Federal Reserve System
FMC	Federal Maritime Commission
GAO	General Accounting Office
GATT	General Agreement on Tariffs and Trade
GDP	gross domestic product
G-7	Group of Seven countries
IDCA	International Development Cooperation Agency
IMF	International Monetary Fund
ITA	International Trade Administration (Commerce Department)
ITC	International Trade Commission
LDCs	less developed countries
MAI	Multilateral Agreement on Investment
MFN	most favored nation (tariff treatment)
MITI	Ministry of International Trade and Industry (Japan)
MNCs	multinational corporations
MTNs	multilateral trade negotiations
NAC	National Advisory Council (on International Monetary and Financial Policies)
NAFTA	North American Free Trade Agreement (or Area)
NEC	National Economic Council
NEP	New Economic Policy
NGOs	non-governmental organizations
NICs	Newly Industrialized Countries
NIST	National Institute of Standards and Technology (Commerce Department)
NSC	National Security Council
NSF	National Science Foundation
NSTC	National Science and Technology Council
NTBs	non-tarriff barriers
OECD	Organization for Economic Cooperation and Development

OIA	Office of International Affairs (Treasury Department)
OMB	Office of Management and Budget
OPEC	Organization of Petroleum Exporting Countries
OPIC	Overseas Private Investment Corporation
OTA	Office of Technology Assessment
PCG	Policy Coordination Group
P.L. 480	Public Law 480 (Food for Peace)
R&D	research and development
STR	Special Representative for Trade Negotiations (renamed USTR, 1980)
TPC	Trade Policy Committee
TPCC	Trade Promotion Coordinating Committee
UNCTAD	United Nations Conference on Trade and Development
USDA	U.S. Department of Agriculture
USTR	U.S. Trade Representative (prior to 1980, known as STR)
WTO	World Trade Organization

Part I

The Unique Nature of International Economic Policy

1   The Content of International Economic Policy

> Economic forces are in fact political forces. Economics can be treated neither as a minor accessory of history, nor as an independent science in the light of which history can be interpreted. . . . The science of economics presupposes a given political order, and cannot be profitably studied in isolation from politics.
>
> —E. H. Carr, 1939

This book examines, explains, and critiques the processes by which the U.S. government formulates and implements a series of measures collectively known as international economic policy. Before turning to these tasks, it is imperative to first explain fully and precisely what is being examined and why its unique nature creates a unique policymaking process. The implicit thesis is that international economic policy should be thought of as existing in a third dimension, not simply as a subset of either foreign policy or domestic economic policy. It is a separate, distinguishable policy that transcends its component policy sectors. The balancing act necessary to reconcile the frequently conflicting priorities of its internal and external elements is what gives international economic policy its substantive importance and unique character. This complex reconciliation act also presents decision-makers with unique procedural challenges.

"International economic policy" is a term infused with value judgment and one that is often misinterpreted. I have used the term throughout this book in lieu of the more commonly used phrase "foreign economic policy." I strongly believe that the former is the preferable term because in today's world, policymaking in this area must take account of too many questions of *domestic* economic and political policy to be considered "foreign." It increasingly is formulated by agencies whose jurisdiction centers on domestic policy. International economic interdependence has blurred the dividing line between domestic economic performance and global economic trends. The term "foreign economic policy" connotes a subdivision of foreign policy and is, therefore, an over-simplification. International economic policy is best viewed as an integrated whole, defying simple classification as domestic or foreign. It should not be compartmentalized into either an international political or a domestic economic policy framework. Downplaying the expanding linkage between domestic economic policy management objectives and international economic relations is inconsistent with a full and accurate understanding of this book's subject matter.

Finally, it is critical not to make the error of equating international economic policy with its most widely recognized component, foreign trade. The former is an umbrella term encompassing many other important issue areas, such as international finance and assistance to poor countries.

DEFINITION AND SCOPE

International economic policies, in the broadest sense, are usually efforts by governments to modify the ways in which goods, services, and capital would otherwise flow across national boundaries if a completely free market situation prevailed. "Policy" in this case is a substitute for the laissez-faire (hands-off) option, that is, the government's choosing to do absolutely nothing to interfere with the outcome of free market forces. Most international economic policies adopted by a sovereign government represent political guidelines designed to limit or expand cross-border transactions in accordance with its collective perceptions of what is in the best interest of the country. These interventions take the form, among other things, of import barriers, export promotion efforts, grants to alleviate poverty in developing countries, and short-term loans to assist countries suffering severe capital flight or speculative attacks on their currencies.

Government officials in every country believe that most of the time they are a better alternative than the greed-driven market mechanism to assure that economic activities, domestic and foreign, are compatible with the national interest and well-being of the population at large. Even in the United States, policymakers justify their efforts to offset market forces by arguing that economic efficiency is not always the highest priority goal. National security or social stability may be deemed to be more important in any given situation. Furthermore, no government feels the obligation to ignore the instabilities associated with occasional "market failure." All governments are prepared to intervene when they perceive markets to be acting irrationally or verging on panic. (This explains, for example, official interventions in the foreign exchange market when currencies are gyrating wildly.)

A second broad definition of the nature of international economic policy applies to those less frequent occasions when it moves in the opposite direction. Governments periodically seek freer markets by negotiating reductions or elimination of governmentally imposed impediments to global transactions, namely, barriers to trade and restrictions on capital movements. A third broad definition applies to sporadic efforts to modify existing regulations of international markets. In this case, policy consists of negotiators pursuing agreements that would broaden the rules of the international trade, monetary, or investment systems and/or enhance the power of an international economic organization to interpret and enforce these rules.

An all-inclusive definition is that international economic policy is the aggregate of a country's ongoing efforts to deal with its disparate and multifaceted relationship with the world economy. It represents the sum total of actions by nation-states intended to affect the economic environment beyond their national jurisdiction. Such policy is a hybrid, combining elements of foreign policy with economic policy.[1]

Sovereign governments constantly assess their precise needs, objectives, and values. International economic policies serve as important means to the end of achieving domestic and external political and economic goals that the official sector has determined would enhance the country's national interests. Whether invoked unilaterally, bilaterally, trilaterally, or multilaterally, these policies collectively set the agenda of economic relations among governments.

An optimum international economic policy expands a country's domestic economic strength, improves international political relations, and enhances global economic efficiency. All too often, however, it is an either/or case, and considerations of global efficiency are unceremoniously brushed aside by perceptions of domestic or international political necessity. First-best international economic policies are less common than second-best measures. All governments repeatedly bend to internal political pressures and provide economic benefits to narrowly focused but vociferous (and sometimes well-financed) interest groups at the expense of the long-term welfare of the general population.

Many criteria can—and should—be used to demonstrate the varied characteristics of international economic policies. Appreciation of the extent of the heterogeneity of substance is critically important to understanding the inevitability of a heterogeneous policymaking process. There can be no "one size fits all" decision-making procedure because there is no single form of international economic policy to be decided. The lack of uniformity in what is being considered necessitates modifications to policymaking dynamics.

One method of disaggregating the broad concept of "international economic policy" is to look at precisely which economic sector is being addressed. In most cases these policies are formulated to affect one of several defined "systems" that comprise the international economic order. The trade and monetary systems are the most important and the systems with the most clearly defined rules and obligations. More informal, abstract systems relate to international financial, investment, development, energy, and science and technology issues. A relatively new "quasi system" involves efforts by the major industrialized countries (the Group of Seven) to coordinate domestic monetary and fiscal policies to enhance international economic stability and efficiency. Sometimes multilateral coordination is replaced by (usually unsolicited) offerings of advice by one government to another on how to remedy alleged deficiencies in existing internal policies, for example, U.S. pressures on Japan in the late 1990s to adopt stimulative economic measures.

A second means of disaggregating international economic policy is to examine the two levels (at least in market-based economies) on which these policies operate. The first consists of government-business relations, a reflection of the fact that the vast majority of international economic activities originates in the private sector. Global commerce continues to grow in size and importance, from trade in goods and services (transportation, tourism, data transmission, etc.) to capital movements (bank lending, short-term speculative money flows, purchases and sales of foreign stocks and bonds, and long-term foreign direct investment). New international economic policies usually arise in response to market-driven changes in economic transactions, for example, increased trade in the information technology sector and the rising propensity of short-term private capital to flow massively into and then out of emerging markets.

Every sovereign government on the planet intrudes in international commercial relations, ostensibly on behalf of its citizens and businesses. As part of their larger agenda to promote the well-being of the citizenry, all governments on occasion implement policies to help the private sector to increase their exports. Official ''enhancements'' include encouraging currency depreciation, providing subsidized export credits, and making demands for reductions in foreigners' import barriers. In other situations, the objective of policy is to restrain the business community's natural impulse to pursue profits. This can be accomplished by imposing controls on currency outflows and on export shipments or by imposing import barriers.

None of these policies is formulated and implemented in a political vacuum. Most governments act to restrict imports only after having been on the receiving end of demands for protection by agitated companies or unions. Similarly, government officials usually make demands on foreign countries to reduce their import barriers only after having been prompted to do so by complaints from domestic farmers and companies who argue that their export potential is being curtailed.

The degree to which the aggregate economic interests of consumers and friendly countries can be ignored when politicians decide to enhance the wealth of special interest groups is underscored by the barriers imposed on U.S. sugar imports. American consumers are forced to pay approximately twice the world market price for sugar as the result of the government's ongoing desire to reward a handful of large and a few thousand small domestic producers with artificially high prices.

The second level of international economic policy activity is formal government-to-government consultations. Issues that touch directly on national sovereignty or on national security—coordination of domestic macroeconomic policy, international monetary reform, imposition of economic sanctions on countries deemed to pose a military threat, and so on—are handled by confidential negotiations among senior officials with little or no input being solicited or received from the private sector.

A third means of diagraming differences in international economic policies is to differentiate at least five different generic kinds of policies:

- long-term initiatives, such as proposing a new round of global negotiations to liberalize foreign trade flows or amendments to the articles of agreement of an international economic organization;
- quick response reactions, such as emergency assistance to a country facing mass starvation or an explosive financial crisis;
- maintenance of the policy status quo, such as rejecting an industry's request for the imposition of import barriers or calls to strip China of its most-favored-nation trade status;
- implementation of incremental policy, such as by making additional demands on China and Japan to further open their markets to U.S. goods; and
- administration of legislatively established programs, wherein policymaking by the U.S. executive branch is unusually circumscribed.

Decisions associated with the administration of international economic programs belong to a distinct stratum of policymaking. Policies are abstract articulations of national goals, whereas programs consist of relatively concrete procedures that are designed to achieve these goals. Foreign aid is a means to the policy-mandated end of helping poorer countries to develop. The escape clause and antidumping laws equate to programs that serve the policy goal of providing avenues of relief to the private sector from the adverse impact of import competition. Export promotion measures help realize the goal of increasing overseas sales of goods and services.

When administering programs, the U.S. executive branch more often than not is simply enforcing congressionally passed statutes. In a literal sense, there may be no policymaking. For example, detailed language instructs the executive branch as to how it investigates accusations that foreign companies are dumping, that is, selling goods in the United States at less than fair value, and how it determines whether such actions are injuring American producers. If both dumping and injury are found to exist, the administration has no choice about what to do next: the law unequivocally mandates imposition of dumping duties equivalent to the estimated margin of dumping of the product in question. Detailed legislative language also spells out the standards of behavior that countries must meet in order to be eligible to receive U.S. foreign aid.

In addition to these procedural criteria, policies affecting international economic relations can also be differentiated according to the relative substantive mix between the economic and political components of a policy action. Decisions on issues that are highly politically charged in the domestic or international spheres obviously require careful consideration at a senior level. Political sensitivity is inescapable in those trade actions that would profoundly affect income distribution, either by restricting imports or by subsidizing a domestic industry targeted for development.

Policy decisions that are relatively non-politicized and technical in nature can be determined by a limited number of officials mostly, not exclusively, on their economic merits. Since policymaking is an inherently political process, no decision can be made that is 100 percent free of political overtones. The Basle Concordat (which sets out complex international standards for banking regulation) and criteria for determining whether "disorderly" trading conditions requiring intervention exist in the foreign exchange markets are two examples of relatively apolitical decisions dominated by a handful of economic specialists. Within the realm of foreign aid, the political-economic mix of decision-making can differ significantly. Determination of which countries get how much money would be a highly political exercise; evaluations of specific projects would be technical in nature; and the provision of emergency disaster aid would mainly be a simple humanitarian gesture.

A final means of disaggregating international economic policy decisions is to plot a vertical axis for ranking policies in a hierarchy based on importance and impact. They run the gamut from high-visibility, high-impact issues that attract the active attention of presidents and prime ministers, through important issues requiring decisions at ministerial level, down to issues that are so technical or narrowly focused that they are dealt with at the working level in the bureaucracy.

At the very top of the hierarchy are broad statements of principle about the desired nature of the systems comprising the global economic order: support for a floating exchange rate system over a fixed rate system or for a liberal trading system in lieu of protectionism. Approving financial aid to Russia or retaining most-favored-nation status for China requires presidential attention. Examples of decisions at the "second layer" of importance include efforts to help Mexico and Brazil deal with their debt crises in the 1980s and requests of Congress to extend the so-called fast-track negotiating authority. Modification of the language in an existing international tax treaty or approval of a small rural development grant to a non-strategic country would exemplify relatively pro forma decisions handled at the office level by a few technical specialists.

THE INTERPLAY OF ECONOMIC AND POLITICAL THEORIES

If the first step in understanding the process by which the United States makes international economic policy is appreciation of the heterogeneity of the policies being formulated, the second step is appreciation of the complex interrelationship of economics and politics in the policies being formulated. If the reader will excuse an old cliche, the economic contents of most international economic issues can be equated with the visible but relatively small tip of an iceberg.

Political considerations subtly extend well below the "sea level" of these issues, even in the arcane sector of international monetary relations.

The process of making international economic policy centers on perceptions, value judgments, the setting of priorities, the making of choices, and the distribution of wealth. At the very heart of most economic policy decisions is the question of equity versus efficiency. Whether to emphasize social fairness or economic efficiency raises the very basic question of the extent (if any) to which government intervention in international economic relations is desirable. All of this is the stuff of politics—even if the vocabulary of economics dominates the discussion.

Political forces do not produce foreign trade flows. The latter usually develop from basic economic considerations: relative efficiency and the pursuit of profits. Cross-border capital flows are influenced by political conditions in countries, but they mostly originate from private financial calculations. Economic, not political, forces dictate the consequences of misaligned currency exchange rates as well as the implications of a country's failure to come to terms with a structural balance of payments deficit. Nevertheless, there probably has never been an instance in which an important international economic policy decision was made solely on the basis of an econometric calculation. At least some subjective criteria are inevitable when governments decide to respond to inward and outward flows of goods and capital. International economic policy substance can be considered the end product of a political process based on debate and compromise.

National security and domestic economic well-being are goals so highly prized by governments that each has generated a large bureaucracy operating in these two separate realms. Both the foreign policy and the economic policy agencies rightly view international economic policy as part of their jurisdiction because it affects their "constituency." Economics has become a central component in world politics, and economic strength is widely recognized as having become part of a broader definition of national security. International economic policies are directly related to the foreign policy objective of fostering the type of international environment that is most conducive to the physical and ideological well-being of that nation. At the same time, these policies directly affect the basic objectives of domestic economic policy management: growth, full employment, and price stability. As explained in the next chapter, the external sector of a country's economy is an increasingly important variable in the performance of the national economy. How well the latter performs regularly determines outcomes of national elections, so political leaders are interested in global economic events.

The growing impact of international economic relations on a country's pursuit of both internal and external goals creates the situation whereby conflicting domestic political pressures, domestic economic policy objectives, and foreign policy priorities are forever being reconciled by the juggling act that typically characterizes the international economic policymaking process. The latter is intrinsically concerned with the core substance of other policy areas. International economic policy is not a completely independent phenomenon. However, its unique mandate to reconcile a number of critical national priorities means that it is more than a subsidiary of domestic economic and foreign policies.

Analyses of international economic relations frequently suffer from the "two-cultures" syndrome. Many political scientists analyzing this policy sphere do not look beyond political concepts such as struggles for power and value maximization. An excessive tilt towards the political element ignores important economic considerations. For example, a liberal trade policy may not be appropriate to all countries at all times. If a country with a structural trade deficit has depleted its monetary reserves and cannot attract additional capital inflows from abroad, it must reduce imports to a level it can afford. A reduction in imports in such circumstances is not considered protectionism or a political sellout to domestic interest groups.

Most American economists analyzing international economic relations also display professional myopia. In their search for optimum efficiency, they tend to dismiss political constraints and social factors as shallow aberrations or boring anachronisms that eventually will be swept aside by the irresistible logic of good economic theory.

Put simply, politics is about the determination of who gets what, when, and how. As such, the political process is an exercise in maximizing power, influence, prestige, and, last but not least, wealth. A number of competing theories have arisen to explain the actions of national political leaders in setting the national agenda, passing laws, administering programs, and determining spending priorities. General interest democracy, pluralist bargaining among competing special interest groups, actions of elites, bureaucratic politics, and rational choice have been used as models to explain how the U.S. government works. All are necessary but not sufficient concepts for explaining how U.S. international economic policy is made.

Economics deals with the production and distribution of limited supplies of goods and services amid unlimited demand. A body of international economic theory has evolved from basic domestic economic theories. At the heart of both internal and external theories are such principles as the need for correcting a structural economic disequilibrium. International economic theory per se deals with the systems comprising the global economy. It includes ideas on why free trade is the optimal form of international commerce, the balance of payments adjustment process, and the means to accelerate economic development in less developed countries (LDCs). Parts of international economic theory are arcane. Some, being more than 200 years old, are of debatable relevance to contemporary international business transactions.

In sum, the international economic policymaking process in the United States and other countries is ultimately the byproduct of the interplay between political needs and economic objectives at both the internal and external levels. Policymakers must tread a fine line between being responsive to public opinion at home and not alienating friendly countries with overly aggressive economic policies. The net result is that an interdisciplinary approach is absolutely necessary for understanding how decision-making works. The body of knowledge accumulated in both economics and political science needs to be applied to the subject matter of this book. This approach gives appropriate attention to the theory of the "second-best," wherein political necessity prevents the selection of optimal economic measures calculated to give "first-best" economic results.

The mix between economics and politics is also evident in heated discussions regarding the most widely accepted international economic theory. Free trade based on comparative advantage creates a situation in which *all* countries gain from the increased efficiencies and output associated with an international specialization of labor based on relative efficiency. Some theoreticians have recently criticized the validity of this hallowed concept. They argue that many assumptions of the theory of free trade (e.g., constant or diminishing returns to scale) have become obsolete in an era of high technology and that a country is better advised to *induce* competitive advantage through supportive economic policies and knowledge creation. The long-running debate concerning the wisdom of the United States' maintaining a free trade posture despite the allegedly unfair and nonmarket trade practices of Japan and other countries involves a subjective clash of economic perceptions that is inherently political.

Decisions about specific foreign aid programs are another example of the interplay of economics and politics in international economic relations. Some bilateral U.S. foreign aid programs have been designed to meet national security interests and placate domestic interest groups. By way of example, neither the form nor the amount of aid given to Israel has noticeably changed for many years, despite the increasing prosperity of that country. Conversely, the nature of U.S. development assistance strategy in most LDCs was radically revised in the mid-1970s after growing empirical evidence that it was not generating adequate economic development. The old emphasis on erecting a modern industrial infrastructure in LDCs failed to produce the expected "trickle-down" benefits to the population as a whole. As a result, Congress rewrote U.S. foreign aid legislation to provide for a new "bottom-up" bilateral development approach that emphasizes such basic targets as agricultural productivity, education, health, and nutrition.

A DISTINCT PHENOMENON

International economic policy is a distinct phenomenon. Neither by process nor substance is it exclusively the economic branch of foreign policy. Nor is it exclusively the external dimension of domestic economic policy management. International economic developments have profound internal effects on every country, and they have an impact on external relationships among sovereign countries. Senior decision-makers sometimes assign the highest priority to foreign policy concerns. However, by definition, international economic policy also touches on the interests and activities of domestic citizens and organizations. Decision-makers at other times will deem it appropriate to give priority to purely internal needs and objectives.

International economic policy, therefore, is a complex and constantly shifting blend of domestic policies, foreign policy, and global economic considerations. It does not fit entirely into any narrow compartment. An entity unto itself, it has its own rules, characteristics, and idiosyncrasies. International economic policy is greater than the sum of its parts. Most importantly, its dualistic nature means that in every country this policy must serve two bureaucratic masters: the domestic economic policy management apparatus and the national security network. Significantly, these are the two most important bureaucracies in the modern nation-state.

When viewed in context, international economic policy can be compared to a strategically situated four-way intersection where very important policies converge. Feeding into a single focal point are domestic political and domestic economic concerns as well as external economic and foreign policy priorities. Policymakers "direct traffic" by subjectively establishing priorities among these four concerns. International economic policy is not an independent phenomenon; it is a composite of other policies. It is unique in that it must simultaneously reconcile economic and political issues, on one level, and external and internal needs, on another. That international economic policymaking, at least among the major industrialized democracies, is an extraordinary balancing act that must accommodate potentially conflicting objectives and perspectives is graphically suggested by the flow chart in Figure 1.1.

The depiction of international economic policy as a distinctive phenomenon involving the reconciliation of usually conflicting priorities of global concerns and domestic economic policy goals has major implications for the procedural, or decision-making, function. The context in which this policy operates is rife with the pursuit of competing, yet perfectly legitimate and perhaps equally reasonable, value judgments. The result is a two-cultures situation. Some advocates want to give top priority to foreign policy considerations because they view international economic policy as being mainly the economic aspect of the pursuit of a stable, friendly, and prosperous global environment. Hence, economic considerations should be subordinate to the primary objective of good relations with other nations. The implication of this viewpoint is that primary responsibility for formulating international economic policy should be in the hands of the national security apparatus; in the United States, that would be the State Department and the National Security Council (NSC).

The second school takes the internal perspective. It attaches top priority to pleasing and strengthening domestic constituencies through a variety of means; they include increasing and protecting jobs, assisting companies and farmers to become more internationally competitive, and retaliating against foreign countries that impose restrictive import barriers. Defining international economic policy as primarily the external dimension of domestic economic policy suggests

Figure 1.1
Flow Chart of International Economic Policymaking

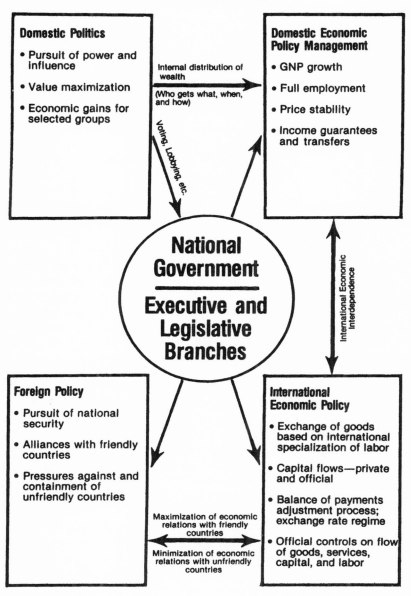

Domestic Politics

- Pursuit of power and influence
- Value maximization
- Economic gains for selected groups

Internal distribution of wealth
(Who gets what, when, and how)

Voting, Lobbying, etc.

Domestic Economic Policy Management

- GNP growth
- Full employment
- Price stability
- Income guarantees and transfers

National Government

Executive and Legislative Branches

International Economic Interdependence

Foreign Policy

- Pursuit of national security
- Alliances with friendly countries
- Pressures against and containment of unfriendly countries

Maximization of economic relations with friendly countries

Minimization of economic relations with unfriendly countries

International Economic Policy

- Exchange of goods based on international specialization of labor
- Capital flows—private and official
- Balance of payments adjustment process; exchange rate regime
- Official controls on flow of goods, services, capital, and labor

that primary jurisdiction should reside in ministries with domestic economic policy responsibilities, for example, the Treasury and Commerce departments.

Both schools of thought are too narrow and, therefore, inadequate. International economic policy is not an either/or choice between foreign policy and economic objectives. It is both. To approach policy formulation by consistently giving one viewpoint dominance would produce skewed policy. "Sensible" international economic policymaking must forever walk the tightrope between the conflicting priorities and values associated with domestic politics, domestic economics, international politics, and international economics.

On a case-by-case basis, and with no permanent guidelines to steer by, the decision on which way to tilt—internally or externally, or politically or economically—is often the essence of the international economic policymaking process. For example, the Clinton administration in 1999 faced a difficult balancing act in deciding how to respond to the onslaught of Russian-made steel that allegedly was being dumped in the U.S. market. Imposition of prohibitive antidumping duties would have blocked further steel imports but deprived the Russians of much needed foreign exchange and possibly destabilized their already shaky economy. However, forcing U.S. steel companies and workers to endure long-term financial hardships from unfair trade practices by America's former cold war rival would have sparked an ugly domestic political backlash. (The issue was resolved by compromise when the Russians responded to U.S. pressure and agreed "voluntarily" to reduce the volume of their steel exports.)

A near-perfect example of the four-fold dynamics of international economic policy formulation was provided by President Ronald Reagan's summer 1986 decision to allow the Soviet Union to purchase some four million tons of U.S. wheat at subsidized prices. The immediate issue was whether to put at risk hundreds of millions of dollars of potential U.S. grain exports by not responding to foreign price competition. The European Union was offering substantial discounts from world prices to the Soviets in order to shrink the massive wheat surplus that had accumulated in Western Europe.

U.S. foreign policy considerations clearly argued *against* the "double whammy" of subsidizing the consumers of a cold war rival while simultaneously offending the friendly wheat-exporting countries (Canada, Australia, and Argentina) that did not want a costly international agricultural price war. Domestic considerations, however, clearly argued in *favor* of providing governmental export subsidies. The then-faltering Midwest farm economy and the then-impending election struggle to retain Republican control of the Senate suggested that a heavy domestic political price would be paid for depriving U.S. farmers of a large, profitable export sale because of national security concerns. The president resolved the not-unexpected schism among his advisers by subordinating his usual tough Soviet stance to his desire to curry favor from the American farm community.

Another example of the four components of international economic policy existed throughout the 1990s in the form of a long-running debate over the relative merits of continuing to extend most-favored-nation (MFN) tariff treatment to China. The debate boiled down to the question of which was more likely to achieve U.S. objectives: providing or denying China the low tariffs associated with MFN status while that country failed to modify a number of social, economic, and national security policies that angered the U.S. government. Within the American political scene, civil rights activists who wanted to apply maximum pressure to force the cessation of repressive Chinese actions clashed with the business community, which advocated "constructive engagement" because it stood to be hurt financially from a downgrade in China's trade status. American importers, facing the prospect of prohibitive duties on the goods they were bringing in from China, warned of the adverse impact on U.S. consumers. Even before China threatened to retaliate with its own increases in import barriers, American exporters of aircraft, agricultural products, etc., argued that the costs to the American economy of denying MFN status would be prohibitive.

Opinion remains divided over whether a hard-line U.S. policy or a non-threatening stance was more likely to induce China to back down and modify the targets of U.S. demands: human rights violations, arms exports (including missiles), unfair trade practices, threats against Taiwan, etc. There is still no definitive answer to the question of how best to nudge Chinese behavior in the direction of American values. The Clinton administration ended the uncertainty by deciding that MFN status would not be terminated and official threats to that end would be muted.

UNIQUE ASPECTS OF U.S. INTERNATIONAL ECONOMIC POLICY

The nature of the international economic policies implemented by the United States since 1945 has been uncommonly distinctive from those of other countries. One source of this distinctiveness is the unique system of government at work in Washington. It features an unusually influential chief executive, supported by a very large number of personal advisers, whose ability to implement these polices is nevertheless heavily dependent on decisions made in the legislative branch.

The other generic source of idiosyncratic policy behavior is a trio of extraordinary economic and political factors that for more than half a century has collectively forged unique U.S. national priorities and attitudes. The first is that the U.S. economy is less sensitive to the vicissitudes of foreign trade flows than any other industrialized economy. One reason for this situation is a simple statistic: compared to all other countries, imports and exports represent a relatively small percentage of total U.S. economic output (gross domestic product). *Total* employment is therefore only marginally affected by trade.

The U.S. economy also has an unusually wide buffer between its domestic and external sectors because the U.S. government studiously avoids economic planning. This means that unlike most of their foreign counterparts, U.S. policymakers do not view trade policy as a tool for use in achieving the larger goals of domestic industrial policy. Most policymakers in Washington, D.C. share the benign American attitude that imports are something benefiting the consumer, not something inhibiting the emergence of an industry targeted for development. Official Washington pays lip service to the idea of export expansion. However, it is not a sufficiently urgent priority that senior politicians would seriously consider promoting exports at the price of abandoning foreign policy or humanitarian objectives, giving preferential financial assistance to a small group of companies, or waiving antitrust and other regulatory provisions.

Second, U.S. international economic policy can never be totally conventional as long as the U.S. dollar serves the extraordinary role as the world's principal reserve and transactions currency. Since World War II, the United States has been the only country that can pay for *all* of its import needs by using its own currency. Every other country must rely primarily on exports to earn the foreign exchange necessary to pay for imports. The bottom line is that the substance of U.S. foreign trade policy reflects the fact that it is the least likely country in the world to observe a bumper sticker warning citizens to "Export or Die." Foreign trade does not permanently occupy a prime spot in the contemporary American psyche.

A third factor contributing to the unique profile of U.S. international economic policy has been the extraordinary role for the last half of the century of the United States in world affairs, first as leader of the free world and then as the world's lone superpower. The singularly broad global vision accompanying this status has produced an unusually frequent subordination of domestic considerations to geopolitical factors. This has manifested itself in the United States' taking the lead in promoting multilateral efforts to reduce trade barriers, an unusually tolerant acceptance (until the 1980s) of overseas barriers to American goods, and an extraordinarily high propensity to impose economic sanctions on dozens of countries in retaliation for what is deemed unacceptable political, military, or humanitarian behavior.

The U.S. government is no longer obsessed with being the chief military protector of the free world against incursions by the Soviet bloc. However, it is still fascinated with the prospect of exercising its considerable power and influence to create a world order consistent with its liberal political and market-based economic values. By comparison, the international economic policies of the rest of the world have more inward-looking and regional orientations. Enhancement of domestic prosperity is a much more pervasive theme in their international policies. To promote domestic growth and employment, most other governments expend far more resources than the United States in providing export loans at concessional rates, extending subsidies and import protection to stimulate favored industrial sectors, and so on. The "Plowden Report" of 1964 surveyed the entire purpose and structure of the British diplomatic service and concluded:

The survival of Britain, let alone her influence, depends on trade. The work of our representatives overseas must be increasingly dedicated to the support of British trade. Economic and political motives intertwine throughout our foreign policy and have always done so; but economic and commercial work has now assumed a position of fundamental importance. It must be regarded as a first charge on the resources of the overseas Services.[2]

The perspective of a country with the global interests of the United States perforce must be broader. Policy reflects purpose. The purpose of U.S. international economic policy "is not simply to defend but to construct, not simply to react to events in a world which others shape but to initiate so as ourselves to shape a world order in which we can live peaceably and prosper," Anthony Solomon has written.[3]

HISTORICAL OVERVIEW

The first manifestation of a cohesive, interactive U.S. international economic policy did not appear until the 1930s. Before then, the U.S. government paid little attention to matters involving the world economy. On those occasions when it was forced to do so, "it played a lone hand without much regard for the interests of other countries."[4] No grand U.S. design for the international economy existed, mainly because the United States was not yet an important enough economic power to need or warrant an ambitious agenda. Amidst a philosophy based on economic nationalism and isolation, there was little vigorous or ongoing pursuit of specific policy objectives in economic relations with foreign governments.

The first sign of change came in the realm of trade relations. For the first 140 years of the Republic, that which passed for U.S. trade policy was minimalist. From the earliest years of its existence, the Congress had listened to the demands of domestic interest groups and unilaterally established the U.S. tariff schedule to protect key constituents. U.S. tariffs were relatively high and inflexible. The interests of exporters mattered little. Since it had minuscule discretionary tariff-setting authority, the administration did little more than passively collect tariffs. Statements were occasionally issued to criticize certain restrictive foreign practices to which the United States objected, for example, the British system of imperial preferences within the Empire.

A historic turning point occurred in 1934 with the passage of the Reciprocal Trade Agreements Act. This landmark legislation authorized the first meaningful transfer of authority to reduce tariffs from the legislative to the executive branch. The State Department thereupon set out to reverse the Depression-era surge in protectionist measures around the world by negotiating bilateral, reciprocal tariff-cutting agreements within the limits authorized.

The short leash provided by Congress notwithstanding, the statute did represent the beginnings of a calculated effort by the executive branch to influence international trade relations as a means to the end of achieving domestic economic and foreign policy objectives. The driving force behind the legislation, the then–Secretary of State Cordell Hull, believed that a direct relationship existed between an open international economy and a peaceful, cooperative world political order. For practical reasons, however, the immediate objective of the newly established Trade Agreements Program was marketed to Congress as a part of the New Deal stimulus package. The anticipated net boost to exports from foreign trade liberalization was promoted as a further means of dragging the American economy out of the depths of the Depression, not as a means of making cheaper imports available to consumers. The next six years of U.S. international economic policy were devoted to bilateral tariff-cutting negotiations, with 28 agreements being successfully concluded. By 1941, the clouds of war had reappeared. Economic policy objectives were quickly subordinated to achieving victory: resources were to be denied to the enemy and provided to allies.

An activist, comprehensive U.S. international economic policy that ventured beyond tariff-cutting negotiations was one of the many far-reaching changes produced by World War II. Prior to 1945, the United States had no ambition to be a political-military superpower; it preferred an isolationist foreign policy. Prior to 1945, the dollar was not the linchpin of the international monetary system; the U.S. balance of payments experienced the same constraints as other countries. Except in South and Central America, the LDCs were mostly colonies of European nations, and no permanent U.S. foreign aid program existed. A growing number of U.S. corporations were operating on a multinational basis, but not on a scale large enough to cause any dramatic impact, meaningful controversy, or need for official policies on foreign investment. Widespread controls severely limited the movement of international capital so that there was infrequent need for policies to deal with destabilizing capital flows.

A permanent leadership role for the United States in the international economic order was inevitable once superpower status was thrust upon it, initially because of its relative economic strength and later because of its military power. The first fruit of American economic leadership was the 1944 Bretton Woods Agreement. It contained the blueprints for key structures—the International Monetary Fund and the World Bank—that would be created once the postwar international economic order was inaugurated. By the late 1940s, the perceived urgency of strengthening the free world and containing Soviet power led U.S. officials at the highest political levels to chart a new global strategy. The United States would use the bountiful resources of its large, strong, and undamaged economy to help finance the rebuilding of the war-shattered economies in Western Europe and Asia (mainly Japan) that remained outside the communist bloc. An implicit bargain was struck. The relatively import-impervious American market would remain wide open to the exports of Western Europe and Japan, and they in turn would follow the U.S. lead in waging cold war.

Postwar U.S. international economic policy has passed through two distinct stages.[5] For nearly 25 years after 1945, U.S. policy was overwhelmingly designed to maximize and accommodate national security needs. Widespread economic destruction in Europe and Asia meant that in the initial postwar period, the U.S. economy, a veritable colossus amidst economic weakness, could easily absorb imports at the same time it could afford to accept temporary foreign discrimination against American goods. More than any other country, the United States pushed for multilateral tariff-cutting negotiations under the auspices of the General Agreement on Tariffs and Trade (GATT), which took effect in 1948. Going one step further, U.S. negotiators until the 1960s were generally willing to concede greater tariff reductions than they demanded, a reflection of the asymmetric distribution of economic power that characterized the early postwar years.

There was little opposition to the proposition that the United States could also afford what was up to then the world's largest foreign aid program by far: the multibillion dollar Marshall Plan to help finance European economic rebuilding. (A separate aid program operated in Japan.) Furthermore, the costs to the United States of the balance of payments deficits that it began incurring in 1950 were minimal.[6] European countries with surpluses eagerly held onto their newly acquired U.S. dollars to build private bank accounts and replenish their governments' monetary reserves. Even the propensity of other countries to periodically devalue the exchange rate of their currencies in order to enhance national competitiveness was of little concern to Washington at this time.

The bottom line calculation was simple. All of these costs constituted a very small economic price to be paid for the far greater political benefits of encouraging restoration of economic prosperity and political stability in the noncommunist world. Furthermore, in the U.S. government's thinking, magnanimity in helping friendly countries to rebuild served to promote a liberal, market-based international economic order that would prevent repetition of the disastrous beggar-thy-neighbor policies of the 1930s.

International economic policy, in short, served foreign policy objectives. Since attention to national security priorities caused no real damage to the U.S. economy through the mid-1960s, there simply was no conflict between "good" foreign policy and "good" international economic policy. Attaining a consensus definition of the U.S. national interest in the initial postwar era was relatively easy. The unprecedented rates of sustained, non-inflationary growth that constituted what became known as the "golden age" of the world economy confirmed U.S. officialdom's confidence in the wisdom of their master game plan.

When they first begin, even massive turnarounds in broad economic trends are usually not detectable. With 20/20 hindsight, we now know that convergence in the relative economic strength between the United States and Western Europe and Japan had subtly, quietly began to build up a full head of steam in the 1960s. Undisputed U.S. hegemony and the very skewed balance of power in the immediate post–World War II period had been transitory phenomena, not a natural or permanent state of affairs. Not until the onset of the 1970s were the effects of this massive shift fully visible, most notably in the long descent of the large U.S. merchandise trade surplus into deficit. With little forewarning, an entirely new era of U.S. international economic policy had arrived.

International economic policymakers and institutions were slow to cope with the speed and severity of unfolding structural changes associated with the ongoing economic resurgence of Western Europe and Japan. To compound the pressures engendered by these changes, isolationist urges in the United States, fueled by popular discontent with the war in Vietnam, had begun to resurface. The burden of acting as the world's "policeman" had brought considerable disenchantment within the United States about its role in world affairs. In addition, President Johnson's refusal to pay for the costs of fighting the war through higher taxes led to relatively high rates of U.S. inflation. This trend accelerated the inevitable decline in relative U.S. industrial competitiveness. The international monetary system by 1970 was being stretched to its breaking point by the chronic balance of payments surpluses of several West European countries and growth in the chronic U.S. balance of payments deficits. Ironically, a significant cause of the deteriorating U.S. economic position, aside from internal mistakes, was the very success of the U.S. external policy priority of restoring the economic vigor of its major trading partners.

Slowly but steadily, the suspicion spread among Americans that the international economic order was now working against them. Many Americans felt that their country was no longer able to "hold its own" in global competition. Edward Fried eloquently described the resulting sense of malaise:

The United States grappled with a stubborn inflation, a deteriorating position in foreign trade, high defense costs, and, beginning in 1969, serious unemployment. Its balance of payments deficit, chronic though reasonably stable for two decades, suddenly grew much larger and became subject to alarmist interpretations. Western Europe and Japan, on the other hand, were characterized by prosperity, continuing balance of payments surpluses, strong foreign trade positions, and comparatively low defense costs. . . . Did not this contrast between the United States and its once economically prostrate industrial partners mean that there was something "unfair" about the ground rules governing our foreign economic relations and something misguided about our foreign economic policy? Was the United States not over-emphasizing the importance of foreign relations in foreign economic policy and thereby paying a heavy economic price?[7]

These questions all were answered in the affirmative when, on August 15, 1971, President Nixon announced what he called the New Economic Policy (NEP).[8] This monumental shift in U.S. economic philosophy can be compared to the swing of a giant pendulum away from a foreign policy–dominant U.S. international economic policy towards a middle ground where domestic interests were no less than an equal partner. What was once the unquestioned priority of cultivating a global environment consistent with U.S. values was pushed aside. The most pressing short-term need was deemed to be restoration of U.S. balance of payments equilibrium through the draconian measures of terminating dollar-gold convertibility (to induce an exchange rate realignment) and imposing a 10 percent tariff surcharge (to encourage reduced trade barriers in other countries). No national security adviser was invited to attend the historic weekend meeting at Camp David when the NEP was quickly crafted and the world economic order was changed forever. In the wake of the decisions made there, an international monetary system based on fixed exchange rates would be effectively ended. The trading system was merely given a severe jolt in the short term by the protectionist act of the leading champion of liberal trade.

The era of "foreign policy imperative" in U.S. international economic policy was over. The rise of U.S. economic problems and the decline of the communist threat to Western Europe and Japan sealed the shift to a new era. That the policy center of gravity had shifted inward in 1971 was vividly demonstrated by the ultra hard-line negotiating strategy pursued by the then–secretary of treasury, John Connally. He effectively ran U.S. international economic policy in the period following the New Economic Policy and saw his mandate as correcting U.S. economic problems, not accommodating the demands and sensitivities of other finance ministers.[9]

From the 1970s through the present, the cumulative record of U.S. international economic policy has been neither dogmatically universalist nor nationalist. Generally speaking, decision-makers have sought a "happy medium" between domestic and external priorities on a case-by-case basis. U.S. policies were generally outward-looking, seeking to liberalize trade barriers or to calm unstable international financial markets. However, domestic economic and political interests were ignored or overruled in few instances—a situation related to the increased presence of Congress in an increasingly politicized U.S. international economic policymaking process.

Beginning in 1973, a continuing onslaught of international financial shocks forced much of U.S. policy to be reactive, that is, it sought to contain unanticipated disruptions that posed an immediate threat to world economic stability. Washington seldom had the luxury of formulating proactive international financial policy in advance. The sudden permanent collapse of the fixed exchange rate system in 1973 necessitated establishment of a new set of rules and arrangements to operate a floating rate system. The swift and large rise in oil prices later that year, commonly referred to as "the first oil shock," produced global inflation, an economic slowdown among oil importing countries, massive strains to the international monetary system, and a frenzied search for palliatives.

Just as stability was returning to the international economy, the Iranian revolution triggered the second oil shock in 1979. To break the back of the double-digit inflation that resulted, central banks in the industrialized countries unleashed extremely tight monetary policy. This action did succeed in lowering inflation. Unfortunately, soaring interest rates also triggered two major crises: (1) the worst worldwide decline in economic growth since the Depression and (2) an external debt crisis among LDCs that slashed their growth rates and put the international banking system at risk when they could no longer service their debts.

When the ramifications of the United States' adopting ''Reaganomics'' materialized, international economic relations hit another turning point. Despite the prophesies of supply-side economists, the slashing of tax rates and a sharp increase in defense expenditures produced a surge in the federal budget deficit. This led to relatively high real interest rates in the United States, which in turn was a major factor in causing the unprecedented overvaluation in the dollar's exchange rate. The end product of this chain reaction was the ballooning of the U.S. trade deficit that continued into the late 1990s. Record-shattering trade deficits failed to elicit the old-fashioned protectionist trade policies that might have been expected. Instead, U.S. trade policymakers opted to correct the trade deficit through increased exports. The specific means chosen to foster this increase was pressuring trading partners to provide ''reciprocity,'' meaning that American goods should be granted the same access to overseas markets as foreign producers have to the allegedly open U.S. market (see Chapter 10). The commitment of recent administrations to export expansion, however, has been limited by a common policy inconsistency. All of them readily resorted (or were required by legislative dictum) to the use of export controls as a means of expressing dissatisfaction with undesirable foreign behavior.

The very inexact science of seeking the right balance between external and internal goals produced a heterogeneous series of policy initiatives in the 1980s and 1990s. The U.S. government during the 1980s continued to make numerous anti–free trade demands on other countries, mostly the rising export powers in Asia. U.S. trade officials convinced them to ''voluntarily'' restrict their exports of automobiles, steel, textiles and apparel, televisions, and so on to the American market. Quite a different policy emphasis prevailed in the 1990s. The United States was in the forefront of promoting regional free trade agreements in the Western Hemisphere and the Pacific Basin and in pushing for a successful conclusion of the Uruguay Round of multilateral trade negotiations.

When Japan's industrial sector seemed poised to push the U.S. economy into permanent eclipse in the late 1980s, public opinion polls showed more Americans believed that Japan, not the Soviet Union, was the greatest threat to U.S. national security. The ''Japanese challenge'' elicited unusually intense U.S. demands that Japan further open its market. It also precipitated heated domestic discussions about the efficacy of a radical departure in American economic ideology: dropping traditional reliance on market forces and emulating the Japanese model of government-business collaboration via industrial policy. Domestic economic policy debates began to merge with external economic policy concerns like never before, leaving no clear delineation between the two (see Chapter 11).

The pace of dramatic, unanticipated shifts in the international order intensified in the 1990s. Within months after starting the decade burdened by self-doubts about the future of their country, Americans watched in pleasant surprise the unfolding of U.S. triumphalism. First, the Soviet Union imploded. This caused complications for policymakers by eliminating the defining element of post–World War II U.S. foreign policy strategy. As the cold war faded into history, U.S. international economic policy could be made with less worry about the need to financially support troubled countries lest they go over to ''the other side.'' Second, downsized industrial sector companies, a booming information technology sector, and an economy enjoying steady, inflation-free growth put the United States on an upward trajectory, just as a slow-growth Japanese economy with a crippled banking sector was on a sharply downward trajectory. As the world's lone superpower, whose visions of capitalism and democracy were spreading throughout the planet, the United States was exerting economic and military power and cultural influence on a scale that perhaps exceeded even the extraordinary level of the late 1940s.

The American public allowed itself only a brief period of rejoicing. On the political-military side, concern grew about threats of terrorism and rogue countries possessing weapons of mass destruction. In the late 1990s, two significant challenges emerged to the continued pursuit of a liberal international economic order. First, an unforeseen protest against the process of ''globalization,'' specifically its impact on relatively less skilled American workers and on the environment, was launched on a number of fronts in the public and private sectors. The second challenge took the form of a sudden disillusionment by some with free markets in general and free movements of international capital in particular (see Chapter 12).

The velocity and crushing volume of private capital outflows from LDCs, first from Mexico in 1994–1995, then from East Asian countries in 1997–1998, and the failure of market reforms to take hold in Russia suggested to some that developing countries should reject the U.S. model and move back toward increased government controls over economic activity. The intense worldwide controversy concerning the lending practices by the International Monetary Fund (i.e., whether they were disastrously restrictive or excessively generous bailouts) symbolized a divisiveness even among economic specialists as to how to deal with the spreading contagion of market instability.

NOTES

1. Benjamin J. Cohen, *American Foreign Economic Policy* (New York: Harper and Row, 1968), p. 10.

2. ''Report of the Committee on Representational Services Overseas'' (London: Her Majesty's Stationery Office, 1972), p. 3.

3. Anthony M. Solomon, ''Administration of a Multipurpose Economic Diplomacy,'' *Public Administration Review* 24 (November–December 1969): 585.

4. Richard S. Gardner, *Sterling-Dollar Diplomacy* (New York: McGraw-Hill, 1969), p. 1.

5. As suggested in Chapter 12, it is possible that U.S. international economic policy

entered a third stage in the late 1990s, when it began to focus on reducing the alleged damage wrought by ''globalization.''

6. The U.S. balance of payments deficits through the 1960s were caused by large net capital outflows from the federal government and the private sector that exceeded the surpluses in the trade account.

7. Edward Fried, ''Foreign Economic Policy: The Search for a Strategy,'' in *The Next Phase in Foreign Policy*, Henry Owen and Morton Halperin, eds. (Washington, D.C.: Brookings Institution, 1973), p. 161.

8. The New Economic Policy was focused primarily on domestic economic problems associated with stagflation. Wage and price controls were the most significant component of the policy package.

9. By unleashing market turmoil that forced countries to let their exchange rates float, the New Economic Policy produced considerable instability and uncertainty in the foreign exchange markets. Secretary Connally for many weeks rejected European and Japanese pleas for a quick agreement to re-fix exchange rates; in late 1970, he was ordered to seek a compromise by President Nixon when foreign policy concerns dictated a settlement.

2 The Importance of International Economic Policy

> The supreme difficulty of our generation . . . is that our achievements on the economic plane of life have outstripped our progress on the political plane to the extent that our economics and our politics are perpetually falling out of gear with one another. On the economic plane, the world has been organized into a single all-embracing unit of activity. On the political plane, [nation-states] have been growing . . . more numerous and the national consciousness more acute. The tension between these two antithetical tendencies has been producing a series of jolts . . . in the social life of humanity.
> —*The Economist*, 1930

> In this post Cold War world, our national security rests more than ever on our economic strength. Our foreign and commercial policies must be integrated if we are to accomplish our objective at home and abroad.
> —William Clinton, 1996

International economic policy is a combination of nothing less than the two highest-priority goals of the modern nation-state: national security and economic prosperity. It has grown steadily in importance because in the largest sense, international economic policy has the daunting task of trying to manage international economic interdependence—the concentric circle linking two global mega-trends of the second half of the twentieth century and beyond:

- The increased intrusion of governments in their domestic economies because electorates hold them responsible for good economic performance; and
- The increased intrusion of economic issues in the day-to-day conduct of international relations.

THE GROWING SIGNIFICANCE OF INTERNATIONAL ECONOMIC INTERDEPENDENCE

It was not until the 1970s that U.S. international economic policy was transformed from an obscure backwater tended by anonymous specialists to a politicized issue deemed important by both political parties, multiple interest groups, and (occasionally) presidents. Politicalization means that political leaders realize that international commerce has grown so much that it is an important pocketbook issue among their constituents and an important vehicle for delivering promises to the electorate. Political leaders in countries more integrated into the world economy than is the United States have long understood the substantial impact of the ever-tightening linkage among national economies on domestic economic policy management. In the new world order of the post–cold war era, ideological hostilities among major countries have virtually disappeared as market-based economies replaced government-controlled, command economies on a nearly universal basis. Meanwhile, the ongoing intensification of international economic interdependence in both quantitative and qualitative terms continues unabated.

Interdependence has no precise, all-encompassing definition. As the term is used here, it has both political and economic characteristics. Politically, interdependence offers opportunities to politicians to achieve economic goals more efficiently in a multilateral context than by unilateral means. The clearest proof that presidents and prime ministers believe that it is important to them is the annual economic summit meeting held since the mid-1970s by the leaders of the seven major industrial countries.

As goods, services, capital, and labor become even more internationally mobile, interdependence creates anxiety by diminishing governments' control over what was once considered strictly domestic policy. Macroeconomic policies sometimes must be changed to conform with externally imposed conditions, inflation can be imported, domestic industries are sometimes swamped by foreign competition, and so on. Suggesting diminished internal control over national economic destiny is absolutely *not* the same thing as asserting that interdependence (often referred to as globalization) has significantly diminished national sovereignty, that is, the government's ability to legally control domestic laws, institutions, and policies. A good case for diminished sovereignty amidst rising interdependence can only be made by pointing to those less developed countries who reluctantly have bowed to tremendous pressure to follow the harsh dictates of the industrial country-dominated multilateral economic organizations, namely the International Monetary Fund (IMF).

The traditional foreign policy adage that countries should not intrude into the internal affairs of other sovereign states has been overtaken by events that have redefined ''internal.'' Today there are few changes in domestic economic conditions in the large industrial countries that do *not* have external implications. The Group of Seven industrialized countries have repeatedly tried to coordinate their monetary and fiscal policies since the mid-1980s. Competition policy and labor standards are gradually being introduced to the agenda of multilateral trade negotiations. Japanese and U.S. trade negotiators have appropriately given each other advice on such "internal" subjects as education, saving rates, length of workdays, antitrust enforcement, land use, and time horizons for planning by business executives.

Economically, interdependence reflects speed in the form of the quickening transmission of global (external) economic events and trends to individual national economies. It represents magnitude in the form of the growing importance of what is happening in other economies as a determinant of economic health in one's own economy. Interdependence explains why the vast majority of economic problems are now beyond the capacity of a single country to solve and require concerted multilateral actions.

To some extent, interdependence is more a matter of perception than empirical measurement. Furthermore, it is incorrect to argue that interdependence among countries is totally new. Only the degree of its intensity and the rising concern it engenders among national political leaders are without precedent. Reliance by countries on foreign suppliers for goods that are unavailable or produced inefficiently at home goes back many hundreds of years. Inflows of foreign capital during the nineteenth century played a pivotal role in the economic development of the United States. Historical data indicate that during the latter part of the nineteenth century, a steadily rising share of industrialized countries' output was channeled into foreign trade. However, this trend was reversed by two world wars and the global depression of the 1930s. Merchandise exports as a percent of world gross domestic product (GDP) are today about twice what they were in 1950, but only about 50 percent greater than in 1913, just prior to the start of World War I.[1]

When interdependence reemerged with a vengeance in the early 1960s, it did so in a very different world. Far more countries were important actors in the international trading system than in the Euro-centric world of the nineteenth century. Infinitely more kinds of goods and services were (and are) being produced and traded. Capital began moving across national boundaries in geometrically greater quantities because of the dismantling of controls and the rapid introduction of cheap and quick computer and global telecommunications technologies.

More importantly, the quantitative and qualitative increase in global interdependence surfaced in a different economic policymaking world. It was only after the Keynesian revolution of the 1930s that governments learned how to apply counter-cyclical fiscal stimuli to cure recessions. As discussed in the next section, governments in the post–World War era accept an exceptional degree of responsibility for the achievement of economic growth, full employment, price stability, and income transfers.

Among major countries, the United States is the least conscious of the spiraling impact of international economic interdependence. The fact that the U.S.

economy is still relatively insulated from the world economy (mainly because foreign trade is a relatively small percentage of GDP and the extraordinary international role of the dollar) is responsible for the average American's being less sensitized to the growing importance of international economics than people elsewhere. Popular recognition of the impact of the external economic sector has grown only very slowly, despite the observation made as early as 1949 in a U.S. government study that ''the traditional line of demarcation between domestic and foreign problems has completely disappeared, and the governmental organization must be shaped to formulate and execute national policies which have both domestic and foreign aspects.''[2] This thought is widely understood in some European countries where upwards of one-half of all goods produced are exported and one-half of all goods consumed are imported.

The extraordinary surge in the intensity and extent of international economic interdependence was caused in part by post–World War II changes in the basic workings of international business. Geographical distances and national borders became less relevant to executives of multinational corporations than at any time in history. Goods can be moved from one side of the world to the other more quickly and cheaply than ever before, thanks to new modes of sea and air transportation. Design engineers and production lines can operate thousands of miles apart thanks to sophisticated data transmission technology. Finally, the lion's share of reductions in and elimination of barriers to international trade and capital movements have been enacted since the 1950s.

The economics of high-tech production are dictating the consolidation of global economic production into fewer and bigger multinational corporations, most of which aggressively sell their goods in every major market on the planet. Economic necessity now precludes large manufacturing corporations from concentrating only on their home market. The ever-rising fixed costs associated with developing and manufacturing capital intensive, high-technology products necessitate economies of scale. Research and development expenses and retooling costs to produce a new generation of jet aircraft, semiconductor, or supercomputer are now measured in billions of dollars. To remain a competitive, low-cost producer in the high-tech sector, a corporation needs to amortize high fixed costs over a maximum sales volume. This is why global marketing strategies have become the norm.

The quest for ''bigness'' and maximum global presence to pay for product innovation, consolidate costs, and prevent being outflanked by fast-growing competitors is repeatedly demonstrated by the endless wave of mergers and strategic alliances being consummated by already large multinational companies (a process described as ''whales consuming other whales''). Financial success and survival by high-tech companies increasingly require a successful presence in the ''triad'': the markets of North America, Europe, and Japan and the Pacific Basin.

Measuring the net intensification of international economic interdependence is a tricky, exacting process. Strictly speaking, there should be demonstrable increases in the sensitivity of individual domestic economies to external trends and in the velocity of transmission effects from country to country. Although the net increment of interdependence cannot be measured precisely (a process that would require voluminous data on price and income elasticities, the effects of exchange rate changes, the impact of overseas wages, etc.), it can be inferred by utilizing the very basic aphorism that everything is relative. Large absolute increases in international trade and investment are not inherently significant to the management of domestic economies *unless* they are increasing *faster* than domestic production. The boom in international trade and finance would not be a statistically significant indicator of increased interdependence if their rise merely kept pace with, or even trailed, the growth in domestic production around the world.

Increases in international trade and capital flows in fact are meeting the criterion of large relative growth. Foreign trade since the 1950s has consistently grown faster in percentage terms than the estimated rate for aggregate world GDP expressed either in nominal or real terms. This relative rate of increase becomes more dramatic if merchandise trade is related only to increased domestic production of goods; in that way, the rapid rise of the service sector as a component of the GDP of industrialized countries is factored out of the statistics. The share of total world production of goods accounted for by exports of manufactured goods almost quadrupled between 1950 and the mid-1990s; exports rose from an estimated 8.9 percent of goods produced worldwide in 1950 to 31.4 percent in 1990.[3]

The volume of world exports expressed as a percentage of total global output rose from an estimated 2.5 percent in the 1950s to 14 percent in the mid-1980s.[4] According to calculations by the World Trade Organization (WTO), trade volume increased by fifteen-fold between the early 1950s and mid-1990s, while real global production increased only six-fold. The proportion of trade as a share of global income tripled during the same period of time from 7 to 21 percent.[5] WTO data also indicate that world exports increased more than twice as much on average as did world GDP between 1987 and 1997.[6] The nominal value of world trade has increased almost sixty-fold since 1955. From an estimated $94 billion in that year, total merchandise trade grew to $903 billion in 1975, and to $5.3 trillion in 1997.[7]

The consistently faster relative growth of trade has a simple statistical effect but significant economic and political implications: the foreign trade sector has been growing as a percentage of virtually every country's gross domestic product. Exports of goods thereby have become an increasingly important source of national economic growth, while merchandise imports have become an increasingly important potential source of domestic economic disruption.

Foreign direct investment also has grown geometrically faster than world GDP since the end of World War II. The data are inexact and incomplete, but one estimate has the value of such investment by all countries increasing by a factor of nearly 25 (more than five times as much as the increase in world GDP), from about $68 billion at year-end 1960 to about $1.8 trillion at year-end 1991.[8] Foreign direct investment from 1986 through 1995 grew more than twice as fast as gross fixed capital formation around the world, "indicating an increasing internationalization of national production systems." A report by the United Nations Conference on Trade and Development goes on to conclude that "The upward trend manifested in all of the indicators of international production, in absolute terms as well as in relation to various macroeconomic indicators, suggests that international production is becoming a more significant element in the world economy."[9]

Economic interdependence is demonstrated even more dramatically by the effects of what has become an integrated global capital market. Armed with instantaneous data transmission and new financial techniques to hedge the risk of financial transactions, tens of thousands of investors, speculators, and corporations in dozens of countries conduct a continuous, round-the-clock, global plebiscite on the relative merits of national currencies, stocks, and bonds. The single largest market in the world today is the foreign exchange market, where *daily* turnover was estimated to be $1.5 trillion in 1998.[10] Foreign exchange transactions dwarf the value of the "hard" international business transactions: foreign trade, foreign direct investment, international purchases of stocks and bonds, overseas bank loans and deposits, and so on. All of these transactions combined probably are little more than $20 trillion annually—the equivalent of about three weeks' turnover in the foreign exchange markets. Therefore, the vast majority of foreign exchange transactions facilitate relatively short-term, "hot money" flows made in response to interest rate differentials or outright speculation about future exchange rate movements.

International borrowing from commercial banks is another category of transborder transaction that has grown geometrically since the early 1970s. Bank lending to foreign borrowers surged almost overnight when the Organization of Petroleum Exporting Countries (OPEC) triggered the first oil price shock in 1973 and wrought havoc with the balance of payments positions of oil-importing countries. Net new international bank lending rose from an estimated $33 billion in 1973 to some $500 billion in 1997.[11] The Bank for International Settlements estimates that the stock of outstanding foreign bank loans grew to $8.5 billion at the end of September 1997—almost 30 times the level of 25 years earlier.[12] Whereas the outstanding stock of international bank lending in 1980 was equivalent to only 4 percent of the industrialized countries' aggregate gross domestic product, this percentage soared to 44 percent of their total output in 1991.[13]

The boom in international bank lending unquestionably helped several developing countries gain access to much needed capital to pay for imports. However, in retrospect, virtually all of these countries borrowed too much, as seen by the onset of the global debt crisis in the 1980s, where the solvency of big debtor countries and many big commercial banks was at risk for several years.

International financial interdependence is also manifested in more frequent concerted movements in stock prices around the world. It is no longer uncommon for sharp price rises or drops in one region to immediately prompt comparable movements in stock markets everywhere else. The increasing sensitivity among the world's investors was perhaps most vividly displayed during the worldwide stock market crash of October 1987 that left no major market unscathed. The unexpected speed and size of worldwide price declines produced a temporary reduction of about $1.2 trillion in global stock market capitalization. Many investors in many different countries dumped stocks because they perceived the stock market debacle occurring in other countries inevitably would be transmitted to their own home market.[14] The deteriorating economic situation in Asia in 1998 put a damper on stock markets around the world; major sell-offs regularly followed announcements of bad news. As the global economic outlook worsened, companies like Coca-Cola and Gillette saw their stock prices tumble because investors aggressively sold shares in American companies with above-average dependence on foreign markets for sales and profits.

In qualitative terms, interdependence complicates the lives of national political leaders and draws them into the vagaries of international economic policy by (1) eroding their control over domestic economic performance and (2) reducing the ability of an individual nation-state to deliver the increased economic prosperity promised in the informal social contract with the populace.

The growing need for countries to pursue economic objectives through regional economic institutions is strikingly illustrated by the ongoing, voluntary surrender of economic autonomy by member countries to the central institutions of the European Union. A pivotal event in world history occurred on the first day of 1999, when eleven European countries surrendered control over their monetary policy to a European central bank and began phasing out their national currencies in favor of the Euro. While military alliances have been necessary for centuries to augment the limited defense capabilities of a single country, recourse to membership in trade blocs to increase national economic performance is a late twentieth-century phenomenon. The increasing need to address economic needs on a multilateral basis can be seen in such disparate tasks as the creation of man-made liquidity in the IMF (special drawing rights), environmental protection, rescues of countries facing financial crises, and application of economic sanctions against Iraq.

The proliferation of new financial instruments and the ability of investors and speculators to quickly and cheaply move massive amounts of capital flows across national borders in search of quick profits have diminished (not eliminated) the abilities of central bankers to follow an independent monetary policy. When the U.S. Federal Reserve Board raised interest rates in 1994, it reduced the incentive to foreign investors to retain riskier assets denominated in Mexican pesos. Higher returns in the United States from the tightening of monetary policy made the international financial community less tolerant of unfolding Mexican economic problems—an attitude that had major negative consequences for that country. The one-world capital market has little sentiment regarding damage to individual countries from massive outflows of money.

The devastating effects on domestic living standards of capital flight and massive selling of the currencies and stocks of the so-called emerging markets have gone far beyond anyone's expectations. Investors and speculators have become so unforgiving of what they perceive as bad domestic economic policies that financial crises can be transmitted with lightning speed from one country to others perceived to have similar problems. In the first instance, the Mexican peso crisis of 1994–1995 triggered a few, relatively mild capital outflows from other countries, an exercise in interdependence labelled the "tequila effect." What started out in 1997 as a barely noticed loss of confidence in Thailand's economy soon mushroomed into the conflagration dubbed "Asian contagion" that sent huge economic and political shock waves throughout that continent. Investor psychology was so shaken that when the Russian government one year later announced a de facto default on its debt, shock waves hit financial markets all over the world. A few months later, in yet another extraordinary demonstration of the grip of global economic interdependence, an obscure governor of an obscure Brazilian state inadvertently unleashed another round of heavy selling in stock and bond markets. He attracted the attention of the world's financial media when he announced a moratorium in his state's debt payments to the federal government and thereby further undermined confidence in the outlook for Brazil's economy. The "flight to quality" induced by global financial contagion was so massive that investors bought so many relatively safe long-term U.S. Treasury bonds that interest rates on these instruments declined to levels not seen in four decades.

Despite a floating exchange rate system that was supposed to insulate domestic macroeconomic policy from external pressures, government officials have less flexibility than ever before in implementing economic policies on the basis of internal rather than external concerns. Floating exchange rates have not been able to arrest an accelerated transmission of macroeconomic policies from one country to another. The steady and large appreciation of the U.S. dollar's exchange rate beginning in 1981 forced western Europe to maintain interest rates far above those appropriate to the virtual absence of real growth in those countries at the time. Cries of anguish emerged, especially from West Germany, which felt compelled to support the deutsche mark with interest rates at levels high enough to discourage large capital outflows into higher yielding, dollar-denominated assets. Interdependence meant that, in turn, other western European countries were forced to follow the leader—West Germany—into a tighter monetary policy that they otherwise would not have adopted in view of stable prices in their home markets. A senior German commercial bank official moaned that the high U.S. rates were "gradually strangling Europe."[15] Otmar Emminger, former president of the Bundesbank, the German central bank, complained in 1986 that "Never before has the fiscal policy of one country . . . had such an enormous impact on the outside world."[16]

Ironically, in 1992 Germany was on the receiving end of an international outcry deploring the injurious effects on other countries of its own high interest rates. The political unification of West and East Germany had produced large increases in budgetary outlays, the effect of which was to stimulate increases in private sector bank borrowing, the money supply, and inflationary pressures that were absolutely unacceptable to the Bundesbank. The central bank thereupon initiated a series of demand-retarding increases in domestic interest rates. Given the fact that other countries in the European Monetary System (EMS) had effectively pegged the exchange rate of their currencies to the deutsche mark, they had no choice but to immediately match these increases in interest rates, even though they were appropriate only to German economic trends. (Interest rate differentials at some point inevitably produce realignments in exchange rates.)

For the same reason, the United Kingdom had no choice but to increase its domestic interest rates in line with Germany in order to keep the pound sterling attractive to investors. The result was that an externally imposed tight monetary policy prolonged and deepened the long British recession, which otherwise would have called for expansionary macroeconomic policies. With growth and employment in Britain (and elsewhere in Western Europe) the innocent victims of German unification, speculators began to pound the pound in (an accurate) anticipation of a depreciation in its exchange rate. The British government eventually decided the costs of interdependence were too great and in late 1992 withdrew its currency from the EMS, thereby allowing a reduction in domestic interest rates and causing the pound's exchange rate to decline.

The intensification of interdependence is not greeted with unequivocal joy by governments; the only thing unequivocal is the sense of importance they attach to it. Increased interdependence suggests a higher degree of economic vulnerability to both changing economic events in other countries and the whims of market forces. It compels sovereign states to discuss and coordinate economic actions that previously would have been considered an off-limits part of their domestic domain. Nevertheless, the vast majority of countries still believe that the cost of international economic interdependence is less than its benefits.

THE EXTERNAL SECTOR'S EXPANDING IMPACT ON THE DOMESTIC ECONOMY

Two factors largely explain why international trade and capital movements have become a major concern of senior policymakers in the United States and elsewhere. The first is the aforementioned acceptance by all governments of responsibility for how well or poorly the domestic economy performs. The electorate's demand for a steady increase in the standard of living means that anything that significantly affects domestic economic performance is an important variable in determining who is president (or prime minister) and which party controls the legislative branch.

The lifespans of democratically elected governments are closely tied to their success in achieving three primary domestic economic objectives: growth, full employment, and price stability. Economic growth, in turn, is essential to a country's achieving social objectives in a non-inflationary environment. The absence of a growing work force or profitable corporations limits the size of the tax base that generates the income to finance the social safety net of income support (retirement income, health insurance, unemployment compensation, welfare, etc.) that all democracies are expected to provide.

No government is willing to fully entrust the invisible hand of the free market with the job of achieving the level of domestic economic performance that will please voters and sustain the political status quo. All countries, some more than others, seek to enhance the market mechanism by providing financial support to, and reducing the regulatory burdens on, favored industrial sectors.

Governments have encroached on the domestic economy in all capitalist countries since World War II. Increases in the percentage of gross domestic product accounted for by governments have become a universal trend. Government expenditures as a percent of GDP in the industrial countries increased from 12 percent in 1913 to an estimated 48 percent in 1997.[17] In the United States, one of the more free market–oriented countries, total governmental expenditures as a percent of total output rose from 18 percent in 1940 to 51 percent in 1996.[18] Twenty-seven new regulatory agencies were added to the federal bureaucracy in the 20-year period commencing in 1960, and 20 of them emerged just in the 1970s.[19] Governments around the world have assigned domestic agencies a greater role in the international economic policy decision-making process because of the growing recognition that the internal impact of external events and trends is pervasive. In administrative terms, the result has been a relative diminution of foreign ministry clout in the formulation and conduct of international economic policy in both the United States and abroad.

The second factor forcing political leaders—more so in Europe, Japan, and Canada—to attach high priority to international trade and finance is what might be called the bottom line of interdependence: the increasing impact of global economic developments on how a domestic economy performs. In the words of the noted management scholar Peter Drucker, the distinction between the domestic and the international economy among industrialized countries "has ceased to be a reality. . . . An unambiguous lesson of the last 40 years is that increased participation in the world economy has become the key to domestic economic growth and prosperity."[20]

As they grow in importance, external factors increasingly enhance, alter, or disrupt domestic economic policy objectives. Policymakers cannot ignore the fact that for three decades, exports as a percent of GDP have been increasing steadily for virtually every major country (see Table 2.1), including the United States. Exports have reached a sufficiently large percentage of the average country's GDP that improving or deteriorating economic conditions among its major trading partners will have a measurable impact on domestic economic conditions. The spread of "financial contagion" beyond Asia prompted Federal Reserve Chairman Alan Greenspan to warn that "it is just not credible that the United States can remain an oasis of prosperity unaffected by a world that is

Table 2.1
Merchandise Exports as Percent of GDP

	United States	Germany	Japan	Canada
1960	3.8	15.8	9.2	14.7
1997	8.5	24.3	10.0	34.7

Sources: "Background Paper" by Robert Solomon in Report of the Twentieth Century Fund, *Partners in Prosperity* (New York: Priority Press Publications, 1991); and International Monetary Fund, *International Financial Statistics*, October 1998.

experiencing greatly increased stress."[21] In some countries, like Saudi Arabia, governmental revenues are overwhelmingly dependent on export earnings. Canadian exports to the United States in the late 1990s had grown to the equivalent of one-third of Canada's GDP.[22] Inevitably, economic conditions in Canada are strongly influenced by trends in aggregate demand south of its border that are beyond the control of the Canadian government.

The unprecedented U.S. hunger for increased imports during the 1983–1986 period was the greatest single force for growth in the world economy during those years. This situation was described in a September 1985 speech by Karl Otto Pohl, then-president of the West German Central Bank:

> This strong performance of the U.S. economy during the past three years was also one of the main reasons why other industrialized countries were able to recover. The U.S. economy . . . accounted for about 70% of all additional growth in this area during that time. So it is only fair to say that the United States acted somewhat like a locomotive which pulled the world economy out of stagnation and recession.[23]

Imports are a classic example of how the external sector can have important positive and negative effects on domestic economic trends. Imports can provide cheaper and/or better quality goods to local consumers. They can offset local shortages. They provide competition and thus an incentive to local producers to minimize costs and maximize attention to consumers' needs. At the same time, however, imports can displace jobs and drive local companies into bankruptcy.

Exports are revered by economic policymakers around the world as catalysts of GDP growth, creators of new jobs, and generators of foreign exchange earnings. Export-led growth can make the difference between stagnation and prosperity for a country. Japan and the Asian newly industrialized countries (NICs) long relied on export growth as a major source of economic growth and industrial development. Between the summers of 1982 and 1985, two-thirds of the increase in West Germany's GDP was due to increased exports of goods and services.[24] Even in the United States, where trade is still a relatively small percentage of GDP, a strong export sector can make a major contribution to overall growth. Increased exports accounted for almost one-third of U.S. GDP growth between 1991 and 1997.[25]

Since the mid-1980s, the U.S. economy has become heavily dependent on foreign investors and lenders to offset its inadequate pool of saving. Massive U.S. current account deficits (the statistical counterpart to investment outlays exceeding saving) were perforce offset by record-breaking cumulative net capital inflows of about $1.6 trillion during the 1985–1998 period.[26] Foreign investors became important sources of financing for the federal budget deficits in the 1980s and early 1990s. Holdings of U.S. Treasury debt by foreigners was estimated at about $20 billion in 1970, or about 9 percent of Treasury debt instruments held outside of U.S. government agencies. By 1997, the foreign share of Treasury securities had risen to $1.3 trillion, about 38 percent of the privately held total.[27] Senior officials in the U.S. Treasury Department became keenly aware of the impact of external factors on domestic interest rates. By the late 1980s, they were actively arguing against a hard-line trade policy toward Japan, a country buying a disproportionately high percentage of the expanding volume of Treasury IOUs used to finance the then–rapidly growing U.S. budget deficit.

One final statistic might usefully be cited in suggesting the significant contribution since the 1980s of foreign capital inflows to U.S. prosperity. In 1960 estimated foreign purchases of U.S. equities and long-term bonds (maturities of more than one year) were $14 billion. That number grew to $2.8 trillion in 1997.[28] Failure to attract the volume of foreign investments and loans needed to offset inadequate U.S. capital formation eventually would have resulted in higher domestic interest rates, depreciation of the dollar's exchange rate, and (presumably) lower U.S. growth rates.

The proliferation of foreign direct investment, another sector of international economic relations, has radically altered the importance of foreign business activity on corporate profit in the United States and many other large industrial countries. For major companies, the aforementioned need to achieve economies of scale means that marketing success in countries beyond the home market is nothing less than a matter of corporate survival. It is now common for the overseas component (which includes both exports and overseas sales by foreign subsidiaries) to account for 40 to 60 percent of total sales and profits of American and European companies. One brokerage firm estimated that in 1998, 40 to 45 percent of the profits of the stocks comprising the Standard and Poor's 500 index came from foreign sales.[29] Another calculation estimated that for the median company in the Standard and Poor's 500, the foreign share of total sales more than doubled between 1985 and 1997.[30] About half of all profits of British corporations are generated by sales outside the United Kingdom, while the United States alone accounts for an estimated one-third of Swiss companies' profits and almost two-fifths of the profits of major Dutch companies.[31]

The rapid spread of multinational corporations (MNCs) has led to an upsurge in intracorporate transactions that may now account for 20 percent of total world trade in manufactured goods. Transactions between U.S. parent companies and their majority-owned foreign affiliates accounted for an estimated 26 percent of total American exports and 17 percent of imports in 1996.[32] Many U.S. companies suffered sizable declines in their per share earnings between 1981 and 1985 simply because the dollar's appreciation meant that overseas earnings in depreciating foreign currencies translated into fewer dollars in their profit-and-loss statements.

As suggested above, interdependence is a two-edged sword. Above and beyond facilitating export-led growth, it also can create "leakage" whereby increased domestic demand induces a bigger increase in imports than growth in domestic jobs and production. For example, an overvalued dollar in the early 1980s raised the U.S. marginal propensity to import. The result was that a relatively rapid increase in aggregate domestic demand did not translate into commensurate growth in domestic output because imports were supplying a growing share of incremental internal consumption. The surge in imports in 1984 and 1985 was the main factor contributing to slower U.S. GDP growth at that time. Imports captured an estimated 52 percent growth in real U.S. domestic demand in the first quarter of 1985.[33]

The potential domestic financial cost of being plugged into the international system has perhaps never before been as effectively dramatized as by what happened to Swedish monetary policy in September 1992 in the midst of turmoil in the European foreign exchange markets. The Swedish central bank acted in dramatic fashion to protect the value of the krona by exploding its overnight lending rate to commercial banks to a spectacular 75 percent. There was a far greater shock when this rate was raised to the staggering level of 500 percent just a few days later.

THE INCREASING ROLE OF ECONOMICS IN INTERNATIONAL RELATIONS

To complete the explanation of the importance of international economic policy, it should be noted that never before in modern history have economic affairs accounted for so much of the day-to-day stuff of international relations. While there is no questioning the ultimate importance of war and peace, international economic concerns dominate the short-term foreign policy agendas of every country not debilitated by political anarchy or a military dictatorship. The concept of national security has been broadened to include economic strength and vitality. The United States and its allies went to war in 1991 to liberate Kuwait from the Iraqi invasion for reasons of economic security: to protect extensive oil reserves there and in neighboring Saudi Arabia.

From the dawn of modern history until the 1960s, countries became regional or global powers only on the basis of their military might and resolution to use it. Since the 1960s, influential state actors—Japan, Saudi Arabia, Kuwait, South Korea, Brazil, etc.—have come on the scene based on a new criterion: economic clout. The most important non-state actors, multinational corporations, also emerged as forces to be reckoned with in the international system because of economic significance. The decisions to lend massively and then to suspend new lending caused many multinational banks to become almost as big a factor as governments in influencing the course of events in the 1980s in the major borrowing countries of Latin America. To a lesser extent, the multibillion dollar investments by "emerging market" mutual funds were major actors in many advanced developing countries in the 1990s.

In a world dominated by democratic, market-based economies, rivalry among the major powers has shifted from territorial and ideological disputes to the industrial, services, and financial sectors. The latter are venues with entirely different rules of engagement than those of traditional international politics. Modern nation-states still compete intensely with each other, but mostly with regard to faster economic growth rates, higher living standards, technological advances, and export promotion. Ideological struggles mainly involve economic questions like the optimal degree of government regulation of markets and job security.

The promotion of economics from the secondary status of "low policy" and its elevation to a major force in international relations is of relatively recent vintage. The long-held notion that international economic issues were sufficiently marginal that they could and should be compartmentalized for handling by second-tier technocrats was discredited only in the 1970s. One of the earliest reasons for this turnabout was the nuclear "balance of terror" that imposed a hopefully permanent end to the way in which powerful countries historically had resolved their major disputes. The horrible destructiveness of nuclear weapons meant that for the first time in modern history, the great powers literally were terrified of military confrontation with one another. In addition, for the first time ever, resort to warfare among the industrialized countries of Western Europe, Japan, and the United States became unthinkable because of a lack of serious political disagreements and because of the common threat from the Soviet Union.

For 20 years after World War II, international economic relations among the noncommunist countries were so harmonious that spillover of international economic disagreements into mainstream foreign policy was nonexistent. As long as the relatively benevolent hegemony of U.S. international economic policy prevailed, the Bretton Woods system of fixed exchange rates worked well and the pursuit of trade liberalization proceeded smoothly. As long as the extremely competitive U.S. industrial sector faced no significant foreign competition, the agencies with jurisdiction in domestic policy management had no problem with leaving responsibilities for the formulation and conduct of U.S. international economic policy mainly to the technicians in the State Department.

However, by the mid-1960s, a new, more complicated era in U.S. relations with the other industrialized democracies commenced. Relative economic power gradually shifted so far away from the United States and toward Western Europe and Japan that economic tensions shifted to center stage. Economic confrontations now strained relations among countries whose political-military relationship was rock solid. The new era of "economic self-defense" for the United States was ushered in by the so-called "chicken war" that began in 1963 with the then–European Community. (The United States imposed higher tariffs on several goods in retaliation for the Community's imposition of prohibitive tariffs on imported frozen chickens.) Later in the decade, the once harmonious U.S.-Japanese alliance would be rocked by trade frictions that would continue unabated through the end of the century. The importance of economics relative to political and military concerns in the foreign policies of the United States and other countries took a quantum leap when the cold war ended. The toppling of Marxism-Leninism as a force in world politics also toppled the uncontested primacy of traditional national security concerns as the centerpiece of world politics—except during relatively infrequent periods of military crisis.

Definitions of self-interest and articulation of goals in foreign policy increasingly are couched in economic terms. East-West and North-South relations during the cold war were dominated by intense, often dangerous struggles between the forces of capitalism and communism. Today, the industrialized countries view the developing countries and the former Soviet republics mainly as a battleground for exports and as countries with balance of payments adjustment problems. Countries in Asia, Africa, and Latin America that were places where the great powers competed for the ideological hearts and minds of the people during the cold war are now markets where businesspeople coldly seek profitable investments.

The unprecedented emphasis in the postwar era on improving living standards and the quality of life is yet another factor contributing to the preeminence of international economic cooperation as a global priority. In the words of Stanley Hoffman, "There is no longer a single international system dominated by strategic concerns. Military security remains an important issue, but the new concerns of world trade, energy, food, raw materials, the world monetary system—each one with its own power hierarchy—have arisen."[34]

A world economy allowing market forces to operate more freely than ever before in modern history provides a unique opportunity to generate and distribute wealth on a global basis. Countries that used to eye each other warily (e.g., Brazil and Argentina; the United States and Mexico) have joined hands in regional free trade agreements. The proven benefits in Western Europe of trading off political autonomy for greater economic efficiency and prosperity led to negotiations on timetables for large free trade areas in the Western Hemisphere and in the Asia-Pacific region. Expanded trade or the prospect of expanded trade has the power to further alter political relations among an endless number of countries whose relative efficiencies complement one another.

The growing primacy of economic relations in foreign policy is not a guarantee of harmony among states. The loss of bonding that once was forged by the common fear of the Soviet Union has made economic diplomacy more necessary than ever. Long-time political allies regularly inflict (deliberately and inadvertently) financial hardships and dislocations on one another. Economic tensions arise between countries that have no political disagreements and harbor no historical animosities. Political and ideological compatibility between countries is insufficient to preclude escalations of economic confrontations in an era of increasing interdependence.

Disagreements among all but so-called rogue states are now dominated by such technical issues as measures utilized by governments to alter export and import flows, techniques for correcting balance of payments disequilibria, and the dangers of destabilizing private capital flows. These kinds of disagreements do not ignite military confrontations, but they do generate anger. A serious backlash against the West is a genuine possibility as countries of Southeast Asia assess the causes, costs, and cures of ''Asian contagion.''

International economic policies are becoming increasingly prevalent at both extremes of foreign policy. In addition to trying to draw countries closer together, they are frequently employed as negative, coercive tactics designed to compel countries to desist from actions that the imposing country or countries find to be dangerous or repugnant. Trade sanctions, withholding of aid, and the freezing of assets are an increasingly used middle ground between armed attack and total inaction when other governments are deemed to be acting in an unacceptable manner. Economic sanctions remain a popular means of inflicting pain and making a statement despite their spotty record in effecting changes in the political, military, economic, and humanitarian policies of targeted countries.

The new world order does not mark the ''end of history.'' Competing political ideologies may be passé, and hunger for additional territory may be over, but mankind's combative nature suggests that international struggles for influence and relative advantage will continue, only through different means. Military power will be a secondary route to international power, influence, and prestige. The new profile of a powerful country is one rich in knowledge, capital, and mastery of the newest technologies. Increasingly, nations will find an inadequate tax base, lagging technology, capital scarcities, and sluggish increases in domestic standards of living to be incompatible with the ability to absorb the economic costs and demands of regional or great power status. Economic strength already begets foreign policy strength, just as economic weakness begets weakness in foreign policy.

NOTES

1. Data source: Matthew Slaughter and Philip Swagel, ''The Effect of Globalization on Wages in the Advanced Economies,'' International Monetary Fund Working Paper WP/97/43, April 1997.

2. Harvey Bundy, ''The Organization of the Government for the Conduct of Foreign Affairs,'' in *The Commission on Organization of the Executive Branch of the Government* (Washington, D.C.: U.S. Government Printing Office, 1949), Appendix H, p. 1.

3. Data sources: David Hummels, Dana Rapoport, and Kei-Mu Yi, ''Vertical Spe-

cialization and the Changing Nature of World Trade," *Federal Reserve Bank of New York Quarterly Review* (June 1998): 79; Douglas Irwin, "The United States in a New Global Economy? A Century's Perspective," *AEA Papers and Proceedings* (May 1986): 42.

4. Data source: Deutsche Bundesbank, *Auszuge aus Presseartikeln*, 24 November 1986, p. 11.

5. Renato Ruggiero, "The High Stakes of World Trade," *Wall Street Journal*, 28 April 1998, p. A18.

6. Calculated from data in World Trade Organization, *Focus* (March 1998): 1.

7. Data sources: various GATT and WTO press releases.

8. Data source: U.S. Commerce Department, Office of Trade and Investment Analysis.

9. United Nations Conference on Trade and Development, *World Investment Report 1997*, p. xvi.

10. Data source: Bank for International Settlements web site: BIS.org/press/index.htm/.

11. Data sources: Bank for International Settlements, *Annual Report*, various editions.

12. Data source: speech of Roger W. Ferguson, Jr., Federal Reserve Board press release dated 16 April 1998, p. 1.

13. "Fear of Finance," *The Economist*, 19 September 1992, survey section, p. 9.

14. Robert Aderhold, Christine Cumming, and Allison Harwood, "International Linkages among Equities Markets and the October 1987 Market Break," *Federal Reserve Bank of New York Quarterly Review* (Summer 1988): 34.

15. Quoted in the *Wall Street Journal*, 26 February 1981, p. 30.

16. Quoted in the *Washington Post*, 8 August 1986, p. K3.

17. Data sources: *OECD Economic Outlook* 63 (June 1998) and Vito Tanzi, "The Demise of the Nation State," IMF Working Paper WP/98/120, August 1998.

18. Calculated from data in *Economic Report of the President*, 1992 and 1998 editions (Washington, D.C.: U.S. Government Printing Office).

19. Data from the Center for the Study of American Business, as reported in the *New York Times*, 15 February 1981, p. 19.

20. Peter F. Drucker, "Trade Lessons from the World Economy," *Foreign Affairs* (January–February 1994): 104.

21. Federal Reserve Board press release dated 4 September 1998.

22. Data source: "Talk of U.S. Slowdown Strikes Fear into Canada," *Wall Street Journal*, 4 December 1998, p. A2.

23. Text of address by Karl Otto Pohl, 19 September 1985, Deutsche Bundesbank, *Auszuge Aus Presseartikeln*, p. 1.

24. Robert Solomon, "Background Paper," in *Partners in Prosperity: The Report of the Twentieth Century Fund Task Force on the International Coordination of National Economic Policies* (New York: Priority Press, 1991), p. 70.

25. Data source: speech of Deputy U.S. Treasury Secretary Lawrence Summers, Treasury Department press release dated 4 August 1998.

26. Calculated from data in the 1998 *Economic Report of the President*, and the Joint Economic Committee, "Economic Indicators," April 1999. Foreign capital inflows into the United States soared to an annual rate of $215 billion in the second quarter of 1998.

27. Data source: Dorothy Meadow Sobol, "Foreign Ownership of U.S. Treasury Securities: What the Data Show and Do Not Show," Federal Reserve Bank of New York, *Current Issues in Economics and Finance* (May 1998).

28. Data source: U.S. Treasury Department, "Report on Foreign Portfolio Investment in the United States," 1998.

29. PaineWebber Corporation, "Portfolio Managers' Spotlight," 13 October 1998.

30. Data source: IBES International, as quoted in the *Wall Street Journal*, 18 August 1998, p. C1.

31. "Dances with Bulls," *The Economist*, 20 April 1991, p. 77.

32. Calculated from data in U.S. Commerce Department, *Survey of Current Business* (September 1998): 54.

33. Manufacturers Hanover Bank, *Financial Digest*, 22 April 1985, pp. 1–2.

34. Stanley Hoffmann, "Toward a New World Order," *New York Times*, 11 January 1976.

Part II

The Policymaking Machinery: The Government and the Private Sector

3   The Executive Branch

Form is substance. A properly organized decision-making process does not
guarantee decisions of high quality, but you are certain to have uneven
decisions without an orderly process.

—Donald H. Rumsfeld

A full appreciation of the functioning of the international economic policymaking system's inner level of activity—by analogy, its brain waves and personality—begins with an understanding of the system's mechanical parts—who and
what are charged with keeping it up and running. This chapter describes the
responsible departments and agencies in the executive branch, the main U.S.
government locus of international economic data gathering, analysis, option enu-
meration, and policy implementation. Description is just a first step, however.
That which can be gleaned from published mission statements and organization
charts of executive branch entities provides only limited insight into the often
subtle rhythms, nuances, and quirks of the decision-making process. Constantly
shifting organizational configurations, the separation of powers within the U.S.
government, the struggle for bureaucratic influence, new international economic
issues where agency jurisdiction is unclear, and the syndrome of the cult of
personality are the major reasons why considerable attention must be paid to
the informal and fluid dimensions of organizational process.

The executive branch is merely the most visible of the three major constituencies in the formulation and administration of U.S. international economic policy. Subsequent chapters deal with the other two key players: Congress and the
private sector. Even a recognition of all the power centers molding policy substance provides only the first layer of comprehending the decision-making proc-

ess. In the next section of the book, the myriad theories and patterns of organizational behavior will be analyzed. Only then will the explanation of the inner workings of the making of U.S. international economic policy be complete.

HISTORICAL EVOLUTION OF ORGANIZATION

Organization and procedures to plan, formulate, implement, and manage a comprehensive U.S. international economic policy were not necessary until after World War II. Although international monetary policy existed, the United States had no need to develop international investment and energy policies. Prior to 1934, trade "policy" consisted of little more than Congress periodically passing laws changing tariff levels. The role of the executive branch in trade policy seldom moved beyond collecting the tariffs mandated by Congress. This situation did not change until passage of the Reciprocal Trade Agreements Act of 1934. The bill created the need for both an increased trade negotiating capability in the State Department and a mechanism for consultations between it and the Agriculture and Commerce departments when negotiating reciprocal tariff-cutting agreements with other countries.

Throughout the late 1940s and the 1950s, U.S. international economic policy followed two tracks. First, it was the servant of national security policy. The United States' continuing global hegemony allowed it to play the role of a benign international economic giant. Given the American economy's near immunity from serious foreign competition, domestic economic policy managers were not overly concerned with external economic matters. Organizational arrangements were fairly simple: the State Department was accepted as the lead agency for formulating and coordinating foreign trade and development policies. Second, international economic policy reflected the American fondness for international law and organization. International economic issues in most cases were neatly confined to the technicians and delegations participating in the international organizations—the International Monetary Fund the (IMF), the World Bank, and the General Agreement on Tariffs and Trade (GATT)—created by the United States and its allies to administer the postwar world economy.

Structural changes in the international balance of economic power and the increasing imprint of interdependence on the U.S. economy subsequently necessitated more intricate policy decisions and therefore a more complex decision-making infrastructure. As international economic policy gradually impacted more Americans and was elevated from "low" to "high" policy, administrative changes were not far behind. The most important change was the growing presence in decision-making circles of domestic departments. Today, the majority of U.S. departments and agencies have some role to play in international economic policy. The inevitable result was a "crowding out" of the State Department and a steady erosion of its once paramount role in international economic relations. By 1998, a majority of the personnel posted abroad at U.S.

diplomatic posts came from domestic agencies rather than foreign affairs agencies.[1]

The continuous blurring of the dividing line between domestic and international economic policy has been reflected in the size of, and activism by, the international divisions of the Agriculture, Commerce, and Labor departments. The single-most significant change in modern U.S. international economic policy organization has been the sustained ascendancy of the Treasury Department's authority and influence in this field. By the late 1990s, it had joined and surpassed the State Department as an institutional superpower in the international economic policymaking process. Being a superpower connotes presence in all sectors of international economic policy formulation as well as the ability to block a final decision below the presidential level.

A second important organizational change was the growing presence and impact of agencies located within the Executive Office of the President. The expansion of presidential authority, the increased need for "in-house" advice for presidents, and the perceived need to situate cabinet-level coordination of international economic policy in the White House are three factors that have created a parallel layer of bureaucracy in the U.S. executive branch above and beyond the line departments and agencies with operational authority.

A third significant change in organization has been the intensification of bureaucratic rivalries. For more than 35 years, the Office of the U.S. Trade Representative and the Commerce Department have quietly and openly vied for leadership status on a variety of trade issues. Throughout the 1970s, the State and Treasury departments struggled mightily on the core issue of whether to tilt international economic policy towards foreign policy or economic priorities.

THE MAJOR CABINET ACTORS: TREASURY, STATE, AND COMMERCE

Any significant global economic issue will, by definition, involve the domestic economy and relations with other countries. Since these are the constituencies of the Treasury and State departments, respectively, they claim jurisdiction in every important issue in U.S. international economic policy. Because these two departments are involved in all sectors—trade, finance, development, investment, and so on—they are the "superpowers" of U.S. international economic policymaking.

The Treasury Department is the "enfant terrible" of this process. The international authority and responsibilities of Treasury have steadily grown, more because of the proliferation of international economic problems than by conscious design or a power grab at the expense of other bureaucratic actors. The steady accrual of its power and influence since the 1960s can be attributed to at least five specific factors working to Treasury's benefit. One was the need for ongoing U.S. government responses to the relative international decline of U.S. economic strength as measured in the deterioration of the U.S. balance of payments in the 1960s and recurring dollar crises that eventually caused the collapse of the fixed exchange rate standard in 1973. The need to reduce the persistent and growing U.S. balance of payments deficits has received very high priority and recurring presidential attention. Balance of payments adjustment, especially in the 1960s and 1970s, became a metaphor for the government's resolve and ability to put its international economic house in order. As a consequence, the external deficit was attacked by a host of corrective programs that grew in number because efforts to restrain U.S. capital outflows were embarrassingly ineffectual. Every dollar spent overseas by the U.S. government or by American businesses and tourists became fair game for Treasury perusal. Every aspect of U.S. international economic policy required a Treasury presence to assure that balance of payments implications received proper considerations. By 1971 the correlation between a secular decline in the U.S. trade surplus and the accelerated deterioration in the U.S. balance of payments position had become fully apparent. Trade policy immediately was added to full-time Treasury preoccupations.

The floating exchange rate system that in 1973 replaced the shattered fixed exchange rate regime utterly failed to introduce what were expected to be smaller, more gradual changes in exchange rates. Sharp downward swings in the dollar's exchange rate in the 1977–1978 period and the extraordinary strength of the dollar in the first half of the 1980s put both the international monetary system and U.S. relations with the other industrialized countries under heavy stress. Decisions on the very important questions of whether the U.S. government should pursue domestic and external policy initiatives aimed at stabilizing the value of the dollar are uncontested responsibilities of the secretary of the treasury.

A second contributing factor to increased Treasury Department authority is the upward spiral in the impact of the external sector on domestic economic policy management discussed in Chapter 2. Treasury's lead role in domestic economic policy management assures that in any significant international economic policy issue it will have a role that is at least the equal of any other department. Hence, the department is influential in policy discussions of import restraints, financial assistance to less developed countries (LDCs), access to foreign-produced oil and raw materials, and inward foreign direct investment. The up-and-down efforts begun in the 1980s by the Group of Seven economic powers to coordinate macroeconomic policy are an important new sector of international economic relations where the Treasury Department is again the dominant bureaucratic actor in preparing U.S. policy. Whereas the president holds the spotlight in the annual economic summits, the treasury secretary represents the U.S. viewpoint in the ministerial-level meetings of the Organization for Economic Cooperation and Development (OECD) and of the Group of Seven meetings held at the finance ministers and deputy levels.

A third factor is the seemingly endless series of international financial crises—yet another undisputed Treasury sphere of influence—that have been wreaking havoc on the global economy since the first oil shock in 1973. Following in rapid succession were the second oil price shock in 1979–1980 and the LDC debt crisis in the 1980s. Precipitous declines in investor confidence in the emerging markets produced the Mexican peso crisis, Asian contagion, and financial instability in Russia and Mexico in the 1990s. Like the finance ministries of all other industrialized countries, the Treasury Department has undisputed jurisdiction over U.S. international monetary policy (exchange rate policy, balance of payments programs, international monetary reform, etc.) and international financial policy (private capital flows and international bank lending). The department also assumed a leadership role in assisting former communist countries to make the transition to market-based economies and took charge of assembling rescue packages (dubbed ''bail-outs'' by critics) for emerging market countries facing destabilizing capital outflows and collapsing exchange rates.

Congressional extension to Treasury of leadership through new economic legislation has been another source of added authority. The Bretton Woods Agreements Act placed the secretary of the treasury in charge of U.S. participation in the IMF and the World Bank. U.S. participation in the regional multilateral development banks (the Inter-American and Asian Development banks, for example) similarly was placed under the overall guidance of the treasury secretary. The U.S. executive directors in the IMF and the development banks usually come from the ranks of the senior Treasury staff, and they receive their voting instructions from that institution. Perception of this department as being ''hard-nosed'' induced Congress in the 1970s to give Treasury primacy in what was then a hotly contested debate about whether the United States should participate in international commodity agreements.

A final contributing factor is that all modern-day presidents formally designated the secretary of the treasury as the senior economic policy official in the U.S. government. This status set the stage for the cabinet superstar roles assumed by John Connally, George Shultz, William Simon, James Baker, and Robert Rubin. Empirical evidence of the effects of this bond include Connally's almost total control of U.S. international economic policy in late 1971 and presidents' naming of subsequent treasury secretaries to chair the senior White House economic policy-coordinating forum.

The bulk of Treasury's international economic activities is concentrated in the Office of International Affairs (OIA). From the relatively obscure Office of International Finance, which in the 1960s numbered well under 50 professionals, a bureaucratic colossus evolved. Now with a trained economics staff about three times as large, along with access to economists in the domestic Treasury bureaus, OIA has the resources to weigh in at every governmental exercise considering any important international economic policy issue. This staff represents the largest single U.S. government body of international economic expertise (with the possible exception of the Central Intelligence Agency).

The scope of Treasury's international policy reach is suggested by OIA's organization chart, reproduced in Figure 3.1. Seventeen offices with functional

Figure 3.1
Organization of the Office of International Affairs

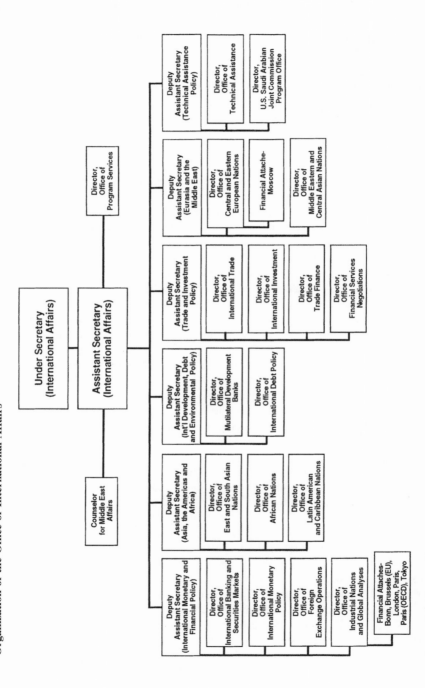

Source: U.S. Treasury Department.

and geographic responsibilities operate under six deputy assistant secretaries. The head of OIA is the under secretary of treasury for international affairs. This post was created in 1989, mainly to placate the demands of David Mulford, who had become assistant secretary for international affairs in 1984. Mulford, a man of uncommon intelligence, ambition, staying power, negotiating skill, and ego, took OIA along for the ride as he shrewdly established himself as one of the most influential international economic officials in any major industrialized country. Be it exchange rate policy, responses to the LDC debt problem, economic assistance to the former Soviet Union, or financial liberalization in Japan, Mulford (in part due to the limited international economic interests of the then–treasury secretary, Nicholas Brady) invariably served as the point man for most important non-trade issues until he resigned in 1992.

The deputy assistant secretary for international monetary and financial policy deals with the heart of Treasury's concerns. The offices reporting to this person provide the staff work that backstops the formulation of U.S. balance of payments policy, financial policies vis-à-vis the other industrialized countries, international banking questions, and U.S. participation in international economic organizations such as the IMF, OECD, and the more informal Group of Seven. Another office monitors the foreign exchange market and will inform senior officials when it thinks that government intervention would be advisable to address "disorderly" markets, that is, excessive gyrations in the dollar's exchange rate.

The offices reporting to four other deputy assistant secretaries represent Treasury's increased interest in the developing countries—including the poorest, the oil-rich, the magnets for private capital, and the countries whose economies are "in transition." These offices assemble the economic data used to prepare the voting instructions for the (highly influential) U.S. executive directors in the multilateral development banks—the World Bank, the Inter-American Development Bank, etc.—and to formulate U.S. debt relief policies for the most heavily indebted LDCs. These offices are also the center of upgraded U.S. government efforts to monitor domestic economic trends in the emerging markets in the effort to head off further unforeseen international financial crises. The OIA provides technical economic advice to former communist countries through the placement of resident and visiting consultants (usually hired on a contract basis); the principal goal is to assist in making these countries' public and commercial financial systems compatible with market-based systems. Finally, another office provides the personnel (again, mostly on a contract basis) to staff U.S. economic advisory functions in the Joint Commission established to encourage close working relations between Saudi Arabia and the U.S. government.

OIA plays an active, albeit subordinate, role in trade policymaking. Despite its financial orientation, Treasury takes an active interest here for several reasons. Liberalization of restraints on trade in financial services and limits on concessional export financing by governments have been added to the agenda of multilateral trade negotiations. Furthermore, the trade balance strongly affects both the U.S. balance of payments position and some important sectors within the domestic economy. Despite the Treasury Department's ostensibly ''inward'' orientation, it is incorrect to assume that it believes import-restrictive measures serve the national interest. The fact that the overall economy is Treasury's constituency, rather than any particular sector, elevates the department's concern about minimizing inflation and maximizing competition above parochial protectionist leanings. The department's role in international investment policy stems from its being designated as chair of the interagency Committee on Foreign Investment in the United States. The latter is charged with implementing the intent of the Exon-Florio amendment, a statutory provision requiring executive branch review of foreign acquisitions of American companies in order to assure that none would damage U.S. national security.

There are offices in the Treasury Department other than OIA that have responsibilities touching on technical dimensions of international economic relations. International tax matters are handled by Treasury, be they tax treaties with other countries or tax regulations to be applied to foreign-owned companies operating within the United States.[2] The U.S. Customs Service has become an occasional factor in trade relations by virtue of being the bureau that rules on what tariff classifications should be assigned to specific imports. This jurisdiction has produced politically sensitive decisions on whether cars imported from Canada have enough local content to qualify for duty-free treatment under the free trade agreement with that country and whether to classify imports of Japanese mini-vans as passenger cars or light trucks (which are subject to much higher tariffs). The Office of Foreign Assets Control enforces economic sanctions that take the form of seizure of the financial assets under U.S. jurisdiction that are owned by targeted foreign countries and narcotics traffickers.

During the 160 years after establishment of the U.S. government, the State Department dominated the conduct of economic relations with other governments. The administrative linchpin of U.S. external economic policymaking in the interwar period was the department's Division of Commercial Policy and Agreements. The department's power in U.S. international economic policy has been eclipsed by the parallel ascent since the 1960s of domestic agencies. It was in this decade that policy began its tilt away from a nearly pure foreign policy orientation towards a delicately balanced internal-external mix reflecting the growing intrusion of interdependence in the domestic U.S. economy.

The department gradually evolved into the role of an important participant in the making of international economic policy rather than one with the mantle of leadership. State cannot match the technical expertise and national political constituencies of the domestically oriented agencies. Nevertheless, the department inflicted some of this decline on itself. It was very late in taking international economics seriously, and State has yet to fully overcome the stigma of being perceived as having a knee-jerk predisposition to accommodate foreigners' interests. When the U.S. government has felt the need to show resolve or place domestic economic considerations ahead of global priorities, the State Department's authority tends to suffer. In 1957, the Trade Policy Committee was established, with the secretary of commerce as chairman, to dilute State's control over the operations of the Trade Agreements Program. This trend accelerated in the 1960s with congressional passage of the Trade Expansion Act that stripped the department of its traditional role as head of U.S. delegations to trade negotiations.

Today, the department has the primary responsibility for only a few international economic issues. On most trade, financial, and investment issues, leadership has gravitated to the Treasury or Commerce departments or to White House offices. The State Department has retained a leadership role in bilateral foreign aid and in a few narrowly focused issues like civil aviation treaties (including landing rights), global rules and liberalization measures in the telecommunications services sector, maritime port access, and scientific issues. The formulation of international science and technology policies is one of the responsibilities of a separate State Department unit, the Bureau of Oceans and International Environmental and Scientific Affairs.

Nevertheless, the State Department's transcendent task of integrating economic interests into overall U.S. foreign policy goals requires it to participate in international economic policy formulation efforts as extensively as any other department—with the sole exception in the 1990s of Treasury. The secretary of state is still the president's chief foreign policy adviser. Most observers agree that the United States' role as lone global superpower requires that at least some attention be paid to the foreign policy implications of both U.S. international economic policy action and inaction in all but the most technical, and therefore apolitical, matters. Despite increased clout by the domestic agencies, the State Department, like the Treasury, is sufficiently influential and ubiquitous in the decision-making process to be in a position to prevent interagency consensus on almost any international economic issue if a clear national security threat can credibly be demonstrated to other departments. Although Treasury, Agriculture, and Commerce economic officers are assigned to the larger U.S. embassies, State officials head the economics sections of these missions, do most of the economic reporting from overseas missions, and control communications between Washington and U.S. embassies and consulates.

The permanent post of undersecretary of state for economic affairs was created in 1972 to increase the department's representative clout in senior interagency deliberations. On a formal basis, this position operates independent of the rest of the department, relying only on a small personal staff. The heart of the State Department's economic policy activities, the Bureau of Economic and Business Affairs (E/B), reports only informally to this undersecretary. As seen in Figure 3.2, this "functional" bureau is currently headed by an assistant secretary who oversees a professional staff of approximately 130, most of whom are foreign service officers with some economics training (this figure is down about 10 positions from five years previously, presumably a reflection of the

Figure 3.2
Organization of the Bureau of Economic and Business Affairs

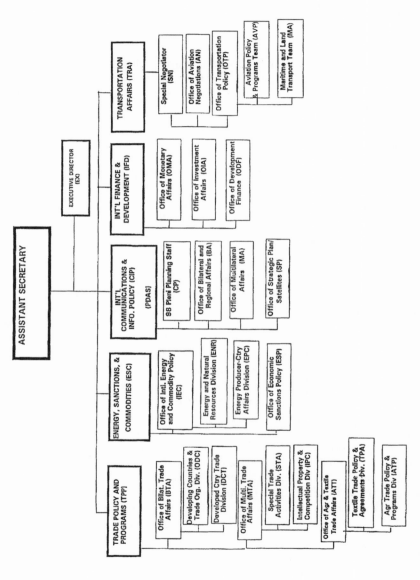

Source: U.S. Department of State.

budget cutbacks absorbed by State). In between these two levels are five deputy assistant secretaries overseeing 20 separate offices clustered around trade policy, international communications and information policies, energy and natural resources, transportation, and finance and development.

A limited version of the bureaucratic politics model of decision-making (to be discussed in Chapters 7 and 8) often applies to the relationship between the economics-oriented technocrats of E/B, on the one hand, and the relatively more parochial political officers assigned to the regional bureaus, on the other hand. The latter's primary assignment is to enhance the U.S. political relationship with specific countries, not worry about economic niceties. The long period of limited internal clout by E/B ended only in the early 1980s, when senior State officials belatedly accepted the fact that neither the increased prominence of domestic concerns in U.S. international economic policy nor the increased importance of economics to U.S. foreign policy were temporary phenomena. The economics bureau is no longer a departmental backwater. The one-time career disincentive to join the economics hierarchy has disappeared, and economics-oriented foreign service officers as a group seem to be able to move up the ranks as quickly as their political colleagues.

Efforts at economics consciousness-raising among the majority of foreign service officers who do not serve in the E/B bureau now occur with some frequency. The then–deputy secretary of state, Lawrence Eagleburger, stated in a November 1989 speech that while his department at times had been perceived (correctly) as letting economic interests play "second fiddle to geopolitics," that was "a luxury" that could be afforded only in an era that "has passed." He told his audience that State "will have to assume a greater and, indeed, more vigorous role in the promotion of our economic interests overseas" because the overall economic health of the United States "may increasingly be seen as the country's number one national security interest."[3]

The world economy became so precarious in 1998 as to be a national security problem. Economic malaise threatened political instability in many countries, like Russia and Indonesia, that are important to U.S. global diplomatic and security interests. Secretary of State Madeleine Albright told a public audience of her concerns about the implications of 100 million Asians being suddenly plunged back into poverty: social and political instability, the potential for backlash against a more open economic system, and labor rights abuses.[4]

Unlike the conceptual policy oversight that characterizes the mandates of the Treasury and State departments, the Department of Commerce is responsible for administering a number of import- and export-related programs that have clearly defined rules and objectives. In addition to these duties, the department's other broad role is to represent its constituency—the manufacturing and service industries—in interagency deliberations on trade and international investment matters. Aggressive commerce secretaries can and do parlay these responsibilities into occasional flashes of influence and public notice for the department. Most recently, this effort can be seen in efforts to expand the agenda of the

Commerce-chaired Trade Promotion Coordinating Committee by defining export promotion in the broadest possible sense (e.g., including advocacy for renewing the president's fast-track negotiating authority).

The department's expertise on the structure of domestic industries and its role as enforcer of most statutes dealing with unfair import competition allowed the late Commerce Secretary Malcolm Baldrige to take charge of many bilateral trade initiatives in the 1980s, including efforts to restrain European steel exports and leadership of the president's trade "strike force," formed to challenge foreign import barriers. A major incentive exists for all future secretaries of commerce to seek opportunities to play a lead role in trade policy: other "juicy" substantive policy issues open to the department have been few and far between, especially on the domestic side.

In terms of policy clout, the United States has the weakest commercial ministry of any industrialized country. The explanation is rooted in the historical pattern of an arms-length distance being maintained between American industry and government, a relationship fostered by both sides. It reflects this country's general abhorrence of economic planning and the desire of private business for maximum freedom from government interference. Most corporate executives remain content to rely on an ad hoc system of contacts in the executive branch and Congress in lieu of a powerful ministry to represent it directly. When the Republicans took control of Congress in 1994, one of their suggestions for smaller government was to abolish the department outright.[5]

Limits on its policymaking clout notwithstanding, the Commerce Department plays an important operational role in the conduct of U.S. international commercial relations. The department is the chief administrator of many U.S. government export promotion programs, as well as chief enforcer of export controls on dual-use (civilian and military) technology. The Commerce Department is responsible for enforcing U.S. antiboycott legislation that limits U.S. business compliance with other countries' boycotts, principally the one imposed on Israel by the Arab League. It also collects and analyzes statistics on U.S. trade and international investment flows.

The Department of Commerce, along with the Office of the USTR, was the big bureaucratic winner in the 1980 reorganization of the trade policymaking process. The realignment significantly added to the department's influence by transferring to it responsibility for administration of two important laws—dumping and countervailing duties—affecting unfair foreign trade practices. The switch was the culmination of growing resentment among critics who charged that the Treasury Department had been too lax in its enforcement of these laws. They alleged that Treasury's culture was far more interested in macro issues such as price stability than in addressing the import grievances of individual American companies. Since 1980, the Department of Commerce has investigated private sector petitions alleging injury from dumping—imports being sold in the U.S. market at prices that are below fair value either because they are below prices of comparable goods in the exporter's home market or because they are priced below production costs. This has been the import-relief statute most often used by the U.S. business sector since the mid-1980s, and Commerce's tendency to rule in favor of domestic companies has generated considerable visibility for and criticism of the department. It also investigates accusations that foreign producers are receiving subsidies from their governments that enable them to artificially lower the prices of their exports. In both cases, Commerce is responsible for the final verdict as to whether and how much relief in the form of import duty penalties is warranted.[6]

Another addition to the Commerce Department's jurisdiction in 1980 was management of the U.S. and Foreign Commercial Service. After years of bureaucratic in-fighting between the State and Commerce departments over control of the overseas commercial representation function, the Carter administration decided to create a separate foreign service specializing in promoting industrial and services exports. In another manifestation of bureaucratic politics, critics long had accused State Department officers of being far more interested in national security matters than in advising businesspeople on exporting and spotting new foreign trade barriers. Hence the new foreign service was assigned to a more export-friendly department. With an emphasis on assisting medium and small-sized companies, the Commercial Service in 1998 had personnel in 144 posts in 78 countries and operated 92 Export Assistance Centers in U.S. cities.[7]

These "field" operations complement the international trade and investment data services provided to the U.S. business community by the Washington-based operation of Commerce's International Trade Administration (ITA). It contains experts on all major manufacturing and services sectors. Their main mission is to provide detailed data on domestic economic conditions to trade negotiators and economic policymakers. The ITA also houses country desk officers on all major markets for U.S. exports and foreign direct investment. For the business community, it operates a "one stop" Trade Information Center, the Advocacy Network to help American companies bid on major overseas contracts, and a database on the countries designated as the "Big Emerging Markets." ITA is also responsible for monitoring foreign compliance with bilateral trade agreements such as those negotiated under the Agreement on Clothing and Textiles (which superseded the Multifiber Arrangement). Another part of Commerce manages some of the programs, most notably the Advanced Technology Program, spawned by increased official efforts to enhance the competitiveness of the U.S. high-tech sector (see Chapter 11).

WHITE HOUSE OFFICES

Flourishing within the Executive Office of the President—colloquially called the White House—is a large, diversified layer of bureaucracy unique to the United States. The entire executive branch of many countries consists of fewer people than the nearly two thousand employees of the Executive Office who serve as presidential advisers, functional specialists such as budget officers and trade negotiators, support staff, and so on.

Four White House offices have a significant role in the making of U.S. international economic policy. Proximity to the chief executive and the prestige of being located in the Executive Office of the President offer great potential to influence the outcome of policy deliberations. But nothing is automatic. The actual degree of ''clout'' held by these White House offices varies according to presidential work styles, personalities and competence of cabinet members, and personal relations between the president and his immediate advisers.

The Office of the United States Trade Representative (USTR) is a structural anomaly: a White House office with specific policymaking responsibilities. As a consequence, it functions at a level midway between its original role as a White House–based ''honest broker,'' or dispassionate policy coordinator, and a line agency trying to directly influence policy substance. The office is charged with developing and coordinating U.S. international trade, commodity, and direct investment policies, and leading negotiations with other countries on these matters. The cabinet-level head of USTR acts as the ''principal trade advisor, negotiator, and spokesperson'' for the president.[8] The policy leadership of USTR is exerted in a number of areas. They include bilateral trade issues and multilateral matters falling within the jurisdiction of the World Trade Organization (WTO); trade, commodity, and direct investment matters dealt with by other international institutions; import policy; export expansion policy; industrial and services trade policy; and trade-related intellectual property rights issues.

By design, the USTR office is supposed to function like the hub of a wheel, with numerous spokes reaching out to all segments—governmental and private sector—of the trade community. The office is the chair of a web of interagency trade policy committees and subcommittees (discussed in detail in the next chapter) that exist at all levels of seniority. USTR officials chair the subcabinet Trade Policy Review Group and the Trade Policy Staff Committee. They also chaired the cabinet-level Trade Policy Committee prior to its being shelved in the 1980s in favor of a White House coordinator. These groups are responsible for formulating nearly all general trade policy positions as well as many case-by-case decisions regarding the operation of programs. The mandate of these committees stretches from articulation of multilateral negotiating strategy to determining whether to impose temporary import barriers under the escape clause statute (in order to assist domestic producers who have been deemed to be injured by fair foreign competition).

For reasons discussed below, Congress and the USTR have maintained an unusually close working relationship. In addition to dozens of formal congressional committee appearances by senior staff, USTR annual reports invariably refer to ''hundreds'' of informal briefings and consultations held annually with members of Congress. By statute, five members of each house are formally appointed at any given time as official congressional advisers to USTR on trade policy. During multilateral trade negotiations, these senators and representatives (as well as other members) are given observer status on the U.S. delegation. In yet another coordination function, USTR serves as the main federal liaison on trade matters with state and local governments.

The USTR is also the administrative overseer of a permanent network of private sector advisory committees that were initiated in the 1970s to assist the executive branch during the Tokyo Round of multilateral trade negotiations. Congress subsequently passed legislation expanding the role of these committees so that they now advise the government on trade negotiating objectives, assist in monitoring foreign compliance with signed agreements, and provide input and advice on the general development of U.S. trade policy. At present, approximately 1,000 private sector experts comprise 34 different committees. At the top of the system is the Advisory Committee for Trade Policy and Negotiations containing 45 people representing all major constituencies affected by trade. Comprising the second level are eight, more narrowly focused policy advisory committees dealing with agriculture, industry, services and investment, labor, intergovernmental (state and local) views, trade and the environment, defense, and Africa. Finally, there are 25 sectoral, technical, and functional advisory committees divided into two areas, industry and agriculture.

The office is headed by the United States Trade Representative, a member of the cabinet with ambassadorial rank, and three Deputy USTRs, one resident in Geneva (site of the WTO) and two in Washington, D.C. There are some 20 other senior staff members, most with the rank of assistant USTR, who head functional offices (general counsel—charged with interpreting trade statutes, WTO and multilateral affairs, industry, agriculture, services and investment, environment and natural resources, textiles, policy coordination, and so on), and five geographic offices.

Congress created the USTR arrangement because of its reading of bureaucratic politics. Misgivings on Capitol Hill and in the private sector about the State Department's ability to drive a sufficiently hard bargain and bring home the most advantageous trade agreement in the then-impending Kennedy Round of tariff-cutting negotiations inspired the Congress to create the position of the special representative for trade negotiations in the Trade Expansion Act of 1962. (The supporting office was created the next year by an executive order.) After considerable debate, it was thought that a White House location would afford the chief trade negotiator maximum objectivity and prestige as the "chief representative" of the United States in negotiations aimed at reducing trade barriers. The USTR has taken the lead in securing congressional support and the necessary supplemental legislation for trade agreements entered into by the executive branch.

From the beginning, senior USTR officials have heard and heeded a subtle message sent to them from Capitol Hill: "what the Congress creates, the Congress can also abolish." They therefore accept the need to retain a balanced perspective between the economic desirability of reducing trade barriers and the sociopolitical necessity of being responsive to the complaints of domestic producers and workers concerning import-induced dislocations and foreign import barriers that curb U.S. exports. The quasi-parental relationship with Congress has kept the office of the USTR from adopting the bureaucratic perspective of knee-jerk advocates of liberalized trade and accommodators of trading partners' negotiating positions. This inter-branch cordiality has also protected USTR when presidents and the Commerce Department have tried to usurp its responsibilities (as was the case in the Reagan administration's proposed transfer in 1983 of the USTR's functions into an expanded Commerce Department).

As first constituted, the Office of the Special Representative for Trade Negotiations (its original name) had a permanent staff of only 20 to 30 professionals. This small size, which lasted through the 1970s, necessitated extensive participation by personnel from the State, Agriculture, Commerce, and Treasury departments, among others, in preparing trade policy positions and staffing the U.S. delegations to major trade talks.

The Trade Act of 1974 gave a major boost to the White House–based trade operation by elevating the position of special trade representative to cabinet status and giving legislated life to the supporting office. These actions reflected in part congressional displeasure with efforts by another White House coordinating group, the Council on International Economic Policy (CIEP), in the 1972-1973 period to absorb the office. The CIEP viewed the special trade representative as a rival within the White House, but the Congress forcefully demonstrated its ''parental'' concern for the smooth functioning of its bureaucratic offspring.

A major step up for USTR in the bureaucratic version of the evolutionary ladder of authority occurred when Reorganization Plan Number 3 of 1979 was implemented on January 4, 1980. As part of the reorganization of the U.S. trade policy machinery, the newly renamed Office of the United States Trade Representative received a broader mandate and doubled in size to approximately 77 professionals. Whereas its original jurisdiction had been effectively limited to multilateral trade negotiations and certain issues of import policy, the USTR became, at least nominally, the lead agency in developing and coordinating the implementation of U.S. trade and investment policies.

The size of the USTR professional staff vacillates up and down depending on whether major trade negotiations are in progress. During the second Clinton administration, the total number of permanent professional slots was about 150. In the private opinion of one trade official (who worked in a different agency), this growth in staff had profound, or critical-mass, implications in that USTR subsequently possessed sufficient human resources to develop positions on, and write interagency talking papers dealing with, most evolving trade issues. When it was smaller and, therefore, heavily dependent on specialists in the line departments for expertise and memo generation, USTR was depicted by this official as being able to chair interagency deliberations as a true honest broker and independent advocate, free of ''pride of authorship.'' In at least one increasingly active coordinating forum, the Commerce-chaired Trade Promotion

Coordinating Committee, USTR is just another participating agency. Dropping any pretense of dispassionate coordinator, it operates exactly like the committee's other members: it is an advocate, submitting and critiquing ideas for new and existing programs that assist American exporters and increase export shipments.

The International Affairs Division of the Office of Management and Budget (OMB) is an influential actor in the policymaking process by virtue of its power to approve or reject annual budget proposals submitted by executive branch agencies to the White House for inclusion in the administration's cumulative budget request that will be sent to Capitol Hill. This power is most evident in the two capital-intensive components of U.S. international economic policy. One is foreign aid. The other involves funding of the Export-Import Bank and numerous export promotion programs scattered in various departments. Another source of OMB significance is its responsibility for coordinating all administration testimony prepared for presentation to all congressional committee hearings.

The three-member Council of Economic Advisers (CEA) was created by the Full Employment Act of 1946 to provide the president with non-political, technical assessments of developments and trends in the U.S. economy and to advise him on policies that would best promote growth and stability. Given CEA's mandate to produce pure, state-of-the-art economic analysis, its members usually are drawn from academia for a limited tour of service. The recognized impact of the external sector on the domestic economy has led to one of the three members of the CEA being assigned international responsibilities, with the support of at least one senior staff economist. Paucity of personnel means that involvement in international economic policy formulation is mainly on a pick-and-choose basis, where potentially serious domestic economic consequences (those issues that threaten economic growth, price stability, or full employment) are perceived. The chair of the CEA heads the U.S. delegation to the Economic Policy Committee of the OECD and traditionally is the chair of that committee.

The National Security Council (NSC) is a fourth White House office directly involved in the making of U.S. international economic policy. It was established by the National Security Act of 1947 for the purpose of advising the president with respect to "the integration of domestic, foreign, and military policies relating to the national security." In practice, this has meant coordinating the high-level policy advice of the State and Defense departments and having the president's assistant for national security affairs provide an in-house perspective on relations with other countries. Traditionally, at least one senior staff person is charged with monitoring international economic issues. This arrangement allows the Council to participate in interagency deliberations whenever such issues affect national security concerns (international energy policy, foreign aid to key countries, trade disputes with strategically important nations, and so on). Prior to 1970, when there was no designated White House coordinating forum dealing with economic policy issues, the NSC functioned by default as the senior convener of interagency meetings and, when necessary, as an arbitrator of subcabinet disputes on these issues. For the past three decades, the NSC has been an active participant when international topics are discussed in the senior White House economic policy coordinating group.

The National Economic Council is the latest in a procession of non-statutory White House groups to play a key role in the international economic policy-making process (see Chapter 4). Since 1971, successive administrations have followed the organizational principle that cabinet-level coordination of economic policies should be controlled by a designated White House group with the active participation of the president, and not by the departments and agencies themselves.

The White House office of science and technology policy in the Bush and Clinton administrations also merits mention because of its leadership in the debates on how to construct a limited American version of industrial policy. The onset of serious concerns in the late 1980s about declining U.S. industrial competitiveness and the alleged need for enhanced governmental efforts to help defray the risks and cost of developing state-of-the-art high-tech industries added domestic science and technology policy to the larger international economic policy mix (see Chapter 11).

THE SPECIALIST DEPARTMENTS AND AGENCIES

Ubiquity in the international economic policymaking process and possession of de facto veto power are the distinguishing characteristics of the Treasury and State departments, and to a limited extent, the Executive Office of the President. Many other departments and agencies have important roles to play in the formulation and administration processes. However, their presence and impact are confined to a limited number of clearly defined international economic issues touching directly on their domestic missions. What follows is a list of the more significant "specialized" bureaucratic actors. A complete list of participants would go on endlessly since almost every department (including Transportation and Education) and every major agency have at least one international program or policy concern.

The fertile land and capital-intensive farming that made the U.S. agricultural sector the world's largest and most efficient also made it the largest single exporter of agricultural products—with an estimated one-third of total U.S. agricultural production sold abroad. The U.S. Department of Agriculture (USDA) therefore cannot avoid being deeply concerned with international agricultural trade issues and with economic policies and trends in foreign markets. An unusually divided constituency makes it nearly impossible for the department to please the entire domestic agricultural community through any single trade policy. Farmers who grow wheat, feed grains, and soybeans are very competitive internationally and prefer liberal trade policies to keep their foreign customers happy. Dairy, meat, and sugar producers are relatively high-cost producers and lobby intensively for protection from imports.

The USDA, through the Foreign Agricultural Service (FAS), is the major force in developing U.S. agricultural trade policy and negotiating positions. Reporting to the under secretary for farm and foreign agricultural services, the FAS provides overseas reporting on agricultural export opportunities, trade barriers, and crop production forecasts. The service has personnel in more than 80 U.S. diplomatic missions and a large staff in Washington, D.C., whose primary mission is operating programs to increase U.S. agricultural sales abroad. To this end, the FAS seeks to reduce foreign import barriers affecting U.S. farm commodities and operates several export promotion and food aid programs. The Commodity Credit Corporation (CCC) provides agricultural exporters with indirect short- and intermediate-term financing support through credit guarantee programs that protect either the exporters or their American lending institutions against the possibility of nonpayment by the importer or its bank. The Export Enhancement Program was inaugurated in 1985 as a means of neutralizing the then-escalating agricultural export subsidies of the European Union, the effects of which displaced a growing number of American sales to third countries. Direct payments are made from USDA to U.S. agricultural exporters when and as necessary to enable them to meet the price competition of other countries' export subsidies.

The Agriculture Department also manages Public Law 480 (P.L. 480), the Food for Peace Program, under which agricultural commodities are sold to developing countries on concessional terms (up to 30 years repayment terms and below-market interest rates). Food aid is provided on a grant basis to the least developed countries and in emergency situations. Above and beyond the short-run objective of reducing world hunger, P.L. 480 has the long-term aim of developing new overseas commercial markets for American agricultural goods.

At the other end of the trade spectrum, the FAS has the lead in setting and administering the quotas maintained by the United States against imports of agricultural commodities, mainly dairy products and sugar.

The Labor Department seeks to ensure that issues important to American workers—employment security, wage levels, and working conditions—get a fair hearing in the interagency formulation of international trade and investment policies. The Bureau of International Labor Affairs, headed by the deputy undersecretary for international affairs, represents the U.S. government in meetings of the International Labor Organization, analyzes the impact of trade agreements on domestic workers, supervises application of the labor cooperation side agreement to the free trade agreement with Mexico, and provides technical assistance for labor market programs in developing countries. The department also takes the lead in assembling data on overseas labor standards—exploitation of children, the right to unionize, worker safety, etc. This is an issue that gradually is becoming part of the international trade negotiating agenda. A separate bureau in the department administers the Trade Adjustment Assistance Program that provides cash payments, retraining classes, and relocation benefits to qualifying workers who have lost jobs because of import competition.

The Defense Department is actively involved in export control and technology transfer decisions. It will advise and advocate on those international economic issues with a direct tie-in to national security or military considerations, that is, U.S. government actions that might antagonize an important ally, destabilize a friendly government, or aid a potential adversary.

The Justice Department applies U.S. antitrust legislation both to U.S.-owned companies abroad and to foreign-owned companies in this country. It is an influential part of U.S. policy deliberations on how to proceed with bringing competition policy into the international trade agenda. Justice publishes an annual report on those persons and groups who are paid to lobby on behalf of foreign interests and have filed under the Foreign Agents Registration Act.

The Department of Energy is the principal supplier of technical expertise and statistics to the formulation and administration of international energy policies. The degree of its international economic policy influence varies; mainly it has been a function of the existence or nonexistence of an energy crisis. With the first and second oil shocks (1973–1974 and 1979–1980) now fading into history, U.S. energy policy consists mainly of reliance on the price mechanism to keep the supply of and demand for oil in balance and on a Strategic Petroleum Reserve for possible use in the event of an acute shortage or an extreme price jump. The Interior Department is concerned with the international aspects of mineral policy, namely U.S. dependence on foreign sources, and with utilization of mineral resources on ocean seabeds.

In terms of direct budgetary outlays, the Agency for International Development (AID) is among the largest bureaucratic actors in the international economic policymaking machinery. The successor to a long line of post–World War II aid-dispensing agencies, AID is a semiautonomous agency reporting to the secretary of state. Organizationally, it consists of two parts. The first is a Washington-based headquarters office providing overall policy guidance and management supervision and dealing with the increasing number of contractors that physically deliver the goods and services provided to recipient countries. The second component consists of about 75 field offices (the number continues to shrink because of downsizing) overseeing various-sized assistance programs in more than 120 countries, all with different development problems and needs. The administrative structure of AID has been reorganized repeatedly because the avowed objectives of the U.S. foreign aid program have been in a state of continual flux and because internal management problems have never been fully corrected. Ongoing efforts to get AID's organizational dynamics on track are not made easier by ever-shifting theories as to how foreign aid actually contributes to the economic development process or by a lengthy list of congressional directives imposing guidelines on AID as to what it should—or cannot—do when considering extending foreign aid loans.

AID is charged with administering the shrinking bilateral development assistance program whose annual budget had declined to the $1.2 billion range in the late 1990s. In accordance with the 1973 "New Directions" initiative of

Congress, this aid program is directed at "sustainable development" in the poorest population segments in the poorest countries, mainly through grants in sectors such as agriculture, nutrition, health, family planning, education, and environmental protection. AID administers a separate, $1 billion–plus development program earmarked for Russia and most of the former Soviet republics that was created after the collapse of the Soviet Union. It also manages several smaller programs, mostly for providing disaster relief and fighting disease. Nominally, AID manages the Economic Support Fund, a separate program budgeted at about $2.5 billion annually, that is specifically tailored to assist less developed countries—mainly Israel and Egypt—with strategic importance to U.S. foreign policy. In reality, the State Department and Congress make most of the decisions as to where these funds will be distributed.

The Export-Import Bank of the United States (Ex-Im) is an independent governmental corporation established in 1934 "to aid in financing and to facilitate exports."[9] The bank's sole responsibility is to promote U.S. exports by assisting in one of the most critical determinants of successful overseas sales of relatively expensive goods: export financing. Its main programs are direct loans, loan guarantees to commercial banks lending to foreign buyers of U.S. goods and services, and credit insurance for exporters that covers commercial and political risks of a foreign buyer defaulting on its payment obligations. Ex-Im support is available when private sector export financing is unavailable or when the U.S. exporter is bidding against a foreign competitor supported by its government's concessional export finance agency. Government-sponsored export finance is of particular importance for high-cost capital equipment like commercial jet aircraft, power generating equipment, and telecommunications equipment. Financing terms for such goods (percentage of down payment, interest rate, and repayment period) can play a critical role in determining who makes and does not make export sales.

Ex-Im has leveraged its annual budget, which in recent years has been in the $650 to $900 million range, to support an estimated $76 billion in exports between 1992 and 1997. Its lending profile in recent years reflects the successful U.S.-led effort to negotiate agreements in the OECD to limit the subsidization of official export financing. The agreements set clear guidelines on how far the export finance agencies of industrial countries can go in providing below market terms.

The Overseas Private Investment Corporation (OPIC) was established to encourage the movement of private investment capital into developing countries and former communist countries in transition to market economies by using its funds to reduce the major risks associated with such investments. It does this by providing American businesses with loans and loan guarantees, insuring investments in these countries against a broad range of political risks, and assisting private investment funds that buy equity capital in foreign businesses.

By setting domestic health, environmental, and safety standards, some U.S. regulatory agencies can influence trade flows in certain product lines. In order to achieve its mission of reducing air, water, and land pollution, the Environmental Protection Agency (EPA) actively solicits the cooperation of other countries to address environmental issues of common concern. Specifically, the EPA works with the USTR to ensure that U.S. trade policies are consistent with the nation's environmental and endangered species protection guidelines and to defend these standards when other countries file complaints in the WTO alleging that these measures illegally restrict imports. The growing overlap between environmentalists and trade policymakers was vividly demonstrated in the inclusion of an environmental side agreement when the free trade agreement was signed with Mexico. EPA provided much of the technical expertise to the U.S. delegation when this agreement was drafted.[10] The agency also seeks to ensure that U.S. obligations under international trade agreements do not hamstring the ability of federal and state governments to enforce relatively vigorous domestic levels of environmental protection. EPA is a key member of U.S. delegations to the trade and environment committees operating in both the WTO and OECD and to negotiations seeking multilateral agreements on environmental protection.[11]

The Federal Communications Commission (FCC) determined the technical standards for the new generation of high-definition television sets (HDTV) to be sold in the United States, a product that may eventually become a multibillion dollar industry. In making its decision in this case, the FCC rejected an already existing, but technologically less advanced Japanese system—thereby rendering those TV sets incompatible with U.S. broadcasting standards and functionally useless in this country.

The Food and Drug Administration (FDA) has an international affairs staff to assure that imports into the United States of foods, pharmaceuticals, medical devices, and cosmetics meet the same safety and disclosure standards required of domestic versions of these goods. The FDA pursues technical agreements to harmonize international standards for such products, and it provides technical expertise for international trade discussions involving food standards (such as in the U.S.-EU dispute on the use of hormones in meat).

The Securities and Exchange Commission has negotiated bilateral agreements with other countries as part of the regulatory and enforcement framework associated with global, 24-hour trading markets in stocks and commodities.

Improbably, the Federal Maritime Commission (FMC), a small and obscure independent agency not versed in trade diplomacy, rocked bilateral economic relations with Japan in 1997. It was instrumental in resolving a long-standing U.S. accusation that foreign (as well as domestic) ships encountered excessive costs and regulations when docking in Japanese ports. The FMC's original tactic of imposing retaliatory fines on the ships of targeted Japanese shipping companies entering U.S. ports was met with a refusal to pay. This set the stage for the dramatic escalation that forced both governments to hastily reach a compromise. The Commission used its legal power to bar all Japanese cargo ships from unloading at U.S. ports; it further ordered the Coast Guard to forcibly turn away all incoming ships and to impound all Japanese-flagged cargo ships currently in port.

As economic and technological considerations have become larger factors in the overall national security equation, the Central Intelligence Agency (CIA) has channeled increased resources into economic intelligence.[12] The CIA remains the chief supplier of covert economic policy intelligence to the policymaking community. It also has developed a large analytical capability in international economics and regularly produces unclassified economic studies and statistical reports. The agency remains reluctant to branch out into the controversial practice, recommended by some, of ferreting out proprietary business secrets from private foreign corporations for the purpose of passing them on to the American business community. However, it does play a counterintelligence role in that it will alert American companies when it discovers that they are the targets of foreign economic espionage efforts.

This discussion of agencies concludes with the International Trade Commission (ITC) and the Federal Reserve System. Because of statutory bases that seek to assure objective and nonpartisan behavior, they are administratively independent of both the executive and legislative branches. The ITC is the renamed Tariff Commission, whose existence traces back to 1916. A once obscure, independent fact-finding and research agency, the commission was elevated to much higher levels of significance as import competition became more severe beginning in the 1970s. With the aid of its professional staff, the ITC's six commissioners (no more than three of whom can come from the same political party) constitute a "quasi-judicial" agency. A primary responsibility is to make non-political determinations concerning the impact of imports on U.S. industry.

The escape clause provision in U.S. trade legislation stipulates a number of criteria for determining whether imports are seriously injuring, or threaten to seriously injure, a domestic industry through fair competition. The ITC is responsible for judging whether injury legally exists whenever an escape clause petition is filed. When injury is found, it is the ITC's job to refer recommendations for remedial action to the president for disposition. After the language of the escape clause was rewritten to make it easier to determine injury, the ITC found itself with a rapidly expanding case load involving multibillion dollar import sectors such as automobiles. Suddenly, the commission emerged as a major factor in U.S. trade relations with other countries, especially in Asia.

The ITC also plays a role in cases of alleged unfair trade practices by other countries. When American companies allege that a foreign exporter is dumping goods or is receiving government subsidies, the ITC determines whether or not the unfair trade practice (the existence of which must be confirmed by a Commerce Department investigation) is inflicting "material" injury on the domestic industry. The ITC also is responsible for investigating under "Section 337" the accuracy of domestic industry accusations that imports are illegally infringing on U.S. patents, copyrights, trademarks, etc. When such unlawful acts are found to exist, the ITC has legal authority to ban outright the entry of all offending goods into the United States.

The ITC has the technical expertise to function as a quasi-scholarly source of analytical and statistical reports on such subjects as the competitiveness of specific industries, the domestic impact of various U.S. trade agreements and programs, and the probable effects of implementing additional reductions of U.S. trade barriers. The chief allure of an ITC-written report to the executive and legislative branches is that the agency's lack of policy responsibility and a constituency to protect is presumed to enhance the staff's objectivity on controversial trade issues.

In order to insulate the important task of managing monetary policy from political pressures, the Board of Governors of the Federal Reserve System (Fed) is also an independent agency. The international economic policy activities and concerns of what is the United States' central bank are largely the outgrowths of the Fed's domestic economic jurisdictions: money and credit aggregates, price stability, interest rates, the banking system, capital markets, and so on. These concerns, together with a highly skilled economics staff, afford the Fed an important but unofficial voice in the formulation and administration of the executive branch's international monetary and financial policies. It also regulates the international activities of commercial banks operating in the United States.

Through its board of governors in Washington, the Federal Reserve System is the junior partner of the Treasury Department in determining exchange rate policies for the dollar, in representing the U.S. government at Group of Seven meetings held at the ministerial and deputies levels, and in formulating responses to the financial turmoil created by such events as the LDC debt crisis in the 1980s and the Asian financial crisis of the late 1990s. The principal short-term instrument used to influence exchange rates is occasional intervention—buying or selling dollars—in the foreign exchange market. These transactions are performed by foreign exchange traders employed by the Federal Reserve Bank of New York but operating under guidelines and instructions emanating from senior U.S. Treasury Department officials. The Fed also operates a network of "swap" agreements with several foreign central banks. (Swaps provide participating central banks with additional foreign exchange balances for use in the foreign exchange markets when they are trying to stabilize a rapidly falling exchange rate.)

ADDENDUM: STATE AND LOCAL GOVERNMENTS

The Constitution clearly empowers the federal government to regulate international trade and conduct the foreign policy of the United States. However, economic interdependence repeatedly nudges state and local governments into efforts to affect U.S. international economic relations by communicating their views and needs to economic policymakers in both the administration and Congress. Groups like the National Governors' Association and the National Association of State Development Agencies analyze and publicly speak out on the likely effects of federal policy on local economies. The Intergovernmental Policy Advisory Committee of state and local government officials is a frequently used conduit to advise the USTR on unfolding trade issues. This committee is concerned, among other things, with the increasing trend of international trade negotiations to set common standards on domestic regulatory practices. It was very active during negotiations to create free trade areas with Canada and then with Mexico.

Most state and local governments provide programs to promote regional exports and to attract inward foreign direct investment. The latter efforts sometimes produce distortions in the form of a bidding war among state and local governments when they offer economic incentives (tax relief, infrastructure improvements, worker training, etc.) to foreign companies whose cumulative costs seem out of proportion to the net number of jobs being created.

Actions by state governments periodically trigger complaints to Washington from foreign governments and threats of lawsuits by aggrieved foreign companies. One example is the state "buy-American" laws that constitute discriminatory state procurement laws favoring domestic producers over foreign bidders. A new source of friction is the increasing propensity of state and city governments to impose localized sanctions to protest actions of foreign countries. A furor occurred in response to the efforts in 1996 of the government of Massachusetts to punish human rights abuses in Burma (Myanmar) by enacting a law effectively denying state contracts to any company, domestic or foreign, doing business in that country. The law was long on moral principle and short on expectations of actually hurting Burma in any measurable way. Nevertheless, Japan and the European Union also acted on principle and announced intentions of filing a complaint against the United States in the WTO. Later, a coalition of U.S. corporations succeeded in having a federal court rule the bill unconstitutional. In 1998, California, New York State, and New York City threatened to terminate business relations with Swiss banks if they did not settle the claims brought against them by Holocaust victims (which they later did).

NOTES

1. Data source: United States General Accounting Office, "International Affairs—Activities of Domestic Agencies," report NSIAD-98–174, dated 4 June 1998, p. 8.

2. One of the more important examples of a tax issue affecting foreign investors in the United States is the periodic proposal to generate more tax revenue by tightening up regulations on transfer-pricing tactics used by some multinational companies in an effort to minimize their global tax liabilities.

3. "International Business: Foundation of National Strength," press release of deputy secretary of state's speech of 30 November 1989, pp. 1–3.

4. "Secretary of State Talking Commerce," *Washington Post*, 1 November 1998, p. A10.

5. The idea had yet to be acted on as of mid-1999, mainly because of problems determining where to transfer the large number of Commerce's component parts whose functions need to be preserved.

6. Foreign exporters are liable for retaliation if the Commerce Department verifies that dumping has occurred or direct subsidies have been received *and* the International Trade Commission determines that the U.S. industry has been materially injured as a result. In such circumstances, Commerce automatically imposes import penalties (dumping or countervailing duties) of sufficient magnitude to neutralize the estimated financial value of the unfair trade practices.

7. Data source: web site of International Trade Administration as of November 1998: www.ita.doc.gov.

8. USTR web site as of November 1998: www.USTR.gov.

9. The original charter of the Bank also spoke of financing imports, but that function quickly and permanently disappeared.

10. The side agreement's main purpose is to encourage enforcement of Mexican environmental protection laws, especially near the U.S. border. This action is designed to discourage manufacturing plants from seeking to exploit the Mexican government's reputation for relatively lax enforcement of antipollution regulations.

11. Examples of major international agreements to reduce global pollution and climate change are the 1992 Convention negotiated at the "Earth Summit" and the 1997 Kyoto Protocol on Climate Change. Both agreements affect the activities and production costs of manufacturing companies.

12. This is a natural reaction to changing demands by the executive branch and the institutional need to retain its importance in the post–cold war era.

4 *The Coordination of International Economic Policy*

> It is time to end the intellectual and bureaucratic separation of economic
> issues one from another, with parts of each specific issue scattered through-
> out the government machinery without any sense of overall purpose and
> general guidance from the top.
> —Former Senators Russell Long and Abraham Ribicoff

When an elected government formulates international economic policy, it must review the needs of four constituencies: the domestic economy, international economic relations, domestic politics, and foreign policy. As suggested by the previous chapter, the number of bureaucratic actors participating in this phase of the U.S. policymaking process is very large. A shortage of participants is not a problem.

The primary organizational challenge is resolving conflicting policy proposals in a manner that assures coherence and consistency. Interagency coordination is the essential means to the end of reconciling different definitions of what constitutes "good policy." Formulating international economic policies in the absence of an organized, cooperative effort would invite outbreak of a bureaucratic version of the law of the jungle. Institutional in-fighting amidst an uncertain chain of command would be the norm.

The necessity of coordination in turn creates the need for a multilayered network of interagency consultative mechanisms. How well the various parts of the administration cooperate in pursuing a consensus view of the national interest can and does affect the quality of a government's domestic and international policies. The stakes are high, but the record of senior-level international

economic policy coordinating groups in the U.S. government has been inconsistent.

SUCCESS AND FAILURE IN COORDINATION EFFORTS:
THE LESSONS OF RECENT HISTORY

If balanced policy and the spirit of fair play were the sole concerns of senior
government officials, they would not question the need for well-organized coordinating groups operating from the cabinet level down to the staff level. Interagency forums are the appropriate venue to develop common long-term goals
and guidelines that cut across multiple jurisdictions. They are also the optimal
venue for providing decision-makers with choice.

A properly functioning coordination process begins with assurance that any
bureaucracy whose jurisdiction is directly affected by a pending decision is not
denied access to the policy formulation process. For the more important decisions, a White House–level coordinating group gives appropriate cabinet members equal ''face time'' with the president. Access is not indulgence; it ensures
that all sides of an argument are carefully weighed before a final decision is
taken. An effective coordination process also encourages a free exchange of
information by treating all participants equally. It assures that notices of meetings and briefing papers are disseminated to everyone who should be part of
the policymaking process.

Absent the highly unusual situation of immediate unanimity among a dozen
or more bureaucracies with different constituencies and priorities, an effective
system of coordination is needed to achieve policy consensus within a reasonable period of time and in a manner deemed fair by all participants. If unanimity
is not possible, a coordinating group can still fulfill its mission by agreeing to
disagree and submitting several options (with the pros and cons of each) to a
higher level for decision. Effective coordination also reduces the possibility that
angry officials might feel themselves disenfranchised and seek to undermine
implementation of a policy they strongly oppose.

While coordination may be desirable in *principle*, the concept is unusually
complicated in *practice* as it pertains to international economic policymaking.
For good reason, the perennial question of whether the foreign affairs or the
economic policy bureaucracy controls the coordinating machinery is a constant
source of dissension among cabinet members. The substance of policy easily
can be affected by whether economic or foreign policy goals get the more favorable treatment in the policy formulation debate.

Political appointees in the U.S. executive branch have but a year or two on
average to leave their personal imprint on policy. The would-be policy mover-
and-shaker knows that an ''end run'' to the president, a quiet contact with a
friendly congressional committee, or an uncleared public pronouncement can
have a much quicker impact than the cumbersome, treadmill-like pace of a
broadly-based committee. In sum, an ambitious cabinet member is more likely

to view a strong White House coordinating group as a burden or threat than a friend. If there must be consultation with counterparts in other departments, most cabinet members would prefer either to unilaterally control the process or, failing that, to informally cut deals among themselves. Power is usually seen as a zero-sum game—the more bureaucratic players, the greater is the dilution factor.

A scholar has suggested that the quest for coordination "is in many respects the twentieth century equivalent of the medieval search for the philosopher's stone."[1] Some observers of policymaking believe that if only the right coordination formula could be found, the U.S. government could harmonize competing and wholly divergent interests, overcome irrationalities in its own structure, and make hard policy decisions about which no one would dissent. Procedural perfection has never been, and probably never will be, introduced on a permanent basis in the international economic policymaking process. No coordinating mechanism can permanently squelch the natural state of affairs wherein a number of bureaucratic actors look at an international economic problem and have diametrically different interpretations as to what tactics and strategies should be employed. The weak link of coordination here is the heterogeneous nature of the policy substance, not the inability to devise sound administrative procedures on paper. Repeated breakdowns in the U.S. international economic policy coordination process are more a symptom of the complexity of the subject than a cause of dysfunctional policymaking.

Nevertheless, it is clear that some administrations have implemented senior-level coordinating groups in international economic policy that have worked much better than others. The history of White House–level coordination efforts presented below suggests recurring patterns of do's and don'ts. Certain variables foster success while others invite failure. The most important factor is the clear and continuing commitment by the president to the unequivocal authority of his senior coordinating group. He needs to serve as an active chairperson who willingly attends meetings when important decisions need to be made or when the cabinet is deadlocked on a recommended course of action. This is not as simple as it sounds. Presidents consistently have displayed less interest in the world economy than in domestic political and national security matters.

The second essential ingredient for success is that the presidential assistant (or treasury secretary) serving as the head of this group possesses a number of attributes. Besides having easy access to and the respect of the president, he or she must be knowledgeable about international and domestic economics and understand the arcane rules of Washington bureaucratic warfare. Equally essential is that the director of the coordinating group be perceived as fair, objective, and non-ideological—someone content to be a dispassionate manager of passionate advice from agencies with operational responsibilities. The director and the staff should be seen as being capable of deterring sloppy policymaking but deferring to the cabinet's authority.

Tepid presidential support of a White House coordinating group and the wrong person to head it are recipes for failure. The degree to which the key line departments (Treasury, State, and Commerce) perceive such weaknesses is directly proportional to the extent they will seek to render the coordinators marginalized observers to decision-making.

A successful White House coordinating group needs authority over a wide range of international economic policy, especially trade. However, it need not claim authority over *all* aspects of policy. The latter is a goal that is unattainable. A few issue areas, most notably exchange rate policy, will always remain under the full control of a single department.

EARLY ATTEMPTS AT HIGH-LEVEL COORDINATION

Senior coordination groups, like U.S. international economic policy itself, did not blossom until the post–World War II period. The only major example of this policy prior to the war, the operation of the Trade Agreements Program, was coordinated through the State Department–chaired Committee on Trade Agreements (with the Departments of Commerce and Agriculture as the other major participants). During the war years, a number of high-level groups existed temporarily in connection either with economic warfare or planning for the postwar period. As early as 1940, an Interdepartmental Group on Post-War International Economic Problems and Policies was formed. Its successors included the Committee on Post-War Foreign Economic Policy (1943) and the Executive Committee on Economic Foreign Policy (1944), both of which were chaired by the State Department.

Since the State Department at this time was clearly the dominant department in formulating and conducting what was then deemed to be the economic dimension of foreign policy, the only major struggle for bureaucratic control in this area was waged between it and the White House staff. Symbolic of this struggle was the creation in 1941 of the Economic Defense Board (later renamed the Board of Economic Warfare). Its duties were to advise the president on the entire range of international economic and communications fields, coordinate the work of the various departments in these sectors, and develop integrated plans for the war years and the postwar period (while leaving policy administration and implementation to the line departments). Chaired by Vice President Henry Wallace, the board quickly became a power to be reckoned with:

While the franchise of the board seemed to absorb all international aspects of economic policy and action, an old inhabitant of the bureaucratic jungle like Mr. [Cordell] Hull knew that Cabinet boards and committees were paper tigers. They made a fine show in a parade but soon dissolved in the rain. . . .

Henry Wallace soon confounded all expectations about the board by a gross departure from the rules of bureaucratic warfare. He introduced into a harmless committee of busy men an executive director in the person of one of the most able, adroit, and energetic administrators whom the war had brought to Washington. Milo Perkins . . . soon had a large organization and began to act through his own people.[2]

The board died a sudden death in mid-1943, when President Franklin Roosevelt lost his patience with jurisdictional quibbling among its cabinet members. It was replaced by the short-lived Foreign Economic Administration.[3]

In 1948, the Economic Cooperation Administration was established. Reporting directly to the president, its purpose was to coordinate the most important program of the early postwar phase of U.S. international economic policy: the $13 billion Marshall Plan that sought to restore the war-torn economies of Western Europe to their prewar vigor. Organizationally, it represented an apparent unwillingness to entrust the State Department with exclusive management of a top-priority program.

The growing involvement of the executive branch in international commercial relations led to a major organizational innovation: the creation in 1954 of the Council on Foreign Economic Policy (CFEP) in the Executive Office of the President. The CFEP became operational pursuant to a letter by President Dwight Eisenhower appointing a special assistant for foreign economic policy. This person was designated chair of the Council and given the role of assisting and advising the president "in accomplishing an orderly development of foreign economic policies and programs and to assure the effective coordination of foreign economic matters of concern to the several departments and agencies of the Executive Branch."[4] His responsibilities included anticipating problems, analyzing economic data, and defining issues. The relation of international economic policy to domestic economic policy was specifically included within the purview of the special assistant. He was also expected to establish appropriate relations with the National Security Council (NSC) and the National Advisory Council on International Monetary and Financial Policies (NAC), the major high-level coordinating groups at the time with international economic responsibilities.

The position of special assistant for foreign economic policy and the CFEP were created because of what would become a permanent theme: the belief that the executive branch lacked an adequate organizational means for senior-level coordination of international economic policy. Letting cabinet departments operate as totally independent fiefdoms was discarded as an acceptable option. At the same time, there was dissatisfaction with the way in which the NSC machinery was dealing with international economic problems, particularly when those problems required the reconciliation of foreign and domestic considerations whose scope exceeded that of the NSC's very limited membership and staff resources.

In retrospect, the Council has to be judged a failure in terms of its two primary objectives: providing overall policy coordination among the many policy threads, and contributing to a systematic and coherent international economic policy. The definitive post mortem of the CFEP's failure was written by the Bureau of the Budget in 1961, shortly before the former's demise. The following passage is of special significance since it is also an ex ante analysis of the

failures of the later reincarnation of the CFEP, the Council on International
Economic Policy:

> Although the range of subject matter considered by the CFEP has been very broad,
> including almost every possible area of foreign economic affairs, it cannot be considered
> the principal interagency forum for any area. Foreign assistance matters are considered
> and coordinated elsewhere. The NAC is the dominant forum for international monetary
> and financial policy, as is the NSC in national security policy. . . . Preparations for trade
> negotiations are considered primarily by the Trade Agreements Committee. . . . The
> CFEP is used to a large extent as a forum for information exchange. Despite the broad
> charter of the Council, it has tended to deal with specific subjects and issues as they
> arise, with the line between broad policy matters and other concerns frequently blurred.
> Because the Chairman has no command authority, decisions must of necessity result
> from agreement or a ''sense of the meeting'' or no decision is forthcoming, unless the
> matter is referred to the President. Frequently, it appears that decisions reached elsewhere
> are merely ratified in the CFEP.[5]

The major reasons why the CFEP failed were the lack of cooperation by the
major line departments and the continuation of independent coordinating groups
in every policy sector. Another reason was that it failed to live up to its advance
billing as a parallel to the NSC in the economics area. The CFEP became more
of a consultative body than an action-forcing organization and more of a specific
issue resolver in special circumstances than an integrator of overall policy substance. The next White House–based council devoted specifically to international
economics would follow virtually the same route in the 1970s.

President John F. Kennedy terminated the CFEP structure in connection with
his overall preference for decentralized, ad hoc decision-making. Responsibility
for advising the president on international economic policy and occasionally
serving as an arbiter of disputes in the line agencies fell to a deputy to the
assistant to the president for national security affairs. Serving as part of the
NSC's senior staff, this aide was supported by a couple of assistants. More
elaborate coordination machinery was provided by an Interdepartmental Committee of Under Secretaries on Foreign Economic Policy and by a cabinet-level
Committee on the Balance of Payments.[6] Lyndon Johnson continued the practice
of relying on a senior NSC staff member for international economic advice and
liaison with line departments. The limited Kennedy-Johnson style in international economic policy coordination had one thing in common with the ambitious CFEP effort of the Eisenhower administration. Both organizational
arrangements arbitrarily separated decision-making on international economic
policies from domestic economic policies.

THE RISE AND DEMISE OF THE CIEP

During its first two years, the Nixon administration retained the limited senior-
level policy coordination mechanism it had inherited from the Johnson admin-

istration. International economics continued to be handled by the national security complex. To the extent there was White House coordination in this area, it fell to C. Fred Bergsten, an experienced economist and middle-level staff member of the NSC. However, as he let it be known after his departure, he had scant access to Henry Kissinger, the NSC's staff director, and even less to the president.

The Nixon administration's willingness to delegate international economic policymaking power to the cabinet was inconsistent with its approach to most other issue areas. Elsewhere, the Nixon White House had methodically set about to centralize its control over the government's policymaking machinery. International economic relations apparently received too low a priority to warrant in-house dominance. Although the NSC was the titular coordinator, the otherwise very powerful Henry Kissinger paid infrequent attention to economics. White House–led coordination in this area was therefore ad hoc and occasional.

The absence of a formal international economic policy coordinating group in the Nixon White House came to an end in January 1971. It was then that the president decided to act on a recommendation made several months earlier by his Advisory Council on Executive Organization for establishment of a new, cabinet-level Council on International Economic Policy (CIEP).[7] The CIEP, along with the new post of presidential assistant for international economic affairs, was created by executive order. The publicly announced purpose of the new organization was to provide a "clear top-level focus" for all international economic issues, to "achieve consistency between domestic and foreign economic policy," and to "maintain close coordination with basic foreign policy objectives."[8] The president was to be its chair, and the other members would be the secretaries of State, the Treasury, Agriculture, Commerce, and Labor (the secretaries of Defense and Transportation were added later), the director of the Office of Management and Budget (OMB), the chair of the Council of Economic Advisers (CEA), the special representative for trade negotiations, and the presidentially appointed executive director of the CIEP, who would be in charge of its small professional staff.

It seemed to be an idea whose time had come. In the early months of the Nixon administration, students of organization had decried the problem of coordinating the 50-odd departments, agencies, and interagency working groups having operational responsibilities in international economic relations. "Gaping voids" had existed in the organization, Roy Ash later testified to a House committee. "There was simply no entity of government, except the president himself, that could examine the whole complex of foreign economic policy issues for consistency and for harmony with United States interests abroad and with programs at home."[9] Congress also reacted positively. It granted the CIEP (temporary) statutory status in 1972 and urged it to provide closer interagency coordination "in the development of a more rational and orderly international economic policy."

The CIEP would never successfully perform such a task. The lack of presidential commitment to the CIEP was a critical factor. From the beginning, formal meetings of the CIEP were rare. The president attended only a couple of sessions. Most of the work was performed by the cabinet-level Executive Committee (headed by then–Treasury Secretary George Shultz); the Senior Review Group, headed by the CIEP's executive director; and the Operations Group, chaired by the undersecretary of state for economic affairs. None of the CIEP's executive directors enjoyed a particularly close professional relationship with the president, nor did any achieve the status of powerful confidant comparable to the average assistant to the president for national security affairs (the head of the NSC staff).

The second major factor causing the early demise of the CIEP was the determination of key bureaucratic actors that they could withhold cooperation from what was regarded as a rival. The absence of presidential commitment stimulated the innate inclinations of top State and Treasury department officials to deal with each other, not defer to the CIEP. For a White House–based coordinating group to function successfully, the two most powerful departments in the making of U.S. international economic policy either need to be directly ordered by the president to use it, or the heads of these departments must themselves ascertain that it is in their mutual interest to do so. The CIEP also suffered from the fact that the Office of the Special Representative for Trade Negotiations fought hard to prevent its role as coordinator of trade policy from being expropriated by the new CIEP. Whether a cause or a reflection of CIEP's inevitable demise, no reduction or streamlining of existing interagency working groups was seriously considered in the wake of the CIEP's creation. Indeed, the number of such groups continued to proliferate.

Despite being launched with the usual over-blown Nixon rhetoric, the CIEP never received direction on how it was to function from people with clout. A study of the CIEP prepared for the Murphy Commission put it this way:

> The fundamental factor responsible for CIEP's failure to carry out its mission is the nature of that mission, its unrealistic scope and great complexity. . . . The mission statement is more an exercise of rhetoric and hyperbole than a realistic statement of purpose. It was impractical to expect any interagency coordinating mechanism to perform such a role, under the existing circumstances.
>
> CIEP was assigned, in vague terms, the difficult and delicate task of coordinating policy and of orchestrating the inputs of numerous, often squabbling, agencies whose relative power varied both with the specific issue at hand and with the particular agency principals involved at the time the issue arose.
>
> In international economic policy, real and ultimate power [lay] elsewhere. CIEP was instructed to recede in favor of NSC in cases of overlap. Two of its members—State and Treasury—are more equal than the others and, when they felt their interests threatened, they moved to exercise their power.[10]

The coup de grace to CIEP's hopes to become the cornerstone of international economic policy coordination was delivered by a seemingly innocuous administration-sponsored amendment to the October 1973 bill that extended the CIEP's life to 1977. The amendment eliminated presidential membership and provided that the chair would be selected from one of the remaining members. The formal loss of the presidential imprimatur meant that from then on the CIEP was relegated to being an occasional coordinator of secondary issues. It now joined the long list of bureaucratic entities whose disuse is irrelevant to their longevity.

Even though CIEP's role as a top-level policy coordinator had ended by early 1973, the fact that it retained a legislated existence meant that it needed to do something. Having been unofficially designated as the international division of the larger economic policy coordinator that absorbed it (see below), the CIEP assumed two kinds of duties. The first was acting as a "last resort" coordinator on specific issues designated by the president's new economic czar (Treasury Secretary George Shultz). This role was activated when subcabinet officials at both the Treasury and State welcomed such a vehicle, when the NSC did not claim authority over a national security issue, or when the CIEP staff itself occasionally took the leadership on a newly emerging policy question of non-critical importance, such as foreign direct investment in the United States.

The second life assumed by the CIEP was that of an additional, marginal bureaucratic actor with no clear constituency needing representation. A careful survey of interagency working groups at this time finds numerous instances of the CIEP's having joined the traditional cabinet departments and long-standing White House offices (OMB, the Office of the Special Representative for Trade Negotiations, CEA, and so on) as a committee member. In effect, the CIEP had been assimilated, like a line agency, as yet another voice into the ranks of the specialized, ad hoc coordinators.

When the CIEP's statutory existence expired on September 30, 1977, no effort was made to extend it. The CIEP in theory was, and still is, a good idea. However, on an operational level, it failed a basic test of achievement: it never provided a consistent and substantial net injection of new effectiveness or efficiency into the coordination process. What CIEP's demise suggests is that however valid may be the concept of White House–based coordination, certain organizational factors must be present to assure effectiveness.

Since late 1972, a single White House–level coordinating group has been responsible for dealing with both domestic *and* international economic policy issues. The creation in December 1972 of the Council on Economic Policy (CEP) formally marked the elevation of the then–treasury secretary, George Shultz, to a position of economic "czar." In addition to being secretary of the treasury, he would be, by the end of 1973, chairman of the all-inclusive CEP, the CIEP, and the East-West Trade Policy Committee. The CEP's purpose, as described by Shultz at a press conference, was to provide an "explicitly identified coordinating group and person responsible to the President for the overall relating of different aspects of economic policy. . . . It cuts across domestic and international spheres."[11]

Although Shultz deferred to the president on all major policy decisions, he did command the process by which the bureaucracy approached all economic issues and sent recommendations to the president. By all accounts, he did this very well. He was a rare individual: a consummate public servant whose intelligence and integrity surpassed his ego. The international economic policymaking process during the Shultz stewardship, not surprisingly, was unusually smooth. Not only did he have easy access to, and the trust of, the president, but he was extremely knowledgeable about economics. Last, but far from least, he was an impartial coordinator, seeking the best overall policy. There were no open accusations that he leveraged his status as presidential assistant to impose the Treasury Department's position (which he occasionally overruled in his presidential adviser role) on other departments. And it was Shultz who mandated what became the CIEP's finest achievement, the coordination of the interagency deliberations that produced the administration's 1973 Trade Reform Act proposal.

CABINET-LEVEL COORDINATION IN THE 1970s AND 1980s

The creation of the CEP at the end of 1972 established a model of White House–level coordination that continued through the end of the 1990s. Although subsequent groups had slightly different names, they were all variations on the same theme. For the purpose of coordination at the highest level, international economic issues were joined with domestic economic policy decisions.

President Gerald Ford approved creation of the Economic Policy Board (EPB) in September 1974. The White House announcement said that the purpose of the new forum was to provide advice to the president concerning all aspects of national and international economic policy; to oversee the formulation, coordination, and implementation of all U.S. economic policy; and to serve as the focal point for economic policy decision-making. Following in the tradition of the CEP, the secretary of the treasury was designated as chair, and the membership again included most of the cabinet (only the secretary of defense and the attorney general were not members) and the heads of the economic offices within the White House. The real guiding force behind the Board's activities was a presidential adviser, L. William Seidman. At the core of the EPB operation was the Executive Committee, which met on a daily basis over breakfast in the Roosevelt Room of the White House. Meetings consisted both of informal exchanges of views and of in-depth presentations on single problems. Task forces were formed to examine major domestic and international economic issues. (Like the CEP before it, the EPB absorbed the CIEP.)

The most difficult coordination problems faced by the EPB concerned international matters. The State Department, headed in 1975 by Henry Kissinger, originally had chosen not to become an active member of the EPB upon its inception. Kissinger apparently viewed the board as a Treasury-dominated enterprise. Additionally, he seemed to prefer using his own private channels into the Oval Office. During his initial months as secretary of state, Kissinger wore two hats by retaining his status as the president's assistant for national security affairs. The belated addition of the secretary of state to the EPB's Executive Committee in July 1975 and the severing of Kissinger's tie to the NSC in November 1975 led to a more active State Department role in the EPB, mainly by the undersecretary of state for economic affairs.

Nevertheless, the State Department still felt more comfortable dealing with the foreign policy–sensitive NSC. The Treasury Department retained its strong preference for dealing with the economic policy–oriented EPB. The result was that both coordinating groups were friendly rivals in the Ford administration's international economic policymaking process. To use one at the exclusion of the other would be perceived as tilting policy either toward foreign policy or domestic economic policy. The administrative outgrowth of the two-track approach to White House international economic policy coordination was the convening of joint EPB-NSC working groups, as well as jointly written memoranda to the president.

The Carter administration retained the concept of a senior all-inclusive economic policy coordinating group at the cabinet level. The renamed Economic Policy Group (EPG) went through two organizational phases in its effort to facilitate policy agreement. Initially, an unwieldy group of up to 40 cabinet secretaries and their deputies, as well as presidential aides, crowded into the Roosevelt Room of the White House for weekly meetings. To make the EPG more manageable, power was soon concentrated in a steering committee. The treasury secretary was elevated from co-chair to chair of the EPG.

By the fall of 1977, President Carter ordered a further streamlining of the steering committee by dropping the secretaries of commerce, labor, and housing and urban development and by pruning the EPG's secretariat to one person. The remaining core of six officials met for breakfast every Thursday morning. Along with the treasury secretary, the members consisted of the undersecretary of state for economic affairs, the head of OMB, the chair of the CEA, and the president's advisers for national security affairs and for domestic affairs. The early integration of the State Department in the EPG's activities produced a relatively harmonious coordinating vehicle for the more important and sensitive international economic policy issues.

International economic policy coordination at the subcabinet level during the Carter administration worked unusually well and harmoniously. The relative absence of intense bureaucratic rivalries in general, and between the State and Treasury departments in particular, reflected for the most part a staffing decision implemented in 1976 by the Carter transition team. As in other policy sectors, senior international economic officials were selected in policy "clusters," not separately by individual departments. A deliberate effort was made to recruit persons of complementary views and approaches to international economic relations.[12] It was no coincidence, therefore, that the two senior international policy officials selected in 1977 for the Treasury Department, Anthony Solomon and C. Fred Bergsten, had earlier served in the State Department. Their outlooks were not significantly different from the views of Richard Cooper, a respected Yale economics professor who became undersecretary of state for economic affairs.

Senior coordination efforts during Ronald Reagan's first term as president were uniquely comprehensive but confusing in structure. In an apparent effort to emphasize government by cabinet, the Reagan administration initially created seven new White House–based interdepartmental councils (some of which dealt strictly with domestic issues). Each was chaired by an appropriate cabinet member. In addition, the NSC was retained without change, and a hybrid called the Senior Interagency Group on International Economic Policy subsequently was created in 1982. Despite this proliferation of formalized groups, an ad hoc group was convened in the early years of the Reagan administration to prepare for economic summit meetings.

International economic policy coordinating authority at the White House level was more dispersed than ever before. No less than seven cabinet-level coordinating groups had some jurisdiction in this field. The substance of global economic issues spanned four of the new Cabinet Councils (Economic Affairs, Commerce and Trade, Food and Agriculture, and Natural Resources and the Environment), the NSC, the just-mentioned Senior Interagency Group, and the Trade Policy Committee (discussed below). In some respects, it was business as usual. Newspaper reports, obviously based on high-level leaks, indicated that the then–secretary of state (and would-be "vicar" of foreign policy), Alexander Haig, pointedly boycotted a meeting of the new Cabinet Council on Commerce and Trade. This move was similar to former Secretary of State Henry Kissinger's decision at one point to boycott the Economic Policy Board. The Cabinet Council meeting had been convened in March 1981 to discuss the East-West trade policy. Haig reportedly voiced a strong feeling that this politically sensitive economic issue belonged under the primary jurisdiction of the Department of State.

The multiple Cabinet Council system proved inefficient. Responsibilities were too widely scattered. There were too many jurisdictional overlaps, and some councils fell into disuse. That too many senior coordinating groups had been created was formally recognized in April 1985 when the seven councils and the Senior Interagency Group on International Economic Policy were consolidated into the Economic Policy Council (EPC) and the Domestic Policy Council. President Reagan assumed titular chairmanship of both groups. The secretary of the Treasury was made the day-to-day operating head of the economics council.

The EPC was given the familiar task of integrating domestic and international economic policy decision-making. As explained in the White House announcement of its creation:

The increasing interrelatedness of the U.S. and international economies illustrates the importance of establishing a process that will examine economic issues in a comprehensive, integrated way. The Economic Policy Council will provide the President with a single entity to advise him on domestic and international economic policy.[13]

Specific efforts were made to assure that the EPC was more a White House institution than an adjunct of the Treasury Department. The agenda of each meeting, usually involving debate on a specific policy issue, was determined by a working group consisting of four White House officials (including the cabinet secretary and an NSC official) and the deputy secretary of the treasury. Any agenda dispute was settled by the president's chief of staff.[14]

The EPC usually met at least once a week in the first year of its operation. "First-stage" meetings typically involved a "presenter," usually an assistant secretary chairing an interagency working group that had previously been established to do the staff work for a given policy proposal or action decision. The presenter's role was to offer a detailed discussion of the issue and to explain the group's policy recommendation, which was occasionally a single proposal, but more often, a list of options.[15] If written memoranda were the vehicle of communication, they would be drafted by the EPC's White House–based executive secretary (a deputy assistant to the president for policy development) and cleared with all departments and agencies participating in a given policy formulation exercise before any paper was sent to the president.

Through early summer 1986, approximately two-thirds of the council's meetings were related to foreign trade matters.[16] While the EPC did not play a major role in non-trade sectors of international economic policy, it had the clout to effectively absorb the preexisting cabinet-level trade coordinating body, the Trade Policy Committee (TPC). By so doing, Treasury Secretary Baker was informally bestowed with a status roughly equal to the U.S. trade representative, the titular head of trade policy formulation and chair of the now dethroned TPC.

The compatible personalities of Treasury Secretary Baker and Secretary of State George Shultz (as well as the latter's decision not to become actively involved personally in international economic matters) and the regular participation of Shultz's top economics deputy minimized allegations of excessive tilt in EPC meetings toward economic priorities and away from national security considerations. During most of 1985 and 1986, senior State and Treasury department officials further bonded by meeting about every two weeks for breakfast discussions of international trade and financial issues.

The EPC continued to function in the same manner during the first three years of the Bush administration. Then it became an indirect victim of the determination that the White House needed a major reorganization in an effort to correct three problems: floundering efforts to deal with domestic economic problems, plummeting approval ratings for President Bush, and indications that the new chief of staff was not efficiently managing the Executive Office of the President. The chosen remedy was the creation of an all-encompassing Policy Coordination Group (PCG) that combined the economics responsibilities of the EPC with the political duties of the Domestic Policy Council.

COORDINATION IN THE 1990s

In the 1992 presidential election, Bill Clinton campaigned first and foremost on the need to reverse the downturn in U.S. economic vitality and competitiveness. Economics, he said, should play a more important role in foreign policy. As the first president elected in the post–cold war era, he promptly sought to deliver on his promise to improve the U.S. economic performance in general and its productivity and technological prowess in particular. Economic policy moved out of the shadow of national security concerns. The organizational manifestation of this important shift in policy priorities was creation of the White House–based National Economic Council (NEC). The president designated himself as chairman; the 17 other members consisted of the vice president, cabinet members, agency heads, and senior presidential advisers (including the national security affairs adviser).

The NEC's stated tasks were coordinating the domestic and international aspects of the economic policymaking processes, coordinating economic policy advice to the president, ensuring that economic policy decisions and programs "are consistent with the President's stated goals," and monitoring implementation of the economic policy agenda with an eye to ensuring that the administration's goals were effectively pursued. The NEC operated on two levels. Formal meetings were held at the principals level, but most of the NEC's day-to-day coordinating duties would be handled at the deputies level.

Although the Clinton White House was otherwise managed in a chaotic fashion in its early years, there was wide consensus that the NEC got off to a very successful start. President Clinton's understanding of economic issues and his commitment to overall White House direction of his economic recovery program were major reasons for the council's success. Another reason was the unusual talents of Robert Rubin, the assistant to the president for economic policy and director of the NEC. A newcomer to Washington, Rubin successfully brought with him the reputation he gained on Wall Street as a highly intelligent person who knew how to ask the right questions. He was also perceived as someone who had mastered the role of an honest broker who made things happen by working quietly but relentlessly to bring people together. He carefully selected an NEC staff (of about 25 professionals) on the basis of both economics expertise and demonstrated ability to work smoothly with others and get things done.

Presidential commitment meant that operating departments and agencies could not ignore the NEC. It was the centerpiece of the president's number one policy concern—economic policy. The ability of Rubin and his staff to assure others that the council was a well-functioning facilitator, not a policymaking competitor, meant that the rest of the cabinet did not especially want to circumvent it. "Through it all, Rubin continued to be master connector to all parts of the presidential team, admired for his skill, sensitivity, and restraint."[17]

Although the NEC's work load mainly consisted of domestic issues and its most notable achievement was coordinating the administration's program to reduce the federal budget deficit, it was also actively involved in international policy. Almost all of the latter involved the big foreign trade issues facing the administration: legislation implementing the NAFTA and Uruguay Round agreements, strategy toward Japan and China, nurturing regional free trade area negotiations in the Western Hemisphere and in the Asia-Pacific region, and so on. The NEC made no move to challenge the authority of the Treasury Department in international financial matters. While it made no inroads on the trade negotiating jurisdiction of the Office of the U.S. Trade Representative, the NEC did absorb most of the USTR's coordinating functions. First, it continued the practice of having the White House economic coordinating group assume the duties of the cabinet-level Trade Policy Committee that originally had been chaired by the USTR. Additionally, the NEC succeeded in having the subcabinet level Trade Policy Review Group (discussed below) report to it rather than the U.S. trade representative. The latter then became just another policy advocate in the committee rather than its neutral chair.

Another factor allowing the NEC machinery to function with a minimum of traditional turf battles was its uniquely close institutional relationship with the NSC. President Clinton's belief that national security and domestic economic strength are closely linked concepts led to two innovations involving White House coordination of those two policies. First, the treasury secretary and the NEC staff director were regularly invited to NSC meetings. Second, it was decided that a single professional international economic policy staff would serve both the NEC and NSC. Two persons were then given the title of NEC/NSC senior directors for international economic policy; they each reported to two bosses, Rubin and Anthony Lake, the president's national security policy adviser. The two senior staff members co-chaired meetings of the interagency, White House–based NEC/NSC "deputies committee" on international economic issues.[18]

In a quick turn of events, the impact and prestige of the NEC declined after 1994—even though its formal responsibilities were left intact. The Republican takeover of Congress put the Clinton administration on the defensive on economic policy. Then Robert Rubin was named secretary of the treasury in December of that year. A major diminution of the NEC's clout was quickly apparent, only partly because it was obviously difficult to find someone with the operating finesse of its first director. The larger blow to the institution came in the symbolic form of presidential disinterest: no new director—not even an acting director—was named for almost three months after Robert Rubin moved to Treasury. It was not until the end of March 1995 that Laura Tyson formally shifted from the chairmanship of the CEA to the president's assistant for economic policy and director of the NEC. Her arrival restored some but clearly not all of the Council's original stature.

In his detailed 1996 study of that institution, I.M. Destler presented contemporary examples of the old story of the vulnerability of senior coordinating committees to waning presidential interest and participation. One incident involved an (unsuccessful) attempt in spring 1995 by the USTR, Mickey Kantor, to circumvent the interagency clearance procedure for a speech that he wrote for the president to deliver on his weekly radio address. The text of the speech was scathingly critical of Japan's trade policies, but Kantor tried to put it directly in the president's hand without first circulating it for clearance in the NEC framework.[19]

IDCA AND DEVELOPMENT POLICY COORDINATION

Like the CIEP, the International Development Cooperation Agency (IDCA) was conceived as an ambitious effort to improve policy substance by means of improving the coordination of decision-making. Also like the CIEP, it faded into functional oblivion. Line departments regarded IDCA, the idea for which originated outside the executive branch, as at best unnecessary and at worst an interloper that needed to be neutralized.

In the late 1970s, interested members of Congress surveyed the organizational arrangements by which the executive branch formulated policies and implemented programs for assisting less developed countries (LDCs). They concluded that the process was excessively decentralized. The International Development and Food Assistance Act of 1978 contained a provision urging the administration to create a new organization to coordinate the "maximum possible range" of U.S. Government agencies and programs dealing with international development.

The IDCA, as originally designed by the Carter administration, looked impressive on paper. It was given the assignment to provide a unified, long-term, and big-picture examination of all assistance programs being administered bilaterally and multilaterally within a single country. On the basis of that review, IDCA was supposed to formulate a strategy that would make the most effective possible use of all development funds contributed to that country. It was also intended to remedy the situation whereby over 31 different agencies took part in a "maze" of interagency committees coordinating U.S. bilateral and multilateral aid programs. Those coordinating committees, the administration argued, often have

too narrow a perspective to be effective. They are often driven by the immediate need to frame a U.S. position on a particular issue by a particular date. As a result, the committees often fail to look at the large policy implication of the issue. They often concentrate on a single bilateral or multilateral program, not on a broad review cutting across different programs conducted by different agencies or organizations. They often adopt the path of compromise and caution, rather than seek the establishment of new or clearer policies.[20]

To remedy these procedural shortcomings, IDCA was established in October 1979. Four organizational changes were implemented in the effort to bring greater consistency to the entire range of U.S. economic policies and development programs affecting the LDCs. First, three entities—the Agency for International Development (which supervises bilateral economic development programs), the Overseas Private Investment Corporation (which provides government guarantees for private investments in the LDCs), and the Trade and Development Agency (which helps finance feasibility studies by American companies interested in bidding for foreign infrastructure and industrial contracts, mostly in less developed countries)—were made components of IDCA, reporting directly to its director.[21]

Second, IDCA was given a number of specific responsibilities, including annual submission to Congress of a comprehensive development assistance budget covering bilateral and multilateral aid efforts. The IDCA director also was designated the principal adviser to the president and to the secretary of state on international development matters. The director was charged with submitting to the president an annual development policy statement outlining priorities and the agenda of activities. Third, IDCA was charged with bringing a development perspective to U.S. trade and financial policies by participating in key coordinating groups and task forces in those policy sectors.

The fourth aspect of IDCA's activities was the trickiest. It involved finding a collaborative role in the areas of U.S. participation in United Nations (UN) programs, participation in the multilateral development banks, and the administration of food aid (P.L. 480). This role required acceptance of IDCA as a new partner by the bureaucratic actors already having primary operational authority over those programs—the State, Treasury, and Agriculture departments, respectively.

An array of memoranda of understanding were produced to recognize IDCA's right to provide overall policy and budgetary guidance for these programs, and to confirm the retention of primary responsibilities for day-to-day administration of these programs with the responsible department. In other words, considerable effort was expended in the preparation of ''peace treaties'' between IDCA and these departments prior to the former's creation. These efforts did not succeed in doing much more than preventing overt efforts by State or Treasury to intercede with the president and Congress to kill the proposal to create IDCA.

Despite the initial support of both Congress and the Carter White House, IDCA's reign as a real coordinator of U.S. economic assistance policies was brief. Its creation resulted in the elimination of absolutely no coordinating groups. IDCA soon became just another layer of bureaucracy that could convene discussions but not force policy change. Then it became a hollow, phantom organization attached to the Agency for International Development with no independent staff. The absence of a clear presidential or congressional mandate ordering a transfer of specific jurisdictional authority to IDCA dealt it the same fate as CIEP: the coordination process remained unchanged and the line departments ignored it. By 1998, IDCA existed in name only: it had no functions and no personnel.[22]

THE SPECIALIZED WORKING GROUPS

The president and his cabinet participate in a relatively small proportion of the executive branch's total coordination effort. If the work of the senior co-ordinating groups described above is compared to a triangle, their efforts would comprise only the small apex. The vast majority of coordinating work is done in lower level groups for two reasons. First, it is here that the relatively time-intensive work of assembling detailed data, articulating arguments and counter-arguments, and enumerating policy options is done. After doing the "leg work," these groups submit distilled briefing memoranda to higher levels for final de-cisions. Second, most of the formulation and conduct of international economic policy involves "routine" matters whose economic impact and political sensi-tivity are sufficiently limited that they can be handled by subcabinet and senior civil servants.

The U.S. government surely is the world's leader in the quantity of inter-agency groups dealing with international economic policy. Some are important, while others deal with obscure issues and merit little outside attention. The large and ever-expanding size of the U.S. international economic policy agenda is a major reason for the abundance of these groups. Interagency committees and working groups continue to be formed in response to an endless array of new issues and legislative mandates that invariably do not fall within the exclusive jurisdiction of any single department. A second reason for the extensive inter-agency network in Washington is that once created, they are very difficult to terminate. No machinery exists to abolish groups whose responsibilities have shifted elsewhere, whose job has been accomplished, or whose mandate has been rendered obsolete by changing events.[23] A final contributing factor to the large number of coordinators is that many interagency groups are subdivided on a vertical basis, that is, they meet at different levels of seniority—office director, subcabinet (assistant secretary or undersecretary), and cabinet.

No one knows exactly how many groups there are. An accurate head count would be difficult because interagency groups and their subcommittees are so numerous, are often so informal that they do not have names, and are often invisible to outsiders because they deal with little-noticed technical matters. For example, in response to a Murphy Commission inquiry, the Treasury Depart-ment listed a total of 58 interagency groups in which its international staff participated in 1975. Quantity of coordinating groups does not necessarily trans-late into either effective coordination or high quality policy. Some groups func-tion more effectively than others. The need to convene an interagency forum containing a dozen or more bureaucracies occasionally does slow the decision-making process to a crawl.

A description of the more important and permanent interagency committees working below cabinet level will provide some appreciation for the systematic (profuse may be the more applicable adjective) means by which international economic policy is formulated in coordinating groups at the intermediate and staff levels.

One of the newest coordinating mechanisms supports U.S. participation in the informal economic policy coordination process of the Group of Seven (G-7) industrialized countries. In preparing for the annual economic summit meeting among heads of government, each of the participating countries has designated a ''sherpa'' to prepare the summit's agenda and to draft preliminary agreements. The part-time position of sherpa in the second Clinton administration was handled by an assistant to the president, who was assisted by two senior officials, one dealing with economic issues (from the Treasury Department) and one responsible for foreign policy issues (from the State Department). Informal consultations between the Treasury Department and the Board of Governors of the Federal Reserve System constitute the limited interagency process that prepares the U.S. government positions for the periodic meetings of the G-7 finance ministers and central bank governors and of their deputies.

Two standing trade policy coordinating committees operate under the chairmanship of the Office of United States Trade Representative (USTR): the Trade Policy Review Group (comprised of undersecretaries and assistant secretaries) and the Trade Policy Staff Committee (meeting at the senior civil servant level). Their work load consists mainly of preparing economic analyses and preliminary policy options pertaining to regional trade strategies, import policy, and actions involving U.S. participation in the World Trade Organization (WTO). The extensive membership in these two committees begins with USTR and goes on to eleven cabinet departments: State, Treasury, Commerce, Agriculture, Energy, Labor, Justice, Defense, Interior, Transportation, and Health and Human Services. Other members are the CEA, OMB, the Environmental Protection Agency, as well as senior staff members from three coordinating bodies, the NSC, NEC, and IDCA.

The USTR-led trade policy coordinating system no longer includes the cabinet-level Trade Policy Committee. Although legally still in existence, it has been functionally inert since the mid-1980s. As noted above, its duties have been assumed by the various cabinet-level groups (mainly the NEC and the EPC) delegated overall coordinating authority in economic policy.

The agenda of the Trade Policy Staff Committee has flourished. At year-end 1998, it had spawned more than 80 subcommittees and task forces:[24]

Geographic Subcommittees

Africa

Andean Countries

ASEAN

Australia/New Zealand

Canada

Caribbean/Caribbean Basin Initiative

Central America

China

Eastern/Central Europe

European Union

European Union Transatlantic Economic Partnership

Free Trade Area of the Americas

India

Israel

Japan

LDC Trade Issues

Mexico

Middle East

North Africa

Russia

Sub-Saharan Africa

South Asia

Southern Cone

Taiwan

Functional Subcommittees

Aerospace Trade Issues

Aeronautical Equipment

Agriculture

Antidumping

Barter and Countertrade

Business and Professional Services

Chemical Trade

Commodity Agreements

Congressional Liaison

Customs (Including Harmonized System & Customs Valuation Code)

Economic Analysis

Energy Issues

European Union Mutual Recognition Agreements

EU Transatlantic Economic Partnership

Export Financing

Fisheries

Generalized System of Preferences

Government Procurement Code

High Technology Trade Issues

Import Licensing

Information Systems

Intellectual Property

Intergovernmental Relations

Investment (bilateral treaties)

Non-Tariff Barriers

OECD Trade Issues

Preferential Trading Arrangements

Pre-Shipment Inspections

Rules of Origin

Safeguards

Section 301

Section 337

Semiconductors

Services

Shipbuilding

Space Industries Trade

Standards

Steel

Subsidies

Tariffs

Basic Telecom

Trade and Competition

Trade and the Environment

Trade and Labor Standards

Trade and Technology

Trade Policy Issues Related to International Finance

UNCTAD Trade Issues

Wood Products

WTO Disputes

WTO Sanitary and Phytosanitary Measures

WTO Regional Trade Agreements

Task Forces

Driftnet Fishing Sanctions

Russian Space Launch

Trade with Guam

Softwood Lumber

Tobacco Import Licensing

Wheat Gluten

WTO Telecom Services

For statutory and historical reasons, a number of interagency trade policy coordinating groups function outside the USTR-chaired framework. Most of them deal with export issues. Three committees exist to resolve disagreements on how to respond to the thousands of export license applications submitted annually by companies for commercial goods having potential military uses (e.g., computers). If staff-level reviewers at the departments of State, Defense, Commerce, and Energy, and the Arms Control and Disarmament Agency[25] disagree on whether to approve an individual license or impose an export control, the application is reviewed by the Commerce-chaired Operating Committee. If the latter cannot reach consensus in a fixed time period *and* the minority dissenter(s) request further review, the matter goes to the more senior Advisory Committee on Export Policy (also chaired by the Commerce Department) for resolution. If there is still no unanimity in a fixed time period and the minority dissenter(s) again demand further review, the application in dispute is evaluated by the cabinet-level Export Administration Review Board. The president is the next and final stop in the appellate process. Export controls on purely military goods are administered by the State Department with the technical advice of the Defense Department.

An informal interagency arrangement prepares the U.S. government's position on export control issues that are to be discussed in meetings convened under the Wassenaar Arrangement. This is the multilateral agreement on common export control standards for conventional arms and dual-use goods and technologies established in 1996 to replace the long-running Coordinating Committee on Multilateral Export Controls (COCOM). If the major participating departments (State, Defense, and Commerce) cannot reach agreement, the issue in question goes to an NSC-chaired working group for resolution. If consensus is still not forthcoming, the debate moves to progressively more senior NSC review levels in a manner similar to the ''appellate'' process for resolving export licensing disagreements.

The determination by recent administrations that the massive U.S. trade deficits should be reduced through increased exports rather than reduced imports, together with pressure from Congress, has generated a growing presence by the Commerce-chaired Trade Promotion Coordinating Committee (TPCC). The latter's importance was significantly enhanced when, in the Export Enhancement Act of 1992, Congress gave the (already existing) TPCC statutory life. The committee was charged with providing better coherence and direction to what was deemed an ineffective and disorganized set of government programs aimed at helping the private sector to increase export sales. To encourage the executive branch to upgrade its export promotion efforts, Congress also ordered the TPCC to produce an annual report called the "National Export Strategy." In responding to this congressional mandate, the 20 departments and agencies comprising the committee have provided detailed reports on their efforts to provide more user-friendly export support facilities to the business sector, identify the fastest-growing overseas markets for U.S. sales, aggressively challenge foreign barriers to American exports, and so forth. More recently, the TPCC became a vehicle for articulating broader export policy priorities.[26]

The politically sensitive issue of textile and apparel imports is overseen by the Commerce Department–chaired Committee for the Implementation of Textile Agreements. Whether meeting at the political appointee or senior staff level, its major concerns are, first, the series of bilateral orderly marketing agreements originally concluded under the Multifiber Arrangement. Under the latter, governments of major textile exporting countries "voluntarily" agree to restrain exports of textile products to the United States and other industrialized countries. Second, the textile committee deals with the more recent multilateral Agreement on Textiles and Clothing that will guide a long-term phase-out of these bilateral export restraint programs.

Relatively informal interagency coordination characterizes the non-trade sectors of U.S. international economic policy. The Treasury Department does not need the specific permission of other departments or agencies to make decisions on international monetary matters. However, it often seeks counsel from other agencies through ad hoc consultations (as opposed to permanent committees). Senior staff members at the Treasury, the Federal Reserve's Board of Governors, and the Federal Reserve Bank of New York participate in a telephone conference call at least twice daily to discuss developments in the foreign exchange market. These conversations determine if and when government intervention in the foreign exchange market is advisable and feasible for trying to moderate large swings in the dollar's exchange rate. The New York Fed's trading desk places the currency buy or sell orders, but only at the direction of Treasury Department personnel, who alone have the authority to order intervention (short of emergency situations).

With increasing frequency, International Monetary Fund (IMF) lending practices involve questions that go beyond the technical one of how a country should best correct its balance of payments problems. Furthermore, Congress has passed legislation urging the executive branch to pursue certain policy goals as part of U.S. support of IMF lending operations. The net result of these developments is a growing need for the Treasury Department to consult elsewhere in the executive branch before giving voting instructions to the U.S. executive director in the IMF (who reports to senior Treasury Department officials). If a proposed loan involves a country accused of such actions as unfair labor practices, Treasury consults with the Labor Department. If the proposed loan recipient appears to have a poor human rights record, excessive military spending, or links to state terrorism, the State Department is consulted. Whenever a proposed IMF loan involves a recipient country of special importance to U.S. foreign policy (Russia would be the prime example), Treasury personnel will seek input from the State Department.[27] The Treasury Department also chairs the only permanent interagency coordinating group dealing with international investment policy, the Committee on Foreign Investment in the United States.

Interagency coordination dealing with U.S. foreign assistance policies and programs is relatively informal. There is no longer any structured interagency coordination machinery guiding the two largest bilateral foreign aid programs. The Agency for International Development (AID) now has a relatively free hand in administering bilateral development assistance grants, most of which are for relatively small dollar amounts. The State Department has an essentially free hand within the executive branch in allocating aid through the Economic Support Fund (ESF) to countries deemed to be strategically important; however, much of the money authorized for this program is earmarked by Congress in specific amounts for specific countries.

The Working Group on Multilateral Aid prepares an interagency position on what instructions to give the U.S. executive director when member countries are asked to approve loans proposed by multilateral development banks (the World Bank, the Inter-American Development Bank, etc.). The Treasury Department chairs this committee because it has primary authority over the multilateral portion of the U.S. aid program. Most loans are approved on a pro forma basis at the senior civil servant level. On the few occasions when controversies arise (e.g., because of allegedly harmful effects on the local environment), the committee deliberates more meticulously and at the political level.

The once-powerful National Advisory Council on International Monetary and Financial Policies (NAC) has been reduced to a usually perfunctory, interagency approval forum at the staff level for export loans and guarantees proposed by the Export-Import Bank, as well as for concessional loans proposed by the Agriculture Department's Commodity Credit Corporation and Food For Peace Program (P.L. 480).

NOTES

1. Harold Seidman, *Politics, Position, and Power* (New York: Oxford University Press, 1970), p. 164.

2. Dean Acheson, *Present at the Creation* (New York: Signet Books, 1970), p. 70.

3. Ibid., p. 78.

4. U.S. Bureau of the Budget, "Organization and Coordination of Foreign Economic Activities" (mimeographed), vol. II, 1961, p. C53.

5. Ibid., vol. I, p. II-9.

6. Kenneth I. Juster and Simon Lazarus, *Making Economic Policy—An Assessment of the National Economic Council* (Washington, D.C.: The Brookings Institution, 1997), p. 13.

7. President Nixon did not act on a second recommendation: a professionally staffed Office of International Economic Policy in the Executive Office of the President. In order to avoid creating new units, the Advisory Council suggested that the Office of the Special Representative for Trade Negotiations be expanded to form the new Office of International Economic Policy. The head of this office (which also would provide the professional staff to the new CIEP) would become the assistant to the president for international economic policy and would retain the legislatively established title of Special Representative for Trade Negotiations.

8. White House press release dated 19 January 1971, p. 1.

9. Statement of Roy L. Ash, ''To Extend and Amend the International Economic Policy Act of 1972,'' Hearings of the House Committee on Banking and Currency, 16 May 1973 (Washington, D.C.: U.S. Government Printing Office, 1973), p. 28.

10. Dominic Del Guidice, ''Creation and Evolution of the Council on International Economic Policy,'' in *Appendices to the [Report of the] Commission on the Organization of the Government for the Conduct of Foreign Policy*, vol. 6 (Washington, D.C.: U.S. Government Printing Office, 1976), p. 123.

11. White House press release dated 1 December 1971, p. 2.

12. Interview with C. Fred Bergsten, April 1981.

13. White House ''Fact Sheet,'' dated 11 April 1985, p. 2.

14. Not-for-attribution interview with a White House official, May 1986.

15. Peter Kilborn, ''How the Big Six Steer the Economy,'' *New York Times*, 17 November 1985, p. 8F.

16. Not-for-attribution interview with a White House official, May 1986.

17. I.M. Destler, *The National Economic Council: A Work in Progress* (Washington, D.C.: Institute for International Economics, 1996), p. 40.

18. Ibid., p. 11. Destler goes on to note that over time, a division of labor developed between the two staffers, an arrangement further enhancing harmonious cooperation between the NEC and the NSC.

19. Ibid., pp. 46–47.

20. U.S. Senate Committee on Governmental Affairs, *Reorganization Plan No. 2 of 1979*, 13 June 1979, p. 5.

21. The Overseas Private Investment Corporation and the Trade and Development Agency were subsequently removed from the IDCA framework and made independent agencies.

22. Information supplied by AID information specialist in a not-for-attribution interview, September 1998.

23. A major exception to this generalization is the termination of ad hoc interagency groups created to support specific trade negotiations, such as those that led to the successful conclusion of the Uruguay Round of trade negotiations and the North American Free Trade Agreement.

24. Data supplied by the Office of Trade Policy Coordination, Office of the U.S. Trade Representative.

25. The Arms Control and Disarmament Agency was absorbed into the State Department in 1998 and will cease being an independent participant in the export control review process.

26. See, for example, the discussion of the need to renew fast-track authority in the

Commerce Department press release announcing publication of the TPCC's fifth annual report on the national export strategy, 24 October 1997.

27. The specifics of the Treasury Department's coordinating procedures were obtained in not-for-attribution interviews with several officials in that department's Office of International Affairs, September and October 1998.

5   The Congress and the
      Judicial Branch

The less people know about the making of sausage and of laws, the better
off they are.

                                        —attributed to Otto von Bismarck

The U.S. Congress's status as joint partner with the executive branch in formulating international economic policy constitutes a decision-making structure
not found in any other country. Nowhere else does the legislative branch even
remotely possess the independent power, capabilities, and inclination to affect
the substance of external economic policies above and beyond the preferences
of the executive branch. Building on its constitutional powers, the Congress has
become sufficiently well-informed and assertive that the administration is often
reduced to the role of high-powered lobbyist. The U.S. executive branch is
unlike that of any other country in terms of the time and energy it expends
trying to convince Congress either to pass international economics-oriented legislation that it wants or to modify congressional initiatives that it does not support.

   It is not possible to comprehend the intricacies of U.S. international economic
policies without an appreciation of the legal, procedural, and philosophical factors that underlie congressional activities in this area. The extent of Congress's
impact on these polices varies from one sector to another, with trade policy
being at the top of its list of interests. This chapter examines the less than precise
organizational dynamics and committee jurisdictions of Capitol Hill. It also ob-
serves similarities and differences in organizational behavior exhibited by the
legislative and executive branches of government. The nature of the uneasy

partnership between the Congress and the administration in the policymaking process will be examined in detail in Part IV.

CONGRESSIONAL POWERS AND INFLUENCE

The concept of the separation of powers among branches of government is uniquely important to the United States. Sometimes characterized as separate branches sharing broad powers, this organizational dynamic has created a complex partnership between the legislative and executive branches in all policy sectors, but especially in the conduct of U.S. external economic relations. There is a deeply imbedded tension in this relationship, the result of two competing prerogatives—that of the Congress in foreign commerce and that of the president in foreign affairs. The resulting battle of wills is an important variable in determining policy substance. It is no exaggeration to suggest that a significant part of the overall international economic policymaking process is the search for consensus between two "subgovernments," the administration and the Congress.

The legal basis of Congress's authority in the trade policy sector is rooted firmly in the Constitution. Article I empowers the Congress "to regulate commerce with foreign nations" and to "lay and collect taxes, duties . . . and excises." These revenue-raising measures include tariffs on imports. One of the very first laws passed in 1789 by the first session of Congress established a national tariff schedule. The authority of Congress to regulate the broadly defined concept of foreign commerce has been held dominant to the broad presidential powers to conduct foreign policy (as inferred in Article II).

In terms of constitutional law, the powers of the executive branch in managing trade policy may be viewed as derivative. Where presidential actions in this field have conflicted with congressional legislative enactments, judicial branch rulings have held the power of the legislative branch to be preeminent. A 1953 court decision ruled that "The power to regulate foreign commerce is vested in Congress, not in the executive or the courts; and the executive may not exercise the power by entering into executive agreements."[1] In the financial realm, the Congress is empowered "to coin money, regulate the value thereof and of foreign coin" and "to borrow money on the credit of the United States."

The principal manifestation of congressional power in international economic relations is the passage of the legislation needed by the executive branch. Although legislation is not necessary for the executive branch to engage in trade negotiations with other governments, it is necessary for the president to be able to implement changes in regulations affecting imports or exports. For example, Congress must pass a statute to authorize implementation of U.S. commitments (e.g., lowering tariffs) made in an international trade agreement and to delegate presidential authority to restrict exports. Authorization and appropriations legislation is required for the expenditure of funds by the executive branch to pay salaries, support bilateral and multilateral economic development programs, and fund official export financing efforts. Senate advice and consent is necessary for completing the treaty ratification process and for confirming political appointees to serve in senior departmental and agency positions. Finally, U.S. adherence to the articles of agreement of such international economic organizations as the International Monetary Fund (IMF) requires implementing legislation from Congress, as do the U.S. government's financial contributions to them.

As seen from the opposite perspective, power has also been exerted by Congress's refusal to pass legislation in accordance with executive branch wishes and needs. Multilateral efforts to create an International Trade Organization, initiated soon after the conclusion of World War II, evaporated in the wake of congressional reluctance to approve the requisite legislation. The Johnson administration's negotiated pledge at the Kennedy Round to abolish the American Selling Price system of tariff valuation drowned in the wake of the congressional refusal to legislate this relatively minor change in U.S. import law. As discussed in Chapter 12, congressional refusal to legislate during the 1997–1998 period triggered impassioned complaints that it was threatening international economic stability by not authorizing additional U.S. funding to the IMF. At the same time, liberal trade advocates accused Congress of undermining the process of trade liberalization by not extending the president's fast-track negotiating authority.

A final source of indirect congressional power stems from its authority to investigate and evaluate the executive branch's performance, substantively and procedurally. As congressional interests and capabilities have grown in the area of international economic policy, so, too, has the utilization of what is termed the "oversight" function. The latter refers to committee hearings that are policy-related inquiries not directly related to pending legislation. The principal objectives of oversight hearings are:

1. To ascertain whether executive agencies are properly administered;

2. To monitor executive branch compliance with programs and policy objectives previously established by Congress;

3. To insure that official policies reflect national needs and goals;

4. To review government programs and activities to determine whether they should remain in existence or whether they should be reduced in scope or eliminated altogether; and

5. To debrief members on the results of major international economic meetings and to inform them of evolving economic trends.[2]

Oversight hearings dealing with international economic relations have been held with increasing frequency over the past two decades. By way of example, these hearings have reviewed the results of the Uruguay Round and North American Free Trade Agreement (NAFTA) negotiations, analyzed the impact of changes in the dollar's exchange rate, investigated causes of and cures for the

Mexican peso crisis and Asian contagion, evaluated import relief and export promotion programs, assessed Japanese trade barriers and executive branch efforts to have them reduced, and appraised U.S. global economic competitiveness.

The increased levels of congressional involvement in international economic policy have increased the work load of the executive branch. Numerous statutes being drafted and more extensive use of the oversight function by congressional committees have forced administration policymakers to spend a significant amount of time preparing for and participating in congressional testimony. For example, a search of the card catalogue in the Treasury Department Library revealed 11 citations in 1968 for congressional testimonies by the treasury secretary, undersecretary for monetary affairs, and assistant secretary for international affairs. In 1978, there were 61 citations. The insatiable desire of subcommittees to have their day in the media has made it not uncommon for key economic officials in the administration to give the identical testimony to two or more subcommittees. Senior USTR officials gave formal testimonies before congressional committees on 41 occasions during 1991, and they made "dozens" of visits to Capitol Hill for informal consultations with individual members.[3] Furthermore, countless hours of staff time in executive branch agencies are devoted to preparing dozens of annual reports demanded by Congress on a wide range of international economic activities.

No matter how numerous inter-branch consultations become, they will never fully dispel partially submerged "turf" jealousies and doubts about the wisdom and intentions of the other branch toward international economic policy management. It is often with an uneasy spirit that the two branches work together in this policy field. The Congress jealously guards its legislative prerogatives, wants to be responsive to constituents' demands, and tends to be suspicious of what it regards as the "internationalist" bias of the executive branch. The latter thinks it better knows the big picture, believes it deserves to have maximum independence, and prefers to keep its dependence on congressional approval to a minimum. However, quick congressional passage of international economic legislation requested by the administration—without additions, deletions, alterations, or insertion of new congressional review mechanisms—has become rare. The main exceptions to this rule were the few cases where requests for trade legislation were submitted under the fast-track provision (discussed in Chapter 9).

AN OVERVIEW OF CONGRESS'S ORGANIZATIONAL DYNAMICS

There is no single theory of behavior that can accurately explain all the attitudes and actions of the two houses of the U.S. Congress. The concept that the vast majority of its members wish to be reelected and therefore are passively responsive to constituents, campaign contributors, and special interest groups is too much of an oversimplification to accurately explain and predict congressional behavior. The U.S. Congress, while often acting in accordance with established theories of organizational behavior and specific academic behavioral models, is just as often a mystifying institution with many important idiosyncrasies. Some readers might be annoyed with my failure to present a unified, all-encompassing theory of congressional decision-making. The fact of the matter is that no integrating thesis is apparent when one closely examines the numerous manifestations of Congress's procedural quirks.

When a member of the House or Senate casts a vote for or against a pending piece of legislation, it is the climax of what is usually a long and elaborate administrative process. If the member belonged to the committee that considered, wrote, and reported the proposed statute, he or she may be intimately familiar with its contents and implications. It is more likely that the member is not personally familiar with, or committed to, a proposed bill and is on the receiving end of arm-twisting advice as to how to vote by administration officials, party leaders in Congress, organized interest groups, or all of the above. It is also possible—especially in cases of amendments to existing bills—that a vote reflects a rushed, last-minute briefing by a professional staff aide who may or may not have closely studied the bill and its amendments. In a private conversation, one former committee aide estimated that during his tenure in the Senate (the late 1970s), more than half the votes cast by members were made on the basis of a quick chat with staff specialists who were asked by their boss, "How should I vote on this?" These consultations are often held only minutes before a floor vote.

It is frequently suggested that only someone who has worked in the legislative branch for many years can fully comprehend the capriciousness and vicissitudes of Congress's operational pattern. There are ample reasons to agree with this:

Item: An article on the power of congressional staffs related the story of an assistant to a senator who produced a requested analysis of a civil rights bill amendment that consisted of a summary, a list of pro and con arguments, and 20 pages of analysis. Upon being handed this document, the senator "weighed the material for a moment, then tossed it back . . . and said, 'you don't expect me to read all this! Just tell me how to vote'."[4]

Item: A former congressman from Michigan (James G. O'Hara) was quoted as saying that "I did not feel strongly about 90 percent of the stuff I voted on [in Congress]. . . . It was just a matter of going along with what the district wanted or what the party wanted."[5]

Item: In a private conversation, a former staff official on the Senate Banking Committee relayed the response to a senator who had asked his opinion on a pending amendment to an export control bill. The staffer presented the positive aspects, but explained his beliefs that the negative factors dominated and that the member should vote against the amendment. The senator said that he agreed with this analysis but added he was nonetheless going to vote in favor of the bill. Why? Because, the senator pointed out, the colleague who was sponsoring the amendment was the chair of another subcommittee, and "I want something passed by that subcommittee."

Item: Members of Congress have been known to tell the floor manager of a bill that they will vote against it—unless their "yea" votes are absolutely required to assure passage. Foreign aid legislation is a prime example of the process whereby many members are anxious to please constituents by voting against it, unless such a vote would actually defeat the proposed legislation.

In recent years the legislative process has become increasingly complex as lawmakers' actions have further flattened Congress's horizontal structure—that is, all elected members ultimately have the same rank and authority in the Senate and House. In a legal sense, there is no pyramidal hierarchy in either chamber. All members are elected in the same way and serve equally. The power and influence that formerly were derived from being elected by one's colleagues to a party leadership post or to chair a committee have been dissipated by a series of reforms begun in the 1970s. Party discipline continues to erode because of the tendency for more candidates to run as independent-thinking, reform-minded "outsiders" and an increased turnover of congressional membership, mostly through retirements.

Challenges to the party leadership of both houses, to the seniority system, and to the power of committee chairs have become the norm. Refusal by newly elected members of Congress to quietly pay their dues has been the hallmark of a new breed of irreverent, self-confident members who have been elected over the past two decades, thanks mainly to their individual campaigning skills rather than party machines. The further decentralization of congressional authority has given freer range than ever before to the interplay of the individual personalities, intellects, ideologies, and constituent interests of the 535 voting members of Congress. (The total is 540 if one includes the limited voting power gained in 1992 by the delegates from the District of Columbia, Guam, Puerto Rico, the U.S. Virgin Islands, and American Samoa.) The result, to some observers, is that Congress is more unpredictable, unmanageable, and obstreperous than ever. A British magazine characterized it as being "composed of 535 one-man parties which combine in small groups and shifting alliances among numberless subcommittees, each led by a chairman jealous of his narrow fief and limited power—which is the power not to promote but to obstruct."[6]

Along with diffusion of power, the growth of professional staff expertise has been one of the most important changes in the legislative process since the mid-1970s. Congress is better informed than ever before (even if it does not always act more quickly and more decisively). The bottom line result is simple and important: elected members are far better equipped than ever before to collect data as well as to develop and evaluate policy options in-house. The desire to be more intellectually self-sufficient is largely an outgrowth of the distrust of the White House that boiled over in the Johnson administration, escalated rapidly during the Watergate era, and hit new highs during the Clinton administration.

When elected members, personal staffs, committee staff personnel, support agencies, district workers, administrative and security personnel, and workers in the Government Printing Office are added together, the U.S. legislative branch's overall work force in 1998 was just under 30,000 people.[7] This total is down from the 38,000 figure in the early 1990s, but still represents a larger work force than the total number of civilian employees in the executive branch of many of the 190-plus sovereign countries in the world today. Annual budgetary expenditures to maintain the U.S. legislative branch now exceed $2 billion (an amount higher than total governmental expenditures in many small countries). The bottom line is that the U.S. Congress by far is the world's best staffed and most expensive legislative body.

The personal staff of members has grown in number from about 2,000 in 1947 to approximately 11,700 in 1997.[8] In addition to the desire to narrow the expertise gap with the executive branch, Congress expanded the size of its professional staff because of a geometric increase in its work load—the result of the increased number and complexity of the issues it must deal with (such as health insurance) as well as more numerous requests for personal assistance from constituents.

Although the number of full voting members has not increased in more than a quarter of a century, Congress has witnessed a proliferation of new subcommittees, each of which provides its chair with the potential for additional political influence and media exposure. During the 82nd Congress (1951–1952), 19 standing (i.e., permanent) committees in the House of Representatives maintained a total of 69 standing subcommittees. In the 105th Congress (1997–1998), 16 standing committees and one select committee in the House were subdivided into a total of 87 subcommittees.[9]

On the Senate side, the total of 66 standing subcommittees in 1950 ballooned to 140 in 1976 (a total that rises to 171 if select, special, and joint subcommittees are included). Consolidation efforts pared the number of subcommittees of standing Senate committees to 68 in the 105th Congress.[10]

Although they were not formally authorized until 1946, professional staff personnel employed by congressional committees increased in the last four decades at a pace even faster than the increases in the members' work loads or numbers of new subcommittees. In 1950, an estimated 300 professional staff personnel were assigned to the Senate's standing committees. In 1997, the comparable figure was 1,216. Committee staff members in the House increased almost ten-fold, from 246 in 1950 to 2,147 in 1993.[11] The Joint Economic Committee listed 5 economists in its 1963 publications; it employed just under 20 full-time professionals in 1998.[12]

The relatively recent arrival on Capitol Hill of career policy specialists, many of whom transferred from executive branch posts, has imbued Congress with an unprecedented level of policy expertise. It also produced a new level of aggressiveness and a keen appetite for independently developing positions on current issues. In 1980, the House Select Committee on Committees warned that some committees had built staff bureaucracies which were "unwieldy, inbred, and self-perpetuating. Members lacking the time to adequately supervise and control staffs often cede to staff the right to determine priorities and to set the legislative agenda."[13]

Research, policy analysis, and program evaluations in the international economic policy sector are also available from many of the 4,000 analysts employed in three "support" institutions created by and reporting to Congress. More than 400 professionals in the Congressional Research Service (CRS), a part of the Library of Congress, provide research on any legislation-related issue requested by Congress. The policy analyses and legislative histories produced are factual and nonpartisan and refrain from providing policy guidance or taking sides on any contentious issue.

The General Accounting Office (GAO) was originally established in 1921 as an independent auditing investigator of executive branch spending. Since the 1970s its mandate has expanded to assist the Congress in reviewing and evaluating executive branch policies, organization, and programs. Its international affairs division has reviewed a wide range of international economic issues, including export promotion programs, bilateral United States-Japanese trade problems, and administration of the steel trigger price mechanism. GAO reports usually conclude with specific recommendations for procedural or substantive changes.

The Congressional Budget Office (CBO) was established to provide analytic support for the reformed budget-creating process in Congress, as mandated by the Congressional Budget Act of 1974. The CBO examines the broad trends of the U.S. economy, analyzes policies and programs, assesses the potential budgetary costs of proposed legislation, and conducts special economic studies upon the request of congressional committees.

CONGRESS AND TRADE

The most important and frequent involvement of Congress in international economic legislation deals with foreign trade, in money terms the most important international economic policy sector to the public at large. It is not an easy subject to handle for someone who wants to get reelected. All legislative bodies must deal with an inherent conflict in the political economy of trade. Economically, the vast majority of people are helped by the free flow of goods and services based on comparative advantage; consumers get cheaper and better goods made abroad and many workers are employed in export-oriented sectors. Politically, the minority hurt by import competition invariably is more vocal and better organized than the majority whose interests are not served by protectionism. People enjoying the fruits of liberal trade seldom communicate that sentiment to their elected representatives. Those being hurt will unhesitatingly and indefatigably exercise their right to demand that government officials ease their burden with new import barriers.

From the beginning of the Republic through 1934, that which "came naturally" to Congress was passage of protectionist legislation. This inclination reflected the fact that it is "a decentralized, undisciplined institution, particularly susceptible to pressure from organized interests."[14] However, Congress has clearly become more sophisticated and discerning in its contemporary approach to trade policy. Congressional forays into trade legislation since the mid-1930s are best understood as an exercise in remaining sensitive to constituents' legitimate demands while preventing repetition of the trade war debacle of the 1930s (this balancing act will be examined in detail in Chapter 9). Most members of Congress enjoy cultivating the image of chauvinistic hardliner—in contrast to the president's image of free trade-loving statesman—even though they do not pass import-restricting trade bills that would justify such a reputation. The average member wants to assure American workers and companies not that they will get immunity from competition with imports, but that they will get a quick, fair, and competent hearing in Washington when import and export grievances arise. The average member feels that trade policymakers in the executive branch are more attuned to the "macro" goal of making the world economy function more efficiently than to responding to the "micro" problems of an individual company and its workers. Congress sees itself as a necessary counterbalance.

Generalizations about international economic attitudes of specific senators and representatives tend to be misleading. Party affiliation and political philosophy often can be irrelevant to accurately predicting voting behavior on international trade legislation. Political conservatives are far more likely than liberals to embrace the concept of a market-based, liberal global trading system. The Senate tends to be more in favor of a liberal international economic order because no state is without a significant free trade constituency, whereas such a presence is not applicable to all the smaller districts served by representatives.

Economic geography is often the dominant variable shaping a member's trade sentiments. Representatives with import-impacted industries like steel, apparel, and footwear in their districts are more amenable to providing import relief than colleagues whose districts are dominated by export-oriented high-tech firms or soybean farmers. Members from oil-producing states tend to favor special import fees on petroleum products (to discourage foreign dependency), while their colleagues from the oil-importing states of New England are adamantly opposed to any measure that would result in higher heating fuel costs. Representatives from major financial centers extol the virtues of free capital movements.

Committee assignments can affect the attitude of a senator or representative towards international economic issues. A congressional variant of the bureaucratic politics model means that the typical member of the outward-looking foreign relations committees views foreign aid in relatively favorable terms and import barriers in relatively unfavorable terms. Members of the armed forces committees tend to take a relatively hard-line position toward controlling the export of advanced technology goods to potential enemies in comparison to the committees whose jurisdictions include export promotion. The agriculture committees take agricultural trade issues far more seriously than the Finance and Ways and Means committees.

THE COMMITTEE SYSTEM: JURISDICTIONS AND JEALOUSIES

In 1885, a political scientist named Woodrow Wilson wrote that "Congress on the floor is Congress on public exhibition, while Congress in its committee rooms is Congress at work."[15] International economic policy is no exception to the rule that U.S. laws emanate mainly from committee deliberations that gather information, pursue political consensus, and draft statutory language. The legislative process dealing with international economic relations is unusual only in the above-average number of committees claiming jurisdiction. Committee responsibilities, especially in the trade and investment sectors, appear to be arbitrarily and excessively scattered. The extent to which jurisdiction is disaggregated is seen in the ten Senate committees and eight House committees having authority over various components of the U.S. foreign aid program. Six committees in both houses have at least a sliver of jurisdiction over global environmental issues. Furthermore, the committee assignments outlined below demonstrate that a committee in one house does not necessarily have parallel jurisdiction with its counterpart in the other house.

The two main reasons for the decentralization and overlap of committee authority are identical to the causes of large numbers of executive branch agencies being involved in international economic policy: the diversity of the subject matter and important linkages to domestic economic policy and to foreign policy. Congress seems well aware of the drawbacks of the resulting administrative overcrowding, and it periodically has sought to reform executive branch organization in international economic policy. For example, it pressured both the Carter and Reagan administrations to streamline the trade policymaking machinery. Occasional efforts in both the House and Senate to rationalize committee jurisdictions have had no success in overcoming the very sensitive "turf" issues associated with transferring power from one committee to another. Outside advice on reorganization is not welcomed, and people in the executive branch and business community long ago learned not to antagonize members by making suggestions on reorganizing committee responsibilities.

Few congressional committees are not involved at least peripherally in legislation and oversight related to international economic relations. Seven standing committees in the Senate and seven more in the House are of major importance in this field. As a group, they deal with the issues of agriculture, appropriations, banking, commerce, energy, finance, foreign relations, and science and technology. In addition, several other committees are responsible for the international aspects of their domestic jurisdictions: environment, labor, government operations, the judiciary, and small business.

The Joint Economic Committee exercises oversight jurisdiction in all international economic policy sectors, but it is not empowered to write or report legislation. Having been exempted from the time pressures associated with drafting new laws, the committee provides a relatively scholarly venue for discussions of evolving trends, the need for structural changes in the global economy (it was the first to actively contemplate the merits of floating exchange rates), and long-term U.S. policy goals.

Senate Committees	International Economic Policy Jurisdiction
Agriculture, Nutrition, and Forestry	Restraints on agricultural imports and export promotion; overseas food aid (P.L. 480).
Appropriations	Funding for bilateral aid and U.S. contributions to international financial institutions; Export-Import Bank and other export promotion programs.
Banking, Housing, and Urban Affairs	Export controls and promotion; Treasury Department's Exchange Stabilization Fund; IMF issues; international banking and debt issues; foreign direct investment in the United States; International Emergency Economic Powers Act; foreign corrupt practices; foreign boycotts.
Commerce, Science, and Transportation	Foreign direct investment in the U.S.; competitiveness of U.S. technology sector; science and technology policy; international telecommunications issues.
Energy and Natural Resources	International aspects of energy policy.
Finance	International trade policy, with focus on U.S. imports and reciprocal trade agreements; international taxation and customs issues.
Foreign Relations	Overall international economic relations; international financial institutions, including the IMF; bilateral foreign aid; confirmation of treaties.

House Committees	International Economic Policy Jurisdiction
Agriculture	Same as Senate counterpart.
Appropriations	Same as Senate counterpart.
Banking and Financial Services	International financial institutions, including the IMF; international banking and debt issues.

Commerce	Import issues exclusive of tariffs; foreign direct investment in the United States; international telecommunications issues.
International Relations	Overall international economic relations; export controls and licensing for dual-use goods; bilateral foreign aid; international investment policy; international information services; commodity agreements; International Emergency Economic Powers Act; Overseas Private Investment Corporation.
Science	U.S. science and technology policy; U.S. technological competitiveness; international environmental and energy issues.
Ways and Means	Same as Senate Finance Committee.

No rational person designing from scratch a system of congressional committee jurisdictions in international economic policy would produce a plan resembling the existing arrangement. The overlapping nature of the issues, historical anomalies, and the need to compromise have led to a splintering of authority that prevents jurisdictional domination as much as it minimizes efficient organization. A number of procedural problems ensue from the sheer numbers of committees involved in international economic relations and the multifaceted nature of many of the issues involved. Problems arise in cases where jurisdiction for the same subject (e.g., the IMF) is claimed by two committees in the same house of Congress. In such cases, both will consider and approve relevant legislation.

Emerging policy issues are more likely to trigger multiple committee claims of jurisdiction because no clear guidelines exist to allocate new lines of authority. When legislation to create export trading companies was introduced in the House of Representatives in 1980, it represented a relatively innocuous attempt to promote sales of U.S. exports, even though it did contain a few controversial technical changes in tax, banking, and antitrust procedures. Expeditiously handled in the Senate and passed by a 77–0 vote in September 1980, the legislation found itself under the scrutiny of four separate House committees: Foreign Affairs, Banking, Judiciary, and Ways and Means. The resultant scheduling problems caused by multiple House subcommittee hearings delayed final enactment of the export trading company legislation until the next session of Congress.

The joint conference committee convened to reconcile differences in the House-Senate versions of what would become the Omnibus Trade and Competitiveness Act of 1988 ranks as one of the largest in congressional history. A total of 199 members represented 14 House committees (Agriculture; Armed Services; Banking, Finance and Urban Affairs; Education and Labor; Energy and Commerce; Foreign Affairs; Government Operations; Judiciary; Merchant

Marine and Fisheries; Public Works and Transportation; Rules; Science, Space and Technology; Small Business; and Ways and Means) and 9 Senate committees (Agriculture, Nutrition and Forestry; Banking, Housing and Urban Affairs; Commerce, Science and Transportation; Finance; Foreign Affairs; Governmental Affairs; Judiciary; Labor and Human Resources; and Small Business). The conference was organized into 17 separate subconferences which collectively produced a trade statute filling more than one thousand pages.

On rare occasions, Congress devises clever improvisations to save itself from its own procedural encumbrances. A classic example was the extraordinary intervention by the House Democratic leadership in the drafting of an "omnibus" trade bill in the spring of 1986. There was at that time a broad and deep consensus among House Democrats about the immediate need for comprehensive trade legislation. Appreciating the inevitable delays in store because of multiple committee involvement, then–House Speaker Tip O'Neill established an extraordinary coordinating mechanism among the seven committees involved. With the concurrence of the chairs of the Ways and Means; Energy and Commerce; Foreign Affairs; Banking, Finance, and Urban Affairs; Agriculture; Judiciary; and Education committees, Majority Leader Jim Wright was designated as a special field general to monitor progress, assign specific drafting responsibilities, and mediate problems arising from overlapping jurisdiction. The outcome of this effort, H.R. 4800, the Trade and International Economic Policy Reform Act, was unusual in two ways. First, there was the unusually diverse nature of its contents (export policy, import policy, international monetary and banking procedures, enhanced educational and training programs for workers, etc.). Second, the legislation was reported for floor action as a leadership bill, not a bill from a specific committee. (Despite this effort, the Senate never approved the act.)

The House's relatively swift passage of H.R. 4800 papered over an intensifying jurisdictional rivalry between two House committees concerning import policy authority. Like the bureaucratic politics model in the executive branch, this committee struggle demonstrated how competing government groups can reach conflicting conclusions as to what is good policy. The once-unassailable dominance of the Ways and Means Committee in drafting import-related legislation (tariffs, as revenue-raising devices, put import policy under its jurisdiction) periodically has been challenged by the House Energy and Commerce Committee. During much of the 1980s, the combination of an outspoken chairman (John Dingell, D., MI), an influx of aggressive new members, the country's declining interest in the energy crisis, and growing anxiety over the soaring U.S. trade deficit, encouraged the Energy and Commerce Committee to seek a larger voice in trade policy legislation. Its jurisdictional claim was justified on the basis of its responsibilities under House rules for "interstate and foreign commerce generally" and assertions that import issues were expanding well beyond tariffs and multilateral reciprocal trade agreements, the unequivocal province of Ways and Means. A staff member on the Energy and Commerce Committee told the author that the committee was merely filling in some of the voids left by the failure of Ways and Means to respond to the many recent changes in the international trading system.[16]

There is more involved here than ego and territory. Deep philosophical differences have periodically surfaced between the chairs of the two committees as to the directions and content of U.S. trade legislation. While serving as chairman of the Ways and Means' International Trade Subcommittee, Representative Sam Gibbons (D., FL) strenuously advocated a liberal trade policy for the United States, the path supported for half a century by the Ways and Means Committee. In contrast to Gibbons's refusal to see any virtue in restricting imports, the more heavily domestic perspective of Dingell and his colleagues advocated aggressive attacks against foreign trade barriers and domestic content requirements mandating a high percentage of U.S.-produced components be used in cars built in the United States by subsidiaries of foreign-owned automakers.

The Energy and Commerce Committee subsequently proposed several initiatives to legislate a stiffer backbone in the U.S. trade negotiating posture. One technique (later enacted into law) transferred certain import restraint decisions from the president to the USTR, who presumably is more sensitive and responsive to congressional sentiment. This proposal first saw the light of day in the Trade Law Modernization Act, H.R. 3777. Approved in November 1985 by the Energy and Commerce Committee, H.R. 3777 was the first general import policy bill in anyone's memory to have been initiated by a House committee other than Ways and Means. The Energy and Commerce Committee indirectly affected trade legislation in the 1980s by pushing Gibbons's trade subcommittee to act in ways that would diminish accusations it was too "soft" on trade. Among other things, the subcommittee was encouraged to toughen trade remedy laws in order to demonstrate concern about the trade problems of important constituencies.[17]

Members of Congress occasionally advocate international economic policy positions in forums other than committees. Informal statements on trade policy have been issued and White House visitations have been organized by some of the 178 partisan and nonpartisan Senate, House, and bicameral "caucuses," each of which deals with a specific regional or substantive issue. These caucuses ebb and flow with hot issues. In the mid-1980s, the roster of economics-oriented groups included a steel caucus, an auto task force, an export task force, a mushroom caucus, and a North American trade caucus. The Competitiveness Caucus, the Senate Science and Technology Caucus, the House Information Technology Working Group, and the Internet Caucus reflected the priorities of the 1990s. On occasion, working groups sponsored by the two main political parties disseminate reports advocating international trade and financial policy strategies. Examples are the Progressive Policy Institute, an affiliate of the centrist Democratic Leadership Council, and the Republican Leadership Council.

THE JUDICIAL BRANCH

The judicial branch has been an infrequent factor in the U.S. international economic policymaking process. The Trade Act of 1974 facilitated court appeals by U.S. corporations and unions whose petitions for import relief from unfair foreign competition had been rejected by the executive branch. Legislation passed in 1980 created the U.S. Court of International Trade by expanding the power and jurisdiction of the U.S. Customs Court. The new court provides a "comprehensive system for judicial review of civil actions arising out of import transactions and federal statutes affecting international trade."[18] It hears appeals in a wide range of trade-related legal disputes, including complaints (from the losing side) about the administrative decisions of U.S. government agencies made in connection with investigations of dumping, subsidies, and escape clause petitions. The Court of International Trade is a potential variable in U.S. trade relations because it has the power to overrule official actions taken in the administration of import relief laws.

The Supreme Court, on rare occasions, has had to settle a contentious trade dispute. In 1978, it decided a protracted legal dispute on whether the rebate of an internal consumption tax on Japanese TV exports constituted an illegal bounty or grant in terms of the U.S. countervailing duty statute. If the Supreme Court had not ruled in favor of the U.S. Treasury Department's contention that no illegal subsidy was involved, the implications for U.S. import policy would have been widespread. In 1983, the Supreme Court declared the legislative veto to be unconstitutional. This action nullified what was an emerging, but untried, congressional tactic to make certain presidential trade actions more responsive to the needs of domestic interests. In the Trade Act of 1974, Congress had given itself the power to override presidential rejections of recommendations of import relief made by the International Trade Commission under escape clause investigations.

The 1993 court ruling that the administration must file a detailed environmental impact statement before implementing the North American Free Trade Agreement suggests a new role for the judicial branch: arbiter of the applicability of domestic U.S. environmental law to foreign trade policy—and vice versa.

Finally, federal courts periodically have ruled state laws affecting international commerce to be illegal (see Chapter 3).

NOTES

1. Peter Buck Feller and Ann Carlisle Wilson, "United States Tariff and Trade Law: Constitutional Sources and Constraints," *Law and Policy in International Business* 8 (1966): 107–108.

2. U.S. House of Representatives, "Task Force to Review Congressional Changes in the 1970's," Final Report of the Select Committee on Committees, 1 April 1980 (Washington, D.C.: U.S. Government Printing Office), p. 47.

3. Data source: USTR, Office of Public Affairs. Federal Reserve chairman Alan Greenspan reportedly testified to congressional committees 32 times in the two-year period of mid-1996 through mid-1998.

4. Maurice Rosenblatt, "At Last, We May End Congress's 'Stafflation'," *Washington Post*, 4 January 1981, p. B1.

5. Bill Keller, "The Pleasure of Losing a Seat in Congress," *Washington Post*, 4 January 1981, p. B4.

6. "Washington Scramble," *The Economist*, 21 December 1985, p. 9.

7. Data source: Congressional Research Service, by telephone to the author.

8. Data source: Norman Ornstein, Thomas Mann, and Michael Malbin, *Vital Statistics on Congress 1997–1998* (Washington, D.C.: Congressional Quarterly, 1998), p. 133.

9. Data sources: U.S. House of Representatives, *Final Report of the Select Committee on Committees*, 1 April 1980 (Washington, D.C.: U.S. Government Printing Office), p. 303; and Clerk of the House of Representatives, *List of Standing Committees and Select Committee and Their Subcommittees of the House of Representatives*, June 1998 (Washington, D.C.: U.S. Government Printing Office).

10. Data sources: *The Senate Committee System, First Staff Report to the Temporary Select Committee to Study the Senate Committee System*, July 1976 (Washington, D.C.: U.S. Government Printing Office), p. 6; and Secretary of the Senate, *Committee and Subcommittee Assignments*, May 1997 (Washington, D.C.: U.S. Government Printing Office).

11. Data sources: U.S. House of Representatives, *Final Report of the Select Committee on Committees*, p. 537; and Ornstein, Mann, and Malbin, *Vital Statistics on Congress 1997–1998*, p. 133.

12. Data source: Joint Economic Committee, by telephone.

13. U.S. House of Representatives, *Final Report of the Select Committee on Committees*, p. 11.

14. I.M. Destler, *American Trade Politics* (Washington, D.C.: Institute for International Economics and the Twentieth Century Fund, 1995), p. 5.

15. Quoted in *The Senate Committee System, First Staff Report to the Temporary Select Committee to Study the Senate Committee System*, p. 5.

16. Not-for-attribution interview with a House staff member, September 1986.

17. Destler, *American Trade Politics*, p. 81.

18. "The United States Court of International Trade," undated brochure produced by the Court, p. ii.

6   The Private Sector: Interest
        Groups and Lobbying

Congress shall make no law . . . abridging . . . the right of the people . . . to
petition the government for a redress of grievances.
                                     —First Amendment to the Constitution

The parasite economy is a disease that has benefitted only the lawyers,
lobbyists and politicians who have flourished as the sickness spreads. . . .
[I]t absorbs not only financial capital but human capital as well. . . . Like
ticks on a hound, the lawyering and lobbying classes are sucking billions
from the economy that might otherwise be used for productive investment.
                                     —Jonathan Rauch

The private sector is the third force, after the executive and legislative branches,
determining the course of U.S. international economic policymaking. Through
a variety of communications techniques, the private sector (a term that includes
both domestic and foreign interests) is organized to transmit to the U.S. government a steady stream of partisan viewpoints. Interest group advocacy seeks
enactment or retention of policies that promote someone's economic interests
or philosophical values. Given the fact that much international economic policy
is made for the purpose of affecting the ways in which the private economy
interacts with the world economy, there is nothing inherently inappropriate about
the private sector speaking up and making demands. Since there are at least two
sides—and, therefore, at least two policy options—to almost every major international economic problem, articulations of different viewpoints, no matter how
self-serving, are legitimate and often useful.
    Input from the private sector is not only appropriate, it is also voluminous.

All conceivable interests, from the completely internally focused to the most overseas oriented, are organized for the purpose of getting their story out and their wishes met.

THE GAMES AND THE PLAYERS

Continuous dialogue—most of it relatively informal—flows between interest groups and the executive departments and congressional committees that have jurisdiction in matters directly affecting these groups. Casual dialogue escalates into intense pressure only when a specific government decision or action is pending that will affect the economic well-being or values of interest groups. Government officials are conditioned to expect pleading from the constituencies within the body politic that they closely work with. ''Iron triangles'' have developed over time among major economic sectors (e.g. agriculture and labor) and the executive departments and congressional committees created to deal with and represent them.

When foreign trade decisions are involved, lobbying is ubiquitous. Winners and losers are created whenever the U.S. government decides to reduce or increase barriers to imports of goods that are also being produced domestically. Imports can cause domestic job losses and bankruptcies, but they can offer consumers lower prices and more choices. Environmentalists see a loss in the quality of life when commercial considerations overrule efforts to reduce pollution and protect endangered species. Export controls also serve to help and harm different interests. They may serve foreign policy purposes, but they also impose costs on would-be exporting companies. U.S. export restraints sometimes have the unintentional effect of handing increased overseas sales to companies in countries that have not joined the United States in imposing trade sanctions. Private sector interventions in matters of foreign investment, international finance, and economic assistance to less developed countries (LDCs) are less frequent and not as well financed as in the trade sector.

When it comes to lobbying efforts in U.S. international economic policy, the ''private sector'' is a very large, diverse community. It consists of the following constituencies:

- The manufacturing sector
- The agricultural and raw materials sector
- The services sector
- Labor unions
- Consumers
- Foreign firms and governments
- Non-governmental organizations concerned with the environment, workers' rights, human rights, economic development, and so on.

Their primary target audience is "inside the Beltway": the executive and legislative branches, independent regulatory agencies like the International Trade Commission, and other interest groups (in the pursuit of coalition building). The secondary audience is the mass media and the general public, even though it usually is difficult to overcome the public's limited interest in international economic relations.

The tactics, strategy, and organization of interest groups may differ, but the ultimate objective of lobbying in any country is narrowly defined: to convince policymakers that a specific set of policy recommendations offer the best definition of the national interest. If politics determines who gets what, when, and how, interest groups are proclaiming "There is good reason to give us what we want, now!" What they want is for the government to satisfy their economic or ideological desires. Since the forms of policy advocacy vary so much, "success" is measured in different ways. Sometimes, specific official action is sought. Sometimes government inaction is demanded, as happened when certain groups successfully urged Congress not to renew fast-track trade negotiating authority.

The art of persuasion in international economic policy varies greatly. Different kinds of lobbying techniques are employed depending on different circumstances. Some activities are specific and intense. Some are mere public relations efforts to suggest that the merits of a particular interest group are worthy of respect. Some activities involve sophisticated technical analyses of economic data. Some involve a raw use of political power through threats of lost votes and political contributions. Capitol Hill is the focal point of lobbying when legislation is involved. The executive branch is the focus when a decision is forthcoming on general policy or administration of an international economic program.

Efforts by people and groups outside of the U.S. government to influence international economic policy decision-making fall into a broad spectrum of activism. At one pole, there is the relatively passive task of absorbing information so that an interest group will be aware of any impending actions, attitudes, and trends that might affect its members and goals. This task is accomplished by reading government documents and technical literature as well as by regularly getting updated from officials in the executive and legislative branches.

Placing the objectives and members of an interest group in the best possible light falls at the center of the activism continuum. Speeches, conversations with policymakers and media people, and production of brochures, web sites, and newsletters usually contain more general information than specific demands. This level of activity represents an ongoing educational process to generate understanding of, and appreciation for, a group's grievances, accomplishments, importance, vision of the future, and interpretation of events. It also is part of what is known as networking: efforts to build friendships and trust among people who might be of help when the time comes to fight for a specific goal.

The activist pole of lobbying consists of direct, overt efforts to assure that policy actions conform with the perceived self-interest and objectives of a specific group. The vast majority of such efforts in international economic relations involves trade legislation and administrative determinations as to whether to impose restrictions on imports or exports. The lobbyist's task here is knowing whom to talk with and when, as well as what to say, and how to say it. The successful lobbyist combines an ability to be articulate and convincing with "access." Senior policymakers and lawmakers, as well as their senior assistants, simply do not have sufficient time to read all relevant material produced internally or externally, answer all their telephone calls, or accept all of their luncheon, cocktail, or dinner invitations. Even the most accurate, best-articulated private sector argument is wasted if the right eyes and ears in officialdom do not focus on it. Access requires the professional skills, reputation, and personal charm necessary to "open doors" and get an otherwise harassed official or skeptical reporter to give a sympathetic hearing to a group's demands or arguments. Another necessary attribute is accuracy and reliability in the eyes of policymakers, who soon learn to ignore anyone who plays loose with the facts.

On a typical business day in Washington, representatives of various import and export interests are cultivating friends through a multitude of visits, telephone conversations, faxes, mass mailings, publication of economic studies, expense account lunches, and so-called Georgetown dinner parties. Voters from back home, perhaps representing an import-impacted industry, may be visiting their representatives' offices on Capitol Hill. More sophisticated forms of access include presentation of testimony before a congressional committee and participation in one of the statutorily established trade advisory committees convened periodically by the USTR office to receive negotiating advice and general policy guidance from specialists in the private sector (see Chapter 3). What might be described as ultimate access, altering the president's priorities or changing swing votes in Congress, is achieved only rarely; it is not the everyday stuff of lobbying.

The private sector is also accorded the opportunity to influence U.S. foreign trade actions through the arguments and counter-arguments presented by their lawyers in cases before U.S. government agencies evaluating petitions for relief from import competition. The U.S. system's preferences for liberal trade substance and legalistic procedure mean that requests for import relief are not provided automatically. Import restraints are adopted by the executive branch only after a relatively transparent, methodical determination that a petitioning domestic producer has indeed suffered injury from either fair or unfair competition as defined by various U.S. trade laws. The tone and direction of U.S. import policy is determined in part by government officials' ruling on the arguments presented in import relief cases by domestic producers and workers, importers, and foreign companies.

Efforts to influence the content of U.S. international economic policy are conducted by a large, heterogeneous array of individuals working for business trade associations, labor unions, law firms, lobbying firms, government relations offices of corporations, non-governmental organizations, public relations firms, consultants, foreign embassies, and coalitions of groups. The *Encyclopedia of Associations* identified some 23,000 of these groups in 1998, up from 4,900 in 1956.[1] Another survey found some 2,400 national trade associations, professional and scientific societies, and unions headquartered in the Washington, D.C. area, the lobbying mecca of the world.[2]

Different definitions of lobbying cause estimates for the number of people engaged in this work in Washington to fall into a wide range of 11,500 to 67,000. Estimates for total expenditures devoted to all lobbying activities run from $1.3 billion to $8.4 billion annually.[3] To comply with the specific provisions of the Lobby Disclosure Act of 1995, more than 3,700 firms and groups paying 7,682 people to represent 9,300 clients (in all policy fields) had registered with the House of Representatives at the end of 1998.[4] The Senate had received registrations from just under 4,300 lobbying entities at year-end 1998 that reported representing about 17,000 paying clients.[5] In addition to professional lobbyists, official attitudes can be influenced by the public utterances of academics and think tank intellectuals, ex–senior government officials, business journalists, and so on.

The drive to influence U.S. international economic policymaking resembles a pyramid of power. At the base of lobbying are thousands of individual companies and organizations, many built around a single issue. The middle layer consists of like-minded companies and farmers linked in trade associations (e.g., the American Soybean Association and the Semiconductor Industry Association). One level above them are permanent, broad-based coalition groups such as the U.S. Chamber of Commerce, the National Association of Manufacturers, the Business Roundtable, the National Foreign Trade Council, and the AFL-CIO. At the apex is a relatively new organizational phenomenon: ad hoc coalitions of coalitions to speak on behalf of multiple constituencies. The Business Coalition on Trade was formed in 1987 by major business coalitions to present unified views to the congressional conference committee putting the finishing touches on the 1988 omnibus trade act.

The stakes and complexity of international economic policy advocacy are sufficiently high to have generated something between an abundance and a glut of lobbyists in Washington. Virtual wall-to-wall representation of every conceivable special interest now exists, at times to the apparent point of overkill. The multitude of lobbying groups is suggested by the ability of a Washington-based IBM employee interviewed by the author to quickly tick off his company's membership in 15 trade associations and coalitions actively involved in international commercial issues. Agricultural associations have grown into a "collective" composed of more than 140 farm, commodity, and agribusiness groups. At least nineteen additional groups in the United States deal just with meat. Makers of machinery have formed nearly 50 trade organizations.

The U.S. version of the international economic policy lobbying game is wide open to the representation of foreign interests as well as domestic producers and workers. The combination of the United States being the world's largest single market and the relative accessibility of U.S. policymakers has resulted in externally generated lobbying efforts whose extent is not matched elsewhere. The record of other governments and foreign companies in influencing U.S. trade policy over the past two decades at times has been as successful and well-financed as that of their American rivals. A *partial* insight into efforts to influence U.S. policy on behalf of foreign interests is provided by the Department of Justice's annual report of filings under the Foreign Agents Registration Act. Nearly 2,800 individuals and firms reported lobbying efforts on behalf of 843 foreign principals in the period ending 31 December 1997.[6] Since most Americans retained by foreigners are not personally endeavoring to change U.S. laws and policy, most are not legally obliged to register under this act. Hence the listings and the earnings to be found in the act's annual report represent the proverbial tip of the iceberg of the multimillion dollar payments by foreign interests wanting to be informed about, and to influence what is happening in, U.S. international trade and financial policies.

Aggressive lobbying activities by Japan and China became sufficiently notorious as to cause a storm of resentment that has embarrassed both countries. Prior to being pressured into lowering its U.S. lobbying profile, Japan had built up the largest, most expensive foreign-run commercial intelligence gathering and policy influencing operation in history.[7] Estimates for total trade policy–related spending in the late 1980s by Japanese government agencies and private corporations were in the $300 to $500 million range.[8] This amount was probably more than that spent at the time by all other countries combined. It reflected Japan's thoroughness, its aversion to surprises, its economic size, and the insecurity that came with being the country having the most numerous trade frictions and biggest bilateral trade deficits with the United States. Japan's network of American lawyers and advisers has provided opinions as to the extent of U.S. bluff and the limits of its patience on specific product disputes. In other words, Americans on retainer have advised the Japanese government as to whether it really needed to offer concessions to forestall threatened U.S. retaliatory measures. In addition to countless other Americans paid to advise and provide "insider" information, Japan's unofficial Washington presence consists of a sizable contingent of its nationals who staff approximately 100 representative offices of Japanese companies, groups, and quasi-governmental agencies.[9]

The China lobby is divided into two camps advocating diametrically different courses of action: maximized economic relations or imposition of sanctions to protest China's poor human rights record and its exports of weapons technology. Some policy advocacy and public relations efforts on behalf of China are funded by the government in Beijing (allegedly including illegal presidential campaign contributions in 1996) and some by export-oriented companies based in Hong Kong.

The most listened-to segment of the China lobby in the United States belongs to American industry and agriculture. Big business and agribusiness unanimously advocate policies that would assist their export and foreign investment activities in a market with nearly unlimited potential. The lobbying campaign of American corporations on behalf of China "has no financial limits. . . . The companies don't care what they spend because the payoff to them is so enormous," California representative Nancy Pelosi was quoted as saying.[10] The Center for Responsive Politics estimated that pro-China American corporations had given more than $20 million in contributions to the Republican and Democratic parties in the year prior to the 1996 vote on extending most favored nation (MFN) tariff treatment.[11] The 800-plus members of the ad hoc Business Coalition for U.S.-China Trade spearhead the business community's day-to-day effort to preserve MFN tariff treatment.

SOURCES OF CLOUT

The continuing ability of private sector activists to be a force in shaping the content of U.S. international economic policy in general and trade policy in particular is based on a number of direct and indirect strengths. First, a lot of time, energy, money, and talent go into the process, since so much money is at stake. As interdependence increasingly affects a progressively less insulated U.S. economy, the United States has learned what other countries have known for decades: trade flows are a critical variable in the determination of gross domestic product (GDP) growth, jobs, profits, and new investment. The relatively high quality of economic policy lobbyists in Washington is directly related to the high salaries and generous expense accounts available to successful practitioners.

Second, a pluralist democracy accepts the argument that the private sector should have a major say in the determination of policy guidelines on how it is supposed to interact with the economies of other countries. Because government presence partly exists to help the private sector prosper, trade policymakers classify relatively little information as secret. Most of what is happening is in the public record. What is not made public soon leaks out. Most executive and legislative branch officials cannot resist confiding in representatives of their constituencies. When involved in internal disputes at the policy formulation stage, these same officials regularly leak their arguments to the media as a means of generating favorable public support. An experienced trade lobbyist therefore does not find it inordinately difficult to glean a sense of mood and direction at an early stage of the policymaking process.

A third factor is the frequency with which the U.S. foreign trade bureaucracy draws on the acknowledged technical expertise of outside sources. Many lobbyists on retainer are skilled analysts and tacticians who have retired from distinguished careers in senior government positions. Corporate officials provide a unique source of hands-on business knowledge useful in the decision-making process. With Washington physically and intellectually distant from the business world, policymakers heavily rely on the business community for details on current import and export trends, foreign trade barriers, domestic market conditions, and so on.

The number of persons working full time on the formulation and conduct of U.S. trade policy is quite small relative to the expanding work load. Personnel resources usually are stretched thin. This is especially true in the Office of the U.S. Trade Representative (USTR), whose professional staff averaged only about 150 during the 1991–1993 period when it was simultaneously conducting two important trade negotiations, the Uruguay Round and the North American Free Trade Agreement (NAFTA). The result is that the typical senior civil servant, being very busy and probably having no experience in business, is partially dependent on private sector sources for data on business trends and product specifications.

The fourth factor enhancing the efforts of lobbyists in the realm of trade policy is the increasing importance of Congress in the decision-making process. Increased voter interest in trade flows means that Congress gives trade policy a high priority. Because members are elected to represent their constituents' interests, they typically exhibit a greater predilection to respond to localized economic grievances than administration trade officials. The increased "democratization" of Congress since the early 1970s has helped make it an even more fertile ground for lobbying. Far more opportunities to influence voting have opened to lobbyists since the days when strong, domineering party leaders and committee chairs ruled the legislative agenda with iron hands. The increased independence of junior members, the growth of subcommittees in number and importance, and the proliferation of professional staff offer the private sector (and foreign governments) numerous access points for influencing legislation.

The final factor enhancing lobbying efforts is the outgrowth of the last two factors just discussed. Congress has written into trade law a comprehensive network of private sector advisory committees whose mandate is to counsel the federal government on the general direction of U.S. trade policy and on specific negotiating objectives in trade negotiations. U.S. trade law further stipulates that members of the advisory committees can be designated as advisers to a trade negotiation delegation and "may be permitted" to participate in international meetings. Before the executive branch can begin the process of securing expedited congressional approval of a trade agreement under the (currently expired) fast-track authority, 34 advisory committees (see Chapter 3 for details of the committee structure) must, by law, first produce evaluations as to whether the proposed agreement serves U.S. economic interests and is compatible with basic U.S. trade policy objectives.

Given the improbable scenario of Congress's passing implementing legislation for a trade agreement that is soundly lambasted by the private sector, the 1,000 private sector persons serving on the advisory committees exert great leverage on what the U.S. government can and cannot agree to in trade negotiations. Although the executive branch is not legally bound by advice of the advisory committees, it is required to inform them in the event of "significant departures from such advice." A de facto limit is thus imposed on the ability of trade negotiators to convince Congress to pass enabling legislation if they have not been responsive to the sentiments of private sector leaders.

If no consensus exists among key business executives that a good, or at least acceptable, trade agreement has been reached, Congress is unlikely to pass legislation ratifying the agreement. As a consequence, trade negotiators since the 1970s have sought an effective two-way dialogue with the business sector and labor community *during* trade negotiations. It was an open secret in Washington that a key element in the domestic phase of the Bush administration's Uruguay Round strategy was to maximize the number of industries and services benefiting from a successful conclusion of the negotiations. The greater the number of business groups supporting the agreement, the more likely it was that the administration could neutralize the opposition on Capitol Hill from groups that would be hurt from reductions in U.S. trade barriers.

AN EMPIRICAL LOOK AT LOBBYING ACTIVITIES

The purpose of this section is to present an overview of how the private sector and foreign governments can be a critical decision-making variable in U.S. international economic policy. The exact nature of this impact varies according to time period and policy sector. As noted above, lobbying is most prevalent in trade relations. Efforts to influence trade policy can be said to have gone through three general phases. Phase I covered the time between the first tariff act in 1789 and the Smoot-Hawley Tariff Act of 1930. Representatives of American industry had a relatively easy time in convincing Congress to periodically ratchet up tariff barriers. Tariffs were the major source of government revenues until the early twentieth century, the United States was still in an infant industry phase, no liberal trade lobby existed, and logrolling was an accepted practice in import legislation. Blatantly protectionist measures being successfully pushed on Congress became the exception instead of the rule only in the post–World War II era—Phase II. A distinctive Phase III may have begun in the late 1990s when non-business interest groups persuaded Congress to delay passing legislation that reduced trade barriers or promoted globalization (see Chapter 12).

This section focuses on Phase II of interest group lobbying. It began at the end of World War II and runs at least through the mid-1990s. (Its interruption in the late 1990s by what I see as a potential third phase may or may not be a brief interlude.) Phase II was a period when protectionist advocates could not turn back the tide of Washington's embrace of a liberal trade policy. The popularity of trade barriers decreased because of the growing number of American companies that became successful world-class competitors having sales and production facilities around the world. This trend in turn meant a great expansion of vested interests wanting to build a liberal global trading order responsive to U.S. exports and foreign investments. Politically powerful coalitions like the

National Association of Manufacturers, the Business Roundtable, and the Emergency Committee for American Trade represent the biggest Americans industrial companies and campaign vigorously for liberal trade policies at home and abroad.

After losing the ability to intimidate Congress into raising U.S. trade barriers in violation of U.S. General Agreement on Tariffs and Trade (GATT) commitments, relatively non-competitive, import-sensitive industries and unions turned their attention, somewhat successfully, to having Congress write statutory language making it easier for them to qualify for temporary measures to relieve import-induced injury. American companies also lobbied, somewhat unsuccessfully, for changes in statutory language that would restrain the administration's ability to restrict exports.

Having proposals become incorporated into trade legislation is among the top priorities of trade policy lobbyists. On rare occasions, lobbyists have gone beyond pushing proposals and de facto have performed the work of government officials. The Burke-Hartke Bill, first drafted in 1971, was a rare example of a bill essentially written from beginning to end by the AFL-CIO. It was an extreme proposal designed to respond to what the labor confederation perceived as legitimate complaints regarding rising imports and extensive U.S. corporate investing abroad. The proposals to impose across-the-board import quotas and punitive changes in U.S. tax laws applicable to foreign direct investment operations were so severe that the bill would have been laughed out of committee if a lesser lobbying force than the AFL-CIO had been the outside sponsor.

It was common knowledge in Washington trade circles that both the administration and the Congress in 1977 opted out of drafting a new section of what later became legislation extending the life of the Export Administration Act. This provision dealt with the emotionally charged issue of U.S. corporate compliance with the provisions of the Arab boycott of Israel. By common consent, a two-sided negotiating team drafted the language of this title. On one side was a task force of lawyers from several of the corporations who belonged to the blue-chip business coalition, the Business Roundtable. On the other side were representatives of a coalition of American Jewish groups that collectively negotiated as the American Jewish Service Organizations. In effect, the U.S. government agreed to (and did) translate their compromise language into the law of the land. The U.S. government thereby avoided the crossfire of two very strong interest groups.

The normal path of interest group impact on the policy process is to press grievances and demands until the legislative or executive branch becomes at least partially accommodating. An outcry from the agricultural lobby caused an overwhelming majority in both houses to pass the Agriculture Export Relief Act of 1998. Congress agreed with farmers' demands, led by the wheat growers, that agricultural goods should be exempted from the sanctions cutting off U.S. government export loans and credits to India and Pakistan. (President Clinton had imposed sanctions on these countries after they tested nuclear weapons.)

The agricultural community strengthened its case by reminding Congress of its promises of assistance in promoting export sales to offset the effects of previous legislation curtailing crop subsidies.

An earlier example of trade policy actions being taken to placate an interest group was the accommodations made to the textile industry in the 1960s and 1970s. Its opposition had to be defused in order to pass legislation providing new presidential authority to reduce trade barriers. Two administrations responded to textile and apparel producers' threats to block this legislation by negotiating "voluntary" export restraint agreements with major foreign suppliers prior to passage of the Trade Expansion Act in 1962 and the Trade Act of 1974. The first restraint agreement involved cotton products, and the second dealt with man-made fibers. Furthermore, the Trade Agreements Act of 1979, needed to implement U.S. commitments in the Tokyo Round of multilateral trade negotiations, would probably have been delayed or blocked in the absence of the Carter administration's acquiescence (in March 1979) to a special initiative that pushed other countries into agreeing to reduce their textile and apparel exports to the U.S. market.

Industry pressure was directly responsible for several key products, such as textiles, steel, glass products, and watches, being excluded from the U.S. tariff preferences scheme designed to assist the export sectors of less developed countries.[12]

The sugar industry provides an interesting case study of how a very small industry can maintain favorable legislation that subverts the free market, hurts American consumers, and strains U.S. foreign policy. To assure high sugar prices at no cost to the U.S. government, the executive branch by law must impose relatively severe import quotas on sugar. This is part of the effort to protect the guaranteed minimum price of sugar provided to an estimated 10,000 domestic sugar growers concentrated in four states and dominated by a few large producers. If it were not for quotas severely limiting imports of cheaper sugar, the U.S. government would be required to preserve the domestic support price by buying virtually the entire domestic sugar crop (because it is not price competitive and consumers would shun it). The result would be a significant budgetary outlay.

The income windfalls accorded high-cost domestic producers by an accommodating Congress do more than deprive several friendly, sugar-exporting developing countries of much-needed foreign exchange. They also impose higher cumulative costs on consumers of $1 to $2 billion annually.[13] Though greatly outnumbered, a handful of large sugar farmers have succeeded in beating back efforts by consumer groups and the U.S. Sugar Refiners Association to ease import barriers on sugar. In an interesting example of strange bedfellows, restrictive sugar quotas have been actively supported by the export-oriented U.S. corn lobby, otherwise one of the staunchest advocates of liberal trade. Sugar quotas are the one trade barrier they like. They reap great profits from the growing use of relatively cheap corn-based sweeteners in American-made soft drinks and food products.

Private sector groups on occasion have served as proxy negotiators in bilateral government-to-government trade talks. The U.S.-Japanese agreement on semiconductors signed in 1986 responded to the complaints of unfair import and export practices lodged by the U.S. industry against its Japanese counterpart. Executives of American semiconductor companies exerted considerable leverage over the U.S. government's negotiating position for two reasons. First, the agreement was tantamount to an out-of-court settlement of the industry's charges of Japanese dumping and discriminatory import practices. Secondly, differences between models of semiconductor chips are very technical and not easily understood by an industry outsider. While industry representatives were never physically in the same room in which the official negotiations were being conducted, the U.S. government to some extent found itself as a middleman. It mainly reconciled the positions of the Japanese on one side and American corporations on the other. When the government of Japan effectively refused to renew the agreement in 1996, the two governments reached a compromise by in effect privatizing the agreement. The U.S. Semiconductor Industry Association and the Electronics Industry Association of Japan jointly created a Semiconductor Council to monitor U.S. chip sales in Japan.

Spokespersons for the private sector sometimes earn their keep by articulating an economic grievance that has not yet been recognized by the bureaucracy and then establishing a public forum for demanding an appropriate policy response. The companies forming the Coalition of Service Industries were instrumental in the 1970s in convincing U.S. trade officials to expand the traditional definition of trade beyond merchandise. The bottom line was the U.S. government's successful effort to have international trade in services added as a major agenda item in subsequent negotiations to liberalize trade barriers.

Similarly, protection of U.S. intellectual property rights—trademarks, patents, copyrights, and so on—from unauthorized use overseas became an active concern in Washington only after affected companies organized to document the extent of intellectual piracy by unscrupulous foreign companies. The lobby's initial efforts were led by two coalitions, the International Intellectual Property Alliance (which consisted of seven trade associations representing 1,350 U.S. companies in 1998) and the Intellectual Property Owners Inc., as well as trade associations in the pharmaceutical, semiconductor, and chemicals industries.

Having seen convincing proof that American firms were losing more than $10 billion annually in export sales to overseas counterfeiters, the U.S. government insisted that an agreement to protect trade-related intellectual property rights be negotiated in the Uruguay Round of multilateral trade negotiations. The intellectual property rights groups (which have expanded to include such rapid-growth business sectors as software, publishing, motion pictures, and music) also were instrumental in convincing Congress to insert into the 1988 trade bill the so-called Special 301 provision. It is used to designate countries deemed to be major violators of U.S. intellectual property and therefore subject to U.S. government demands for corrective action. Intellectual property rights groups play an indirect role in implementing Special 301. Unlike any U.S. government entity, American trade associations and companies devote considerable resources to regularly monitoring business practices abroad for violations of their intellectual property. Reports from their field investigations serve as the major source of original data in USTR decisions on which countries to place on the Special 301 "watch lists."[14]

The free trade agreement signed with Mexico in 1992 arguably became the most hotly contested, widely lobbied single trade issue in U.S. history. The divisiveness and the multimillion dollar lobbying campaign associated with the congressional vote on legislation approving U.S. membership in NAFTA were based on both calculations of economic self-interest and a variety of social and political concerns.[15] Opponents saw the agreement as hurting relatively unskilled American workers and the environment. Supporters saw it as mutually beneficial to the U.S. and Mexican economies and vital to good overall political relations between neighboring countries.

With the Clinton administration forcefully promoting the agreement and with a majority in the Senate favorably disposed, lobbying focused on the House of Representatives, where approval was very much in doubt. Mexico's government and business sector hired as many as 70 firms at a total cost estimated in the press as exceeding $15 million to present the positive side of bilateral free trade to Congress and the American people at large. American companies formed one of the largest private sector lobbying groups ever. The Coalition for Trade Expansion quickly attracted a membership of more than 500 companies, trade associations, coalitions, and lobbying groups to voice support for approval of NAFTA. After successfully arguing for the extension of fast-track negotiating authority (needed to assure congressional approval of the final trade agreement), the coalition was superseded by a new, still larger super-group. U.S.A.-NAFTA attracted a loosely-knit membership that exceeded 1,200 companies and trade associations. Anti-NAFTA lobbying was less capital-intensive, but highly visible. It was led by the AFL-CIO and the Citizens Trade Campaign coalition, which coordinated the efforts of approximately 70 labor, business, farm, environmental, religious, and animal rights groups to defeat NAFTA.

The strong anti-NAFTA sentiment that prevailed in the House was narrowly beaten back by the combination of big business being solidly in favor of it and the lack of unity among groups opposing the agreement. All but one of the senior trade advisory committees endorsed NAFTA (the Labor Advisory Committee was the lone dissident). Congressional members throughout the southwestern United States, the geographical region that stands to benefit most from free trade with Mexico, were avid supporters. Even the usually trade-monolithic textile industry was split on the issue. Many companies saw Mexico as a growing market for fabrics and fibers as well as a source of low-paid labor to reduce production costs. There also was a split among the fourteen environmental organizations that were actively involved in the events leading up to the vote on NAFTA. One faction believed that the defeat of NAFTA would be more detrimental to Mexico's lagging environmental protection efforts than its implementation and success. (Economically prosperous countries spend more to protect their environment than poor countries.) Another set of groups feared an upsurge in U.S. companies relocating across the border to exploit Mexico's relatively less strict enforcement of antipollution regulations.

The entrance of the environmental lobby into the realm of U.S. trade policy was formally announced when several of its member groups filed a lawsuit demanding that the U.S. government submit an environmental impact statement on the effects of NAFTA. Although the suit was later rejected by a court decision, the Bush administration (which had initiated the free trade negotiations with Mexico) saw the need to give environmental concerns the highest priority ever in trade negotiations. The administration sought to demonstrate its sensitivity to the trade-environment link by assuring the active participation of government experts on environmental affairs in negotiations with the Mexican government. The position of assistant USTR for the environment was created. In addition, the White House ordered a comprehensive interagency review of bilateral environmental issues. To make the NAFTA trade-negotiating process more interactive, the interagency environmental group publicly circulated draft copies of its study, receiving and acting on comments before the final version was released. In addition, six prominent environmental activists were placed on six of the USTR's senior private sector trade advisory committees to broaden the perspective of these groups.

The debate on NAFTA was one of two events that drew the politically powerful environmental lobby into the U.S. trade policy decision-making process. The other event started out as an obscure GATT decision rejecting the applicability to U.S. import policy of a U.S. law protecting dolphins. In August 1991, a GATT panel ruled in favor of Mexico in its allegation that a ban imposed by the U.S. government on imports of yellow fin tuna from Mexico violated American foreign trade obligations under GATT. The ban had been imposed under provisions of the environmentalist-inspired U.S. Marine Mammal Protection Act that seeks to prevent dolphins from being killed by the driftnets that occasionally are used to catch tuna. The GATT panel decision alarmed environmentalists because it created what they saw as a dangerous precedent—giving international trade agreements higher legal standing than domestic environmental laws.

Subsequent events heightened the anxiety of environmental groups. For example, a World Trade Organization (WTO) dispute panel in 1998 determined that the United States had violated its trade commitments by prohibiting imports of shrimp from those countries that did not use a device that protects the endangered sea turtle from deadly entanglement in the nets of shrimp boats. There was growing reason to fear that use of import restrictions to bolster enforcement of domestic legislation protecting the environment and endangered species might be regularly overruled for countries adhering to the GATT articles of agreement (now incorporated into the World Trade Organization). The articles do not contain any explicit references to environmental concerns and therefore imply that prohibitions against the imposition of unilateral trade barriers take legal precedence over national environmental protection laws. Another major concern to the environmental lobby is the potential drift to least-common-denominator environmental standards as countries try to enhance their international competitiveness by reducing antipollution standards imposed on domestic industries to levels prevailing in less strict countries.

The bottom line was the advent of an irreversible link between international trade negotiations and the interests of organizations concerned about sustainable development; resource depletion; water, air, and land pollution; and food safety. A representative from an environmental group proved quite prescient when he predicted to a USTR official in 1992 that the environmental lobby would force substantial changes in the procedures of the GATT just as they previously had imposed changes on the World Bank and the International Monetary Fund (IMF)—namely in altering their operating procedures so as to give greater consideration to appropriate environmental conditions and policies in countries seeking loans.[16]

Having come to see unregulated free trade as a threat to their priority concerns, environmental protection organizations soon found a natural ally in labor unions opposed to further reductions in U.S. trade barriers. A new private sector alliance was born, one that would last long after Congress voted to approve NAFTA. A natural affinity exists between unions who feel that freer trade eliminates too many jobs and environmental groups wishing to prohibit imports of goods whose production is deemed to be environmentally damaging.

A well-researched and well-marketed lobbying program can be effective in influencing a White House decision on whether to accept the recommendation of the International Trade Commission (ITC) to grant relief from fair import competition to an industry found injured under the terms of the escape clause statute. (In cases where injury results from proven unfair trade practices, the president lacks discretionary authority.) The initiative launched by the copper fabricating industry was instrumental in convincing the Reagan administration to reject the ITC's 1984 recommendation to impose temporary import barriers to relieve the injury inflicted by imports on the copper mining industry. The Washington law firm hired by the copper fabricators assembled and then transmitted economic data to administration trade officials showing that the number of workers and value of production in copper fabrication were much larger than in copper mining. This supported the argument that reduced access to competitively priced copper imports would place far more manufacturing jobs and value-added production at risk in companies incorporating copper into their products than the few hundred mining jobs that might be preserved through copper import controls. (Increased dependence by domestic copper fabricators on higher-priced U.S. produced copper would likely cause increased inroads by cheaper foreign-made fabricated products.) Members of Congress from districts with major copper fabricators were enlisted to lobby the administration to reject the imposition of unilateral import barriers.[17]

A demand for fair play backed by the prestige of one of the fastest-growing sectors of American industry resulted in the Clinton administration's adamantly opposing Japan's proposed implementation of changes in software standards that potentially would have jeopardized U.S. exports there. A cabinet-level response was inevitable after the USTR received a request for intervention jointly signed by six groups representing the backbone of the critically important information technology sector: the American Electronics Association, the Business Software Alliance, the Electronic Industries Association, the Information Technology Industry Council, the Software Publisher Association, and the Telecommunications Industry Association. The message to the USTR from the trade associations was followed up by letters from the chief executives of some two dozen major high-tech firms. U.S. government pressure was instrumental in convincing the Japanese government to withdraw its proposed change and keep its software standards consistent with international specifications.

Astute private sector lobbying can prevent a planned policy change from being implemented, at least temporarily. A group of major exporting companies joined forces in the early 1980s to try to preserve and enhance the Export-Import Bank's subsidized export-lending activities. The Reagan administration had proposed phasing out the bank's loans and guarantees as part of its larger attack on all government subsidy programs. The first task for the lobbying campaign was to avoid the image of soliciting welfare for big, wealthy companies while it argued that curbing the bank's export lending programs would be penny wise and pound foolish. The nobly named Coalition for Employment through Exports launched a public relations offensive based on data disaggregated by state and congressional district showing how export sales by a single large corporation (e.g., Boeing) benefited hundreds of subcontractors from coast to coast. By providing members of Congress with numbers describing how regional jobs and production were tied into export sales, the lobbying effort transformed the abstract concept of export finance into a local pocketbook issue. The efforts at sensitivity training on Capitol Hill by the 48 business organizations, 14 labor groups, and 14 governors in the coalition convinced Congress to restore most of the cuts in appropriations that it tentatively had made at the request of the administration.

The massive lobbying efforts by foreign companies and governments in the United States launched in the late 1970s have added a major new dimension to policy advocacy. Big-name U.S.-based lobbyists retained by foreign interests, mostly Japanese, became masters of forging alliances with sympathetic domestic interests that wanted to preserve an open U.S. market and to avoid retaliation against other countries' trade practices. By the late 1980s, the Japanese lobby had gained the reputation for wielding so much power and spending so much money that many Americans feared the balance of lobbying power had tilted too heavily in its favor.

Part of the backlash against Japanese-financed lobbying activities focused on what was dubbed the "revolving door." A growing number of senior trade officials were "trading up" on their valuable insiders' experience to become handsomely paid lobbyists for foreign interests. A study by the nonprofit, non-partisan Center for Public Integrity determined that between 1974 and 1990, nearly half (47 percent) of former senior officials in the Office of the U.S. Trade Representative had registered as foreign agents, mostly on behalf of Japanese clients.[18]

The massive lobbying campaign conducted by the Toshiba Corporation during 1987 and 1988 demonstrated how far growing American dependence on Japanese imports had reduced the leverage of U.S. government threats of retaliation against alleged trade transgressions of Japan. The Toshiba effort sought to defeat Congress's proposed five-year, comprehensive import ban on that company's products. Stiff retaliation was intended as punishment for a subsidiary's sale (in violation of Japan's export controls) of advanced machine tools to the Soviet Union. The machine tools were used to make propeller blades that enabled Soviet submarines to operate much more quietly.

Toshiba succeeded in reducing sanctions by spending millions of dollars in a textbook effort to change U.S. public opinion. First, it argued that the parent company knew nothing about the illegal sale. More importantly, Toshiba's lawyers and lobbyists unleashed an avalanche of complaints on Capitol Hill. Letters and calls opposing sanctions flowed in from numerous American high-tech companies (many of whom were Pentagon suppliers) explaining their dependence on imports of Toshiba-made parts, and from several thousand workers in Toshiba's plants in the United States whose jobs would be at risk if the embargo was enacted. Clever, but truthful, lobbying quickly transformed Toshiba's image as a dispensable seller of generic consumer electronics products to that of an irreplaceable vendor of specialized components to American manufacturers. Convinced that its constituents would be harmed more than Toshiba, Congress retreated and settled for imposition of nominal import sanctions.

The sheer volume of lobbying activities in the trade sector nearly obscures the more limited activities in other areas of U.S. international economic activity. The Israeli lobby for years has been an important catalyst in perpetuating the relatively large amounts of U.S. economic assistance given to that country even after it became a relatively prosperous, developed country. Despite Greece's relatively advanced economic status, it received military aid in amounts linked to aid given to Turkey until 1998. This long-lasting arrangement was due to effective lobbying by the Greek-American community.

A relatively new advocacy trend is private sector efforts to influence the substance of relatively arcane international monetary policies. The Bretton Woods Committee is comprised of some 250 individuals, many of whom are well-known members of the financial and business communities. The committee's goal is to promote public and congressional support for U.S. participation in and financial support of the key multilateral lending institutions: the IMF, the

World Bank, and the regional development banks. Policy recommendations re-flect committee members' belief that these international institutions play a major role in providing the economic growth and stability in the developing countries that is important to the United States and the other industrial countries.

In an unusual crossover between policy sectors, lobbying by a handful of industrial companies succeeded in having Congress insert trade-related limita-tions in the legislation appropriating funds for the U.S. contribution to an IMF quota increase. A few alert executives sought to assure that the fund's financial bail-out of Korea did not provide funds that would be used to enhance the international competitiveness of companies competing with American industry. A provision of the 1998 bill directs the administration to oppose further dis-bursement of any IMF funds to South Korea under its 1997 standby agreement unless the secretary of the treasury can certify to Congress that several precon-ditions have been met. One is that no IMF resources made available to Korea were used to provide financial assistance to the semiconductor, steel, automobile, shipbuilding, or textile and apparel industries. Another precondition is that the fund has neither guaranteed nor underwritten the private loans of companies in any of these sectors.[19]

ASSESSING THE IMPACT OF LOBBYING ACTIVITIES ON U.S. INTERNATIONAL ECONOMIC POLICYMAKING

Domestic and foreign groups have had a mixed record over the past half century in their efforts to influence U.S. international economic policy substance. No fool-proof standard exists to quantify the impact of lobbying over an ex-tended period of time. Policy advocates usually fail to get 100 percent of what they demand, and partial successes are tricky at best to assess. Furthermore, successful lobbying comes in various forms. One consists of having the gov-ernment undertake an action it had not already planned to do, such as adding a special interest provision in new legislation or demanding that other countries initiate voluntary export restraints to ease the burdens of a particular American industry. Another measure of success is the absence of government action, that is, preventing something from happening. A citizens coalition was successful in the late 1990s in convincing Congress to ignore the administration and big business and not extend fast-track authority. It is usually easier for special in-terest groups to kill someone else's proposal (perhaps by making it controver-sial) than it is to create something from scratch.

Large numbers of supporters, a big war chest, and a major industry facing crushing economic problems certainly do not hurt a lobbying effort. However, these factors guarantee no results in an increasingly competitive and crowded marketplace of ideas about optimal international economic policy. The proba-bility that the U.S. government would act on the trade policy demands of a large, mobilized, persistent, articulate, and loud special interest group has fallen from a 99 percent certainty prior to the early 1930s to mere likelihood today.

"America Leads on Trade" is a super-coalition of some 675 companies, trade associations, and coalitions. It was formed in the mid-1990s to advocate extension of fast-track trade negotiating authority. The 73-member Agriculture Coalition for fast track has been working alongside this group. Despite this impressive array of political and economic power, the two groups were unsuccessful in the latter half of the 1990s in their efforts to convince Congress to extend fast track. In the words of one trade Washington lobbyist, "I tell my clients: 'I can get you a hearing. I can get your case moved to the top of the pile. But don't expect me to move it across the finish line unless the merits are there.' "[20]

The argument that a cause-and-effect relationship exists between big money and successful lobbying is undermined by the fact that ability to exert political clout in trade policy is influenced by a number of other variables. On the import side, an important question is whether domestic producers are alleging injury from fair or unfair import competition. Presidential discretion in imposing restrictions is near zero if unfair trade practices have been found to have inflicted material injury on a domestic industry. Four additional variables are rooted in timing. Doing something to alleviate the impact on a large domestic producer of a surge in imports becomes more appealing to presidents and legislators if national elections are looming. Second, efforts to restrain imports also are more likely if unemployment is already a problem. They are also more likely if Congress is considering trade legislation so that it could quickly add relatively severe protectionist provisions to punish an allegedly overly soft trade stance by the administration. A final timing variable is the level of need to combat inflationary pressures in the domestic economy (import barriers tend to cause price increases and are therefore unattractive to domestic macroeconomic policy managers).

By definition, the universal absence of an absolute policy of free trade means that all sovereign governments are accommodating *some* of the economic needs and political pressures of *some* special interest groups. It is a question of degree. The steady, albeit gradual reduction of U.S. import barriers (and those of other countries) discredits the argument that a single group of powerful, like-minded interest groups dictates a steady procession of protectionist trade measures. It is true that the measured pace of trade liberalization is dictated by deference to domestic pressures fearful of import-induced injury. Nevertheless, governments would not have steadily pressed forward with initiatives to lower trade barriers without encouragement from liberal trade-minded interest groups.

The political economy of U.S. trade policy was dramatically reshaped by the rise of a powerful lobby, led by multinational corporations, to champion freer movements of goods, services, and capital. The full impact of a powerful and well-financed liberal trade lobby did not make itself felt until the 1970s. As size and competitive success became synonymous with a global presence, American multinational corporations deserted the historically protectionist leanings of industry. Multinationals oppose governmental restrictions on international economic transactions. Such restraints inhibit their global business strategy that prefers making decisions with little or no regard to the existence of national borders.[21]

The limited impact of even the biggest corporations to modify government mindset is especially visible in export policy. Despite nearly unanimous opposition by the American industrial sector to what it considers excessive export controls, it has had little success in moderating the extraordinarily high propensity of the U.S. government to impose trade sanctions on other countries for foreign policy reasons and human rights violations. U.S. government attitudes towards exports still contrast sharply with the blatantly mercantilist policies practiced elsewhere. Even the largest companies have had limited success in convincing the government to relax export controls, even when they can demonstrate that other countries are shipping comparable products to targeted countries.

A classic case of American big business failing to make a dent in what was a dubious administration policy occurred in the early 1980s. One American manufacturer after another loudly complained about the impact on their international competitiveness of the extraordinarily large appreciation in the dollar's exchange rate. Nevertheless, the Reagan administration doggedly clung to its faith in market forces and remained serenely indifferent for years to the growing burdens placed on domestic industry and agriculture as imports became cheaper and exports began to be priced out of world markets (see Chapter 10). It is difficult to believe that the parliamentary governments in Western Europe and Japan could have survived the torrent of criticism and red ink in the trade balance if they stubbornly accepted the economic consequences of a grossly overvalued exchange rate for as long a time as did the Reagan administration.

The uncertain outcome of seemingly powerful business voices to influence policy substance has been compounded by an old political fact and a new one. Imposition of import barriers always has hurt some companies even while helping others. Today, however, business lobbying has become so pervasive that when an American company or industry determines that its economic well-being is threatened by proposed import restraints, it can be expected to launch a counter-lobbying campaign. Import restraints are perceived as undesirable (read costly) policy by any or all of the following groups: export-oriented industries (who do not want to risk being hit by foreign retaliation), discount retailers, purveyors of trade-related services (banks, ports, longshoremen, etc.), importers, and domestic end-users of imported raw materials and components such as steel and semiconductors. The propensity for lobbying in the trade sector to breed counter-lobbying was discussed in *American Business & Public Policy*, a classic study of the politics of U.S. trade policy:

> The stereotype notion of omnipotent pressure groups becomes completely untenable once there are groups aligned on both sides. The result of opposing equipotent forces is stalemate. . . . It would be interesting to know how much of the generally held notions

about pressure groups come actually from propaganda the pressure groups have put out about themselves and the opposition.[22]

If business no longer speaks with one voice in trade, no single vested interest can dictate U.S. trade policy. The lobbying equation must be recalculated when efforts by one economic sector to increase trade barriers on imports regularly engender offsetting lobbying efforts by another sector opposing resort to protectionist measures. Divisiveness within the business community enables the executive and legislative branches to remain true to a preexisting, underlying philosophy as to what is the optimal trade policy action for the country as a whole. Since the late 1940s, the collective vision of first-best policy in Washington, D.C. has leaned toward liberal trade.

Opposition by makers of finished goods to the prospect of losing access to the cheapest inputs (no matter where they come from) lest they suffer a loss in their own price competitiveness against foreign manufacturers has been one of the most common causes of offsetting lobbying efforts in import policy. This consideration explained the successful opposition by copper fabricators to the efforts discussed above to limit imports of relatively cheap raw copper. It also explained opposition by American computer manufacturers to the 1986 semiconductor agreement with Japan that resulted in higher Japanese export prices for memory chips. Reduced access to cheap components angered U.S. computer makers in 1991 when dumping duties were applied to certain Japanese flat-panel display screens used in portable computers. (When foreign-assembled computers are imported into the United States, they are not hit with the same dumping duties that are applied to imports of individual components like memory chips or display screens. Japanese and other foreign-made computers therefore gain a price edge equivalent to any higher costs imposed on imported components that are incorporated into domestically assembled computers.)

Companies that assemble steel into finished products actively opposed the domestic steel industry's 1989 drive to extend foreign restraints on steel exports. The resulting deadlock in the Bush cabinet will be examined in Chapter 8. Similarly, President Bush faced a sticky situation when the American peanut lobby screamed angrily at the effort by the Peanut Butter and Nut Processors Association to temporarily repeal the tight U.S. quota on peanut imports. A drought in the southeastern United States caused a peanut shortage severe enough to trigger a sizable jump in the price of a jar of peanut butter. President Bush wound up approving an increase of only 100 million of the 300 million pounds of additional peanut imports recommended by the International Trade Commission in order to alleviate domestic shortages.[23]

Another version of counter-lobbying sprang from the inherent conflict of interest between domestic manufacturers of labor-intensive apparel and discount retailers. Two business coalitions publicly disagreed over the economic wisdom of enacting the textile quota bill passed by Congress but vetoed by President Reagan in December 1985. The Fiber, Fabric, and Apparel Coalition for Trade spoke on behalf of the import-induced problems of the domestic industry. On the other side, the Retail Industry Trade Action Coalition opposed the proposed legislation on grounds that its members would suffer from a reduced ability to purchase low-cost foreign-made apparel. Both groups had an impressive nation-wide membership and engaged in extensive lobbying in Congress. Both groups published polished, eloquent reports that gave diametrically different economic analyses of the logic and implications of further restricting imports of textile and apparel goods. Not unexpectedly, the split voice of industry meant that the American apparel industry secured only a small fraction of the increased protection it was seeking and through easily reversible administrative means, not legislation.

At least two politically active industries have failed to achieve all they wanted when requesting the U.S. government merely to restrain the *growth rates* of imports. Liberal traders decry the protection that the steel and textile and apparel industries have received almost continuously since the 1960s. However, workers and executives in these industries sincerely believe that in having only part of their demands met, effective import protection for them has been a case of too little, too late. By U.S. standards, these industries have indeed received considerable relief from foreign competition. Conversely, U.S. government import policies toward the steel and apparel industries have remained relatively liberal by international standards when measured by import penetration as a percentage of total domestic consumption.

Deteriorating global economic conditions at the end of the 1990s forced many foreign companies to look to export-led growth and to the booming American market. One empirical result was the 66 percent increase in U.S. imports of key steel products—and the 157 percent jump in steel imports from Japan—recorded during the first ten months of 1998 over the comparable period in the previous year.[24] The Clinton administration refused to assist the allegedly reeling domestic steel industry except to promise quick enforcement of the antidumping statute.

Willingness to protect the domestic apparel and textile industries led to creation of the Multifiber Arrangement, which became the single most restrictive U.S. import barrier. Still, its ability to stifle total imports of these goods is open to serious question. That the U.S. market is hardly closed can be seen by government data showing that the ratio of imports of textile and apparel goods to total U.S. consumption increased from 11 percent in 1977 to 47 percent in 1998. As measured by volume, total textile imports increased almost seven-fold between 1979 and 1998, jumping from 3.9 billion to 26 billion equivalent square meters.[25]

In sum, private sector efforts to instill protectionist trade policies became the victim of their overwhelming success in encouraging passage of the notorious Smoot-Hawley Tariff Act of 1930. Nevertheless, as long as U.S. international economic policies are largely made in consultation with the private sector and not behind locked doors, a good lobbying effort can make a decent argument out of a dubious case and an excellent argument out of a good case. The result *may* be at least a partially sympathetic response from an administration or Congress not previously disposed to protecting the petitioning industry or union.

The private sector is properly an unofficial junior partner in the formulation of at least the trade and investment segments of U.S. international economic policies. Most of these policies are designed to assist the private sector. There is no good reason for a democratic government not to at least listen to the trade-related desires, data, and complaints (as well as the promises of political support) expressed by the private sector. The government must be resolute and smart in this dialogue because interest group presentations are not known for being objective and unselfish. Policymakers should never lose sight of the economic difference between protecting the overall public good and protecting narrow special interests, and they should never forget that the former is far more desirable than the latter.

NOTES

1. *Encyclopedia of Associations* (Detroit: Gale Publishing Company, 1998), pp. v, ix.

2. *National Trade and Professional Associations of the United States* (Washington, D.C.: Columbia Books, 1998), p. 18.

3. Data sources: web site of the Center for Responsive Politics, www.crp.org.pubs/lobby98/summary.htm/ (for low-end estimates) and ''Washington's Lobbying Industry: A Case for Reform,'' report issued by the Office of Representative Dick Armey, June 1996 (high-end estimates).

4. Data source: House Legislative Resource Center, by telephone.

5. Data source: Senate Office of Public Records, by telephone.

6. Department of Justice web site, www.usdoj.gov/criminal/fara/, as of January 1999.

7. For a more detailed description of the Japanese lobby in Washington, see the author's *An Ocean Apart—Explaining Three Decades of U.S.-Japanese Trade Frictions* (Westport, Conn.: Praeger, 1998), pp. 188–207.

8. See, for example, ''Japan's Clout in the U.S.,'' *Business Week*, 11 July 1986, pp. 64–75; and Pat Choate, ''An Open Letter to Mr. Miyazawa,'' *New York Times*, 26 July 1992, p. IV-13.

9. Calculated from the 1991 membership list of the Japan Commerce Association, Washington, D.C.

10. Ken Silverstein, ''The New China Hands,'' *Nation*, 17 February 1997, p. 12.

11. *Ibid.*

12. Not-for-attribution interview with business lobbyist, November 1980.

13. See, for example, President's Council of Economic Advisers, *Annual Report*, 1992, p. 197; and U.S. General Accounting Office, ''Sugar Program—Changing Domestic and International Conditions Require Program Changes,'' report number RCED-93–84, April 1993.

14. Not-for-attribution interviews with a USTR official, December 1992, and a representative of the International Intellectual Property Alliance, January 1999. This organization posts data on alleged overseas intellectual piracy at its web site: www.iipa.com/.

15. Canada is the third member of NAFTA; however, the free trade agreement with that country never caused major political controversy in the United States.

16. Not-for-attribution interview with a USTR official, October 1992.

17. Not-for-attribution interviews with private sector lawyers, June 1986.

18. Press Release of the Center for Public Integrity, dated 7 December 1990, p. 1.

19. *Congressional Record*, 19 October 1998, p. H11103.

20. Burt Solomon, "Hawking Access," *National Journal*, 3 May 1986, p. 1052.

21. Multinational corporations also dislike their home government imposing trade barriers or capital controls because they run the risk of antagonizing governments in countries where overseas subsidiaries are located.

22. Raymond A. Bauer, Ithiel de Sola Pool, and Lewis A. Dexter, *American Business and Public Policy* (Chicago: Aldine-Atherton, 1972), pp. 398–399.

23. *Washington Post*, 6 July 1991, p. A4.

24. Data source: White House press release on the administration's plan for responding to increased steel imports, 7 January 1999.

25. Data sources: Economic Research Service, U.S. Department of Agriculture, *Cotton and Wool Situation and Outlook*, February 1999; U.S. International Trade Commission, 1992 annual report on "U.S. Imports of Textiles and Apparel under the Multifiber Arrangement;" and Department of Commerce, Office of Textiles and Apparel web site: www.otexa.ita.doc.gov/.

Part III

Executive Branch Decision-Making: Theories and Models

7 Theories on How U.S. International Economic Policy Is Formulated

> The size and the performance of the existing administrative apparatus impose a certain inflexibility on the direction of policy. Large-scale organizations display a number of characteristics which reduce their responsiveness to political control: attachment to precedent and continuity, loyalty to the organization as such and to its clients, established routines for handling business and established views of the environment in which they operate. . . . Decisions once made must be followed through; where political objectives conflict with organizational habits or objectives, they are likely to gain ground only slowly.
>
> —William Wallace

The previous section of this book dealt with the institutional "hardware" of U.S. international policymaking. This chapter and the one that follows examine the "software," that is, the behavioral principles that make policymakers and institutions "tick" and the abstract forces that influence the ways in which they interact with one another.

The chapter begins by examining the several theoretical constructs that have been advanced in the quest for a unified explanation of government officials' actions in making international economic policies. The first section catalogs the organizational and non-organizational factors that have been cited as major factors affecting policymakers' thinking and actions. It does not rank or evaluate the relative merits of the theories advanced. Nor does it decry the abundance of their numbers, a source of obvious frustration to those political theorists who are dedicated to finding the decisive element in policymaking behavior that comprehensively explains past decisions. The remaining sections of the chapter elaborate on theories of organizational behavior and its impact on policy substance, which is, admittedly, only part of the total policymaking equation. In examining "macro" theories about why the government collectively produces the kinds of policies that it does, this chapter sets the stage for the next chapter's examination of the various "micro" models that depict the means by which specific international economic policies have been made.

SCHOLARLY APPROACHES TO THE STUDY OF INTERNATIONAL ECONOMIC POLICY

The international economic policies of the United States are the outgrowth of five basic forces. The first is the combination of perceptions, ideologies, priorities, and force of personality of the president and his senior economic and national security advisers. The second is the sentiment of Congress, as transmitted by both legislation and informal means of communication. The third force is the international economic environment, principally the institutions and practices that constitute the international trade and monetary regimes as well as economic trends in other countries. The fourth consists of pressures from domestic interest groups. How the executive branch is organized to transform ideas into international economic policy is the fifth and final variable. Organizational factors are important, but they are not everything.

Academics have incorporated these five forces into a number of theories that attempt to construct a broad explanation of U.S. government actions affecting international trade. There is relatively little literature devoted to other areas of international economic policy, partly because of the prominence of trade policy and partly because political scientists can easily relate to the relatively heavy political overtones of import policy. The objective of these theorists is to identify the most important and permanent variables that shape the thinking and actions of decision-makers. In so doing, they hope to establish cause-and-effect relationships in the policymaking process. If such relationships can be demonstrated, the ability to forecast government behavior in the future would be significantly enhanced.

Many different models of U.S. decision-making have been constructed. All are accurate and applicable in some circumstances. However, none are universally applicable, even within trade policy. Any number of theories can be supported by carefully picking a limited number of case studies from the massive and disparate record of decision-making episodes in international economic relations.

The diversity of academic analysis in this field is appropriate. However, its contributors are openly frustrated at the crowded marketplace of ideas. They remain determined to distill a single model with universal applicability that can comprehensively explain the past and accurately predict the future. The argument that diverse models of causality can and should coexist seems to be anathema to most political theorists. The quest for a universal hypothesis that is more than a generalized least-common-denominator approach continues unabated, notwithstanding a significant body of empirical evidence to suggest that the quest itself is misguided.

Theorists usually overlook the important generic differences in kinds of policies and decisions, as described in Chapter 1. Behavioral principles that may be applicable to one specific situation cannot necessarily be applied to other kinds of decisions. Government officials are subjected to a wide range of pressures to act that vary according to the situation at hand. Consider the diversity of international economic policymaking suggested by a minuscule sample of what needs to be done: deciding how to respond to an International Trade Commission (ITC) recommendation to impose new trade barriers under the escape clause statute; weighing the merits of imposing trade sanctions on a foreign country; determining which specific requirements of internal economic reforms should be established before additional International Monetary Fund (IMF) loans are approved for Russia; preparing the agenda for an international economic summit; or calculating how to lobby a reluctant Congress to extend fast-track negotiating authority. Despite the heterogeneity of the policy process, most scholars cannot be content with the first of two scholarly approaches to social science described by Max Weber: causal analysis of individual actions, structures, and personalities—the approach to understanding the policymaking process that is offered in the next chapter of this book. Instead, they emphasize the second alternative, namely, the construction of concepts and typologies and the discovery of general laws.[1]

A new generation of theoretical literature in international economic policy has emerged. While the first generation produced competing, irreconcilable theories of what makes the policymaking system function as it does, no one model was sufficiently persuasive or universally applicable to prevail.[2] In contrast, the second wave of efforts sought to synthesize carefully delineated lists of disparate theories into broader, less exclusionary approaches. The introductory article of a special issue of the journal *International Organization* identified three major approaches:

1. International, or system-centered, approaches explain international trade policies as shaped primarily by norms enshrined in international regimes and by the opportunities and limitations imposed by a nation-state's relative position in the global economy. A "hegemonic" state like the United States, for example, exerts leadership in creating a liberal trade regime that seeks to constrain unilateral protectionist actions.

2. Society-centered explanations see the government as a relatively passive actor responding to the interests of the groups or coalitions that dominate the struggle for influence within the trade policy arena. In this case, domestic politics, not external forces, determine policy decisions.

3. State-centered approaches emphasize policy constraints imposed by institutional relationships within the government. Executive branch officials operate as independent actors within these constraints to manipulate policy outcomes in accordance with their personal preferences and conceptions of the "national interest." According to this

theory, the relatively "weak" or decentralized structure of the U.S. federal government limits the policy instruments available to U.S. policymakers relative to their counterparts in "strong" states where governments take a pro-active role in economic planning. Hence, it is argued that U.S. trade officials cannot act as purposefully or coherently as those in many other countries.[3]

The journal's concluding article offers two approaches for synthesizing systemic, societal, and state-centered variables. The first focuses on the properties of issue areas, while the second focuses on the dynamics of institutional structures and on the manner in which those structures constrain and shape societal and governmental actors.[4] An institutional analysis of international economic policy, concludes the author, G. John Ikenberry, may provide the best synthesis of the variables, but it is "an approach and not a theory" that "does not pretend to provide the basis for a formal and parsimonious set of propositions that researchers can test in a simple fashion."[5]

In a literature review article, John S. Odell identifies four major theoretical themes. He, too, accepts none as definitive.

1. The market perspective states that while the majority of citizens recognize that liberal trade is the best policy for a nation as a whole, some interest groups are inevitably injured by import competition. They, in turn, initiate an intense lobbying effort for protectionism that inevitably produces strong political pressures to impose import barriers. The extent of protectionism is determined by a complicated mix of factors, such as business cycle conditions and the presence in a given country of multinational corporations that may be so heavily dependent on international commercial flows that they actively lobby against the imposition or trade barriers by any country.

2. The cognitive perspective assumes that policy ideas, while affected by material interests, are not identical to them. Deeply held values and beliefs of the public and of policymakers have independent effects (of indeterminate degree) on policy content. Leaders at times define the national interest and, therefore, they may create policy in terms of the subconscious values that they brought with them to the job.

3. The institutional perspective emphasizes the constraints that domestic political structures impose on individuals and groups, and it claims that institutional change (such as the transfer by Congress of tariff-cutting authority to the president) affects the broad patterns and content of trade policy.

4. The international perspective, which is identical to the initial entry in the first list.[6]

As with the *International Organization* study, Odell emphasizes the need for synthesizing the different approaches, since he too notes that each of the models individually proves inadequate as a single unifying vehicle. He welcomes what he sees as an integrated theory of trade policy formulation emerging in a form that encompasses individuals, groups, and states as actors. The new consensus theories are said to recognize that policy preferences "are partly shaped according to ideologies, theories, and political institutions and processes that vary across countries and change through time.''[7]

A study by Robert Baldwin limited to U.S. import policy is comfortable with the notion that an eclectic approach is warranted. His study determined that it was not a case of an either-or selection between two basic models, but a combination of: (1) government officials acting as intermediaries between interest groups and (2) government officials taking the initiative in pursuit of their own public policy preferences formed on the basis of personal values.[8]

The second generation of theoretical literature is an improvement over the first-generation efforts to develop general theories of U.S. international economic policy decision-making. Nonetheless, the question remains as to whether a broad synthesis of several models will collapse from the weight of complexity and qualifying assumptions. Can any single theoretical structure transcend the diversity of the individual sectors that comprise international economic policy? The answer is no. Even when viewed collectively, the multiple approaches just delineated should not be considered definitive. None of the models is fully appropriate for non-trade issues (e.g., international financial crises). None focuses adequately on Congress and the complex dynamics between it and the executive branch, a major shortcoming in view of Congress's pivotal role in determining U.S. international economic actions.

The route to definitive theory has many more detours. A relatively well-defined international regime exists in international trade, but regimes in other sectors range from the murky (international monetary relations) to essentially nonexistent (foreign aid). Interest groups have been active in trade policy but mostly absent in balance of payments policy. The Treasury Department has been nearly autonomous in making international monetary policy, in contradistinction to trade policy, where a host of competing power centers participate. This fact indicates that society and the characteristics of governmental institutions at times may be merely minor determinants of the policymaking process. In sum, the *kind* of international economic policy being formulated influences the relative distribution of power among government officials, the international regime, and the private sector.

The interactive nature of policymakers' values, interest group pressures, and the discipline imposed by regimes obscures the direction of cause-and-effect relationships, thereby confounding builders of unified models. Under such circumstances, there can be no single, consistent procedural formula for reaching decisions in international economic policy. Conflicting values and priorities abound in this field. The key question is how they will be reconciled and converted into policy. And the answer is: it depends. In some cases, the decision will simply reflect the personal values of senior government officials; in other cases, the decision will be heavily influenced by exogenous variables. The exact form of organizational dynamics will differ, depending on the nature, circumstances surrounding, and gravity of the issue at hand.

THE RELATIONSHIP OF ORGANIZATIONAL PROCESS TO POLICY SUBSTANCE

At the highest level of generality, governmental organization is concerned with the relative allocation of power—the power to dominate the policy formulation process, to draft options memoranda for the cabinet or the president, and the power to administer policy after decisions are made. Policymaking is a political process—especially in international economic relations. As economics is more of an art than a science, senior policymakers must rely far more on judgment and compromise to guide them than on absolute truths. The strongest, shrewdest advocates—as opposed to the best ideas—often dominate the outcome of decision-making.

The importance of government organization and procedures in general was well articulated in the 1970 final report of the Commission on the Organization of the Government for the Conduct of Foreign Policy (the Murphy Commission):

> Good organization does not insure successful policy. Nor does poor organization preclude successful policy. But steadily and powerfully, organizational patterns influence the effectiveness of government.
>
> Policymaking on any subject of importance requires adequate information, careful analysis of the implications of that information, consultation with the various parties legitimately concerned, and balanced assessment of the alternative courses of action. Once a decision is made, it must be clearly communicated to those responsible or affected by it, carefully monitored in its implementation, and evaluated for its actual effects. . . . But organization affects more than the efficiency of government; it can affect the outcome of decisions.[9]

Government organization directly affects the substance of international economic policy by determining how the different views, goals, self-interests, and recommendations of the participating bureaucracies are to be introduced into the policy formulation process and assigned weights and priorities. By definition, major international economic issues must reconcile the usually incompatible needs of domestic politics, domestic economics, foreign policy, and international economics. The participation or nonparticipation of particular departments and agencies, accessibility of cabinet members to the president, procedures for resolving interagency disagreements, and budgets for personnel are some of the organizational variables that either will benefit or penalize competing values and interests. Therefore, a critical organizational question is: Which perspectives on how to serve the national interest are introduced, when, by whom, and with what degree of importance attached to them?

The struggle to maximize the values of a particular constituency when policy priorities are being determined lies at the heart of organizational politics. Energetic bureaucracies seek to do this by protecting their domain and autonomy and by enhancing their budget. Sheer size can be an effective tool in the bureaucratic struggle by assuring that a pool of talent is available, first to provide an agency position, and then to overwhelm competing agencies with a barrage of expertise and argumentation. Access to the president's office is another organizational means of affecting policy. This can be done by maneuvering to be the last official to talk with the president before he makes a final decision, or by being able to add a cover note commenting on the memoranda submitted by the responsible departments on a given matter.

The focus, chairmanship, and membership of the various groups comprising the interagency coordination process (see Chapter 4) can affect the outcome of a policy formulation exercise. Each international economic policy-related coordinating group has a distinctive institutional culture; departments seeking approval (or rejection) of a policy proposal will prefer to utilize a "friendly" group with a comparable perspective. This was the reason for the State and Treasury departments each adopting a preference during the Ford administration for different White House coordinating bodies (the National Security Council and the Economic Policy Board, respectively). The perceived "tilt" of certain coordinating groups also explained the ploy by certain agencies to use the White House's Economic Policy Group (chaired by the secretary of the treasury) rather than the Trade Policy Committee (chaired by the U.S. trade representative) in 1980 to consider the possible reinstitution of the Trigger Price Mechanism to effectively impose a relatively high minimum price on imported steel. Opponents who charged that higher prices for steel imports would be unacceptably inflationary urged the interagency decision-making process be placed in the Economic Policy Group, a forum whose focus was macroeconomic policy not trade policy (where a better political case could be made for encouraging higher steel import prices).

Chairing an interagency working group can be turned to an agency's advantage if it is possible to dominate the setting of the agenda, voting procedures, or the selection of participating organizations. Consider an extreme example that occurred in 1981 during the initial phase of a cabinet-level formulation of a policy response to the financial crisis affecting the "Big Three" U.S. automakers. The then–secretary of Transportation, Drew Lewis, an ardent supporter of import restraints to help the industry to regroup, was designated by the newly inaugurated Ronald Reagan to chair a special task force on the automobile industry. Its mandate was to determine how best to deal with the combination of rapidly rising imports flowing in from Japan and the torrent of red ink flowing in Detroit. In an important meeting held early in the process, Lewis arranged the agenda so that virtually all of the 30 minutes allotted for the session was allocated to his presentation and those of fellow cabinet members (the secretaries of Commerce and Labor and the USTR) who publicly had supported his position. "The Cabinet Council meeting . . . had been rigged by Lewis. He didn't plan to hear from the other side," wrote David Stockman in his memoirs.[10]

A good deal of international economic policy consists of outgoing instructions to U.S. negotiating delegations and embassies overseas. The absence or presence of a given agency, or bureau within an agency, in the process that clears outgoing communications from Washington, D.C., could affect the contents or the overall nuance of the policy position being transmitted to the field. Conversely, control over the cable traffic written by embassy staff for transmission back to Washington can affect policymakers' attitudes at home.[11]

A final relationship between process and substance is the potential for confused or overlapping organizational procedures (e.g., multiple coordinating groups handling the same issue) to delay final decisions and dissipate bureaucratic energies before engaging in negotiations with foreign counterparts. The absence of a clear chain of command or presence of overlapping bureaucratic vehicles encourages internal bureaucratic gamesmanship, not decisive policy implementation. Bureaucratic wheelspinning, in turn, works to the advantage of skillful lobbyists and foreign governments who are determined to influence the outcome of decision-making.

Organizational issues, in sum, are much more than academic pondering as to where to move boxes on a chart. They involve struggles for position and power. Adroit government officials know how to orchestrate the lines of command to tilt interagency debates in their favor. Finessing the procedural aspects of policymaking can: (1) provide more time for discussion of one viewpoint over another; (2) give the views of selected departments more access to the senior-most ranks; (3) manipulate the contents of briefing papers to favor one analysis over another; (4) assure that some issues rise to the top of the government's agenda faster than others; and (5) and mobilize the right private sector interest groups to lobby government agencies and Congress. As one former national security official noted, some organizational procedures facilitate certain kinds of policy while other procedures facilitate other kinds of policy.[12]

Values influence organization, just as organization translates values into policy. A country's policymaking structure and process do not develop in a vacuum. They reflect not only basic economic values, but basic approaches to governmental structure at the national level. For example, the proliferation in Washington of cabinet-level departments, agencies, White House offices, and congressional subcommittees reflects the American propensity for allowing every major point of view to have representation in the policymaking process.

The constitutional imperative of checks and balances between the three branches of government puts the executive branch in a subordinate role to the legislative branch in certain aspects of policymaking: legislation, appropriations, and confirmations of senior appointees and treaties. When other congressional functions, such as policy and program oversight, are added to the equation, the U.S. international economic policymaking process is clearly differentiated from countries with a parliamentary form of government. As discussed in subsequent chapters, only in the United States is the inter-branch model central to the international economic policymaking process. The need for inter-branch consensus makes U.S. decision-making in this area relatively complicated and often cumbersome.

The fact that senior policymakers are political appointees who come and go more frequently than the career civil servants who staff all but the top ministerial post in parliamentary governments suggests yet another unique variable in U.S. policymaking. There are costs and benefits from this arrangement. U.S. international economic policy is more amenable to change thanks to a relatively rapid turnover at the senior ranks of policymaking. Although it is a good thing in principle to be able to constantly adjust policy to changing conditions, the relative absence of institutional memory can create excessive inconsistency and an occasional effort ''to reinvent the wheel'' by returning to unsuccessful initiatives tried earlier.

Another exogenous variable creating unique U.S. organizational arrangements for formulating import policy is the combination of the country's preference for open, transparent conduct of government business and its ideological preference for letting the market mechanism determine economic transactions to the maximum extent possible. One result is a clearly spelled out administrative system to determine on a case-by-case basis whether import restraints are justified to protect a domestic industry from injury inflicted by fair or unfair foreign competition. Although official attitudes towards import policy disparage protectionism and the U.S. market is relatively open, the complex body of U.S. trade law has been labeled a non-tariff barrier by some trading partners. To affected exporters, the time, effort, and costs of arguing against U.S. companies' efforts to obtain import relief under the escape clause, the antidumping statute, and so on constitute a major obstacle to successfully selling in the U.S. market. To Americans, this is simply the offshoot of a litigious society. Whereas some countries take care of import problems in a back room, attorneys specializing in U.S. import relief statutes become central actors in what at times are legalistic and administrative—not economic—determinations of whether certain U.S. imports should be restricted because of injury to domestic producers or unfair foreign trade practices.

That the United States has what is arguably the weakest ministry of industry (the Commerce Department) among the industrialized countries is another organizational manifestation of the relatively intense U.S. preference for market-based neutrality in lieu of government interference. The absence of any conscious effort to implement industrial policy means that the United States neither has nor needs an equivalent of Japan's powerful Ministry of International Trade and Industry (MITI). The United States has been described as a regulatory state that concerns itself with the forms and procedures of economic competition, but not with planning economic growth. Japan, conversely, has been characterized as a plan-rational, or developmental, state giving priority to industrial policy.[13] The United States has no strategic, or goal-oriented, approach to domestic economic policy management. Hence it does not need to deal with imports, exports, and international capital flows as intrinsic parts of a domestic economic grand design.

The industrial sector of the United States has never demanded strong representation in Washington through a cabinet department. Presidents and Congress have never volunteered to give them one. Instead of an activist's urge to help promote targeted industrial sectors, the "culture" of the U.S. executive branch in the post–World War II era has been to react in a less than positive and enthusiastic manner to most of the demands by industry for relief from fair import competition. Many industries requesting import barriers have been viewed by policymakers as laggards who want to cooperate with the government only when the free market turns against them.

THE ORGANIZATIONAL POLITICS OF INTERNATIONAL ECONOMIC POLICY

There is no single universally accepted answer to the question of what is the ultimate, *overriding* objective of U.S. international economic policy. Is it to prevent international chaos and warfare? Is it to increase the relative wealth and comfort of U.S. citizens? It is to contribute to the domestic political base of the Democratic or Republican parties? Is it to contribute to a more equitable distribution of the world's income? Or is it a vehicle to increase the profits of those American companies, investors, and entrepreneurs engaging in overseas business transactions? Then there is a basic chicken and egg dilemma. Is a strong, stable domestic economy the prerequisite for an effective and domestically popular U.S. involvement in the world political order? Or is a world environment favorable to U.S. political and economic interests the long-term prerequisite for a strong, stable domestic economy and a flourishing industrial sector? The best answer to this conundrum may well be not to exclude any of the options just presented on the grounds that they are all relevant. International economic strength and geopolitical power feed off each other.

International economic policy is complicated and multifaceted. On a day-to-day basis, it requires the constant reconciliation between ever-changing priorities in domestic politics and economics and global politics and economics. These competing interests cannot be quantified and indefinitely assigned fixed degrees of importance. As a consequence, there can be no unambiguous, self-apparent strategies or tactics in U.S. international economic policy on an across-the-board or permanent basis. Trade-offs always will be required given the absence of objective truths. Strategy is a series of variations on a number of themes. Inexact shortcuts are more likely to be used than an idealistic process of determining what is in the overall national interest at any given time. The policy search is more likely to embrace the acceptable than the excellent.

To comprehend the U.S. international economic policy decision-making process, it is absolutely necessary to move beyond the overly simplistic notion that this policy is made by like-thinking administration officials who objectively define and then pursue a mutual vision of the national interest. In the first instance, looking only at the executive branch is totally inappropriate. The role of the legislative branch has become so important that it is no exaggeration to speak of Congress as a co-partner in formulating foreign trade policy and most other sectors of U.S. international economic policy. No theory can be adequate without considering at least three aspects of an inter-branch model of policymaking: what Congress does, which administration requests it refuses to act on, and how the executive branch modifies its policy preferences to be compatible with prevailing sentiment on Capitol Hill.

Several theoretical approaches, originally devised to explain how values are translated by the executive branch into U.S. foreign policy, are appropriate to international economic policy. One school concentrates on the cognitive/psychological aspects of the people who are making policy. The thesis here is that policymakers filter new information through a preestablished set of values and perceptions developed over a period of many years. This approach to decisionmaking has limited applicability to international economic policy because all modern U.S. presidents (and most secretaries of the treasury and state) have come into office with little or no direct exposure to the intricacies of international economic relations.

There are many instances when direct presidential intervention or perfectly shared perceptions in the bureaucracy have determined international economic policy. An example of the first situation was the crude bullying of Japan between 1969 and 1971 by the Nixon White House to restrict that country's textile exports to the U.S. market. On other occasions, policy has flowed easily from a wide consensus among departments, as exemplified by shared values that an essentially ''open-door'' approach should be maintained rather than placing any new limits on foreign direct investment within the United States.

The bureaucratic politics model of decision-making, also spawned by scholars looking to explain the formulation of U.S. national security policy, provides useful insight into a high percentage of international economic policymaking. The model is based on the assumption that in more cases than not, there will be differences of opinion within any large national government as to what policy in a given circumstance serves the long-term national interest. Gray-area assessments vastly outnumber black or white absolutes. Given the frequently contradictory needs between domestic economics and politics and between international economics and politics, the choice of optimal international economic policy is seldom a simple one.

The bureaucratic politics model suggests that policy decisions can best be understood as the outcome of bargaining among participants in various parts of the bureaucracy. Policy frequently emanates not from a centralized, totally neutral decision-maker, but from a patchwork of bureaucracies and officials imbued with different missions, perceptions, and priorities. Often disagreeing among themselves about what is the best course of action by the government in a particular situation, agencies actively compete against each other in attempting to determine governmental strategy and tactics.[14]

In point of fact, relatively few global economic problems suggest a response or course of action that is unambiguously, unequivocally correct and compatible with everyone's priorities and preferences. All too often, policy is determined by a committee-bred consensus that everyone can live with. In such cases, the final product is more likely to represent a line of least resistance than sparkling brilliance and the pure pursuit of optimal policy. At times decision-making is a bruising power struggle between conflicting diagnoses of appropriate policy, and at other times it is a pragmatic search for a mutually acceptable course of conduct.

Four reasons can be cited as to why international economic policy in the major industrialized countries is especially fertile ground for bureaucratic dissent over what, in a specific situation, is optimal policy:

- The inherent tensions between economic and political priorities as well as between internal and external priorities.
- The large number of bureaucratic actors involved.
- The frequency of unclear, overlapping jurisdictions.
- The imprecision within the economics profession, as seen in the high propensity of economists to disagree among themselves on both technical analyses and policy prescriptions.

The bureaucratic politics model argues that pursuit of the "national interest" is such a gross generalization that it is an inadequate guide to understanding the international policymaking process. Producing a definition of the national interest with which everyone agrees usually requires strenuous effort and a lot of flexibility. It is insufficient to argue that the United States government simply adopts international economic policies that maximize its citizens' prosperity. First of all, national security concerns sometimes take precedence over corporate sales and profits, as exemplified by export controls. Second, in cases where private sector requests for import relief are being debated, only some departments and agencies will believe that the path to domestic prosperity is temporary import barriers that would allow an import-impacted sector to regroup. Other bureaucratic entities will oppose barriers because they would be seen as inflicting unacceptable harm on the American economy by reducing competition and increasing prices.

The image of U.S. government agencies thinking identical thoughts over a long period of time and marching lockstep toward a common international economic grand design is therefore a chimera. In the abstract, countries do pursue broad national interests. In real life, bureaucracies play politics. They engage in maneuvers in order to maximize individual values and goals in a milieu of differing opinions as to what exactly is "good policy." Each bureaucracy is created and its staff is paid to perform a specified function, worry about a relatively narrow piece of the policy "waterfront," and defend certain priorities. Government officials will examine any policy proposal at least in part to determine whether it will increase the effectiveness with which the mission of their particular organization can be carried out. The interests of the constituencies they represent help define officials' perceptions of all issues. "All organizations seek *influence*; many also have a specific *mission* to perform; and some organizations need to maintain expensive *capabilities* in order to perform their mission effectively."[15]

The success or failure of a bureaucratic entity's drive to maximize certain values is partly a function of how the government's decision-making process listens to and evaluates the various bureaucratic inputs. If organization is biased in favor of, or against, certain values, it probably will tilt policy priorities toward the favored constituency.

Yes, people make policy decisions. However, bureaucratic affiliation can and does affect the nature of people's opinions as to what policy option should be selected for implementation. In most cases, bureaucratic actors sincerely believe that advancing their constituency and their institutional values will best serve the national interest. They have no reason not to covet as much influence as possible for enhancing their viewpoint and containing opposing positions. There is nothing wrong with a vigorous debate on subjective values that seeks to assign a sliding scale of importance to different goals. Keeping the decision-making process fair, well-informed, and expeditious is what matters most.

Policy officials' viewpoints typically become identified closely with those of their agency, which is where their careers, reputations, and professional self-esteem are either made or broken. In the course of their duties, the average political appointee and public servant seldom perceive any major conflicts, either between their personal views and those of the organization, or between their organization's attitude and their view of the national welfare. In the first place, individuals are not likely to be attracted to, or to flourish in, organizations whose missions are antithetical to their personal values. A resident of an East Coast city who is totally indifferent to the farm community would not be confirmed by the Senate in the unlikely event that such a person was nominated for the post of Secretary of Agriculture. Few people who are openly antagonistic to big business would seek career employment with the Commerce or Treasury departments. Barring crass hypocrisy, bureaucrats who do develop a philosophic difference of opinion with their agency's constituency would seek transfer to another part of government or move to an interest group with a more compatible viewpoint.

The jurisdictional arguments that arise frequently in international economic policy formulation are surrogates to a significant degree for deep-rooted cleavages in basic perspectives and self-interests. Discussions of jurisdictional and coordinating problems often mask what are really conflicts about which of the elements comprising international economic policy should be given priority.

This policy can be viewed as being primarily an extension of domestic economic policy management *or* as primarily the economic aspect of foreign relations. All may agree on the long-term destination of a growing and stable market-oriented world economy, but there is unlikely to be unanimity on the timetable for, and best means of, reaching this end. Resolution of these completely legitimate conflicts will often be determined to some extent by which bureaucratic players have the most power and influence.

Most departments actively engaged in U.S. international economic policy-making have a reasonably predictable visceral reaction to policy issues. It is usually possible for an informed outsider to accurately predict the gist of a departmental position that will be advanced in an interagency group. Agency positions are directly related to bureaucratic ''essence''—the dominant view held in each organization concerning its mission and needs. Stupidity and venality are rarely the reasons that executive branch officials seldom bring a common vision of how best to react to a new issue. The fact is that they are all searching for ideal policy, but from different angles and on behalf of different values.

One way of illustrating the effects of bureaucratic politics is to suggest different reactions if officials in a variety of departments and agencies were asked what is their number one concern about China. Some would name trade barriers and violations of intellectual property rights; some would speak of exports of highly lethal weapons and weapons technology; some would name human rights violations; and so on and so forth.

When dealing with Japan, perhaps the United States' most important bilateral relationship, three different views on what constitutes ''good'' policy have existed for decades within the executive branch. The departments responsible for U.S. national security policy (State and Defense) are predisposed to placing strict limits on how far the U.S. government should go in pressing trade demands on Japan. In their view, commercial quarrels should not, and must not, undermine the close, all-important bilateral political and military relationship. The defenders of free trade ideology, the Council of Economic Advisers (CEA), Office of Management and Budget (OMB) and (usually) the Treasury Department, suggest a low-key attitude towards trade frictions by reciting the economic theory case: the United States is the clear winner in raising the national standard of living to the extent that a mercantilist Japan is willing to exchange on a net basis real economic resources for paper money. A third perspective comes from the trade specialists in USTR and Commerce who look at bilateral trade relations and see the United States being hurt by the restricted ability of American business to compete in the world's second largest market. Their recommendation has long been the adoption of aggressive efforts to force Japan to stop stalling and genuinely liberalize its economic and trade practices to the standard allegedly practiced in Western Europe and the United States. The value judgments of the reader will determine which of these three rational, legitimate, and competing ideas he/she thinks would best advance the U.S. ''national interest.''

Not surprisingly, some of the most vivid examples of the bureaucratic politics model in international economic policymaking have come in the form of disagreements between the State and Treasury departments. The State Department exists to worry about U.S. foreign policy and manage the country's role as global superpower. It will construct its response to a problem primarily in terms of how a U.S. action or attitude will be received in other countries, not in terms of the impact on a domestic interest group. It will prefer give-and-take negotiations over unilateral acts that might isolate the United States or alienate allies or potential allies.

The Treasury Department's raison d'être, constituency, and perspective are different. It is responsible for promoting a good overall performance by the U.S. economy. In seeking to protect and enhance its unusually broad, complex constituency—the American economy—the Treasury has the most complex job of any agency in determining optimal policy. Despite its seemingly inward-looking orientation, the department's general embrace of free market economics frequently causes it to vote against import barriers in the belief that such a move would discourage competition and encourage inflation.

Just as businesspeople look for profits, Treasury and Commerce look to the advancement of U.S. domestic economic interests and values as the main indicator of sound international policy. These departments, unlike the State Department, exist to worry about U.S. economic security, not traditional national security. Countries are judged to be friendly or hostile mainly in terms of their impact on the U.S. economy, not on the more traditional basis of political orientation and military strength. A major implication of this situation is that the Treasury Department tends to have a "nondifferentiated-adversary attitude" toward international relations. Political allies deserve no special economic favors at the cost of the U.S. economy.[16] Relative to the State Department, which actively seeks the cooperation of foreign governments, and the Defense Department, which worries about foreign military bases, the Treasury Department has less dependency on the goodwill of other countries.

The Treasury and State departments have experienced relatively few policy clashes in recent years. Their move toward common ground has been due in part to the increased clout of the trained economists in State's Bureau of Economic and Business Affairs relative to the regional bureaus. This trend in turn reflects both the greater sensitivity of most foreign service officers to American domestic economic problems and the growing appreciation of the importance of international economics by recent secretaries of state. An additional factor has been the undisputed jurisdiction of the Treasury Department in dealing with the financial crises that have dominated international economic relations in the 1990s.

CONCLUSION

A single theory identifying universal truths about the forces driving U.S. international economic policymakers to shape decisions remains beyond the reach of academic theorists. Causality comes in a number of forms, depending on the many variables associated with numerous *kinds* of decisions in numerous *sectors* of international economic relations. For many, a generalized guideline about the decision-making process will suffice: invariably, there is a need to reconcile, or trade off, any number of different values and priorities in a manner that is reasonably consistent with a number of operational influences. The latter include: the beliefs of senior policymakers, domestic economic needs, international economic principles and ideology, public opinion, and the need to support the foreign policy responsibilities of a global superpower. Any or all of these five factors will be present in a constantly changing mix, depending on the circumstances surrounding the issue at hand.

Procedural factors only on occasion decisively tip the scales in certain directions. Beliefs are always important in decision-making. However, the organizational factors affecting how those beliefs are "marketed" can and do determine bureaucratic winners and losers in the interagency formulation of U.S. international economic policy.

NOTES

1. Max Weber, *Economy and Society*, as cited in G. John Ikenberry, "Conclusion: An Institutional Approach to American Foreign Economic Policy," *International Organization* 42 (Winter 1988): 241.

2. For an excellent sample of first-generation writings, see footnotes 1–3 in G. John Ikenberry, David A. Lake, and Michael Mastanduno, "Introduction: Approaches to Explaining American Foreign Economic Policy," *International Organization* 42 (Winter 1988): 1–2.

3. Ibid., pp. 1–12.

4. Ikenberry, "Conclusion," p. 222.

5. Ibid., p. 241.

6. John S. Odell, "Understanding International Trade Policies—An Emerging Synthesis," *World Politics* 43 (October 1990): 140–57.

7. Ibid., pp. 160–161.

8. Robert E. Baldwin, *The Political Economy of U.S. Import Policy* (Cambridge, Mass.: MIT Press, 1985), pp. 176, 180.

9. [Report of the] *Commission on the Organization of the Government for the Conduct of Foreign Policy* (Washington, D.C.: U.S. Government Printing Office, 1975), p. 21.

10. David A. Stockman, *The Triumph of Politics* (New York: Harper & Row, 1986), p. 154. Secretary Lewis's ploy was not completely successful, in large part because it so angered then–Treasury Secretary Donald Regan that his department launched a strong fight against any unilateral U.S. restrictions on auto imports. A compromise eventually was reached that induced Japan to "voluntarily" restrain its auto exports.

11. See, for example, the discussion of efforts in the U.S. embassy to block outgoing messages critical of Japanese economic policies, in Clyde Prestowitz, Jr., *Trading Places* (New York: Basic Books, 1988), p. 270.

12. Roger Hilsman, *The Politics of Policy Making in Defense and Foreign Affairs* (New York: Harper and Row, 1971), p. 152.

13. Chalmers Johnson, *MITI and the Japanese Miracle* (Stanford, Calif.: Stanford University Press, 1982), p. 19.

14. Graham Allison and Morton Halperin, "Bureaucratic Politics: A Paradigm and Some Policy Implications," Reprint 246 (Washington, D.C.: Brookings Institution, 1972), p. 42.

15. Morton Halperin and Arnold Kanter, eds., *Readings in American Foreign Policy* (Boston: Little, Brown, 1973), p. 10. (Emphasis in original.)

16. My first job after graduate school was in the international bureau of the Treasury Department in the mid-1960s, a time when the French were actively buying large amounts of U.S. gold to pressure the United States to reduce its balance of payments deficit. I had no problem accepting the departmental "culture" that viewed France as being at the time at least as much of a threat to U.S. national security as the Soviet Union.

8   The Many Models of Executive Branch Decision-Making

> We make [international economic policy] . . . in the most disorganized, fragmented, and incoherent way imaginable. If there is consistency among decisions we make in our relations with less developed countries, trade negotiations, selling agricultural products abroad, and so on, this is purely coincidental. . . . [We] have a non-system.
>
> —Sidney Weintraub

The specific decision-making procedures followed by executive branch officials lie at the heart of the U.S. international economic policymaking process. Literally speaking, policy is determined after the various bureaucratic actors described in Chapter 3 deal with the pressures and priorities discussed in Chapter 7 and then reconcile their often conflicting assessments of the "national interest." The eight models of intra–executive branch decision-making presented in this chapter are not sufficient to explain all major U.S. international economic policy decisions. This is not surprising: just as the substantive terrain of international economic policy varies greatly, so too does the procedural terrain. Which model is used in any given situation is determined by a constantly changing mix of circumstances. Many decisions are made in accordance with the ninth model, inter-branch dynamics, that is described in the next chapter. Some are sui generis, and some are an amalgam of two or three of the nine major decision-making models; they are discussed in this chapter's concluding section.

To enhance relevance to the contemporary scene, only policy actions that have occurred since 1970 will be examined.

OBSTACLES TO CONSTRUCTING A UNIFIED THEORY OF INTERNATIONAL ECONOMIC POLICYMAKING

Several obstacles impede a scholarly analysis of how U.S. international economic policies are formulated and implemented. The process over any extended period of time is disparate, ad hoc, inconsistent, and often just plain disorganized. A journalist's description of the U.S. regulatory process is totally applicable to international economic policymaking: "a hodgepodge of the smart and the perverse, the elegantly precise and the miserably flat-footed, the extraordinarily cost-effective and the grotesquely wasteful."[1] How much the erratic performance of policymakers harms the national interest cannot be calculated on a scientific basis. The ultimate purpose of this or any other form of government decision-making is not to win an award from a public administration society for its well-oiled efficiency, but to produce "good" policy. The degree to which an individual agrees with the substance of policy is likely to be the primary determinant of whether that person judges as good or bad the policymaking process that produced it.

There is no guarantee of method to the occasional madness. Nor is there any easy route to making the decision-making process more straightforward and consistent. Process reflects substance. International economic relations are a dynamic phenomena. The lack of orderliness, consistency, and predictability in the commercial, financial, developmental, energy, competitiveness, and environmental issues that collectively constitute international economic policy is a major cause of an uneven, constantly reconfigured decision-making process. Even if the policy priorities of successive administrations did not change, there would still be dissimilarities in the organizational preferences of the hundreds of new senior-level political appointees who arrive with every new president. Furthermore, no organizational chart can be so perfect as to easily digest all of the new issues, such as international energy and environmental concerns, that constantly burst unexpectedly onto the scene and require new deliberating forums, often with a new combination of bureaucratic actors.

The heterogeneous nature of international economic "policy" is at the heart of the difficulty of constructing a unified theory of policy formulation. In fact, the use of the singular form of the noun probably is a fundamental error. The term *policy* falsely suggests a degree of consistency and homogeneity that is not consistent with the decentralized nature of international economic relations. There are a number of different, albeit related, policy sectors (trade, monetary, aid, etc.), and within each, many different kinds of governmental actions are called for. As noted in Chapter 1, policy in this area is an umbrella term whose elements can be disaggregated and discretely defined in a number of ways, such as importance and nature.

All things considered, the premises, priorities, perceptions, and personalities from which international economic policy emanates all can be characterized as "fluid." Different kinds of official responses are necessary and different constraints are involved, depending on the nature of the issue at hand. Policy questions have different dynamics, depending on several factors, such as whether the U.S. economy is growing and competing well against other countries, how important are technical economic questions relative to political factors, and whether two branches of government are involved.

The bottom-line result is a nearly infinite variety of possible configurations in decision-making patterns. The balance of power between domestic and foreign policy departments varies on a case-by-case basis as does the complexity and make-up of decision-making forums. Different combinations of bureaucratic actors and the variety of official actions involved preclude postulation of uniform cause-and-effect relationships except at the highest level of generality. Policymaking can be quick and intimate. Decisions on intervention tactics in the foreign exchange market consist of relatively brief technical dialogues held daily between a select few Treasury Department and Federal Reserve Board officials that normally involve no input from anywhere else. As seen in Figure 8.1, however, sometimes the number of participants and length of discussions seem to spiral out of control. The complexity of formulating textile trade policy in the 1980s resulted in so many lines of communication that even the savviest bureaucrat must have been perplexed.

Only two patterns of behavior are visible in all models of U.S. international economic policymaking. The first is that rational policymakers consider, at least briefly, four basic questions:

- what are the probable short-term economic and political costs and benefits of various policy options to their personal and institutional positions;
- how would the country's long-term national interests best be served;
- what are the consequences of favoring one set of demands from domestic constituents or foreign governments and ignoring others;
- what about timing, that is, how urgent, if at all, is the need for action?

Any of several techniques—depending on the circumstances and personalities at hand—will be employed to resolve these questions.

The second consistent pattern in the decision-making models is that all will assemble value judgments by assigning weights, or priorities, to each of the four elements of international economic policy: domestic politics, foreign policy, domestic economic policy, and international economic objectives.

Consistency does not exist below these generalized common denominators. Many pivotal U.S. international economic policy decisions and actions have been made on a highly idiosyncratic basis. Some were quickly devised in crisis situations; others grew by inertia. Furthermore, the dynamics of decision-making in one sector and in a particular year are not necessarily representative of those in other sectors, or even in the same sector in different years. The problem with attempting to construct a single, comprehensive theory of the internal and ex-

Figure 8.1
Textile Trade Policy

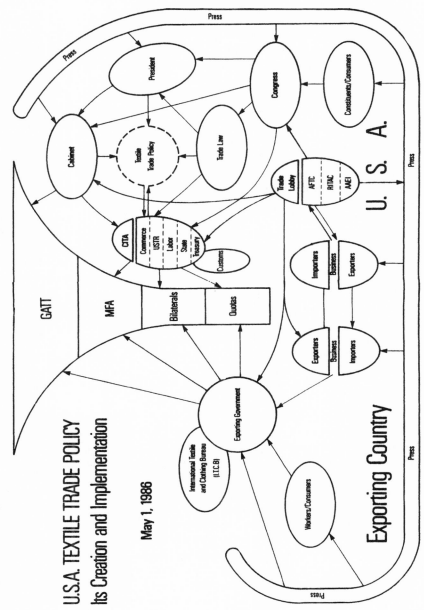

U.S.A. TEXTILE TRADE POLICY
Its Creation and Implementation

May 1, 1986

Source: U.S. Congress, House Ways and Means Committee.

ternal forces shaping the U.S. government's international economic decision-making process is that no one model appears to be even close to universal validity. All the major models utilized in the foreign policy (national security) decision-making process can be shown, both in pure form and in variations, to be applicable at one time or another to international economic relations. To suggest that this decision-making process is too ad hoc to lend itself to a unified model of action is not necessarily a criticism of either officials or existing procedures. The changing mix of governmental entities that have a right to be heard on any given issue and the endless procession of new global economic issues do not lend themselves to neat consistency.

The implication of the empirical evidence is that multiple models of decision-making exist, and that any one of them might be operational in a given policymaking exercise according to prevailing circumstances. It is still not possible to know a priori exactly which model will be relevant for any given issue. A theory whose task is to explain and predict U.S. international economic policy decisions must respect the inevitability of diversity. Students of the one-model school are guilty of either an insufficient disaggregation of the term "policy" or of utilizing too narrow and selective a set of supporting case studies to demonstrate purportedly universal truths.

Recurring patterns in decision-making do exist. However, they are far from being sufficiently significant or numerous to lead to categorical theories or assertions. For example, the eleven case studies in international economic policy decision-making written for the Commission on the Organization of the Government for the Conduct of Foreign Policy (and published in Volume 2 in the Appendices to its report) were vivid and expensive evidence of the fallacy of trying to capture the essence of universal truths about the organizational system from a small, randomly selected sample. Collectively, the case studies provide no means to either understand the system as a whole or to predict future behavior.

The inherent limitations of the case study method in producing universal truths would be minimized if hundreds of separate decisions and operations were to be examined on a comprehensive basis and then meticulously cross-referenced according to very specific criteria. Even so, a relatively brief time frame would need to be chosen in order to examine a system reflecting similar presidential styles and prevailing global realities. A random sample of ten to fifteen events is likely to produce interesting and illustrative anecdotes, but could not be extrapolated on any scientific basis to produce a systemic diagnosis. A carefully preselected sample of decisions, however, could be employed to arbitrarily defend any specific hypothesis embraced a priori by the person conducting the study.

In an effort to present the fullest, most realistic perspective, the remainder of this chapter is devoted to two separate means of examining the diversity of the decision-making process. The first is an examination of the characteristics of the major intra–executive branch decision-making models and how each corresponds to specific policymaking exercises. The second technique uses case studies to examine organizational dynamics that either utilized more than one of the models presented or did not conform to any of them.

EIGHT MODELS OF INTERNATIONAL ECONOMIC DECISION-MAKING

A number of theories have been advanced to explain the principles that guide the U.S. executive branch in formulating economic and national security policies. This section focuses on eight of the nine models that collectively illustrate how the vast majority of post–World War II international economic policy decisions have been reached (the model incorporating Congress is discussed at length in the next chapter). No one method is necessarily better than another in terms of the quality of the policy substance produced or the speed that it is arrived at. It is a strength of the U.S. system that it is sufficiently diverse to provide a number of options for reaching policy decisions. It is the system's weakness that the method of decision-making used is more the random byproduct of case-by-case circumstances—a situation that encourages bureaucratic infighting—than a logical, predetermined process. Nevertheless, a homogeneous set of policies produced by a mechanically repetitive policymaking process is unlikely to be applauded by those who object to the substance of these policies.

Presidential Fiat

Decisions under the presidential fiat model reflect the direct intervention and clear dictation of the president—with little or no advance input from senior advisers and career specialists. The president's values, interests, and operating style are important decision-making variables only in the most sensitive policy decisions. In theory, all U.S. international economic policy could be made by a highly centralized White House, but in practice, very few such decisions have been made this way. Historically, presidents only infrequently have elevated international economic concerns to sufficiently high levels as to warrant their paying a lot of attention to them. In most of these cases, presidential involvement was not so much pro-active as a reaction to the need to either ratify a consensus cabinet recommendation or to arbitrate a cabinet stalemate. A flow of direct, forceful presidential direction from early policy formulation through implementation constitutes the purest and rarest form of this model.

An unusual exhibition of intense presidential involvement in a long-running international trade issue revolved around Richard Nixon's unrelenting, top-down demand throughout the first three years of his presidency that Japan and other Asian textile-exporting countries be made to ''voluntarily'' restrict shipments of man-made textile fibers to the U.S. market. The economics of the issue were subordinated to the political imperative of fulfilling a campaign pledge designed to obtain domestic political support. The administration's position was ''perfectly clear'' throughout the 1969–1971 period. From beginning to end, U.S. policy never wavered. It attained its objective, even if it never made sense in purely economic terms.

Presidents have participated actively in the international economic policy formulation process during the periodic crises associated with chronic U.S. balance of payments deficits. A classic example was President Nixon's 1971 decision to terminate dollar/gold convertibility and to impose a 10 percent import surcharge as part of the New Economic Policy. This drastic and abrupt shift in economic policy was part of a larger package of mainly domestic measures constructed by the president and a handful of senior advisers during one fateful August weekend at Camp David.

The parallels between this decision and the textile dispute are striking. U.S. policy was formulated quickly and enunciated at the highest level. Objectives were then pursued singlemindedly by the administration with relatively little regard to foreign political sensitivities. No one from the foreign policy community was invited to the economists-only Camp David sessions. Once again, maximum concessions were eventually extracted from other countries with relatively little offered in return. The U.S. government successfully attained its international economic objectives, but at a cost of deep foreign resentment. Offsetting the clear direction from the chief executive was the absence of a process to ensure that relevant foreign policy concerns were introduced and integrated with the economic dimensions of the issue at hand.

Another example of decision by presidential fiat was the embargo of 17 million metric tons of U.S. grain that had been ordered by the Soviet government. Announced by an angry President Jimmy Carter on January 4, 1980, this decision was a direct retaliation for the Soviet military invasion of Afghanistan that had unpleasantly surprised the White House when it had been launched the previous month. This policy response was orchestrated exclusively from the White House. The president and two of his close advisers, Zbigniew Brzezinski (assistant for national security affairs) and Lloyd Cutler (counsel to the president) were the principal actors. Key departments and agencies (including Agriculture, State, and the Office of the U.S. Trade Representative) reportedly were consulted only after the decision to act had been made. They had no hand in the policy formulation process; they were asked only to provide operational support after the fact. In a private conversation with the author, a U.S. trade official suggested that the reason for this procedure was the president's desire for a quick response and his feeling that international economic policy officials were not essential to what was perceived as being mainly a national security–oriented affair.

There was no impasse needing resolution in the preparation of the U.S. government's position in the 1992 UN Conference on Environment and Development. President Bush and several of his senior advisers had long made it publicly known that the administration was not prepared to go very far in subordinating economic growth to environmental concerns. The administration's negotiating position at Rio was as clear as it was unpopular among the more than 175 participating countries—even after President Bush had gained some concessions from other countries following his threat to boycott the meeting.

The genesis of the controversial U.S.-Mexican free trade agreement can be traced to a single meeting in mid-1990 between presidents Bush and Carlos Salinas of Mexico. With no prior public debate or detailed U.S. government review, the two chief executives agreed to initiate negotiations, an act setting in motion the self-perpetuating process that eventually produced the North American Free Trade Agreement (NAFTA).

The Bureaucratic Politics Model

The majority of U.S. international economic activities involves incrementalism: modest additions to, or shifts in, existing policy guidelines. Most individual decisions involve neither great changes nor great impact. Well over 90 percent of decisions are made below the presidential level and involve relatively narrow, unspectacular determinations of how to proceed. The relative absence of White House command and control results in a number of U.S. international economic policy decisions being made in accordance with the bureaucratic politics model. The core idea of this model, as discussed in the previous chapter, is that policy substance often takes the form of the end product of bargaining and consensus building by a cohort of bureaucratic entities. Natural consensus seldom exists because each agency possesses a different array of perceptions, goals, constituencies, and vested interests—a situation that usually produces multiple interpretations of the "national interest." This theme is often summarized in the axiom "where you stand depends on where you sit."

There is nothing inherently venal in bureaucracies bringing competing values and agendas to interagency deliberating bodies. Domestic priorities do not necessarily overlap with external priorities, and bureaucracies are not specifically charged with weighing both perspectives on a even-handed basis. No one has a monopoly on truth and wisdom when it comes to international economics. An unequivocal answer is seldom written in the stars stating exactly which policy option absolutely would maximize the national interest along with global economic efficiency in a given situation. At least two sides to the story and an extremely large gray area are present in every significant international economic policy issue. There is nothing inherently wrong with efforts to chart a middle-ground course of action among conflicting, often self-serving bureaucratic perspectives. The real question is how efficiently, intelligently, and equitably the reconciliation process resolves differences.

The reaction by the U.S. government in the mid-1970s to the economic demands of the less developed countries (LDCs), collectively known as "the new international economic order," was a classic case of bureaucratic politics at work and deserves an in-depth examination. From the official birth of the new international economic order debate in the spring of 1974 at the Sixth Special

Session of the United Nations General Assembly, until May 1975, the United States maintained a negative attitude. Like most other industrial country governments, the Nixon-Ford administrations refused on principle to accept the LDCs' argument that systemic changes to reduce free market forces were necessary to correct the existing international economic system's alleged bias against poorer countries. Documents written by the LDCs contained a long shopping list of demands to redress the imbalance of world economic wealth. They included advocacy of international commodity agreements to raise and fix commodity prices above their market-determined levels, elimination of limitations on expropriation of foreign direct investment, including the requirement of fair and prompt compensation, and a general moratorium on repayment of debts owed to industrial country governments.

Underlying differences in the perspectives of the State and Treasury departments eventually caused a head-on collision on specific strategy, made all the worse by blurry lines of jurisdiction, ambitious political appointees, and random events. It escalated into a public, no-holds-barred rivalry that continued for a painfully long period of time because no arbitration mechanism was readily available to force a compromise that would end the internecine warfare. With glacial speed, the U.S. response evolved in uneasy fashion from unequivocally hostile to highly conditional flexibility.

Predictably, the Treasury Department assumed an orthodox free market approach, decrying all suggestions that government intervention and budgetary funds be used to rig the international economic system to favor the LDCs. Free market advocates viewed most of the demands comprising the new international economic order as wrong-headed, interventionist economics whose enactment would hurt, not help developing and industrialized countries alike. Although the State Department did not embrace the underlying economic philosophy espoused by the LDCs, it far preferred a flexible dialogue and partial accommodation over alienating more than 100 countries with an uncompromising hard-line.

Separate studies by the State and Treasury departments of the international commodity agreement issue had begun in 1974, but were merged into an interagency task force on international commodity agreements in February 1975. This group in turn reported to two other review groups, the Economic Policy Board (EPB) and the National Security Council (NSC), the former having a spiritual and intellectual affinity with Treasury, and the latter with State. Thus, while a more efficient cooperative effort resulted, neither State nor Treasury yielded any degree of control over the ongoing policy review process. Some consensus eventually emerged. The principal conclusion reached by the task force was that the United States should be prepared to discuss commodity price and supply arrangements on a case-by-case basis and should avoid a single grand approach to commodity agreements.[2]

In late April, then–Secretary of State Henry Kissinger was reviewing the text of an upcoming speech concerning North-South relations. Reportedly, he thought it to be both too tentative and unresponsive to the existing issues. By the time the rewritten text had been approved within State, there was time only for a perfunctory, eleventh-hour clearance at the very top levels of the Treasury Department. And so Kissinger announced that the United States was prepared to discuss "new arrangements in individual commodities on a case-by-case basis as circumstances warrant." A major policy decision had been forged by Kissinger's sudden public enunciation of a new U.S. posture on commodities. Interagency consensus had been superseded by unilateral speech-making.

Dr. Kissinger's speech mainly consisted of a carefully hedged, least-common-denominator approach that committed the United States to very little in the way of specifics. Nevertheless, the speech triggered a savage bureaucratic counterattack as senior Treasury officials immediately developed second thoughts about the Secretary of State's initiative. The Treasury Department then launched a number of broadsides against State, contending that U.S. policy had not really changed in this case. In a late May 1975 White House meeting, Treasury Secretary William Simon attempted to impress upon the president that nothing Kissinger had said, or would say, would bind this country to anything specific. Assistant Treasury Secretary Gerald Parsky told a press interviewer shortly afterward that "no decision has been made to make a change in the basic thrust of this country's policy in the commodities area, which is to maintain to the maximum extent the free functioning of the marketplace." An official of the Special Trade Representative's Office summed up the confused situation this way: what Kissinger said was settled U.S. policy; however, what it *means* was not yet settled.[3]

The commodity cartel question assumed a life far out of proportion to its actual merits and importance. In fact, it became a symbol of the larger ideological question as to whether occasional government intervention in the international markets for commodities was ever justified to meet the demands of the poorer countries for higher prices that would generate more foreign exchange earnings for them.

The approach of the UN Seventh Special Session, in September 1975, meant another speech and the opportunity for another U.S. public initiative. Not wishing to repeat the coordination fiasco associated with the May speech, the State Department initiated well in advance an ad hoc series of consultations, primarily with the Treasury and Agriculture departments. Once it was decided in principle to have Secretary Kissinger's speech include a major series of resource-transfer proposals, each one was negotiated and cleared at all levels of the other agencies. Intra–U.S. government feuding subsided. The harmony would be short-lived, however.

Senior officials at the Treasury Department were still adamant about keeping a lid on the extent and costs of commodity agreements. The policy-by-speech syndrome returned when Assistant Treasury Secretary Gerald Parsky told a San Francisco audience in January 1976 that "there appears to be a growing willingness to sacrifice economic principles for the sake of political gains. . . . If, for political reasons, we agree now . . . with demands for a new economic system, it will be impossible to justify on economic grounds our desire to preserve our system later.''[4] He also announced that the United States would not sign the then-pending international cocoa agreement.

None of this speech had been cleared with a horrified State Department. The latter had been hoping to push positively for a revision of the cocoa agreement's proposed language, not opt for a public declaration of opposition. Parsky's very equivocal clarification of U.S. policy on commodity agreements issued to the press the next day did nothing to clarify the situation. Despite a written statement's reiteration of the principle of a case-by-case approach to commodity agreements, he allegedly told the assembled reporters verbally that U.S. policy in principle opposed the concept of such agreements. The vehemence with which senior officials in the State and Treasury departments pursued bureaucratic politics in this case exacerbated a unique flaw in the U.S. government's way of disagreeing: a propensity to publicly air conflicting interpretations of ''good'' policy for all to see.

Bureaucratic politics dominated the formulation of a U.S. position on an international food policy in the 1970s. Efforts to construct a position on the magnitude of the U.S. food aid commitment that would be announced in 1974 illustrated differing emphases on a short-term attack on world hunger, domestic agricultural policies, and budgetary restraints. The bureaucracy debated the aid issue inconclusively for months while awaiting the final forecasts of the fall crop to determine available supplies. However, a decision had to be made prior to the president's scheduled address to the General Assembly on September 18, 1974, when he would have to discuss U.S. food aid policy. Agreeing with Secretary Kissinger that the United States should substantially raise the value of its food aid, President Ford selected an increase to about $1.5 billion.

The theme of the [president's] speech was victory for Kissinger, but everything else was a compromise. On the level of increase, the difference was roughly split between Kissinger, who wanted about $1.8 billion as the new total, and [OMB and CEA heads] Ash and Greenspan, who argued for holding the level at $900 million. In the middle, ranging from those advocating less aid to more, were the CIEP, Treasury, and Agriculture. And the $1.5 billion figure was more a general target than a firm decision. Indeed, a month later there was still disagreement about what Ford had decided.[5]

Another example of pure bureaucratic politics involves the question of export promotion. Among the many basic questions involved here is whether it is necessary and proper for the government to provide financial resources to help the private sector increase sales and profits. If so, what are the most efficient and effective techniques, and how much funding is appropriate and necessary? There are two opposing points of view on the specific issue of subsidized (below market rates) export financing by the Export-Import Bank. One side argues that a critical determinant of U.S. export success is an activist Export-Import Bank that responds to the generous export financing agencies operated by all other industrialized countries. A major advocate is the Commerce Department, with its business orientation and its own export promotion programs. Opponents see no justification for a U.S. government institution providing subsidies to foreigners buying American goods. The Office of Management and Budget and the Federal Reserve System's Board of Governors during the 1970s openly voiced opposition to the scope of the bank's operations. They argued that use of U.S. budgetary funds to support a handful of exporters violates free market economic theory and government impartiality.

The bureaucratic politics model also explains the administration's decision in April 1976 on how to respond to the ITC's recommendation that the U.S. footwear industry be granted relief from import competition. President Ford accepted the liberal trade option recommended by his cabinet-level Trade Policy Committee that funds for adjustment assistance be made available to help the industry modernize and to retrain workers. The option of imposing higher tariffs or quotas was rejected. In addition to the predictable votes of departments on the committee (State on the liberal side, and Commerce and Labor on the protectionist side), the Department of Defense's vote exactly conformed to its mission and constituency. Two of the major shoe-exporting countries to this market at that time were Spain and Italy. Both countries were sites of important military bases, and Italy was a North Atlantic Treaty Organization ally facing serious economic difficulties and an increasingly powerful Communist party. Since domestic suppliers of footwear to the U.S. military were secure from foreign competition, the Defense Department cast its vote against a resort to protectionist measures.

This decision-making exercise also provided a valuable insight into the limits of the bureaucratic politics model and the need for inside information to comprehend all of the twists and turns of bureaucratic behavior. The Office of the U.S. Trade Representative (USTR) is charged with negotiating the worldwide reduction of trade barriers. As such, fears of retaliation and angry trading partners must weigh heavily in the spirit of its bureaucratic "essence." Nevertheless, its vote was cast with the protectionist side in this footwear escape clause.[6]

The USTR's behavior made sense only if one was aware of its active marketing efforts at this time to assure congressional passage of the Trade Act of 1974. USTR officials emphasized to representatives of import-sensitive industries that the bill, if passed, would provide them with easier access to governmental import relief programs. In fact, the "sales pitch" went further. The USTR promised that after the bill became law, it would not play an active role in denying relief to petitioning industries that had been declared qualified for it under the newer, more flexible language. When USTR voted with the protectionist bureaucratic actors in the 1976 footwear case, it may have been acting contrary to its immediate bureaucratic mission. But it was demonstrating commitment to a promise that had been extended in conjunction with the pursuit of a larger interest: passage of major new trade legislation.[7]

George Bush was confronted early in his administration with bureaucratic deadlock on steel import strategy. His cabinet was unable to reach consensus on the tricky issue of whether or not to extend the five-year "voluntary" export restraint agreements that had been signed with major steel-exporting countries. The agreements, negotiated under the Reagan administration to meet domestic assertions of pervasive unfair trading practices overseas, were due to expire in late 1989. One reason for the Cabinet's indecision was the materialization of a lobbying gridlock. The American Iron and Steel Institute pleaded for a second five-year period of foreign export restraints. Domestic steel companies argued that they were almost but not yet fully back on their feet, and they threatened again to overload the system with multiple filings of antidumping and counter-vailing duty complaints to prevent being injured by the alleged continuation of unfair foreign trade practices. Leading the opposing side was the Coalition of American Steel Using Manufacturers, representing several hundred U.S. companies that incorporated steel in their finished products. Restricted access to the cheapest steel raised their production costs and harmed their competitiveness. Caterpillar, Inc., one of the United States' biggest manufacturing companies and a major user of steel, was the driving force behind this lobbying coalition. Other liberal trade advocates argued that the steel industry had regained its international competitive edge, thanks in part to restraints on imports that had been in place almost continuously since the late 1960s, and that no continuation of the export restraints was justified.

President Bush's final decision reflected a simple arithmetic compromise between two perfectly legitimate but irreconcilable viewpoints. In what was hardly a daring policy ploy, he decided to negotiate a one-time extension of the steel export restraint program for two and one-half years.

In addition to bureaucratic politics reflecting an axis running from free trade to protection of domestic industry, the model applies to the spectrum separating economic and national security priorities. The Department of Defense is viewed as most pro–national security, the Commerce Department is judged to be the most pro-export, and the State Department falls somewhere in between. A classic agency split resulted from the December 1992 consideration of an export license for what would have been the first American supercomputer shipment to China. The Defense Department and the Arms Control and Disarmament Agency opposed the sale on the grounds that the supercomputer could be diverted to military purposes from its supposed use in weather research. The State and Commerce departments supported the sale because of their inclinations, respectively, to improve political relations with China and to increase American exports. Neither had any problem assuming that adequate safeguards could be devised to prevent diversion of the computer to military purposes.[8]

Congress's perception that the Commerce Department had gone too far in putting export promotion ahead of national security concerns led it to pass legislation in 1998 specifically ordering the return of export licensing authority for commercial communications satellites to the State Department. Upset at the flow of sensitive technology to China, Congress took the initiative and passed a bill reversing a 1996 executive action by President Clinton that had transferred this responsibility from State to Commerce. The legislators believed that the former's licensing procedures for dual-use technology was more rigorous than the latter's. The bill also increased the Defense Department's review authority over licensing satellite exports as an additional safeguard to assure adequate weight for national security considerations.

The bureaucratic politics model was very much in evidence in the public postures taken by three senior officials in early 1986 on the question of the desirability of increased dollar depreciation (above and beyond the considerable amount that already had occurred). Central bankers are paid primarily to worry about inflation and financial instability. Accordingly, the then–Federal Reserve Chairman Paul Volcker was concerned that continued dollar weakness could rekindle domestic inflation and that prolonged depreciation eventually could trigger a free-fall in the dollar's exchange rate. He told a House Committee in late February that he believed that the dollar had "fallen enough" and warned that "it is very easy to overshoot on the downside" in pushing a currency lower.[9]

One day earlier, the far more politically engaged treasury secretary, James Baker, told a Senate committee that he "wouldn't be displeased" with a further decline in the dollar's value. This de facto talking down of the dollar was fully consistent with his reported desire to promote adjustment in the mammoth U.S. trade deficit so as to hold off the protectionist pressures swelling on Capitol Hill. Concerned that his industrial constituency was suffering from stagnant exports and severe import competition, Commerce Secretary Baldrige publicly explained his differences with Volcker's worries about a depreciating dollar: "The effect wouldn't be as severe as the Chairman fears because businessmen think like businessmen, not like economists."[10]

Different constituencies and different organizational cultures explain conflicting views taken on the subject of the Strategic Petroleum Reserve, a key element in U.S. international energy policy. National security-conscious agencies view the reserve as an invaluable insurance policy that can be cashed in during times of oil shortages or soaring prices. In the 1980s, their priority was to accumulate as big a reserve as possible and to do it quickly. In fact, the stockpiling of oil was slowed considerably because of opposition to extensive governmental oil purchases by the Office of Management and Budget. Its priority was minimizing the costs to the federal budget by holding down spending.

Dealing with a politically sensitive, albeit financially shaky, foreign country is fertile ground for revelations of how rival bureaucratic cultures serving different "constituencies" create different interpretations of what good policy is. The mushrooming scandal involving Iraq and an American branch of Banca Nazionale del Lavoro forced the release of a torrent of internal Bush administration documents detailing its relations with the government of Saddam Hussein prior to the invasion of Kuwait. One important decision was on the proposal to extend another $1 billion in new loan guarantees from the Agriculture Department's Commodity Credit Corporation (CCC), mainly as a means of improving strained political relations between the two countries. In order to gain interagency agreement on this additional funding, the State Department and the National Security Council had to go through elaborate procedures to overcome Agriculture Department hesitance and to reverse outright opposition from three other agencies that were seriously worried about Iraq's creditworthiness, that is, its ability to repay the agricultural loans.

As noted in a confidential State Department memorandum, Treasury, the Office of Management and Budget, and the Federal Reserve Board initially opposed any further financial commitments to Iraq because that country had failed to make payments on some of its debt to non-Arab creditors. The memo asserted that the State Department's power of persuasion had to be focused on these three agencies inasmuch as the other members of the National Advisory Council, where the final vote on the CCC program would be taken at the political level, were not opposed to the billion dollar program. ''AID can generally be depended upon to follow State's lead and [the Export-Import Bank] has privately indicated support, since it has its own short-term program of credit guarantees.''[11]

Shared Perceptions

Many international economic policies of the United States are routinely handled by a cabinet or bureaucracy that is unhampered by real differences of opinion. In most cases, U.S. policy on international investment smoothly flows from several shared assumptions. The dominant one is that the market mechanism should be allowed to function wherever and whenever possible. No agency has openly argued in the post–World War II period against the essentially opendoor policy for U.S. companies wishing to invest overseas or for foreign companies wishing to invest in the United States. Similarly, no agency has claimed that a resort to comprehensive import barriers or export subsidies would be a sensible or long-lasting solution even as the U.S. trade deficit reached one record level after another in the 1990s.

There is no major bureaucratic dissent on the broad principles of U.S. international energy policy. With the exception of the explosive State-Treasury feud in 1975 on the concept of a guaranteed floor price for oil, no continuing, serious differences of opinion have emerged. The State, Treasury, and Energy departments and the concerned White House offices all want to minimize U.S. vulnerability to future embargo threats through stockpiling oil and international supply sharing arrangements.

The shared perceptions model was applicable to the identical economic analyses and policy recommendations emanating from the State and Treasury departments in response to the LDCs' demands in the 1970s for generalized debt relief from obligations to repay bilateral foreign aid loans. Unlike the ideological split complicating U.S. policy on international commodity agreements, this aspect of the North-South economic dialogue never became a contentious issue.

The State and Treasury departments agreed at the time that no universal debt crisis existed. Hence, a generalized, or across-the-board write-off of the LDCs' external development loans was deemed unjustified, the political pressure from the LDC bloc notwithstanding. Both departments agreed that requests for debt relief should be handled on a country-by-country basis in the so-called Paris Club meetings of creditor governments. Generalized debt relief, it was agreed, would disproportionately benefit a few big debtor countries that accounted for most of the LDCs' accumulated bilateral external debt from official development loans. Both departments feared congressional anger at the "back door," that is, non-appropriated, foreign aid implications of debt forgiveness, and they worried about the precedent that would be set by allowing debtors to void their past contractual commitments to repay lenders.

No one in the executive branch or in the Federal Reserve System proposed that the U.S. government turn its back on Mexico's surprise announcement on a hot weekend in Washington in August 1982. A delegation of senior Mexican officials arrived to inform their startled U.S. counterparts that their country was about to run out of foreign exchange reserves and would have to suspend service on its external debt the following week if emergency financial assistance was not forthcoming. Given fears of a possible international financial panic following an unforeseen Mexican default, the U.S. government orchestrated an interim loan package literally on an overnight basis.

More recently, the deteriorating economic situation in Russia following the breakup of the USSR was met by the shared perception that potential economic anarchy in a former superpower possessing more than 20,000 nuclear weapons was a combustible mixture and that financial assistance from the international community was necessary.

Multiple Advocacy Model

Decisions taken under the multiple advocacy model involve the forceful management of competitive bureaucratic viewpoints by a dispassionate, neutral adherent to a presidential perspective. Power brokering is removed from the direct control of cabinet departments. It is usually a White House official who becomes the chief coordinator with responsibility to ensure that all agencies with appropriate jurisdiction have an equitable share of information, participation, and if necessary access to the president. The president may be an active participant at critical points in the decision-making process.

An excellent example of multiple advocacy was the interagency deliberations in 1972–1973 that produced a proposal for major trade legislation. The latter was submitted to Congress in April 1973 and eventually became the Trade Act of 1974. The process by which the trade bill was drafted reflected two principal realities. First, this was a time when the "agonizing reappraisal" of the U.S. commitment to liberal trade was near the high-water mark. It is no cliche to suggest that U.S. trade policy was at a major historical crossroads. Intellectually,

the questions of where and how to proceed legislatively were exceedingly complex. Even the basic question of the wisdom of submitting a comprehensive trade bill to the Hill had to be thrashed out. Second, the number of bureaucratic entities with an overall or specific interest in major trade legislation was unusually large. More than a dozen departments and agencies regularly participated in the interagency drafting sessions. Others attended occasionally. About 25 persons reportedly attended a typical meeting.

The so-called Trade Legislative Committee, the interagency group that handled the statute-drafting chore, was established within the Council on International Economic Policy (CIEP) machinery by George Shultz, acting in his informal capacity as ''economic czar'' and in his formal capacity as head of the more senior Council on Economic Policy. By late 1972, work began in earnest to finalize the language of the bill with Shultz acting as the president's alter ego. Although he was the treasury secretary, Shultz's personal traits and style permitted him to play the role of neutral supervisor, custodian of the presidential perspective, and consensus builder. His firm commitment to producing a good trade bill was reflected in his occasional opposition to Treasury positions.

Differences in goals and viewpoints abounded in the continuing interagency deliberations. State and the Office of the Special Representative for Trade Negotiations shared a preference for a very liberal trade-oriented bill with a maximum of negotiating authority. The Treasury and Commerce departments were anxious to protect and promote the balance of payments and the business sector, respectively. The Agriculture Department wanted to rectify what was presumed to be an insufficient agricultural liberalization package produced in the Kennedy Round. All of these viewpoints were valid inputs in considering many difficult questions. When an immediate consensus was not forthcoming on a relatively minor issue, the Trade Legislative Committee's chairman, Deane Hinton, deputy executive director of the CIEP, would make a ruling, in effect on behalf of the president. Substantive disagreements and appeals immediately would be sent up to the CIEP's Executive Committee for a decision. If no consensus developed there, the president's economic chief, Shultz, personally would make the final decision or request a presidential decision. In the end, the proposed statute elicited broad support in the administration.

A second example of the multiple advocacy model involved an issue of a much more narrow scope, but which offered nonetheless a classic representation of an international economic policy dilemma: economic interests, political virtue, and the national interest were tinged with soft nuances, not clear truths. President Carter in 1978 ordered the drafting of a formal policy statement on the export of hazardous substances whose use had been banned for safety or environmental reasons within the United States, but whose use was legal overseas.

The two and one-half year effort and five written drafts that preceded the finalization of this policy statement reflected the inherent difficulty of achieving consensus among the more than 22 bureaucratic entities that constituted the task

force assembled to draft the document. Eleven cabinet departments were regularly represented (only the Department of Housing and Urban Development and the Department of Education were absent). Other participants included the Consumer Product Safety Commission, the Environmental Protection Agency, the Export-Import Bank, the Agency for International Development, the Office of Management and Budget, the U.S. Special Trade Representative, the Regulatory Council, the Overseas Private Investment Corporation, and the Nuclear Regulatory Commission. Co-chairing the task force was a member of the president's Council on Environmental Equality and the president's consumer affairs adviser. At various times, the Office of Domestic Policy, the Council of Economic Advisers, and the Office of Science and Technology (all in the Executive Office of the President) also participated in the deliberations. Six sets of public hearings were held between the interagency task force and representatives of interested industries and consumer groups. Task force members periodically testified to congressional hearings that were independently considering revisions in various statutes affecting exports of the various hazardous substances (drugs, pesticides, nuclear materials, etc.).

Substantively, the debate revolved around the trade-off between, first, the unilateral application of U.S. standards and statutes externally to governments that did not agree with or accept them, and second, the concern about the potential harming of human beings and the environment in other countries. While no agency advocated an active effort to export the products deemed the most hazardous, there was disagreement over the need to further tighten the existing sets of export restraints and regulations. The compromise reached by the task force established a dual export control system: a few extremely hazardous items would be withheld outright from export, while other designated items could be exported if full disclosures about potential dangers were made before shipment to the would-be customer in the importing country.

At the height of its influence under Robert Rubin, the Clinton administration's National Economic Council often replicated the multiple advocacy model (see Chapter 4).

Single Agency Domination

Shared jurisdiction among bureaucratic entities is the predominant, but not universal, feature of international economic policymaking. When specialized expertise is involved, it may be that only one department or agency matters. The most frequent and important example of single agency control is the Treasury Department's dominance of U.S. international monetary and financial policies. The latter encompasses balance of payments problems, the dollar's exchange rate, financial rescues of emerging markets (Asia, Latin America, Russia, South Africa, and so on), and the International Monetary Fund's (IMF) guidelines on lending. Since the Reagan administration terminated the International Monetary Group, no formal interagency coordinating mechanism has existed in this policy sector. In most cases, Treasury decides when and how to "reach out" to other agencies on issues in the international financial sector.

Outside of Treasury, the State Department is the only cabinet department having significant staff expertise in international monetary and financial relations. The Federal Reserve System, which formally is independent of the executive branch, is unique in sharing with Treasury, through the Federal Reserve Bank of New York, operational responsibilities in exchange rate policy.

The Treasury position can be implemented with little or no outside approval for anything below momentous international monetary policy issues (like the dollar devaluations in 1971 and 1973). In November 1975, a number of technical decisions involving exchange-rate flexibility were relegated to the finance ministries of France and the United States. With only a few points preventing final agreement on a monetary reform package, the finance ministers of the other countries participating in that year's economic summit charged the financial officials of those two countries (who usually have the most divergent opinions on international monetary issues) to reconcile the few remaining differences. The feeling was that whatever final language was agreed upon by the two delegations, it would be one with which all of them could live. The finance ministers of the five largest industrial economies were so much in command of the monetary reform exercise that they were in a position to select a two-nation subcommittee to reach a final understanding affecting the entire world.

The combination of strong Treasury secretaries and recurring financial crises in the so-called emerging markets has allowed the department to dominate many important contemporary decisions. It was Treasury that virtually monopolized U.S. responses to ameliorate the Latin American debt crisis in the 1980s and the Mexican peso crisis in the mid-1990s. Concerns about Japan's weak economy and increasingly fragile banking system had grown so serious by 1998 that the Treasury Department had informally suspended three decades of trade-based bilateral economic relations. It replaced them with the administration's urgent campaign to induce Japan to implement stimulative domestic economic policies and address its banking crisis.

Other highly specialized economic issues handled by a single agency with minimal interagency clearance include bilateral double taxation treaties negotiated by the Treasury Department and routine General Agreement on Tariffs and Trade (GATT) business attended to by USTR.

The Personality Factor

Strong personalities backed by powerful political connections can short-circuit established organizational charts. When the cult of personality prevails, another decision-making model takes over. In the aftermath of the abruptly implemented New Economic Policy of August 1971, the fixed exchange-rate system temporarily collapsed, replaced by the uncertainties of floating exchange rates moving in response to supply and demand in the foreign exchange market. Investors

around the world, traumatized by Richard Nixon's dramatic policy shift, began massively selling dollars. The resulting exchange rate gyrations were highly unsettling to the top financial authorities of all industrialized countries—except in the United States.

The late John Connally, who was then secretary of the treasury, personally dominated U.S. international economic policy during the last quarter of 1971 as the result of his extraordinary relationship with the president and his hard-driving personality. His goal was simple: a reduction in the large and growing U.S. balance of payments deficit. His strategy was to press hard on other industrial countries to substantially revalue their currencies upward and to reduce their barriers to U.S. exports, all the while refusing to change any U.S. policies. He cared little about ruffling foreign feathers or about the intricacies of the international monetary system. The United States was relatively insulated from international monetary chaos, and Connally was playing his strong hand for all it was worth.

Had the State Department been able to exert strong leadership and influence at this time, a classic confrontation of bureaucratic politics would have developed. An economic hard-line was causing strains in U.S. relations with its most important allies. The timing was particularly inopportune for creating disarray in the Atlantic alliance, since presidential summit meetings with China and the Soviet Union loomed on the horizon.

An informal partnership to alter U.S. policy gradually developed between Henry Kissinger, in his role as the president's national security adviser, and Arthur Burns, chairman of the independent Federal Reserve Board. Peter Peterson, head of the CIEP, and Robert Hormats, Kissinger's assistant for economic affairs, reportedly played supportive roles by raising questions within the White House, noting that the U.S. demands on the Europeans and Japanese were not attainable in full and were damaging to larger U.S. foreign policy objectives. The immediate problem was tactical: the sheer force of Secretary Connally's personality and his close relationship with the president suggested the folly of a frontal attack. The opposition therefore opted for a quiet end run in the form of a low-key conversation with the president suggesting it was time to rein in Connally.

Differences in the priorities and values of two successive treasury secretaries, Donald Regan and James Baker, provided the pivotal factor fomenting a fundamental shift in U.S. exchange rate and trade policies in 1985. The role of personality and the nature of these differences are examined in the case study that comprises Chapter 10.

The unassailable clout of Treasury Secretary Robert Rubin in formulating the U.S. response to the financial crises in the emerging markets was buttressed by wide-scale perceptions of his mastery of the operating principles and psychology of financial markets. By virtue of his successful stint on Wall Street, his brilliant advice to President Clinton that reducing the federal budget deficit would reduce interest rates and significantly increase U.S. economic growth, and consistently favorable media coverage, no one in the administration publicly challenged his financial assessments or policy strategies.

International Financial Judgments

This model existed in obscurity until the 1980s. A subset of single agency domination in decision-making, the financial judgment model is mostly associated with Treasury Department efforts to define the U.S. national interest in international monetary and financial matters. The latter tend to be highly arcane economic questions on the surface but political in nature below the surface. In the late 1960s, Treasury represented the U.S. government in multilateral negotiations that eventually agreed on the properties of a new international reserve asset called Special Drawing Rights. With virtually no outside scrutiny, the department formulated and successfully pursued a strategy to ensure that the creation of this reserve unit did not damage the dollar's role as an international reserve asset. U.S. policies responding to the Latin American debt crisis of the 1980s were mostly formulated in accordance with this model. What resulted was a series of U.S. government financial plans, mostly Treasury-inspired, to ease the debt burdens of debtor countries without imposing unacceptable financial damage on their creditors—commercial banks, most of which were U.S.-based.

The international financial judgment model became much more visible in the 1990s as Treasury officials were required to hurriedly devise strategies to contain multiple outbreaks of a new kind of international financial crisis. The genesis of these crises was the relatively recent phenomenon of massive flows of private capital (bank loans and equity investments) moving quickly into and then just as quickly out of the so-called emerging markets. Senior Treasury officials had little in the way of precedents or unambiguous economic theory to guide their responses to the Mexican peso crisis of 1994–1995 and the Asian financial crisis that erupted in 1997. Their responses can be categorized as educated judgments shaped by an economic philosophy (often referred to as the ''Washington Consensus'') based on the twin beliefs of reliance on market forces and the need for financial discipline.

Custom designing rescue packages to cope with these unprecedented, quick-to-erupt financial crises has been an exercise in making difficult choices among ambiguous options. The ultimate question is how best to stabilize Thailand, South Korea, Russia, Brazil, and other emerging market countries experiencing or facing massive capital outflows, collapsing exchange rates, and chaotic financial markets. Few would assert that there is an unequivocal argument for choosing just one of three broad strategies available: (1) limited aid conditional on painful internal ''reforms'' being implemented to restore investor confidence; (2) extensive and unconditional aid designed to restore economic growth and alleviate human suffering; or (3) the ''tough love'' option. The latter entails refusal to extend financial assistance in order to provide a bitter, expensive lesson to these countries and their creditors that domestic mistakes in economic policies and business practices can be prohibitively expensive and should not be repeated.

Decisions have been made mostly but not totally in-house. The Board of Governors of the Federal Reserve System is closely plugged into the international banking system and must be consulted on how the major commercial banks are reacting to the problems faced by their foreign borrowers. Because many of the emerging market countries facing economic crises are strategically important to the United States, Treasury officials apprise the National Security Council of policy intentions.[12] Furthermore, before endorsing programs of internal reforms, senior Treasury officials consult foreign political leaders to ascertain which externally imposed demands would and would not be politically palatable in the affected countries.

The desire to reduce the likelihood of unexpected and explosive financial crises in the future created a new, highly esoteric multilateral exercise to explore ways to strengthen the ''architecture'' of the international financial system. Treasury Secretary Robert Rubin, Deputy Secretary Lawrence Summers, and a handful of senior aides—in an atmosphere more closely resembling a post-doctoral seminar in international political-economy than a consensus-seeking government forum—produced U.S. proposals on such abstractions as increased transparency of international financial transactions, improved regulation of commercial banks, and more specific standards for IMF rescue packages.

Righting Foreign Wrongs to the U.S. Private Sector

Academic models of trade policymaking traditionally focus on private sector efforts to induce governments to impose protective barriers against imports. A quite different form of lobbying effort has figured prominently in trade policy demands from U.S. industry since the 1980s. The private sector has become the major conduit for alerting the U.S. government to foreign practices that have severely diminished their overseas sales. Once ascertaining that these complaints are legitimate, U.S. trade officials have acted on the notion that they have an obligation to defend domestic producers from injurious foreign practices. The U.S. government's response in these cases is not based simply on a desire to placate interest groups or to protect an international regime, and it has not required compromises between warring bureaucracies. This model explains why the U.S. government successfully made the non-negotiable demand that the Uruguay Round include two first-of-their-kind multilateral trade agreements. One dealt with protection of intellectual property rights. Overwhelming evidence existed that U.S. companies were losing tens of billions of dollars annually in export sales because of violations of their patents, trademarks, and so on. The second negotiation demanded by the United States produced an agreement that established the first multilateral guidelines for reducing international barriers to trade in services, the fastest-growing sector of the American economy.

This model also explains why the U.S. government demanded that European countries reduce the official subsidies being given to Airbus to help it reduce the development and production costs of its aircraft.

SPECIAL CASES IN POLICYMAKING

The eight models cited above do not represent a definitive list of the international economic policymaking techniques utilized in every significant decision. This section examines a small sample of the many additional policymaking exercises that were either an amalgam of several of these models or were sufficiently unique that they did not fit the mold of any of the offered paradigms.

The "non-decision" by the Reagan administration in 1981 to indirectly coax the Japanese into unilaterally restraining automobile exports to the U.S. market exemplifies how a difficult policy decision can pass through a number of distinct phases, each of which exhibits the characteristics of a different policymaking model. Three models—bureaucratic politics, inter-branch politics, and presidential fiat—were in evidence at various times. The complexity of the issue stemmed from the inherent difficulties of constructing an objective cost-benefit analysis for restrictions being imposed in the early 1980s on imports of Japanese-made cars. The logical arguments that could be raised both for and against import restraints created a tailor-made situation for encouraging and sustaining subjective bureaucratic differences in priorities, perspectives, and remedies.

On the one hand, a key domestic industry was, at that time, "on the economic ropes." The U.S. auto industry was suffering from unprecedented corporate losses (about $4.2 billion in 1980), high unemployment (more than 200,000 automobile workers and a multiple of that number in automotive supplier industries had been laid off by early 1981), and the loss of more than 25 percent of the U.S. market to imports. The industry faced an estimated $80 billion price tag for retooling and new capital equipment to make the smaller cars that Americans wanted to buy. On the other hand, allowing consumers unfettered access to imports encourages competition and minimizes price increases. The stampede by American consumers to smaller cars was the direct result of the second oil shock of 1979–1980 that had sent gasoline prices soaring. It therefore made sense to maximize the use of energy-efficient cars to minimize gasoline consumption. The shortage of small, gas-efficient automobiles produced within the United States raised serious questions as to the efficacy of imposing import controls to assist an industry unprepared to deal with a major shift in consumer demand. For this very reason, the International Trade Commission in 1980 had rejected a request for import relief filed by Ford Motor Company under the escape clause statute. The commission concluded that energy-related, non-import factors were the most important source of the industry's problems. This decision deprived the administration of clear legal authority to unilaterally impose import barriers.

Press reports of the cabinet meeting held by the newly installed Reagan administration on March 3, 1981 (and confirmed by conversations with government officials) noted a predictable bureaucratic politics-style split into protectionist and liberal trade camps. The Transportation, Commerce, and Labor departments, with an eye to assisting their industrial and worker constituents, favored imposition of import restrictions to hold Japanese imports below their 1980 levels. Speaking on behalf of liberal trade and against import barriers were Secretary of State Alexander Haig, Treasury Secretary Donald Regan, Director of the Office of Management and Budget David Stockman, and Murray Weidenbaum, chairman of the Council of Economic Advisers. A "pragmatic" middle ground was staked out by the new U.S. trade representative, William Brock. Continuing the tradition cited above of the trade representative being sympathetic to domestic needs, Brock was quoted as telling reporters that restrictions of "a limited application or duration" against Japanese cars might be "politically acceptable."[13]

Congress played an important indirect part in the decision-making process by performing a classic version of its role of volatile "bad cop" as counterpoint to the enlightened reason emanating from the administration's "good cop" posture. Congress began drafting automobile quota legislation that would have severely cut back imports from Japan. The signal emanating from Capitol Hill was clear to veteran observers: the domestic automobile industry needed at least a modest breather from import competition. The administration and the Japanese government therefore would be well-advised to reach a meeting of the minds if they wanted to remain in control of the situation.

The presidential fiat model appeared when Mr. Reagan personally had to make the final decision on how to proceed, partly because of the big money stakes of the issue and partly because of the inability of his cabinet to reach consensus on a course of action. It was he who approved a strategy of unusual subtlety that was a middle ground between desire to help the domestic automakers and desire to retain his public image as free market/free trade advocate. His instructions were that the administration would make no overt demand on the Japanese that they restrict auto exports. Instead, it would provide a friendly recitation to the Japanese of the potentially serious costs associated with unabated increases in U.S. imports of Japanese automobiles: unilateral U.S. legislation, the bankruptcy of one or more U.S. automakers, mounting resentment of Japan by American public opinion, and so forth.

The final phase of U.S. government strategy was influenced by some unusual signals emanating from Tokyo.[14] In March 1981, the Japanese government was dropping increasingly clear hints that it would respond to public arm-twisting by the Reagan administration by negotiating an orderly marketing agreement. The receptiveness of the Japanese government to an orderly marketing agreement most likely was the manifestation of a Japanese version of bureaucratic revenge. Many years previously, the Ministry of International Trade and Industry (MITI) had been rebuffed in its efforts to restructure Japan's automobile industry in the form of consolidation into a few large firms. A voluntary export

restraint agreement would necessitate the imposition of some form of administrative guidance over the industry by MITI, providing, in effect, the long-desired
leverage over the independent-minded automobile companies. The Japanese
government eventually announced its intent to unilaterally impose a ceiling on
auto exports after being unable to convince the USTR, William Brock, to give
them a formal request and a specific export quota number. Acting on instructions, Brock remained inscrutable. He refused to provide anything more than
informal advice on what he thought would be a cutback of their exports adequate
to prevent Congress from enacting severely restrictive auto quota legislation.

Actions related to the development of one narrow aspect of international energy policy, the imposition of oil import barriers, also reflected three different
decision-making models. In March 1978, the Carter administration initiated an
investigation under Section 232 of the Trade Expansion Act of 1962 to determine whether rising levels of oil imports threatened to "impair the national
security." The investigation elicited submissions from the departments of Treasury, State, Energy, Defense, and Commerce, as well as the Council of Economic
Advisers. Shared perceptions produced the identical conclusion that the growing
U.S. dependence on imported oil was potentially damaging to U.S. national
security interests and that greater reliance on domestic sources was advisable.
Action was taken by presidential fiat. On April 2, 1980, President Carter announced the impending imposition of a gasoline conservation fee of $4.62 per
barrel on imports of crude oil.[15]

The import duty was short-lived. It was killed by domestic political pressure
against gasoline price increases and skepticism by some congressional members
about the legality of administrative action, taken under a trade statute, that had
major federal revenue-raising implications (estimated annual revenues from the
oil import duty were put at $10 billion). The Congress thereupon invoked the
inter-branch politics model by overwhelmingly approving a bill that withdrew
presidential authority to impose the duty. The overwhelming override by Congress of the subsequent presidential veto of this bill was the first time in more
than 25 years that a Democratic Congress had turned back a Democratic president's veto.

Efforts to implement a free trade agreement with Mexico involved a policymaking process that, at various times in its long history, can be viewed as
incorporating four decision-making models. A telephone conversation between
presidents George Bush and Carlos Salinas de Gortari in the early months of
1990 resulted in the unusual situation of a presidential imprimatur on a bilateral
free trade agreement. President Bush ordered U.S. trade officials to look into
the suitability of a free trade agreement with Mexico. After closely studying the
improving economic scene there, a U.S. interagency working group determined
that a bilateral free trade agreement was a sound economic idea. An important
supporting argument was the assumption that the inherent discipline of free trade
with the United States would serve to make permanent the market reforms and
economic progress then emerging in Mexico.[16]

A face-to-face meeting between the two presidents in June 1990 resulted in a presidential fiat to commence informal consultations. The latter subsequently expanded to include Canada, so that the issue at hand became the creation of a North American Free Trade Agreement (NAFTA) among the three countries. The shared perceptions model explains the subsequent consensus among executive branch agencies that concluding a free trade agreement with Mexico would be advantageous on balance to the U.S. economy. This consensus no doubt was encouraged by perceptions that President Bush personally favored it, mainly for foreign policy reasons.

At the onset of formal negotiations, the sheer volume of technical issues on the agenda necessitated the use of a broad participatory process approximating the multiple advocacy model. The office of the USTR, acting in the dual roles of coordinator and active participant, assembled all relevant agencies into 20 specialized negotiating groups organized around six broad trade and investment issue areas. The groups were chaired by different agencies selected mostly on the basis of jurisdiction and expertise.

Negotiations with Mexico were the easy part in comparison with the policymaking follow-up at home, namely, the need to gain public and congressional approval of the agreement. A long, difficult procedural road could have been predicted: conflicting interests needed to be sorted out before such approval could materialize. There would be winners and losers. Labor intensive industries and relatively unskilled workers were most at risk from increased imports from Mexico. Consumers would benefit, and some industries and workers would be helped by increased export shipments to a less protectionist, more market-oriented Mexico. The introduction of environmental and labor standards issues as new variables in the trade policymaking equation further complicated the decision-making process.[17] A number of interested groups saw a clear and present danger of environmental damage from accelerated industrialization in Mexico, a country with a reputation of relatively lax enforcement of its environmental protection laws. Other groups questioned the logic of free trade with a much less developed country having significantly weaker worker protection laws and lower wages. The Bush administration and most members of Congress from states in the southwestern United States (the region with the greatest potential for increased exports to Mexico under free trade) quickly embraced the terms of the agreement eventually negotiated. Elsewhere, skepticism and outright opposition were much in evidence.

The last phase of the NAFTA policymaking process evolved into the interbranch model of decision-making. The unprecedented outburst of opposition to the proposed free trade agreement with Mexico came from businesses and union groups who felt they would be adversely affected by the proposed free flow of trade as well as from many environmental groups who envisioned intensified industrial pollution on the Mexican side of the border. Together, they created a clear and present danger that the House might refuse to pass implementing legislation (a bare majority of senators were in favor).[18] As part of a vigorous marketing effort to attract the necessary votes, the USTR and the interagency negotiating groups held ''nearly 1,000'' briefings and consultations with Congress, private sector advisers, trade associations, business groups, and the public, with an average of three briefings per work day after the formal talks were launched.[19] In the final analysis, passage of NAFTA was assured only after an outpouring of last-minute promises by the Clinton White House to wavering House members, ranging from increased federal spending in their districts to special trade treatment for goods important to their constituents, as well as last-minute special understandings with Mexico concerning sensitive products.[20]

Beyond the several models and combinations thereof just reviewed, some decisions are—and probably always will be—made through an idiosyncratic process where logic and consistency are in short supply.

Export policymaking has been the most fertile field for demonstrating the absence of coherent decision-making models. The resulting organizational foibles are ultimately the outgrowth of the long-standing inability of the U.S. government to develop consistent policies on the two major segments of export policy—controls and promotion. This ambivalence in turn has been produced by national security and economic policy factors peculiar to the United States: the primacy of global foreign policy pursuits and the unique lack of need to earn foreign exchange from exporting to pay for imports. Serious disagreements over the relative priorities between foreign policy and commercial priorities lead to ongoing disputes over the proper extent of trade sanctions being imposed on countries engaged in objectionable behavior and over the appropriate limits on exporting dual-use technology to potentially unfriendly foreign countries. In addition, disagreements rage over how high a priority export promotion should be for the U.S. government. The bottom-line result is a system of transitory, overlapping, and imprecise organization with an ad hoc mentality, unable to integrate individual situations into a coherent whole.

The idea of asking the chief executive officers of the ''Big Three'' American automobile companies to accompany President Bush to Japan in January 1992 was especially ill-conceived. The decision to invite members of the business community on the trip originated with White House staff who wanted to give a no-nonsense U.S. business promotion veneer to this presidential visit. Confusion then set in on the issue of who would compile the invitation list. Responsibility eventually was given to the Commerce Department. Because it was the lead agency in the preexisting program to increase American exports of automobiles and auto parts to Japan, Commerce thought it a good idea to invite a large entourage from the automobile industry. Little or no thought was given to the notion that the heads of the automobile Big Three at that time epitomized what many Japanese most disliked about American industry—fabulously well-paid executives who headed money-losing, internationally non-competitive companies. Furthermore, no one in the administration thought to seek consensus among business and government officials on three critical questions: what was the ultimate purpose of the visit, what should the Japanese reasonably be expected to concede, and what kind of follow-up mechanism would be implemented to monitor progress?[21]

Two classic examples of the U.S. system's failure to foresee and effectively respond to unexpected contingencies involved agricultural export situations in the 1970s. The first was the federal government's being caught flat-footed by massive Soviet grain purchases in 1972. The belated realization of the magnitude of Soviet buying increased domestic prices because of resulting reserve shortages, and it wasted perhaps $300 million dollars in unnecessary wheat subsidies. In its haste to unload what were then major grain surpluses, the Agriculture Department ignored reports by its own attache in Moscow concerning the major shortfall in the Soviet harvest. Because it did not collect and collate data on the magnitude of the sales contracts handled by private grain exporters, the U.S. government had no way of foreseeing the depletion of reserves or the strain on transportation facilities. Nor was there any mechanism to terminate wheat subsidies once it became apparent that only the United States had significant supplies of exportable wheat and therefore would effectively establish the world price. "At virtually every step . . . the grain sales were ineptly managed." Agriculture Department policy was "inadequate, short-sighted and dictated by . . . philosophies ill-equipped for a changing world" concluded the Senate's Permanent Subcommittee on Investigations.[22]

Interagency coordination broke down in the case of the ill-advised soybean export embargo of 1973. The decision began with the convergence of a well-below-average domestic soybean crop, growing foreign demand, and the continued use of price controls by the Nixon administration. As increased numbers of soybean dealers and shippers came to believe that export controls on soybeans (to restrain domestic prices) were imminent, they sought to protect themselves by signing export contracts far above their immediate needs. It was a self-fulfilling prophecy. An Interagency Task Force on Food Export Controls, chaired by the CIEP, looked at the export contract filings and assumed that the domestic supply of soybeans was about to be exhausted. It recommended to the White House that export controls be adopted, and they were. Unfortunately, the interagency group lacked the expertise to recognize, and adjust for, the immense padding of "phantom" export contracts written as a hedge against later controls. The unfortunate long-term legacy of the brief embargo was an undermining of the U.S. government's long-standing assertion that American farmers were such dependable suppliers of agricultural commodities to world markets that foreign restraints on agricultural imports were unjustified.

U.S. East-West trade policymaking after the peak of the cold war was especially devoid of consistency. During the 1970s and 1980s, most of the decision-making models were in evidence at various times. The General Accounting Office (GAO) published a stinging critique of U.S. East-West trade policy in a 1976 report that found "no consistent pattern of study, analysis, and decision-making." The interagency process "has not insured that agency positions are clearly defined and properly analyzed before decisions or implementation plans are made'' and ''there has been no guarantee that true interagency consultations will occur'' once an agency has assumed the lead in particular negotiations, argued the GAO. An inadequate pursuit of the ''balance of benefits'' in East-West trade was said to be the result of too many agencies having limited horizons and limited authority.[23]

In April 1999 President Clinton refused to culminate his face-to-face talks in the Oval Office with China's Premier Zhu Rongji with an agreement to support that country's application to join the World Trade Organization (WTO). His unexpected negativism illustrated both a combination of identifiable international economic policy models of decision-making and the potentially critical presence of linkage to other policy concerns. In a narrow sense, this was a clear example of the presidential fiat model, inasmuch as Mr. Clinton made the final decision to overrule the advice of his USTR, secretary of state, and national security adviser to accept the terms agreed to by Premier Zhu. In a broader context, the complex reasoning behind his decision—as well as the extraordinary events that shortly followed—made this decision more than a simple illustration of presidential engagement. According to press reports, Mr. Clinton made additional demands for trade concessions that his guest rejected. To the president and his personal advisers, the time was not propitious for accepting anything less than a ''super-deal'' in which China went beyond the already sizable list of market-opening measures that it had agreed to. Premier Zhu left town empty-handed.

Most Republican members of Congress at the time were vehemently attacking the administration for allegedly having been too lax in protecting highly sensitive nuclear weapons secrets from Chinese spies and too avaricious to detect illegal campaign contributions from persons acting as middlemen for the government of China. Liberal Democrats were lukewarm to a deal because of fears by unions that, absent agreement to prevent import surges, WTO membership would set the stage for a massive increase in shipments of Chinese-made textiles and apparel. The inter-branch model further entered into the equation by virtue of the fact that following China's accession to the WTO, Congress eventually would be called on to pass legislation conferring permanent MFN (now termed ''normal trade relations'') status on that country. This change would deprive hard-liners on China of their annual opportunity to recommend termination of temporary MFN status because of human rights violations, military threats against Taiwan, and so on.

This decision was unusually short-lived. On a nearly overnight basis, a second set of pressures was orchestrated that caused President Clinton to reverse course. The political counterforce was created by a masterful public relations triumph fashioned by Mr. Zhu in his post–Washington, D.C. tour of the United States. In a series of speeches, he forcefully outlined to high-powered American business audiences how they stood to reap large economic benefits from the concessions he had offered the administration. Zhu then warned that the promised market liberalization measures were subject to being withdrawn if no agreement was forthcoming. His exhortations provoked a torrent of criticism from the U.S.

business community and the media denouncing the president's timidity in rejecting a WTO deal. The breadth and harshness of this spontaneous outcry apparently was sufficient to put congressional hardliners on the defensive and to goad the president into hurriedly assuming a more conciliatory posture.[24] After a telephone conversation with the Chinese premier, Mr. Clinton announced his support in principle for the idea of China's joining the WTO before the end of the year.

The administration of official export promotion programs was so decentralized and the overall results so disappointing that reports from the GAO eventually convinced the Congress to try forcing a rationalization of the process through passage of the Export Enhancement Act of 1992. Prior to 1992, meaningful coordination in export promotion did not exist, and the various export financing programs were funded arbitrarily, not on the basis of a government-wide strategy or set of priorities. To quote the GAO:

Much more might be achieved with existing resources if they were allocated according to national priorities and were administered by a more rational agency structure. This is not now being achieved, with the export promotion effort spread amongst separate programs with separate budgets in separate agencies that are not integrated under any unifying strategy or rationale.[25]

The most striking demonstration that some rationalization did follow from the congressional push for a unified export promotion strategy is the large reduction in the Agriculture Department's (USDA) outlays for export loans and general promotion purposes. As late as the early 1990s, its annual expenditures of $2 billion-and-up dwarfed those by the Commerce Department ($195 million). This situation made little economic sense given the facts that farm goods account for less than 10 percent of total U.S. exports and that much of USDA's expenditures were made in support of a few large agribusiness corporations. The agricultural community's powerful friends in Congress were not predisposed to voluntarily slashing these appropriations, however. The Agriculture Department's outlays for export loans and loan guarantees in fiscal 1991 were nearly as much as those of the Export-Import Bank on loans for advanced industrial products, a sector accounting for far more exports and employment.[26]

Sometimes the effects of policy linkages can push aside normal decision-making procedures. In these cases, the pursuit of international economic excellence takes a back seat to another, presumably larger objective. The reasoning behind the Caribbean Basin Initiative and the U.S.-Israeli free trade area agreement lay overwhelmingly with foreign policy objectives, not compelling economic logic or domestic political pressures.

Another version of the linkage concept emerged during a senior-level discussion in the Carter administration about the sugar subsidy program. The then–Secretary of the Treasury Michael Blumenthal had made a presentation that for anti-inflation reasons recommended a much lower sugar support price than that which was being demanded by interested congressional leaders. Since import quotas are linked to the support price, Robert Strauss, at that time the U.S. trade representative, had an important stake in these deliberations. When Blumenthal was finished, Strauss rebutted his colleague's proposal with the opinion that an excellent idea to reform sugar program had just been proposed. However, he declared, ''we are running a government, not a sugar program.'' He argued that the administration would not be able to get approval for major legislation from the Senate Foreign Affairs Committee (then chaired by Senator Frank Church of Idaho) or the Senate Finance Committee (then chaired by Senator Russell Long of Louisiana) if the price support level was not increased sufficiently to appease representatives from those sugar producing states.[27]

Finally, on rare occasions the policymaking process can spontaneously mutate into extraordinary forms, especially when high stakes and high frustration cause events to career out of control. The mutation syndrome was vividly demonstrated during the bitter three-year-long struggle to convince the Japanese to ''voluntarily'' restrain their textile exports. The combination of an unrelenting demand by President Nixon and an equally unrelenting refusal by the Japanese to comply unleashed an occasionally bizarre chain of events. Negotiations that dragged on between 1969 and 1971 were pursued through front channels, secret back channels, and informal discussions. Interspersed with official negotiations among a long series of officially designated negotiators were back channel talks by a secret Japanese envoy with the president's national security affairs adviser, Henry Kissinger; unofficial talks between the Japanese and Congressman Wilbur Mills (then chairman of the Ways and Means Committee); and even more unofficial talks between Japanese authorities and business leader and presidential friend Donald Kendall. Noticeably absent among the plethora of active U.S. government officials were the bureaucracies most experienced in trade negotiations and foreign relations, the USTR and the State Department, respectively.

There is no reason to assume that all decision-making models already have appeared and that no additional ones will emerge in the future. Any new international economic issue possessing unique characteristics, such as the competitiveness–industrial policy debate, has the potential to forge a new model of decision-making.

NOTES

1. Peter Passell, ''A New Project Will Measure the Cost and Effect of Regulation,'' *New York Times*, 30 July, 1998, p. D2.

2. ''U.S. Takes First Hesitant Steps toward Shift in Commodities Policy,'' *National Journal*, 21 June 1975, p. 915.

3. Ibid., pp. 915–916.

4. U.S. Treasury Department press release dated 15 January 1976.

5. Leslie Gelb and Anthony Lake, ''Washington Dateline: Less Food, More Politics,'' *Foreign Policy* (Winter 1974–1975): 183–184.

6. Not-for-attribution interviews with former U.S. trade policy officials, 1978–1979.

7. Ibid.

8. *Washington Post*, 5 December 1992, p. A3; and *Wall Street Journal*, 2 December 1992, p. B7.

9. "Dollar Recovers as Volcker Says It 'Fell Enough'," *Wall Street Journal*, 20 February 1986, p. 3.

10. *Washington Post*, 27 February 1986, p. El.

11. *Congressional Record*, 2 March 1992, pp. H866–867.

12. Not for attribution interview with U.S. Treasury Department official, January 1999.

13. As quoted in the *Wall Street Journal*, 5 March 1981, p. 4. Brock added that in the pursuit of freer trade, "there are times when you have to take some steps backwards to go forward."

14. In preparation for the anticipated talks with the Reagan administration on the auto issue, the Japanese government succumbed to a rare bout of publicly displayed bureaucratic politics. A scramble to lead the Japanese negotiating team that would discuss an orderly marketing agreement developed between MITI and Japan's Special Representative for External Economic Affairs, Saburo Okita, who worked closely with the Ministry of Foreign Affairs. The Japanese prime minister reportedly settled this turf battle by securing a consensus that Okita would handle the overall bilateral negotiations, but the vice minister of MITI would accompany Okita during the talks and the MITI minister would have responsibility for the "final decision." See, for example, "Japan's Infighting over Auto Export Policy," *Business Week*, 23 March 1981, p. 57.

15. The figure selected was designed to raise prices of imported gasoline by ten cents a gallon.

16. Not-for-attribution interview with USTR official, March 1993.

17. The complexity of the environmental issue required a large number of agency participants. They consisted of the USTR; the Environmental Protection Agency; the departments of State, Treasury, Justice, Commerce, Transportation, Agriculture, Interior, and Labor; the Food and Drug Administration; the Fish and Wildlife Service; the Council of Economic Advisers; and the Office of Management and Budget.

18 This situation forced the Clinton administration and the Mexican government to quickly negotiate so-called side agreements on protection of workers' rights and the environment.

19. "Report of the Administration on the North American Free Trade Agreement and Actions Taken in Fulfillment of the May 1, 1991 Commitments," 18 September 1992, p. 65.

20. See, for example, "Oink Oink," *Nation*, 20 December 1993, p. 752; and Sharyn O'Halloran, *Politics, Process, and American Trade Policy* (Ann Arbor: University of Michigan Press, 1994), pp. 170–171.

21. Not-for-attribution interviews with trade association executives, January and February 1993.

22. U.S. Senate, Committee on Government Operations, *Russian Grain Transactions*, 93rd Congress, July 1974, pp. 55, 58.

23. General Accounting Office, "The Government's Role in East-West Trade— Problems and Issues," February 1976, pp. 4–5, 56–57.

24. See, for example, "How Push by China and U.S. Business Won over Clinton," *New York Times*, 15 April 1999, p. A1, and "A Magical Lobbying Tour," *Newsweek*, 26 April 1999, p. 47.

25. General Accounting Office, "Export Promotion—U.S. Programs Lack Coherence," congressional testimony of Allan Mendelowitz before the House Committee on Government Operations, 4 March 1992, p. 3.

26. Data source: U.S. General Accounting Office, "Export Promotion—Federal Approach Is Fragmented," congressional testimony of Allan I. Mendelowitz, 10 August 1992, p. 7. Agreements in the Uruguay Round to limit agricultural subsidies also were a factor in restraining the U.S. Department of Agriculture's export promotion activities.

27. Not-for-attribution interview with former U.S. trade policy official, January 1981.

Part IV

Congressional-Executive Relations: The Uneasy Partnership

9 The Inter-Branch Model of Decision-Making in Concept and Practice

> The question is not whether Congress or the president dominates decision-making; clearly, both branches of government play an integral role in trade policy formulation. The relevant question is how does Congress structure the delegation of authority to control policy without reverting to legislative [logrolling]?
>
> —Sharyn O'Halloran

> In recent years . . . the most effective trade actions of our government have emanated from the Congress and been embraced only reluctantly—frequently at the last minute—by an administration desperate for ideas. What passes for administration trade policy is actually a patchwork of congressional trade initiatives.
>
> —Former Senator Lloyd Bentsen

The extensive and intensive role of the Congress in the making of U.S. international economic policy means that a full understanding of how this policy is formulated and administered is not possible if only intra–executive branch decision-making models are used. The occasionally decisive role of Congress and the unique sharing of power between the U.S. executive and legislative branches have bestowed critical importance on what I call the inter-branch model of decision-making. The model encompasses two main concepts. The first is the divergent attitudes and objectives between the two branches that jointly shape U.S. international economic policymaking. The second element consists of the control mechanisms used by Congress either to delegate measured amounts of authority to the executive branch to conduct these policies or to block the implementation of policies desired by the administration.

THE INTER-BRANCH MODEL

A not-insignificant number of U.S. international economic policies—especially in foreign trade—have been created solely within the Congress. An even larger array of policies was formulated through protracted negotiations between the two branches acting as friendly rivals haggling over details.

An elevated form of bureaucratic politics is on display as the two branches weigh the priorities of international economic policies from different perspectives because they are subject to different pressures and harbor a different sense of mission. The result is dissimilar assessments of the optimal balance between pursuit of global priorities, on the one hand, and looking out for the home front (i.e., protecting the interests of domestic companies and workers), on the other hand. It is said on Capitol Hill that part of Congress's job is to remind the rest of the U.S. government for whom they are working. The executive branch is confident that it has an excellent sense of perspective and yearns for maximum discretion in policy formulation and administration. The Congress has long suspected the executive branch of harboring excessive interest in external policy priorities. It therefore sees the national interest as best served by assuring that the executive branch operates within international economic policy parameters established by congressional consensus. In sum, periodic tension between the branches is inevitable.

An empirical review of inter-branch relations reveals five distinctive patterns of interactive behavior, that is, variants of the model. The *first* involves directives unilaterally imposed by legislative fiat on the executive branch. A greater sense of independence and expanded professional staff since the 1960s have made it commonplace for senators and representatives to put themselves out in front of the executive branch by espousing new tactics and strategies in international economic relations. Although some of these initiatives have been designed to serve constituent needs and facilitate reelection, other displays of congressional leadership have been the byproduct of a genuine intellectual commitment to produce better policy.

The record has shown that administrations at various times may be favorably disposed, neutral, or opposed to congressionally ordered changes in U.S. international economic policy. Treasury officials were amenable to most of the reforms in the procedures of the International Monetary Fund (IMF)—more transparency, discouraging "bail-outs" of irresponsible behavior by charging relatively high interest rates for countries suffering balance of payments problems brought on by a sudden loss of market confidence, and so on—mandated by Congress in the 1998 bill appropriating the U.S. contribution to the agreed-upon increase in the IMF's currency holdings. Conversely, the Carter White House was angered by the somewhat humiliating 1980 legislation repealing his imposition of a special duty on imported petroleum, a presidential action severely disliked by most members even though it had national security overtones. The limitations imposed on the president's extension of nondiscriminatory (most-favored-nation) tariff treatment to communist bloc countries by the Jackson-Vanik amendment to the Trade Act of 1974 exemplifies Congress triumphant in its desire for a policy stance more demanding of foreign concessions than what was thought appropriate by the administration. In this case, administration acquiescence to a congressional initiative turned to regret when the Soviet Union later decided it would not comply with the terms of the amendment by providing assurances of eased barriers to emigration.

The debates in the late 1970s concerning the need to reorganize the executive branch's trade policymaking process originated in the Congress. Congress also took the leadership in pursuit of the so-called level playing field in trade relations. By creating and passing the "Super 301" provision in 1988, Congress compelled a reluctant Bush administration one year later to forcefully demand that "priority" foreign governments (Brazil, India, and Japan) remove or reduce designated import barriers. Pressures from Congress subsequently helped convince a reluctant Bush administration to relax its aversion to providing governmental assistance to enhance U.S. commercial competitiveness in the high-technology sector (see Chapter 11).

As discussed previously, Congress eventually lost patience with the haphazard performance of the government's dozens of export promotion programs. Successive administrations had been unconcerned about their lack of coordination and an integrating strategy and the fact that they presented the business community with a confusing labyrinth of bureaucratic offices. The Export Enhancement Act of 1992 directed the Commerce Department to set up consolidated export assistance centers and ordered the Trade Promotion Coordinating Committee to report annually to Congress on its progress in rationalizing export promotion strategy and its implementation.[1]

Congress has taken the lead in expressing dissatisfaction with foreign governments by passing economic sanctions legislation not asked for or wanted by the administration. In 1986 both houses independently passed legislation and then overrode a presidential veto in their determination to increase U.S. economic sanctions against South Africa to a level beyond what the Reagan administration said was acceptable. The Clinton administration in 1996 reluctantly signed two sanctions bills that had originated in Congress and that threatened to complicate relations with friendly countries. One, the so-called Helms-Burton bill, expanded existing sanctions against Cuba mainly by threatening retaliation against foreign companies using seized American property in that country. The second threatened sanctions against Western companies making substantial investments in the energy sectors of Libya or Iran.

The Nixon administration neither encouraged nor discouraged Congress to act on its conviction that U.S. foreign aid was in need of a major overhaul. Members responded to mounting data that the aid program was doing little to generate economic development (because of the inadequacies of the "trickle-down" strategy emphasizing large, capital-intensive projects) by rewriting U.S. foreign aid legislation in 1973. The Agency for International Development (AID) was directed to concentrate on small projects to help the poorest segments of the population in the poorest countries.

Sometimes Congress has been out in front in generating new ideas that only later were accepted by the administration. The benefits of a floating exchange rate regime (as opposed to fixed rates) were being hailed by a subcommittee of the Joint Economic Committee for many years prior to the reluctant acceptance of them in 1973 by the U.S. Treasury Department. During the 1979–1980 period, the most articulate governmental analyses of the causes and nature of U.S.-Japanese trade problems, as well as the means to address them, came from the studies released by the U.S.-Japan Trade Task Force of the Subcommittee on Trade of the Ways and Means Committee.

The *second* variant of the inter-branch model involves a non-adversarial, cooperative effort by both branches to develop new statute-based policies. The drafting of major trade legislation in 1962, 1974, and 1979 exemplifies positive, give-and-take consensus formation. The process by which the Congress considered and then modified the Trade Reform Act, as originally submitted in 1973 by the Nixon administration, reflected harmonious congressional-executive working relations at their best. A close working relationship developed between the two congressional committees that wrote the statute and the three senior officials of what was then called the president's special representative for trade negotiations. These White House aides often were allowed to attend the markup sessions of the bill and provide further justification for the requested legislation. The 1988 omnibus trade bill does not qualify for the list of cooperative efforts because most of the bill was written by Congress and because of the administration's hostility towards many of the proposed provisions of a bill that wound its way through an unusually long (three-year) drafting process (see Chapter 10).

The *third* variant consists of actions undertaken by the executive branch in *anticipation* of possible congressional action. Congress does not necessarily have to physically pass legislation to influence policymaking. The introduction of a bill or a proposed joint resolution in the Congress is sometimes viewed as an early indicator of future legislative action. Even the perception of potential legislation-by-rancor can provide sufficient leverage to convince executive branch officials and foreign governments to cooperate with congressional activists in order to avoid provoking their wrath. From time to time, the administration feels it necessary to abandon its preferred course of action either to prevent undesired congressional action or to assure that a desired action is forthcoming.

More through effective role-playing than action, Congress has cultivated a tough-guy image in foreign trade matters. The image as champion of domestic interests persists despite Congress's unbroken restraint since 1930 in passing any outright protectionist legislation. Members have said absolutely nothing to try to dispel this exaggerated, but useful reputation as a fire-breathing, interest group–beholden, foreigner-baiting, trade issue–oversimplifying legislative body. When negotiating with trading partners, the executive branch on occasion deliberately cultivates the persona of an enlightened force for moderation and reason, ostensibly to tame the potentially explosive temper of an emotional Congress.

Threats by Congress to pass draconian legislation set the stage for the Washington version of the old Hollywood tandem of "good cop/bad cop." In the oft-repeated final act of this drama, foreign governments feel compelled to cut a deal with the good cop lest the tempestuous Congress unleash metaphorical violence, for example, a quota mandating a severe rollback of imports. Several of the "voluntary" export restraints negotiated with other countries and much of Japan's liberalization of its import barriers during the 1970s and 1980s can be traced to that country's sensing a seething Congress itching to legislate severe retaliatory measures.

The Congress savors its role as would-be protectionist because this is a stratagem that can simultaneously generate a modicum of relief for the import and export problems of its constituents without actually having to legislate unilateral protectionism or retaliation. As articulated by a friend who formerly worked on Capitol Hill, the "responsible way for Congress to act on trade is to act irresponsibly." The stronger the appearance that Congress is about to go legislatively berserk, the greater the likelihood that foreign governments will embrace the "wise counsel" of the executive branch.

It is important to distinguish between expressions of congressional moods and actual enactment of new laws. The former represents a desire, while only the latter is invocation of policy change (short of a successful presidential veto). If the desired response to the signal is achieved, the likelihood of legislation is diminished. As Robert Pastor has written:

A Legislator introduces a bill to send signals forcefully to different groups, governments, the executive branch or particular bureaus or departments. The purpose is to inform injured or adversely-affected groups that the Congress or a particular Legislator is listening and aware of their plaint; to signal to potentially countervailing groups the beginning of a debate on an issue which could affect them adversely; to indicate to a foreign government that the U.S. intends to pursue its interests more forcefully in international negotiations; and most importantly to signal to the executive branch that its administrative or negotiating behavior has either not been satisfactory or not been responsive to the law's intent.[2]

The existence of a large number of members of Congress—even a majority—speaking on behalf of a specific course of action or cosponsoring legislation may or may not result in a law being passed and sent to the president for signing. Delaying actions through parliamentary maneuver, the end of a congressional session, the rejection by one house of a bill approved by the other house, or a presidential veto can thwart even the most impressive legislative momentum. Nevertheless, none of these contingencies totally eliminates beforehand the chance of congressional action, and outsiders' strategies often are based on a disinclination to gamble that nothing will happen. The bottom line is frequent acceptance of the old axiom that discretion is the better part of valor.

A good example of the executive branch altering its policy preferences to prevent potential congressional action was demonstrated in March 1976 by the cabinet-level Trade Policy Committee (TPC). It needed to formulate the administration's response to the International Trade Commission (ITC) recommendation that, under the escape clause statute, import quotas be imposed for five years to relieve import-induced injury to the domestic specialty steel industry. The committee's decision to press for voluntary export restraint agreements was connected to its concerns about being countermanded by Congress if it chose to take the liberal trade option and refused to assist a politically influential industry. Although it would be overruled by the Supreme Court in 1983, Congress had given itself a legislative veto over a number of executive branch actions, including escape clause decisions.

Normal bureaucratic politics in the specialty steel case almost certainly would have seen a majority recommend against the imposition of import quotas, with the Commerce and Labor departments in the minority. In the first place, questionable economic analysis had been used by the ITC to ''prove'' import-induced injury to the specialty steel industry. Second, this action was occurring amid major trade liberalization talks in the Tokyo Round. Skepticism about the timing of restricting imports of specialty steel was overwhelmed by pragmatism. Ominous warnings were coming from Capitol Hill. Several members vowed that the legislative veto would be used for the first time to override a presidential refusal to respond to the ITC's recommendation of escape clause relief, thereby causing great embarrassment to the administration.

The decision by the Reagan administration in 1986 to accept the ITC's recommendation (in an escape clause case) that higher tariff duties be imposed on cedar shakes and shingles seemed puzzling. Imposition of trade barriers angered Canada at a time when negotiations were commencing on creation of a free trade area between the two countries. A second, less obvious timing factor apparently swayed the decision-making process. The Reagan administration's protectionist stance was announced on the same day that the House was voting on H.R. 4800, an omnibus trade bill containing several protectionist provisions strongly opposed by the administration.

The specter of congressional action can affect negotiations with foreign governments as well as internal executive branch strategizing. ''The Congress will never buy this'' is an argument used by administration negotiators in an effort to make other countries more responsive to U.S. demands for market-opening measures and export restraint agreements, or to ease foreign countries' trade demands on the United States. Congress used hearings and action on a restrictive quota bill to send a clear signal in 1981 that it wanted the Reagan administration and the Japanese government to come to an understanding that would restrain automobile exports to the United States. Neither the administration nor the Japanese government wished to call Congress's bluff. They opted instead for a ceiling on Japanese car exports as a means of helping Detroit work through its production problems.

On rare occasions, Congress escalates demonstrations of its impatience with imports and actually passes protectionist legislation. On three separate occasions beginning in 1985, Congress finalized and sent to the president legislation ordering unilateral import quotas on textile products. None were enacted. All were "veto bait." The real key to accurately gauging the prospect of protectionist legislation opposed by the president becoming the law of the land is not the fact that it was passed by Congress. Instead, it is the (unlikely) availability of votes to override an almost guaranteed presidential veto. The protectionism drama in the case of textiles was more suspenseful than usual. The critical variable was that the three presidential vetoes were accompanied by modest administrative adjustments to tighten up existing restraints on textile imports (mainly through the Multifiber Arrangement). The resulting dip in the growth rate of these imports was sufficient to placate swing voters in Congress and sustain the vetoes.

A friend who at the time worked as a Senate aide told me of an incident in which one of his contacts at the Office of the U.S. Trade Representative (USTR) called to ask him if his boss would assist in an effort to rebuff a minor trade concession being pressed by Brazil. As subsequently arranged, the USTR staff member quietly sent over a draft letter urging stiff resistance to the demand. The paper was retyped, signed by the senator, and mailed. Clayton Yeutter, the USTR at the time, then relayed the gist of its contents to the Brazilians as evidence of the domestic pressures he was facing.

The *fourth* variant of the inter-branch politics model is an inconclusive struggle over policy substance, the result of deadlock over which branch's competing ideas should take precedence and be implemented. A prime example was the heated debate on strategy that sprang up in the early 1990s between a mostly Democratic group of legislators and the Bush administration over the terms for continuation of most-favored-nation (MFN) tariff treatment to China. The crux of the problem was not the undesirability of certain Chinese practices, such as overseas sales of weapons technology and human rights abuses, nor was it the simple desire to protect American companies from Chinese imports. The larger issue was and is whether a hard- or soft-line approach would be most effective in convincing the Chinese government to stop violating a number of humanitarian, political, and economic practices that most Americans readily agree are abhorrent. Human rights activists and foreign policy hard-liners want the United States to take the moral high-road and punish China. The business community and others advocate commercial engagement as the preferred means of promoting growth of a middle class that one day might rebel against totalitarianism and of encouraging less restrictive Chinese import practices.

The subtle nuances of inter-branch relations were demonstrated in the events that transpired after Congress in 1992 overwhelmingly passed the United States-China Act. The bill demanded a number of changes in Chinese behavior before the president could annually extend that country's MFN status. President Bush's promised veto was overridden in the House, but it was sustained by a narrow margin in the Senate. Congress then stopped passing legislation actively seeking to restrict MFN renewal. The most likely reason for this new-found moderation was the inauguration of a new president who might actually sign such a measure. Without assurance of a presidential veto, Congress lost its aggressiveness. It was not about to risk setting into motion U.S. trade actions that might spur Chinese retaliation that would keep American goods and services out of the world's fastest-growing market. President Clinton eventually delinked human rights abuses from extension of MFN, but the debate over optimal policy continued.

The *fifth* and newest variant of inter-branch decision-making consists of Congress's outright refusal to pass legislation strongly supported by the administration (and the business community). The Clinton administration's plan to provide a multibillion dollar loan guarantee to help Mexico cope with its peso crisis had to be abandoned in January 1995, when it became clear that a majority in both houses opposed what they perceived to be a "bail-out" of bad loans and would vote against the legislation authorizing the loan guarantee. As discussed in Chapter 12, in the late 1990s Congress rebelled against the post–World War II U.S. tradition of championing a more open international economic order. Among other things, it refused to approve extension of the expired fast-track negotiating authority and delayed for months the U.S. contribution to the latest in a long series of capital replenishments of the IMF.

CONGRESS'S IMPACT ON INTERNATIONAL ECONOMIC POLICIES

The imprint of Congress is not uniform across the several sectors of international economic policy. A hierarchy of congressional interest exists among these sectors based on their perceived impact on constituents. Congress's willingness to defer to the executive branch in the conduct of a given sector of U.S. international economic relations is inversely correlated to constituent interest. The degree of "politicalization" of an international economic issue is a function of voters' beliefs that it is important to them.

Trade is the most important "pocketbook" issue in international economic relations because of its direct implications for domestic jobs and profits. The result has been intense levels of citizen concern and interest group lobbying of such magnitude that trade policy is often mistakenly equated with international economic policy as a whole. Once beyond trade, members of Congress and lobbyists spend less time considering global economic issues.

Congress employs a number of checks and balances to limit the administration's freedom to implement trade policy. Broadly speaking, the general direction of U.S. trade policy has been determined by the passage of new trade legislation. On a more specific level, the conduct of U.S. trade relations is influenced by the unique contents of a relatively informal inter-branch dialogue that includes committee hearings, one-on-one informal conversations, and the accreditation of members of Congress to U.S. trade delegations.

After the United States lost its post–World War II economic hegemony and foreign competitiveness began to take a domestic toll, a surge in congressional involvement in trade policy quickly followed. This presence was most visible in questions of the extent to which U.S. import barriers could be reduced, how to restrain undesirable levels of imports, and how to pressure other countries to reduce their barriers to American-made goods. A Congressional Research Service study summarized the trade policy role of Congress in these terms:

> The development of the Congressional involvement in Presidential import relief actions from a simple reporting requirement to the present rather broad direct intervention authority reflects the increasing desire of the Congress to have an active part, indeed, possibly the final word, in the procedure designed to protect the domestic industry from the harmful impact of import competition. It also reflects the trend toward increased safeguards that has marked the involvement of the Congress in matters of foreign trade in general since the early 1950s, although this trend has been, in part, a counterweight to the increasing authority granted to the President to reduce barriers to U.S. trade, particularly to imports, embodied in the same progression of trade and tariff legislation.[3]

Foreign economic assistance is the international economic policy sector receiving the second greatest degree of congressional scrutiny. Congress's impact on U.S. foreign aid policy can be viewed from at least three different perspectives. The first is its absolute control over appropriations to fund assistance programs. The perennial absence of a powerful constituency for foreign aid, either in the public at large or within Congress, frequently delays and diminishes appropriations levels requested by the administration. Aid funding can be used to exemplify what was once described by C. Fred Bergsten as "a virtual stalemate system of governance" containing "a plethora of checks with very few balances." In recalling his experiences (as assistant secretary of the Treasury in the Carter administration) in trying to get congressional approval of U.S. financial commitments to the multilateral banks, a frustrated Bergsten went on to write that "Program managers must spend an inordinate amount of time 'working the Hill' rather than improving their programs, and must cater to the whims of that willful minority that can stop the process dead in its tracks." Quantifying the dimensions of the problem, he added:

> A major systemic problem is that any money program that does not enjoy permanent authorization must clear at least 27 separate legislative steps to become effective. Three distinct processes are involved: one or more budget resolutions, authorization, and appropriation. Each process usually encompasses nine steps: Each House votes on a bill at both the subcommittee and committee levels and then again on the floor, with a conference committee reconciling the inevitable differences and shipping the bill back once more to each body for final passage. Even programs with permanent authorization face 20 or so separate Capitol Hill hurdles each year.[4]

From a second perspective, Congress's impact on foreign aid can be described as innovative and constructive. As mentioned above, it was Congress, not the administration, that in the 1970s altered U.S. development policy objectives and program funding priorities. In producing the "New Directions" approach in 1973 and in authorizing a means of providing external debt relief in 1978 to the poorest aid loan recipients, Congress acted without presidential requests for changing the status quo. In both instances, congressional actions reflected the conceptual desires of supportive legislators and professional staff experts to make U.S. foreign aid efforts more effective.

A third perspective is the occasional decision by Congress to "micromanage" policy, even where the executive branch theoretically is in control. This tendency is most evident in the national security–related sphere of foreign aid. The Economic Support Fund (ESF) is that part of the overall U.S. foreign aid program that channels funds to countries mainly on the basis of practical foreign policy considerations rather than the recipients' demonstration of economic need. Congressional appropriations bills contain unilateral directives to the administration as to which countries under this program are to get what amount of money during a given fiscal year. In the most extreme example of this phenomenon, Congress one year (in the early 1980s) earmarked 100 percent of appropriated ESF funds to specific countries, temporarily leaving the administration with no discretionary funding whatsoever.[5] Upwards of 80 percent of ESF appropriations is still earmarked because of the relatively large funding going to Israel and Egypt. Congress more recently has operated on the principle that in the fast-changing post–cold war era, the executive branch needs some flexibility in determining the other recipient countries of this fund.

The arcane nature of international monetary relations had long kept congressional involvement in this policy sector to a perfunctory concern. This changed when the domestic economic dislocations caused by overvaluation of the dollar in the early 1980s created an unprecedented degree of scrutiny in the links between trade flows and exchange rates. Relatively apolitical issues such as exchange rate policy, balance of payments programs, and U.S. participation in the IMF had never before provoked controversial legislation or attracted anything more than a tiny coterie of interested and knowledgeable members of Congress. By 1985, the Congress was considering a number of legislative proposals—successfully opposed by the administration—that would have ordered active foreign exchange market intervention whenever the dollar's value was found to have risen so high as to materially hurt U.S. international competitiveness.

Congress's anger at the Clinton administration's decision to use the Treasury Department's Exchange Stabilization Fund to aid Mexico during its 1994–1995 currency crisis without congressional concurrence led to legislation potentially limiting presidential authority. Since the stabilization fund was created in 1934, the secretary of the treasury had had authority to use its currency balances to address instability in the foreign exchange markets. The situation changed when

Congress gave itself the power during 1996 and 1997 to pass a binding reso-lution disapproving any proposed loan from the stabilization fund to a foreign government in excess of $1 billion and for more than 180 days. This statutory restraint played a critical role in the administration's decision not to tap the Exchange Stabilization Fund's resources to assist Thailand contain its 1997 fi-nancial crisis, the event that would trigger ''Asian Contagion.'' To directly commit U.S. funds, the administration feared, could provoke a congressional override that might fan investor nervousness.

Congressional initiatives on U.S. international investment policy were non-existent until the late 1980s. An inter-branch consensus held that the U.S. gov-ernment should not interfere in decisions by private corporations to build production facilities abroad. Neither the balance of payments concerns in the 1960s about dollar outflows associated with outward foreign direct investment nor the AFL-CIO's lobbying in the early 1970s for taxation changes to dis-courage foreign direct investment inspired any restrictive legislation. Only the rise of apprehensions in the late 1980s about the effects of increasing *inward* foreign direct investment in the United States, mainly from Japan, inspired two important congressional efforts to legislate changes in the administration of in-ternational investment policy. The Reagan administration strongly opposed both initiatives. It defeated an effort to increase the extent of financial disclosure on individual foreign investment projects. The Exon-Florio bill became law only after Congress agreed to dilute its original contents. The final statutory language provided the president with discretionary authority to block any foreign takeover of an American company if the purchase was deemed to be a threat to national security.

A major wild card in the impact of Congress at any given time on the making of U.S. international economic policy, particularly in the trade sector, is the personal and working relationships among key congressional and administration officials. The extent to which the administration and the Congress succeed in meshing their assessments, strategies, and recommendations into a relatively coherent whole often reflects the amount of mutual respect and trust between personnel in the two branches. The willingness by the president to compromise and to consult early and fully about impending trade actions of significance is important to eliciting congressional cooperation or lack of opposition. Congres-sional willingness to accommodate the executive branch's trade desires is closely correlated to partisan concerns to be sure, but members also want to know that their needs are being heard, understood, and acted on.

The positive results of executive branch responsiveness to congressional sen-timents on trade issues have been demonstrated empirically on many occasions. Congress's efforts in the early 1980s to pass textile quota, domestic content, and reciprocity legislation all dissipated in the wake of incisive responses taken by the Reagan administration. They ranged from explaining the negative con-sequences of proposed legislation to negotiating tighter ''voluntary'' export re-straints in textiles. The replacement in early 1985 of a politically callous secretary of the treasury, Donald Regan, by the politically astute James Baker halted a rising protectionist backlash on Capitol Hill. Baker's responsiveness defused the near-boiling-point anger in Congress at the administration's inflexible hands-off stance on taking exchange rate and trade measures to deal with a sharply deteriorating trade balance.

When the Trade Reform Act was first submitted to Congress in early 1973, there was widespread concern that protectionist sentiment engendered by the deteriorating U.S. trade balance, together with the hostile Watergate atmosphere, would ignite congressional action that was long on import restraints and short on the requested executive authority for negotiating reciprocal reductions in trade barriers. Members of Congress were assiduously cultivated as part of a textbook case of congressional "stroking" by senior trade officials. The bill that ultimately emerged, the Trade Act of 1974, provided extensive negotiating flexibility and relaxed criteria for approving private sector petitions for import relief. However, it contained no outright import barriers.

The administration's strategy also included astute and widespread solicitation of private sector support for the 1975 trade act. One part of a two-pronged lobbying effort promoted support from liberal-trade and export-oriented interest groups and industries on the basis of the bill's setting the stage for negotiations leading to further reductions in trade barriers overseas. The second part consisted of telling import-sensitive industries about the bill's provision for greater accessibility to relief from both fair and unfair foreign competition. By the time that the overwhelmingly favorable House and Senate votes were taken, only the AFL-CIO was voicing strong opposition.

HOW AND WHY THE CONGRESS ATTACHES STRINGS WHEN IT DELEGATES TRADE POLICY AUTHORITY TO THE EXECUTIVE BRANCH

The short leash on which Congress keeps the executive branch in the foreign trade sector lies at the center of a behind-the-scenes relationship that literally shapes U.S. trade policy. In partially delegating its constitutional authority to regulate foreign commerce, Congress has created an inter-branch balance of power unique in the world. Only Congress has the power to modify or terminate this balance of power. Decision-making models that exclusively consider the executive branch start from the point at which Congress has delegated power to it. A serious intellectual gap results. The considerations that preceded this delegation of authority and the nature of the strings attached are too important to be ignored by serious students of U.S. trade policy.

The trigger for the carefully measured transfer of trade authority to the administration was a legislative mistake so grievous that for 70 years Congress has worked conscientiously to prevent its being repeated. The legislation creating the Smoot-Hawley Tariff Act of 1930 symbolized a bad system exploding out of control. Congress had long demonstrated a limited ability to resist constituents' demands for high tariff walls. To quote E.E. Schattschneider, a pioneer scholar in this area, "In tariff making . . . Congress writes bills which no one intended."[6] The tariff schedule legislated in 1930 remains the most egregious example of the protectionist snowballing effect that is unleashed when Congress starts setting import barriers on the basis of political favoritism rather than compelling economic logic.

What became the Smoot-Hawley tariff act began as a modest, albeit ill-advised, effort to placate farmers by trying to raise domestic prices on agricultural goods by increasing tariffs on food imports. Members of Congress representing industrial districts agreed to go along only on the condition that higher tariffs also be imposed on manufactured goods. At the end of the day, the statute inflated into the highest tariff wall ever erected by the United States. The timing could not have been worse. When the depression in the United States spread around the globe, other countries resorted to similar trade barriers. The outbreak of the worst trade war in modern history created a negative-sum game. World trade imploded, export-sector jobs were lost, and economic efficiency declined. The results served to worsen and prolong everyone's economic misery.

Congress came close to repeating this process only once. An extreme case of legislative logrolling occurred in 1970, after Japan's prolonged refusal to restrain textile exports caused the White House's frustration to hit the boiling point. The Nixon administration thereupon abandoned the tradition of presidential commitment to liberal trade and unexpectedly offered public support for textile quota legislation that had been introduced in the House Ways and Means Committee. As the suddenly reinvigorated bill continued through the legislative process, the dubious economic justification for such import restraints encouraged other members of Congress to assert that they would vote for the bill only if import barriers on goods produced by their favored constituents were added. The bill had originated as a "bad cop" stratagem by the powerful chair of the Ways and Means Committee to scare the Japanese and U.S. governments into an amicably negotiated solution to the Nixon administration's demands for "voluntary" export restraints on man-made textiles. Following endorsement by the administration, the proposal snowballed into a massive protectionist bill whose various provisions made it potentially more trade-restrictive than the Smoot-Hawley tariff. The bill died when the 91st Congress adjourned in January 1971, before a conference committee could reconcile differences in the two versions passed by the House and Senate.

The massive breakdown in 1930 in Congress's ability to say no to the demands by interest groups for import protection scared that institution into creating procedures for deflecting such pressures to the executive branch. Give-and-take is at the heart of a deceptively complex formula. Congress delegates significant power to the executive branch to implement trade policy, but on a highly conditional, temporary basis that limits the latter's independence.

The process utilized by Congress to avoid another Smoot-Hawley fiasco has been based on a number of separate measures, not on a carefully crafted master plan. Through trial and error, Congress has institutionalized its desire to contain pressures from constituents for relief from import competition. It is willing to voluntarily restrain its political reflexes because the vast majority of representatives and senators intellectually accept the economic truism that the population as a whole pays the price of protectionism while only a small few reap the rewards. To understand exactly how the qualified delegation of authority works in practice, it is necessary to avoid two oversimplifications. First, Congress has provided neither an absolute nor irreversible delegation of trade authority. Secondly, it is not forever plotting to increase trade barriers to reward constituents, its cultivated image of trade hard-liner notwithstanding.

Since the end of World War II, Congress has consistently supported the process of multilateral trade liberalization. Beginning in the late 1980s, it has approved U.S. participation in regional free trade areas. The price of its endorsing reductions of trade barriers is a vigorous congressional insistence that a fair shake in Washington be guaranteed for import-impacted companies and workers. Members of Congress believe that the U.S. government owes a quick and fair hearing to those companies alleging economic injury from fair or unfair foreign competition. Carefully delineated trade remedies must exist to meet legitimate grievances. These beliefs reflect both a sense of political responsibility to assist the people who elected them and a calculated means to protect the forever-fragile domestic liberal trade coalition.

"Controlled sensitivity" to import-induced domestic dislocations explains Congress's middle of the road response to rising complaints from the steel industry in 1998 that foreign companies were massively dumping steel in the American market. It passed legislation requiring the Clinton administration to send to Capitol Hill a special report detailing how it planned to respond to the surge of low-priced steel imports that had been driving down domestic prices and forcing the closing of some U.S. steelmaking plants. Controlled sensitivity also caused the House in early 1999 to pass a tough steel quota bill, mainly to make a statement on behalf of the domestic industry. Some members admitted the bill had no real chance of becoming law. Senate approval was unlikely and a presidential veto would be inevitable.

Since passage in 1934 of the Reciprocal Trade Agreements Act, congressional sentiment can be summarized as a belief that reduction of trade barriers must be done on a steady, gradual, and equitable basis. The process should maximize benefits to society as a whole while keeping the costs inflicted on import-impacted workers and companies to "manageable" levels of dislocation. Congress insists unequivocally that foreign countries reciprocate with comparably open markets and generally fair trade practices—or risk retaliation. This multilevel philosophy is clearly visible in the contents of the major trade bills passed by Congress in 1962, 1974, and 1988.

The bottom line is an intricate, highly nuanced set of mechanisms whereby legislators enjoy the best of two worlds. They largely remove themselves from the everyday rough-and-tumble tensions of foreign trade relations while assuring that the executive branch cannot stray too far from Congress's collective preferences. In their classic study of the politics of U.S. foreign trade, Bauer, de Sola Pool, and Dexter described congressional efforts to situate the executive branch between Capitol Hill and the demands of constituents for specific import barriers:

> Congress has found it far more comfortable to decide matters of general tariff policy and the procedures for seeking favors, but to leave individual decisions in the hands of administrators. This means that the individual business interest appeals to Congress only for an intermediate goal, namely, that general rules be framed in ways likely to result in favorable action on later petitions. That fact reduces the frequency and urgency of appeals to the congressman. By thus passing the buck, Congress has reduced its own power. A congressman's power is in large part the favors he can perform. If patronage is eliminated . . . if tariff-rate setting is turned over to the executive, the legislator is deprived of ways to win the support of constituents. But each of these powers is a two-edged sword. If there are more appeals for help than he can handle and if the intensity of them is such that they generate threats and anger against him, then he may be glad to yield a part of his power, letting someone else take the blame for decisions and reserving to himself only the role of critic and issuer of statements.[7]

Members of Congress have enhanced the trade policy power of the executive branch as part of a conscious effort to keep themselves sympathetic in principle to requests for protection by constituents but without having an obligation to actually impose import barriers. The main result of this arrangement, in the words of I.M. Destler, is not so much protection for industry as protection for Congress. Instead of giving priority to protecting American industry, members of Congress give priority to protecting themselves "from the direct, one-sided pressures from producer interests that had led them to make bad trade law." Product-specific trade decisions would be channeled "out of the committees of Congress and off the House and Senate floors to other governmental institutions."[8] An additional motive in willingly delegating trade power has been the growing sentiment on Capitol Hill that the administration of trade policy was becoming too complicated and detailed for effective handling by the relatively cumbersome procedures and smaller staff of Congress.

Since Congress changed course on trade policy in 1934, it has consistently passed statutes granting the president authority to reduce trade barriers on a reciprocal basis and to conduct trade relations in general. At the same time, Congress consistently has placed multiple limitations on that authority. The president's power to unilaterally reduce trade barriers has always been limited to a fixed number of years and to tariffs only. Furthermore, the criteria for domestic industries to obtain relief from fair and unfair import competition have been amended to make relief more easily available whenever Congress believed that eligibility had become too restrictive.

Another important aspect of the metaphorical short leash on the executive branch's trade authority is the special institutional ties established by Congress with two agencies discussed in Chapter 3. These ties are a calculated move to limit the independence of presidents in implementing trade policy. The U.S. International Trade Commission is neither part of the executive or legislative branch, yet it is more fearful of Congress than the White House. It is the recipient of detailed statutory guidelines from Congress on procedures to determine the existence of import-induced injury. It is dependent on Congress for its budget. Furthermore, the six commissioners tend to be well-versed in the congressional mind-set because it is not uncommon for three or more of them to have been nominated for their position while serving as professional staff members of Congress.

The second special relationship involves the Office of the U.S. Trade Representative (USTR). Congress relentlessly hints to the USTR that the office risks being eviscerated if its actions stray too far from congressional sentiments on what constitutes the appropriate balance between liberal trade and minimization of domestic economic disruption. The 1988 trade act added to the USTR's existing consultation requirements by ordering submission to Congress of an annual statement setting forth trade policy objectives and priorities, actions and legislation to achieve them, and progress made toward their accomplishment. This law also enhanced the directive that the office of the USTR seek advice from the five congressional advisers on trade policy selected by each house (they are the same members who are accredited as official advisers to U.S. delegations to trade negotiations and meetings).[9] These procedures joined preexisting requirements that USTR officials consult with the private sector advisory groups and testify regularly before congressional committees.

The special negotiating authority known as fast track is an excellent case study in the subtlety of the strings attached to congressional delegation of trade authority to the executive branch. When Congress first passed this vehicle to expedite its approval of executive branch agreements to reduce non-tariff barriers, some interpreted it as a major surrender of legislative branch trade power. On the surface, Congress seems to be bending over backwards to assure that trade agreements involving more than simple tariff reductions will get final approval. This is not an accurate depiction of the situation, even though all comprehensive U.S. trade agreements (including NAFTA) since the Tokyo Round agreement in the 1970s have used the fast-track procedure for final legislative approval.

True, the fast-track statute establishes two extraordinary changes in Congress's procedural rules. Bills submitted under this authority cannot be kept from a floor vote. In addition, Congress denies itself the right to amend legislation implementing a trade liberalization agreement negotiated by the administration. This is extraordinarily important. It eliminates the possibility of converting what started out as a trade liberalization bill into a ''Christmas tree'' festooned with protectionist amendments that would have serious consequences for U.S. trade relations and would likely be vetoed.

Prior to formally submitting implementing legislation, the USTR makes it a practice to consult informally with key congressional members on the terms of the just-concluded trade agreement and the contents of the bill that will be submitted for fast-track approval. This informal process has been institutionalized to the point that it has become known as the "non-markup" session. The Trade Agreements Act of 1979 had been so thoroughly pre-screened on Capitol Hill that it passed the House and Senate by votes of 395 to 7 and 90 to 4, respectively.[10] Similarly, support by congressional leaders assured that fast-track approval of the Canadian free trade agreement passed by overwhelming margins in both houses. Conversely, informal inter-branch consultations revealed serious congressional opposition to two alleged shortcomings of the free trade agreement that had just been signed with Mexico. To avoid the bill being voted down, the Clinton administration had no choice but to negotiate side agreements with the Mexican government that proposed additional safeguards for workers' rights and for the environment.

The self-imposed discipline of having to make a simple up or down vote masks a number of choke points where Congress can limit the effects of fast track. Legislation enacted under the fast-track provision is not all that "fast." In the first place, this authority always has been granted for a fixed number of years. When it expired in 1994, Congress refused to renew it. Moreover, legislators can threaten to vote no, thereby either killing a trade agreement outright or forcing the administration to reopen negotiations with the countries that were co-signatories. In the latter case, foreign governments would be asked to agree to modify provisions of the agreement in order to make it palatable to Congress.

Congress further strengthened its position in 1988 by inserting a "reverse fast-track" provision in the law. A vote by both houses can repeal the application of the fast-track procedure to a pending trade agreement before the administration submits an implementing bill. Congress can pass such a resolution if it believes the executive branch has not provided adequate advance consultations with the appropriate committees about a trade negotiation.

The cumulative impact of the strings attached to Congress's delegation of trade authority is to keep it actively, but selectively, involved in the formulation of trade policy, the management of import and export programs, and the conduct of trade negotiations with other countries. If provoked, Congress will use its power to legislate new policy, modify existing statutory provisions, or limit the executive branch's discretionary authority. "Although it is not usually thought of as such, trade policy has essentially become regulatory policy." So many rules, procedures, and obligations to respect private sector interests are imposed on the executive branch that trade negotiations, at one time viewed as one of the president's diplomatic prerogatives, "are now treated much as any other executive branch regulatory proceeding."[11]

NOTES

1. U.S. General Accounting Office, "Export Promotion—Issues for Governmentwide Strategy," report dated 26 February 1998, pp. 2–3.

2. Robert Pastor, *Congress and the Politics of U.S. Foreign Economic Policy, 1929–1976* (Berkeley: University of California Press, 1980), p. 192.

3. Vladimir N. Pregelj, "Legislative Veto or Positive Approval of Executive Action under the Trade Act of 1974 and Related Legislation," House Rules Committee, *Studies on the Legislative Veto* (Washington, D.C.: U.S. Government Printing Office, February 1980), p. 718.

4. C. Fred Bergsten, "Congress's Stalemate System," *New York Times*, 30 January 1981, p. A27.

5. Interview with Larry Q. Nowels, Congressional Research Service, October 1992.

6. E.E. Schattschneider, *Politics, Pressures, and the Tariff* (New York: Prentice-Hall, 1935), p. 13.

7. Raymond A. Bauer, Ithiel de Sola Pool, and Lewis Anthony Dexter, *American Business and Public Policy* (Chicago: Aldine-Atherton, 1972), pp. 455–456.

8. I.M. Destler, *American Trade Politics*, 3rd ed. (Washington, D.C.: Institute for International Economics and The Twentieth Century Fund, 1995), p. 14.

9. George D. Holliday, "The Changing Role of Congress in Trade Negotiations," Congressional Research Service report number 92–231 E, dated 14 February 1992, p. 7.

10. I.M. Destler and Thomas Graham, "United States Congress and the Tokyo Round—Lessons of a Success Story," *World Economy* 3 (June 1980), pp. 64–67.

11. Sharyn O'Halloran, *Politics, Process, and American Trade Policy* (Ann Arbor: University of Michigan Press, 1994), pp. 181–182.

10 The System Responds to Exchange Rate and Trade Balance Disequilibria, 1985–1986

> I will not stand by and watch American businesses fail because of unfair trading practices abroad. I will not stand by and watch American workers lose their jobs because other nations do not play by the rules.
>
> —President Ronald Reagan, 1985

> I'm fed up with those in Washington who talk like Rambo but act like Bambi where trade is concerned.
>
> —Senator John Glenn, 1986

The U.S. trade and exchange rate positions occasionally sink into structural disequilibria. Twice in the post–World War II period an overvalued dollar has caused a major deterioration in the trade account. On both occasions, the resulting *Sturm und Drang* sent shock waves across the bow of U.S. international economic policy that dwarfed the relatively gentle vibrations of incrementalism that usually characterizes the policymaking process.

In August 1971, President Nixon decisively dealt with the first of these two exchange rate disequilibria by suddenly and unexpectedly using his executive authority to the maximum in imposing the so-called New Economic Policy. The closing of the gold window and imposition of an import surcharge eventually produced an unprecedented series of negotiations that culminated in massive exchange rate realignments as well as agreement to initiate the Tokyo Round of multilateral trade negotiations. Indirectly, this dramatic presidential action had the effect of inducing a real, albeit short-lived, adjustment in the U.S. trade balance, mainly through dollar devaluation. The aftermath of the New Economic Policy also had the effect of extinguishing the protectionist fires that were raging on Capitol Hill during the 1970–1971 period. A comparable chain of events occurred in the mid-1980s.

THE CONGRESS SIZZLES AT THE ADMINISTRATION'S ICY COOL

The U.S. international economic situation at the beginning of 1985 was both similar and dissimilar to the situation prevailing in 1971. Once again, the exchange rate of the dollar was overvalued in terms of U.S. international commercial competitiveness, producing the inevitable deterioration in the U.S. trade balance and swelling discontent in Congress with the trade policy status quo. But even adjusting for inflation and economic growth, the magnitude of the exchange rate and trade disequilibria in the mid-1980s was far greater than in the early 1970s. Nevertheless, the Reagan administration adopted a defiant hands-off posture that, in effect, refused to second-guess the market mechanism in determining either the dollar's value or the flow of goods into and out of the United States.

The administration's indifference to the mounting costs and distortions produced by the resulting economic disequilibrium unleashed a political disequilibrium in executive-legislative branch relations. To attribute the inter-branch strains during the 1980s to partisan politics between a Republican White House and a Congress controlled by the Democrats is to oversimplify the situation. The strains emanated mainly from two strongly held, very divergent institutional and ideological beliefs about the appropriate course of U.S. international economic policy. The result was a kind of "mega-case study" in how critically important U.S. international economic policies are formulated under extreme stress.

In a typical parliamentary democracy, trade policy would be formulated discreetly, mainly within the confines of the cabinet's meeting room. The outcome of high-priority discussions probably would be forthcoming within a very few weeks. Approval by parliament would be assumed as automatic. The unusually severe U.S. external disequilibrium that existed by 1985 produced a vivid display of how much more public, protracted, and complex is the U.S. decision-making system. International monetary and trade policy decisions made in Washington that year provided a classic example of the dynamics and virtues in the system of checks and balances built into the U.S. government.

The magnitude of the U.S. external disequilibrium in 1985 can be empirically measured, even if an interpretation of the implications perforce would be subjective. According to the exchange rate index published by the Federal Reserve Board, the nominal value of the dollar increased from an index of 85 in the middle of 1980 to a peak of 165 in late February 1985. This incredible 94 percent appreciation had no foundation either in terms of relatively low U.S. inflation or in increases in the ability of U.S. businesses to compete with their foreign competition. The dramatic increases in the dollar's value against virtu-

Table 10.1
Growth in U.S. Imports of Key Manufactured Goods, 1980–1985 (imports on C.I.F. Basis)

	1980	1985	Rate of Increase (percentage)
	(millions of U.S. $)		
Chemicals	9.0	15.3	70
Power generating machinery	3.9	9.1	133
General industrial machinery and parts	4.1	8.5	107
Telecommunications apparatus	7.0	19.1	173
Electrical machinery (includes apparatus)	8.3	18.2	119
Passenger cars	17.8	37.6	111
Automotive parts	5.0	10.2	104
Clothing	6.8	16.0	135

Source: U.S. Commerce Department, *United States Trade, Performance in 1985 and Outlook* (Washington, D.C.: Government Printing Office, 1986), p. 129.

ally every currency (approximately 150 percent against the French franc, 125 percent against the British pound, 90 percent against the German mark, and 17 percent against the Japanese yen) were rooted in noncommercial factors: unusually high real rates of interest in the United States, a favorable business climate, and pure speculation.

The growing gap between the dollar's rising overseas value and the relative decline in the U.S. competitive position was an important contributor to the biggest trade deterioration in world history. (Among the other important causes of the increased trade deficit were a large, persistent federal budget deficit that was largely responsible for the United States spending more on consumer and capital goods than it produced; relatively high U.S. growth rates; the debt problem that hurt U.S. trade with Latin America; and foreign trade barriers.) The total U.S. trade deficit nearly quadrupled in the six-year period beginning in 1980, soaring from $36 billion to $148 billion. Total U.S. imports increased by almost 50 percent during this period, rising from $257 billion in 1980 to $362 billion in 1985. Particularly dramatic was the near doubling of manufactured goods imports, going from $138 billion to $269 billion in these same years. By 1985, it was clear that increased imports represented a serious drag to real U.S. gross domestic product (GDP) growth as foreign producers were providing a disproportionate share of the goods that met incremental domestic demand.

The increased suffering and declining competitiveness of the U.S. manufacturing sector is displayed in import growth data found in Table 10.1. Equally disquieting (to most non-administration officials, at least) was the dismal export performance, as the dollar value of U.S. exports in 1985 was less than the comparable figure for 1980.[1]

The administration's response was minimal, except to reaffirm its basic faith in the market mechanism and to call for additional federal spending cuts as the means for reducing the budget deficit. The White House was unshakable in its commitment to the broad principle of a noninterventionist international economic policy. The need for extensive import restrictions or retaliation against foreign barriers was summarily rejected by the Reagan administration.

The rising exchange rate of the dollar seemed to be viewed more with a sense of pride (the "America is back" syndrome) than a sense of alarm by the president and his treasury secretary at the time, Donald Regan. In February 1985 President Reagan stated that the "main problem is not the strength of the dollar; it's the weakness of foreign currencies." At a press conference one week later, the president argued that many other countries "have a ways to go in changing some rigidities in their customs, in their methods of doing business and in industry, and what we really need is their recovery to bring their money up in value comparable to ours."[2]

Extensive intervention in the foreign exchange markets to stem the dollar's rise in value had been dismissed unequivocally as being a waste of time and representing a false belief that a handful of government officials somehow knew better than tens of thousands of private sector people what the proper value of an exchange rate should be. Exporters and import-sensitive businesses were told to try a little harder to overcome the burdens of a strong dollar—a cavalier attitude that was so costly, inflexible, long standing, and inflammatory to the private sector that it would have brought down most parliamentary democracies.

In testimony to the Senate Finance Committee in March 1984, R. T. McNamar, then the deputy secretary of the Treasury, denied that the dollar had become overvalued when measured in the broadest sense. Describing economic trends that have a close similarity to those of the late 1990s, he argued that

> The major factors influencing market perceptions of real rates of return to capital over the past three years have been: fundamentally better U.S. economic performance and prospects; weaker performance and prospects in other major industrial countries; and the threat posed by economic and political turmoil in the Middle East, Latin America, and Eastern Europe. Our economic program brought a historic turnaround in U.S. inflation performance, followed by vigorous recovery. As a result of our non-inflationary recovery, deregulation, and more favorable depreciation allowances under the Economic Recovery Tax Act of 1981, the profitability of American business investment has improved dramatically. Foreign economic prospects and business conditions, especially in Europe, did not keep pace with ours. . . . Under those circumstances, there was nothing we should—or could—have done to keep the dollar from appreciating, short of weakening our own economy to match the rest of the world.[3]

In contrast, the then-chairman of the independent Federal Reserve System's Board of Governors, Paul Volcker, would soon be publicly exuding a sense of discomfort. Typical of his fear of the trade-exchange rate disequilibria was this statement to the Senate Foreign Relations Committee in early 1985:

> Economic analysis and common sense coincide in telling us that the budget and trade deficits of the magnitude we are running are not sustainable indefinitely in a framework of growth and prosperity. They imply a dependence on foreign borrowing by the U.S. that, if left unchecked, will sooner or later undermine the confidence in our economy essential to a strong currency and to prospects for lower interest rates.[4]

By the middle of 1985, Congress was seething at the categorical refusals of the administration to admit that something was seriously amiss with spiraling trade deficits or to alter what could be viewed as an unswerving commitment to an increasingly obsolete liberal trade ideology. At a minimum, the administration had maintained a blind eye to the consequences of its failure to respect the cardinal domestic political rule of maintaining trust and mutual responsiveness between itself and Congress. The administration's indifference to the mounting trade woes of the U.S. agricultural and industrial sectors forced a change of strategy by the business community. Faced with ''nonproductive'' meetings with senior administration officials, the industrial sector shifted its lobbying to Capitol Hill. The result was a barrage of pleas for relief from external problems in business's de facto appellate court: the Congress.

Few members of Congress relish this role. The executive branch had ceased performing its traditional buffer role as lightning rod, absorbing and deflecting the heat of protectionist demands away from elected members of Congress. ''Because of its lack of credibility on trade, the administration . . . was doing the opposite, diverting those pressures to Capitol Hill.''[5] The legislative branch thus had no choice but to give a sympathetic hearing to domestic complaints about debilitating foreign competition. Impressed with the economics and politics of the industrial sector's case, Congress assumed the role as spokesman for a very credible school of thought. The latter argued that there were dangerous cumulative implications in the lingering refusal to deal with the mounting U.S. trade deficit that in large part was a function of the exchange rate misalignment, that is, the overvalued dollar. The external disequilibrium arguably had risen to unsustainable levels, economically as well as politically.

A growing number of members of Congress wanted the White House to adopt a more flexible, pragmatic international economic position. It did not happen. To try to get their message across, legislators felt it necessary to begin acting and talking in a way that suggested they might abandon more than 50 years of self-restraint in dealing with import policy. Why did such a basic shift take hold of congressional emotions? The answer, according to Senator John Danforth (R., MO), was that ''the executive branch, which should be the place to manage specific trade problems, is now closed to industries seeking import relief. When the executive branch is closed for business, Congress is the only place to turn, and the remedy Congress offers is quota legislation.''[6] Chairman of the House

Ways and Means Committee Dan Rostenkowski (D., IL), explained the situation in similar terms:

> People are beating down the doors of Congress because government has no clear plan to shore up our international competitiveness; no plan to reduce the overvalued dollar to allow U.S. exports to compete abroad and domestic goods to compete with imports at home; no plan to minimize the impact of rapidly increasing imports that this high dollar now causes; and no plan to systematically eliminate unfair practices of barriers abroad.[7]

In the largest sense, a growing segment of Congress was suggesting that the invisible hand of the international marketplace needed some degree of official guidance. The legislative branch also agreed on two other things. First, there would be partisan benefits in seizing the initiative in the trade issue, as well as costs for ignoring it. Second, the expansion of import relief petitioners beyond basic manufacturing to include high-technology industries had created an extraordinary coalition on behalf of protectionist policies.

The symptoms of rising congressional anger and frustration were manifested in a spate of legislative activity not requested, wanted, or supported by the Reagan administration. The objective was simple: to get the executive branch's attention and convince it that the international trade and monetary status quo was unacceptable. Many observers accepted the premise that the Congress was performing a useful function in mirroring the business community's sentiments and seeking a basic shift in international policies away from laissez-faire, and toward governmental efforts to induce U.S. balance of payments equilibrium. For those agreeing with this premise, the outpouring of protectionist trade and exchange rate intervention bills demonstrated a previously cited political aphorism: sometimes, the responsible way for Congress to act, is to act irresponsibly.

To see how dramatically the tone of inter-branch trade relations had changed by 1985, it is necessary to go back only one year to demonstrate the product of the traditional give-and-take in executive-legislative mutual trust and responsiveness. Despite efforts to include product-specific import restrictions and the existence of a trade deficit that was heading beyond the symbolic $100 billion mark, the largely liberal trade-leaning Trade and Tariff Act of 1984 was almost devoid of even quasi-protectionist measures (due in no small part to the efforts of the USTR).

But for the perceived failure by the administration to deal adequately with the two external disequilibria, the Congress would have not been bothered with trade legislation so soon after the passage of the 1984 trade bill. No time-sensitive issues were at hand. Nevertheless, legislative activity and rhetoric heated up in 1985 as wide-ranging, uncoordinated efforts to send the administration a message on international economic policy spontaneously arose in both houses through oversight hearings, speeches on the floor, efforts to pass new laws, and at least one major effort to overturn a presidential veto.

Approximately 300 bills designed to impede imports in some form were introduced in the 99th Congress of 1985–1986. Many were out-and-out protectionist in content, while many were designed to force the administration either to successfully negotiate reductions in identified foreign barriers to U.S. exports or impose retaliatory trade barriers. Since the early 1980s, Congress has responded to perceptions of the executive branch's being too lax in defending U.S. commercial interests overseas by threatening to restrict the executive branch's ability to accommodate the economic needs of other countries.

The first tangible manifestation of congressional anger was aimed at Japan. The latter is a country with a long, impressive record of export growth and a pattern of resistance to increased imports of manufactured goods relative to economic growth or liberalization of import barriers. At this time, it possessed the largest single bilateral trade surplus with the United States and was once again seen as dragging its feet in responding to the perennial U.S. government demands for greater access to the Japanese market. With minimum fanfare, the chairman of the Senate Finance Committee's international trade subcommittee, John Danforth, drafted a nonbinding concurrent resolution that portrayed Japan as an unfair trader, maintaining trade practices that are "unjustifiable, unreasonable, or discriminatory and burden or restrict United States commerce," and then instructed the president to take "all appropriate and feasible action" to rectify the situation.

As word of the document circulated in the Senate, unsolicited offers of co-sponsorship began to pour in.[8] The groundswell of support culminated in March 1985 in a Senate vote of 92 to 0 in which Japan's trade practices were roundly damned. A similar nonbinding resolution sailed through the House by a 394-to-19 vote a few days later. That there were two layers of meaning to the resolution's swift and dramatic success can be found in an explanation of what was going on by an aide to a Senate Republican: "The target isn't the Japanese; it's the White House."[9] A binding version of this resolution was overwhelmingly passed in April 1985 by the Senate Finance Committee. However, a procedural quirk prevented a floor vote.

The next legislative shock was registered in mid-July, when three prominent Democrats (Senator Lloyd Bentsen, Chairman of the House Ways and Means Committee Dan Rostenkowski, and Representative Richard Gephardt) introduced legislation mandating unilaterally imposed import surcharges on countries running large bilateral trade surpluses with the United States. The proposed statute's most controversial provision called for imposition of a 25 percent duty on all imports from "major trading countries that maintain an inequitable surplus in their trade with the U.S. or with the world as a whole." A complex formula was provided to trigger the surcharge that could be terminated following removal of a foreign country's unfair trade barriers or specified reductions in the size of its bilateral surpluses. Despite the prestige of its authors, the Trade Emergency and Export Promotion Act was never passed.

The only protectionist legislation to be passed by both houses of Congress and reach the president's desk in 1985 was textile quota legislation that would have caused a significant rollback in absolute terms of U.S. imports from many countries. (Provisions dealing with reductions in footwear and copper imports were also included.) The apparent initial failure of the Reagan administration to take the bill seriously and lobby actively against it helped to generate support for it in Congress, and it passed handily in the House and Senate. Although the president vetoed the bill in December, the administration got the message that textile imports had to be tempered.

The outline of an inter-branch deal began to materialize when the Congress began signaling its desire for a tough U.S. negotiating position in the then-ongoing efforts to secure the third renewal of the Multifiber Arrangement—a much tougher stance than that preferred by the more liberal trade-minded executive branch. The dynamic tension of executive-legislative branch trade relations was clearly in evidence by the congressional decision to delay, until the late summer of 1986, the vote to override the president's veto of the textile quota bill. By that time, the textile negotiations would have been concluded and new bilateral textile export restraint agreements would have been implemented. The message of these inter-branch machinations to the major Asian exporters was simple: be flexible in response to the good cop's demands or face the wrath of the bad cop. The strategy worked. The agreed-upon rate of growth in 1987 for textile imports from the major suppliers was cut significantly back, to 1 percent. Still, the vote in the House to override the veto was close: 297 to 149, a scant eight votes short of the required two-thirds majority.

Later in the year, Congress would turn to a new, previously ignored area of legislation. Although the dollar had peaked in value at the end of February 1985, the perceived need to address exchange rate factors as a cause of the deteriorating trade position led several members of Congress to introduce bills requiring executive branch intervention in the foreign exchange markets under certain circumstances. The objective would be to alter the value of the dollar when certain criteria had been met (e.g., the current account deficit reached certain levels and the dollar's exchange rate was judged to be too high to induce current account equilibrium).

This entree into international monetary relations was caused in part by growing sentiment that the deteriorating U.S. trade position could not effectively be dealt with by the traditional, narrow staples of trade policy: export promotion and import restrictions. A decline in the dollar's rising exchange rate, a reduction in the U.S. federal budget deficit, and increased economic growth in the other large industrial countries were clearly essential ingredients to a cost-effective move to a sustainable equilibrium in the U.S. trade and current account balances.

THE ADMINISTRATION RESPONDS: BASHING THE DOLLAR, LASHING AT TRADING PARTNERS

A dramatic turnaround in U.S. international economic policies followed in the wake of Donald Regan's being replaced in February 1985 as treasury secretary by James A. Baker III. The latter's switch from presidential adviser to operational policy manager ended his predecessor's hard-edged, uncompromising free market approach and initiated a new, more pragmatic approach to international economic policy substance. The decisions that brought about major international economic policy changes encompass at least three of the models discussed in Chapter 8: the personality factor, single agency domination, and inter-branch policymaking.

James Baker was perceived in Washington as a pragmatic lawyer who had a less well-defined economic philosophy but a much greater sense of political realities and necessities than his predecessor, Donald Regan, the former head of Merrill Lynch. It did not take Baker long to become very alarmed at the prospect of passage of protectionist trade legislation by an increasingly frustrated Congress. He thereupon set out to topple the economic status quo and to defuse Congress's growing political anger at the growing U.S. trade deficit. The result was reorientation of the international economic policies that were being widely criticized as callously ignoring the needs and demands of the domestic industrial sector. In their place came a more accommodating and less pure market approach, especially on the international monetary policy side, than would have been acceptable to the Regan-led Treasury.

In May 1985 a memo went up to the treasury secretary through the assistant secretary for international affairs dealing, among other things, with a range of possible actions to deal with the foreign exchange market situation. A favored option was to build on the apparent turn in market sentiment away from the dollar, whose exchange rate was slowly retreating from its late February peaks. The Treasury staff suggested that an opportunity presented itself to "go with the flow" of declining enthusiasm for dollar buying that was developing, but might not last. Given the upward trend in the U.S. trade deficit, the staff believed that the government "had to be seen to be doing something" to assure that the dollar's exchange rate continued moving in the "right direction."[10]

The initiative that would eventually produce the so-called Plaza agreement apparently was hatched in Secretary Baker's mind by early summer. At a June meeting of the Group of Ten industrial countries, he privately met with the Japanese finance minister about the possibility of organizing a small group to attempt to bring about further changes in the foreign exchange markets, namely additional dollar depreciation. His counterpart was amenable, and they agreed to follow through on the proposal. The secretary's first-phase strategy had been successful. The Japanese were to be brought on board first, and then the Germans.[11]

The rest of the summer was devoted to work by economic technicians of what was then known as the Group of Five industrial countries. They assembled contents of the package of economic measures that would be announced on September 22, at the Plaza Hotel in New York City. Specific agreement was sought and reached on what exactly was expected from each country to move the "orderly appreciation of the main non-dollar currencies against the dollar" from the realm of "desirable" to actual, and on specific magnitudes of change desired.[12]

At least 90 percent of the U.S. government's effort to bring about the Plaza agreement and its subsequent success in lowering the dollar's value was handled within the Treasury Department. Presidential approval was secured. Secretary of State George Shultz and Chairman of the Federal Reserve Board Paul Volcker, both former senior Treasury Department officials, were the only ones in their agencies consulted; they did not have any major problems with Baker's idea. Only the president's new chief of staff, Donald Regan, derided efforts to try to push aside market forces and find a more commercially realistic exchange rate for the dollar.[13]

Although the largest, most important international component of the United States' trade problem was handled through an aggressive change in exchange rate policy, Baker also saw fit to complement it with a splashy but relatively moderate substantive shift in trade policy. While Treasury Department officials were working entirely from within on the exchange rate front, they joined the Office of the U.S. Trade Representative (USTR) and the Commerce and State departments in the Economic Policy Council (EPC) to develop a consensus plan on how to demonstrate a new aggressiveness in trade without abandoning liberal trade and embracing protectionism.

In the summer of 1985, the interagency Trade Policy Review Group had a mandate to forward ideas on trade policy initiatives up the chain of command to the EPC. The economics of the rising trade deficit and the intensity of political pressures from Capitol Hill were sufficiently serious to deter bureaucratic politics from impeding movement toward consensus. No one rose to challenge the viewpoint attributed to Secretary Baker in an EPC session, which, as reconstructed by other participants, went like this:

> Look, nobody wants to sell out our free-trade policy. Nobody is arguing we shouldn't veto the textile [quota] bill. But we've got to be damn sure we can sustain the president's veto. And to do that, we're going to have to do some things. We're going to have to recognize the political problem with Congress. We're going to change our language and tell our allies they have to open their doors [to U.S. exports]. We're going to have to start being a little tougher on enforcement [of unfair trade practice laws].[14]

The decision to implement the aggressive trade package also was based on the theme of linkage. The Reagan administration had decided in August 1985 to reject the International Trade Commission's (ITC) recommendation of temporary escape clause relief from import competition for the U.S. footwear industry. It was a classic dilemma situation. On the one hand, there was legitimate doubt that this labor-intensive industry could ever achieve competitiveness, even with temporary import protection. On the other hand, the domestic industry was demonstrating a high degree of injury from imports, having lost all but about 25 percent of the U.S. market to foreign competition. This rejection was a slap in the face of domestic constituents and an indirect slap in the face of Congress. It provided a new sense of urgency within the administration that a comprehensive trade initiative was quickly needed to prevent an upsurge of protectionist sentiments.[15]

On September 23, 1985, one day after the Group of Five finance ministers announced the Plaza agreement, President Reagan delivered a tough-sounding speech declaring that other countries had to do their share to help the United States ensure an open trading system. Among the new policy measures announced as part of this new emphasis on the need to protect U.S. trade interests was a series of self-initiated investigations by the executive branch of foreign trade practices that allegedly discriminated against U.S. products. A second major announcement was that a "trade strike force" was being established (and placed under the Commerce Department's chairmanship, allegedly to please Secretary Baldrige) to "uncover unfair trading practices used against us and develop and execute strategies . . . to promptly counter and eliminate them." Significantly, the president stated his interest in "working with the Congress to put into place any necessary legislation that would help us promote free and fair trade."[16]

The policy changes initiated in 1985 induced enough economic changes to put the United States on the path of balance of payments equilibrium. Improving economic conditions in turn produced political equilibrium, for the time being, in inter-branch relations. The "system" had worked rather well in many respects. Arguably, the administration had overstayed its "everything is okay" posture on the trade and exchange rate policy fronts. Congress thereupon emitted sufficient smoke to induce a new, more pragmatic—and some would say more economically desirable—set of actions without actually setting fire to "good" international economic policy.

ENDGAME: PASSAGE OF "AGGRESSIVE" OMNIBUS TRADE LEGISLATION

The executive branch response in 1985 to Congress's long-running message about the need for remedial action was effective. It led to a moderate improvement in the U.S. competitive position, and it radically altered the legislative equation. A credible threat by Congress that it would pass protectionist trade legislation and override a presidential veto disappeared in the aftermath of the administration's efforts to correct the exchange rate misalignment and its export expansion initiative. There was justifiable confidence that there soon would be restoration of much of the American competitiveness lost during the era of the overvalued dollar.

Although an economic cycle had ended, Congress's secular discomfort with perceived presidential permissiveness in dealing with unfair foreign trade practices continued unabated. It was transformed from the abstract to the concrete by virtue of the need for new trade legislation in connection with the initiation of the Uruguay Round of multilateral trade negotiations. The trade act enacted in 1988 was the culmination of an effort begun by Congress in the mid-1980s to alter the tone of the administration of U.S. trade policy. The nature of the bill as well as the process leading up to its passage offer a lesson in microcosm of how the separation of trade powers in the U.S. government functions in practice. Partisan politics, gamesmanship in the form of extreme legislative proposals never intended for enactment, threatened vetoes (the trade bill that was passed in 1986 by the House, but not the Senate, was branded ''kamikaze legislation'' by President Reagan), and an actual veto in early 1988 were all part of the scenery in the long, drawn-out, and circuitous three-year endurance contest to produce major trade legislation that could only happen in Washington, D.C.

Underneath the multitude of complex substantive issues involved, three key, interrelated process questions had to be resolved, mainly through trial and error, before the 1988 trade bill could be enacted:

- How best to achieve the stated goal of reducing the U.S. trade deficit through export expansion rather than import reduction.

- How Congress could legislate maximum presidential backbone in an effort to correct the perception that all presidents were reluctant to play ''hard ball'' in dealing with foreign trade practices that disadvantaged American business interests. The average member of Congress believes that presidents, past and present, place foreign policy interests and belief in the theory of liberal trade consistently—and excessively—ahead of domestic economic concerns.

- The extent to which Congress, without incurring a presidential veto, could legislate reductions in presidential discretion (i.e., flexibility) to choose not to retaliate against restrictive foreign trade practices.

The 1988 trade act is a classic balancing act between two branches of government with different priorities. The legislative branch was determined to attain the mystical ''level playing field'' in trade relations and to accelerate reductions in the still large U.S. trade deficits. The executive branch was determined to preserve its discretionary authority in trade policy management and to pursue further reciprocal reductions in trade barriers on a global basis. The end result was a 1,000 page bill, the Omnibus Trade and Competitiveness Act of 1988. On the one hand, it was devoid of both unilateral, head-on protectionism and mandatory actions imposed on the White House. Many provisions contained in earlier incarnations of the omnibus trade bill that were vehemently opposed by the administration were either removed or watered down. On the other hand, it was a statute with enough new teeth to force immediate adoption of at least a marginally more aggressive U.S. trade stance. Its core theme was the need to expand U.S. exports, mainly by aggressively attacking foreign import barriers.[17]

The 1988 trade act contains a number of provisions that impose more specific guidelines on the administration in the conduct of trade relations. The basic delegation of power to the executive branch to conduct trade policy was not challenged, but discretionary authority was restricted and new procedures were mandated by congressional dicta. For example, Section 301 of the Trade Act of 1974 (which is used to challenge foreign trade practices that discriminate against American exports) was amended in several important respects. The changes included the imposition of tighter deadlines on final determinations of Section 301 investigations in an effort to halt the perceived willingness by administrations to allow such cases to drag on indefinitely without retaliation against governments that refuse to reduce their trade barriers; additional definitions of what constitute unfair foreign trade practices; mandatory retaliation against foreign violations of trade agreements with the United States unless one of several "back-door escape hatch" circumstances exists; and transfer of final authority for determining retaliation from the president to the (more congressionally sensitive) USTR.

The trade act also created, for a two-year period, the "Super 301" provision, which directed the administration to annually identify "priority practices" of "priority" foreign countries that adversely affected U.S. commerce. Initiation of negotiations with these countries was supposed to follow. The goal was reduction or elimination of the practices discriminating against U.S. goods; the statute urged retaliation in kind for non-responsive countries. Although unwanted by the administration and lambasted by foreign countries, Super 301 was a considerably diluted revision of the so-called Gephardt amendment to the original 1986 House trade bill. This provision directed that any country running "large and excessive" bilateral trade surpluses with the United States and maintaining a pattern of discriminatory trade practices should negotiate meaningful reductions in them or face retaliation.

The 1988 bill included the demand for closer, more frequent consultations on trade policy by the administration with relevant congressional committees. The president, through the USTR, was required to submit to Congress an annual "National Trade Policy Agenda" which, among other things, must outline the administration's major trade objectives and priorities for the upcoming year and actions envisioned for their achievement. Other examples of congressionally mandated trade policy aggressiveness in the act were the delegation of increased authority to the executive branch to address circumventions of the U.S. anti-dumping law by foreign companies, and the requirement that it annually identify foreign government procurement practices that hurt U.S. goods and services exports and to seek their removal. With regard to foreign direct investment in the United States, an increasingly concerned Congress handed a reluctant administration the explicit power to reject new investments by foreigners if, after a review process, they are deemed to impair national security.

In connection with the central theme of export enhancement, the 1988 bill contained a number of new non-trade provisions designed to enhance U.S. competitiveness in the high-technology sector. These provisions included improved education and training programs, establishment of a Competitiveness Policy

Council, and several modestly funded government programs (most notably the Advanced Technology Program) designed to help American companies commercialize new scientific discoveries and improve manufacturing technologies.

The most important single difference between the trade policy of the Bush administration and its predecessors was that it was the first to be subject to the new mandates of the Omnibus Trade and Competitiveness Act of 1988. Despite the slow but steady decline in the U.S. trade deficit, the Bush administration was limited in its ability to extend the laissez-faire economic doctrines it practiced in the domestic sector to the foreign trade sector.

Unrelenting congressional pressures in the 1980s nudged two Republican administrations into a more aggressive trade posture than they would have preferred. "The Congress kept moving the goal posts" is how a Senate staffer described this process in a conversation with the author. On the broad, "macro" level of principles and goals, the design and basic administration of U.S. trade policy from the mid-1980s to the Clinton adminstration's second term has mostly exemplified the inter-branch model of decision-making.

EPILOGUE

In the second half of the 1990s, a combination of economic factors again caused the U.S. current account and trade deficits to soar to record levels while the dollar's exchange rate continued strong. Unlike the mid-1980s, however, there was hardly a murmur in either the private or official sectors about the needs to protect domestic jobs from the onslaught of foreign competition and to restore American competitiveness. This dramatic difference can be attributed to the unanticipated, extraordinarily strong overall performance of the American economy. Also contributing to the lack of great concern for the rising red ink of the trade deficit was the fact that it was a lower percentage of the booming U.S. GDP than it was in the 1980s. The debilitating financial crisis faced by many Asian economies made inevitable a slowing of U.S. exports. The singular lack of interest in restricting imports and threatening trading partners if they did not reduce their import barriers reflected full employment and rising living standards in the United States. The number of production-line workers losing their jobs to imports and being unable to find alternative employment was not statistically significant. Imports were largely viewed as a desirable safety valve preventing inflation by helping to meet the surging aggregate demand associated with eight consecutive years of U.S. economic growth. Furthermore, most of the growth in imports of manufactured goods was in relatively labor-intensive, low-technology sectors that long ago had withered domestically in the face of cheaper overseas production. The weak link in this rosy scenario, of course, is that sustained growth and low unemployment in the American economy cannot continue indefinitely.

Although traditional protectionist sentiment was minimal, a more complex, subtle reaction to trends in the global economy began to surface among many interest groups and in parts of Capitol Hill. The implications for U.S. international economic policymaking of an emerging backlash against globalization are examined in Chapter 12.

NOTES

1. U.S. Commerce Department, *United States Trade, Performance in 1985 and Outlook* (Washington, D.C.: U.S. Government Printing Office, 1986), p. 128.

2. "Reagan Says U.S. Not to Blame for $," *Financial Times*, 14 February 1985; *Washington Post*, 22 February 1985, p. A13.

3. U.S. Treasury Department press release dated 23 March 1984, p. 6.

4. *The United States in a Global Economy*, Hearings of the Senate Committee on Foreign Relations, February 27, 28, and March 6, 1985 (Washington, D.C.: U.S. Government Printing Office, 1985), p. 5.

5. I.M. Destler, *American Trade Politics—System under Stress* (Washington, D.C.: Institute for International Economics, 1986), p. 237.

6. John C. Danforth, "A Rip in the Trade Laws," *Washington Post*, 23 October 1985, p. A23.

7. Quoted in Raymond J. Ahearn and Alfred Reifman, "U.S. Trade Policy: Congress Sends a Message," 24 July 1985 (processed), p. 5.

8. Not-for-attribution interview with professional staff member, Senate Finance Committee, August 1985.

9. Destler, *American Trade Politics*, p. 106.

10. Not-for-attribution interview with U.S. Treasury Department official, October 1986.

11. Ibid.

12. Text of the Group of Five's Communique, Bureau of National Affairs, *Daily Executive Report*, 24 September 1985.

13. Not-for-attribution interview with U.S. Treasury Department official, October 1986.

14. Paul Blustein and Art Pine, "The Upper Hand: Baker, Darman Regain Role in Policy for the U.S. Treasury," *Wall Street Journal*, 17 April 1986, p. 13.

15. Not-for-attribution interview with a U.S. Treasury Department official, November 1986.

16. *New York Times*, 24 September 1985, p. D26.

17. Whether a more aggressive stance was in fact needed is a value judgment with no conclusive answer. The same can be said of the necessity to reduce presidential "wiggle room" in avoiding confrontation and retaliation in cases of discriminatory foreign trade practices.

11 The Merging of Domestic and International Economic Policies: The Competitiveness/Industrial Policy Debate

Our previously overwhelming lead in technology is declining. . . . This situation will not be remedied if we do not take action, and put in place a coherent, well-defined technology policy.

—Erich Bloch

Major premise: socialism is a failure. . . . Minor premise: private enterprise capitalism is the only system that has been able to combine prosperity with human freedom. . . . Conclusion: the U.S. needs more socialism! The conclusion is a clear logical fallacy yet . . . whatever problem you talk about . . . the only solution generally regarded as possible is more government intervention, throwing more money at it, passing more laws, more regulations.

—Milton Friedman

The U.S. international policymaking apparatus created a new venue in the mid-1980s. It gradually would erase the last vestiges of a separation between the formulation of internal and external economic policies, and it would accelerate the redefinition of national security to include economic strength and stability.

The new policy exercise was an unusually complex and contentious debate on whether the ability of U.S. industrial companies to compete in global markets was eroding to dangerous levels, and if so, what to do about it. Alarm about the global competitiveness of domestic producers grew more widespread in the wake of steady growth in the U.S. trade deficit and the discomforting sight of a steady stream of American manufacturing companies being decimated by seemingly unstoppable Japanese companies. Steadily increasing foreign competition—some of it supported by foreign governments—was extinguishing the logic of viewing the U.S. industrial sector in a strictly domestic context.

At the heart of this policy debate was the question of whether there was need for the U.S. government to adopt a more proactive role in assuring a ''competitive'' U.S. industrial sector. In a sense, the United States was the last entrant in the game of how to use government resources to enhance both exports and the ability of domestic manufacturers to compete against imports. Virtually every other country had long embraced the idea of government-business cooperation in lieu of complete reliance on the invisible hand of the marketplace. The uniquely American propensity to treat domestic and international economic policies as two distinct functions reflects the previously discussed, uniquely U.S. economic characteristics such as: relegation of trade policy to secondary status because of an unusually small percentage of GDP accounted for by trade; the absence of strategic policy planning in international trade because of the absence of strategic planning in the domestic economic sector; and the lack of a need to earn foreign exchange because of the ability to use dollars to pay for all desired imports.

HOW IDEOLOGY CAN SHAPE DECISION-MAKING AND ORGANIZATION

An economic policy formulation exercise—different in substance and procedure—emerged in the 1980s to deal with an escalating debate on U.S. competitiveness. This debate was not about allocating priorities between foreign policy and domestic economic policy objectives or allocating income and resources among special interest groups. It consisted of a conceptual examination as to whether a radically new economic problem had emerged and the best means of addressing the situation at hand. Noticeably absent as important players in the competitiveness dialogue were such international economic policy stalwarts as the Treasury and State departments, and the USTR. Instead, these discussions were led by a new cast of protagonists.

The initial phase of the competitiveness policymaking process was dominated by a contest of wills between those congressional Democrats who believed in greater governmental efforts to promote U.S. industrial strength and Republican administrations (Reagan and Bush) with strong beliefs in unfettered markets and small government. On another level, domestic and international economic policymakers, heretofore dwellers in two compartmentalized ''cultures'' with infrequent cross-communication, suddenly were working side-by-side in the emerging competitiveness policy debate.

As discussions on this issue continued, a separate dialogue developed between two cultures with very divergent mind-sets. On the one side were executive branch policymakers steeped in the notion that government and business were adversaries. On the other side were those elements of the managerial, scientific, and engineering communities who had become worried that U.S. industry was falling dangerously behind other countries in technology, manufacturing processes, and product innovation. Despite their widely divergent backgrounds, all the participants in these new dialogues did share one trait: they all were amateurs in quantifying the extent of the U.S. competitiveness problem and articulating an optimal policy response.

Efforts to enhance U.S. industrial dynamism took place within a policymaking process significantly different from the traditional trade, financial, and aid issues discussed in previous chapters. Whereas a running theme of this book is that the policy substance of international economic issues is often shaped by organizational process, the competitiveness debate is a case in which ideological and philosophical beliefs shaped organization. The reversal of the usual cause-and-effect relationship is due to the fact that the various versions of U.S. competitiveness-enhancing strategy imply different kinds and degrees (including none at all) of government support.

Numerous organizational configurations are possible, each one appropriate to administering and coordinating specific kinds of programs to assist and subsidize domestic industry. At one extreme would be nothing more than making sure that new domestic economic policies damaged international competitiveness to the least extent possible. At the other extreme, unrestricted government involvement could turn Uncle Sam into the world's biggest venture capitalist, providing direct funding of basic and applied research projects in targeted industries, some of which probably would be designated on the basis of political clout. U.S. lawmakers and policymakers to date have reached consensus only on acceptance of a flexible, ill-defined gray area that goes beyond the first option, but stops far short of the second. The extent to which one advocates creation of new, elaborate, well-financed organizational arrangements is therefore mainly a function of the extent to which one believes increased governmental activity is, or is not, warranted by an inadequate U.S. industrial performance relative to its major trading partners.

The debate on competitiveness policy and the resulting policy responses provide a rare portrait of the Washington economic policymaking process breaking new ground. These debates are too new and amorphous to have generated entrenched "iron triangles" among specific agencies, congressional committees, and special interest groups sharing the same self-interests and priorities. Instead of bureaucracies shaping policy substance, competing philosophies in Congress, the White House, and the private sector clashed over the efficacy of expanding and altering the existing bureaucratic order.

Substantive issues raised in the competitiveness debate were and are uncommonly ambiguous—starting with the conundrum as to whether a problem requiring a greater government presence really exists.[1] Although there was consensus that most parts of the U.S. industrial sector had been performing relatively poorly since the 1970s, there is no unanimity as to why it happened, how serious it was, or whether the alleged problem could be cured by government officials in Washington, D.C., arrogantly "picking winners and losers" among competing economic interests. Increased governmental involvement in the industrial sector is seen by some (such as Erich Bloch, quoted at the beginning of the chapter) as an absolute necessity in alleviating alleged competitive shortcomings brought on in part by the willingness of most governments to actively support their industrial sector. However, to others (like Milton Friedman), the means to a stronger economy is still limited government interference and free markets that provide maximum freedom to entrepreneurs.

Decision-making in this case has been mostly a groping for answers to a series of previously unexplored issues, with few analytical guidelines and no U.S. governmental forums with experience in dealing with them. Imprecision extends even to labeling the subject matter discussed in this chapter. What has been referred to here as competitiveness policy in most countries is dubbed industrial policy. Opponents to a reliance on U.S. government largesse to enhance industrial strength succeeded early on in equating the term ''industrial policy'' with an excessive, uninformed, and wasteful intrusion of the U.S. government into decisions best left to the marketplace. Because it came to suggest bureaucratic excess and a slide down the ''slippery slope'' to socialism, ''industrial policy'' gradually disappeared from Washington jargon, replaced by a more constrained and benign term: ''science and technology policy.''

Whatever it is called, the bottom-line policy question is the same: if and how a *limited* increase in U.S. government involvement in the economy can be a cost-effective catalyst for improved industrial competitiveness. There is a vast mix of policy and program measures that can be implemented, and selectivity lies at the crux of the debate. To oversimplify slightly, the options advanced in the United States since the early 1980s may be categorized according to three levels of intensity. The first is competitiveness enhancement policy only in an indirect, macro sense. Favored by economic conservatives, this option has the fewest implications for the budget and would necessitate no new federal programs or organizations. This low-intensity level would consist of regulatory reform and maintaining a mix of monetary, fiscal, and regulatory policies that consciously provides corporations with the most supportive business environment possible. A pro-competitive atmosphere would be produced mainly by an optimal monetary policy that kept both inflation and corporate borrowing costs (interest rates) at low levels, by a fiscal policy that provided low corporate income taxes and appropriate investment incentives (e.g., permanent tax credits for incremental corporate research and development). Efforts to protect a domestic industry or encourage its restructuring through imposition of temporary import restrictions would also fit into this category.

The second level consists of new, modified, or better financed official programs. Typically, they include such initiatives as increased governmental financial assistance for scientific research in the early stage of development of commercial, non-defense technology and manufacturing processes; improvements in the education system and expanded worker training programs; and less vigorous antitrust enforcement.

Box 12.1
The Stages of Research and Development

> *Basic Research*—Consists of original experimental and/or theoretical investigations designed to advance knowledge in scientific and engineering fields. In industry, basic research seeks to advance knowledge, but lacks a specific or immediate commercial objective.
>
> *Applied Research*—Is aimed at gaining knowledge or understanding to determine the means by which a specific, recognized need may be met. In industry, applied research includes investigations oriented to discovering new scientific knowledge that has specific commercial objectives with respect to products, processes, or services.
>
> *Development*—Is the systematic use of the knowledge or understanding gained from research directed toward the production of commercially useful materials, devices, or methods.

Source: Adapted from National Science Board, *Science and Engineering Indicators 1996* (Washington, D.C.: Government Printing Office, 1996), p. IV–9.

The third level, closest to the generalized concept of industrial policy, would include massive funding by the government of those emerging civilian industrial sectors and technologies that were "targeted" to receive extensive official subsidies. Government support would move beyond basic research and into pre-commercial development of new technologies (see Box 12.1). This strategy would require an expanded bureaucracy to include a new cadre of analysts to select which sectors deserved favorable treatment, new agencies to disburse government loans and grants to businesses and research organizations, advanced technology training facilities for smaller American companies, and an extensive information operation to monitor technological advances abroad and disseminate data to domestic businesses.

The U.S. science and technology policy/competitiveness debate has been further complicated by the fact that the United States long has had a de facto industrial policy. However, it has been produced in bits and pieces—unconscious, unplanned, and uncoordinated. In some respects, it seems irrelevant to be arguing over whether to create something that already exists. Even if they are only occasional and inadvertent, government actions constantly affect decisions and performance in the industrial sector. Many have argued that the U.S. government for more than four decades has operated a powerful, well-financed technology-promotion department. The Department of Defense is the closet counterpart in Washington to Japan's Ministry of International Trade and Industry. Cold war priorities promoted a partnership between the U.S. government and defense industries that has successfully created much of the most sophisticated military and aerospace technologies ever produced, from incredibly accurate missiles to the Internet to tremendously powerful spy satellites. As long as an argument can be made that a military tie-in exists, even the most ardent free marketeers have not questioned the merits of the Pentagon's financing state-of-the-art private sector research in dual-use (military and commercial) technologies, such as computers, semiconductors, and composite materials, or the military's funding of a program to improve the manufacturing of clothing.

For years, opponents of industrial policy have downplayed the de facto industrial policy characteristics of a steady spillover of Pentagon-funded technology into such commercial realms as aircraft. To the consternation of laissez-faire advocates, the Defense Advanced Research Projects Agency (DARPA) became the shining example for competitiveness policy activists that positive results can be delivered by a small, highly competent, and independent group of technocrats in the government operating with a relatively limited budget (about $2 billion annually). The agency amassed an impressive track record for supporting private sector research in a number of high-risk/high-payoff research projects that advanced state-of-the-art military and dual-use technologies. Few Americans doubt the historical contribution of the U.S. Department of Agriculture to the development of one of the world's most productive agricultural sectors, and still fewer have criticized the medical advances supported by the budget of the National Institutes of Health. Even self-proclaimed free market presidents like Reagan and Bush repeatedly assisted favored industries by granting relief from import competition. Curiously, controversy is only triggered about the ability of the U.S. government to help promote commercial technology, arguably the single most important sector determining the rate of future productivity and innovation in the U.S. economy.

THE INITIAL PHASE OF THE DEBATE: IDEOLOGUES EVOLVE INTO PRAGMATISTS

To stretch a point, the advocacy of industrial policy in the United States can be traced back to Alexander Hamilton, the first secretary of the treasury. More than 200 years ago, he wrote of the "expediency of encouraging manufactures in the United States" and suggested that "To produce the desirable changes as early as may be expedient may . . . require the incitement and patronage of government."[2] Hamilton's views on the promotion of manufacturing were sharply opposed by Thomas Jefferson, whose beliefs were summed up in his dictum that the government that governs least, governs best. Direct U.S. government support for the development of commercial technology goes back at least to 1836, when Congress appropriated $30,000 to subsidize Samuel Morse's first telegraph line between Washington, D.C., and Baltimore, Maryland.[3]

The contemporary debate on how to respond to the alleged U.S. industrial competitiveness problem formally emerged in the 1982–1983 period when a number of congressional Democrats began holding hearings and introducing what was unabashedly described as industrial policy legislation. As long as a Republican sat in the White House, agencies of the executive branch remained aloof from the emerging competitiveness policy debate. They had nothing to offer except to advocate the policy status quo and to suggest a presidential veto of any dramatic new legislation. This was the reason that the decision-making process in this case followed an intra-legislative branch model until Bill Clinton was inaugurated in 1993.

Discussions about possible need for a more activist U.S. science and technology policy were encouraged by two phenomena. The first was a substantial decline in the rate of increase in U.S. productivity and an increasing number of import-induced dislocations in basic manufacturing sectors such as steel, automobiles, and consumer electronics. Pessimists began forecasting the deindustrialization of the United States, warning that the industrial strength of Japan increased the possibility that the United States risked emulating Great Britain's economic decline. The second phenomenon consisted of the emerging ideas and literature, produced by academics like Robert Reich and Lester Thurow and business persons like Felix Rohatyn and Ira Magaziner. Collectively, advocates of a more aggressive competitiveness policy elaborated on the growing deficiencies of American industry, noted that technological advance was responsible for up to one-half of U.S. economic growth,[4] and argued that since the U.S. government was inevitably involved in the performance of the country's industrial sector, the only real question was whether it could do so in a more supportive manner.

One faction of congressional Democrats, which was pro–industrial policy, favored the reestablishment of a Reconstruction Finance Corporation to revitalize existing, import-impacted industries (e.g., steel and automobiles), while a second faction, dubbed the "Atari Democrats," focused attention on promoting new high-tech industries. The first wave of industrial policy proposals, introduced by Democratic members of Congress in 1983, proposed relatively ambitious changes. In retrospect, they were far too extreme to generate the political support needed to be passed and enacted into law. Typical were the National Industrial Strategy Act and the Industrial Competitiveness Act, both of which proposed creation of a federal industrial development bank. The two proposed bills also would have created a national council, consisting of leaders from business, labor, government, and the public, whose main task was to develop consensus and make policy recommendations for a national industrial strategy. This first wave of proposals also included expanded government funding for research and development (R&D) in new civilian technologies.

Industrial policy discussions were defined largely in terms of partisan politics for several more years. An increasing number of Democrats serving in Congress in the 1980s felt the need for the federal government to "jump start" what was perceived to be a flagging U.S. industrial sector. However, most of their Republican counterparts, while accepting the need for macroeconomic policies more favorable to business interests, were steadfast in their belief that waste and market distortions were the inevitable results of increased governmental subsidies and interventions in microeconomic policies. The 1984 reelection of President Reagan, a believer in small government and free markets, took the wind out of the sails of the Democratic proposals. The public demonstrated little open enthusiasm for Walter Mondale's support of industrial policy in his unsuccessful presidential campaign.

The idea of greater government activism on behalf of the industrial sector did not fade from the scene; instead, it underwent a metamorphosis. An important first step in the eventual narrowing of the gulf between the interventionists and the free market purists came in 1985 from an unlikely source: President Reagan's own Commission on Industrial Competitiveness. In retrospect, the commission's final report was instrumental in shifting the debate from an all-or-nothing, up-or-down vote on a broad-based industrial policy to the more narrowly focused, decentralized, and politically palatable concept of science and technology policy. The report pulled no punches in disagreeing with the "morning in America" theme of the Reagan administration. It cited "compelling evidence" of a relative decline in U.S. economic performance and declared that the ability of the United States "to compete in world markets is eroding."[5]

The report then recommended a mildly activist plan for new government initiatives to restructure the tax system, increase private R&D expenditures, reduce the cost of capital to private corporations, improve public education, create a Department of Trade as part of an effort to make foreign trade a national priority, create a Department of Science and Technology, and so on. These proposals were so poorly received by the Reagan White House that it refused to formally accept the report (which was presented, instead, to Commerce Department officials). Nevertheless, the commission's findings struck a responsive chord outside the Reagan administration and helped legitimize the growing argument that the absence of any advances into competitiveness policy was shortsighted and eventually would be prohibitively costly.

Shortly after the report's release, business advocacy of a national industrial "strategy" to enhance U.S. science and technology capabilities began hitting critical mass. The chair of President Reagan's Commission on Industrial Competitiveness, John Young, was president of the Hewlett-Packard Company, a successful and highly respected computer products firm. He became one of the more visible examples of the expansion of business support for governmental activism that went beyond declining basic industries hoping for government bailouts. A growing number of executives from high-technology and services sectors were now going public with their concerns about the ability of their companies to continue competing successfully in world markets. One year after the commission report was issued, Young helped found the privately run Council on Competitiveness to serve as a forum for discussing and recommending public policy changes aimed at enhancing the competitive position of American industry. The council quickly attracted the participation of executives of such influential high-tech American companies as IBM, Boeing, and Motorola.

Other business-supported advocacy groups were soon created to nudge the U.S. government toward a pro-active competitiveness policy. They included the National Coalition for Advanced Manufacturing, a 225-member lobbying effort by corporations and educational groups advocating federal support of advanced manufacturing technology; the National Advisory Committee on Semiconductors, established by federal law to produce a national strategy for this critical sector; and the Computer Systems Policy Project (an organization composed of 13 American computer manufacturers that advocated public policies to promote technologies critical to the success of their industry). A group calling itself Rebuild America enhanced its message of "investment economics" and "industry-led strategy" by having a member of Congress serve as its chair for several years.

Further legitimization of a more vigorous science and technology policy came from the American scientific and engineering communities. The National Academy of Sciences and affiliated groups, the National Academy of Engineering, the National Research Council, and the Manufacturing Studies Board began issuing a series of reports whose tone was identical: U.S. industrial and technological preeminence was at risk unless industry and government began to respond more effectively to the new, tougher realities in international competition. A joint panel of the National Academies of Science and of Engineering and the Institute of Medicine argued that the changing economics of advanced technology required U.S. science and technology policy to move beyond basic research to include the next step, applied or pre-commercial R&D. In August 1992, the National Science Board, an offshoot of the National Science Foundation, issued a report concluding that the American industrial R&D system "is in trouble" because the United States "is spending too little, not allocating it well, and not utilizing it effectively."[6] Policy activism was also the watchword of a series of reports issued by the Carnegie Commission on Science, Technology, and Government.

Private sector advocacy of a more aggressive stance moved up yet another notch in the initial report of the Competitiveness Policy Council in March 1992. The twelve people on this federal advisory board created by the 1988 trade act were all appointed by the president or Congress. Finding that U.S. competitiveness was eroding "slowly but steadily," their first annual report called for the establishment of a "serious" national competitiveness strategy focusing on six priority areas: saving and investment, education and training, technology, corporate governance and capital markets, trade policy, and health care costs.[7]

Broadening public support and the deteriorating U.S. trade numbers increased the ranks of members of Congress amenable to a more activist competitiveness policy. By the 1990s, the debate on U.S. competitiveness policy focused on the relatively narrow issue of how to modestly increase government funding of basic civilian research, not on a ground-breaking, budget-intensive industrial policy. A bicameral, nonpartisan Competitiveness Caucus was founded in 1987 and soon saw both its membership grow (to more than 200 members of Congress) and its agenda expand. Members of the 100th Congress introduced what was then a record total of 611 bills dealing with competitiveness, but this figure was eclipsed by the 666 bills introduced on the same subject into the 102nd Congress during 1991 and 1992.[8] Nevertheless, enthusiasm in the business community and on the Democratic side of the aisle was sufficient to inspire only a limited number of changes in actual policy.

THE LATTER PHASE OF THE DEBATE: SILHOUETTES EVOLVE INTO SUBSTANCE

The absence of a grand design for science and technology policy created a situation whereby the United States gradually developed a kind of "stealth" competitiveness strategy. Yes, a growing number of bits and pieces were put into place, creating the general outlines of a policy vehicle. However, even after ten years of evolution, the effort was neither sufficiently comprehensive and integrated nor sufficiently well-funded to produce a forceful, coherent science and technology policy that materially enhanced U.S. industrial competitiveness.

The U.S. policymaking process still has not succeeded in forging an ideological synthesis between respect for the principle of free markets, on the one hand, and assumptions of benefits to society from a more activist government role in spurring advances in commercial technologies and manufacturing procedures, on the other hand. Nor is there a well-established system of interagency coordination (as in international trade and monetary policies) to conduct such vital tasks as minimizing duplication among federally financed R&D programs, minimizing the extent that domestic economic policies do not work at cross-purposes with international economic objectives, and so on.

The mid-1980s saw the initial passage and enactment of a few ad hoc, relatively modest statutes designed to enhance U.S. science and technology efforts. Collectively, these uncoordinated measures began redefining the acceptable degree of government involvement in encouraging the development of new commercial technologies.[9]

The little-heralded National Cooperative Research Act of 1984 significantly relaxed the application of antitrust laws to joint corporate research and development efforts. By 1992, more than 250 cooperative ventures were created under the aegis of this act for the purpose of sharing the cost and risk of advanced R&D. They ranged in size from tiny operations up to Sematech, which started out as a $200 million-per-year effort, approximately half of which was funded for several years by the Pentagon. (Sematech is a research consortium of high-tech corporations seeking to expedite advances in the manufacturing know-how of American semiconductor producers and of builders of machinery for making semiconductors.)

The Federal Technology Transfer Act of 1986 created cooperative research and development agreements to stimulate joint R&D projects between the hundreds of federally funded laboratories and the business community and universities. In most cases, private companies are allowed to retain title to inventions resulting from research performed under cooperative agreements.

The Omnibus Trade and Competitiveness Act of 1988 was so named because the Democratic leadership in Congress made a decision in 1986, at the onset of deliberations on the bill, that it needed to go well beyond traditional trade policy measures and include provisions enhancing American technology and applied manufacturing skills. The act contains various provisions designed to improve worker training and retraining, and to enhance math, science, and engineering education.

Arguably, its most significant expansion of the boundaries of competitiveness policy was creating the Advanced Technology Program (ATP) within the National Institute of Standards and Technology (NIST), part of the Commerce Department. The ATP's main function is disbursing matching grants to encourage private companies to conduct applied research on cutting-edge, "pre-competitive, generic technologies" and manufacturing processes. The program is designed to provide limited seed money for high-risk (not readily attractive to private lenders or investors) R&D work that is past the basic research stage but not yet at the commercialization stage. The first round of matching grants to industry awarded in fiscal year 1990 amounted to only $9 million (pocket change by Washington standards). NIST was selected to administer these new programs because the Senate Commerce Committee, whose jurisdiction includes NIST, emerged from a floor fight as the winner in a spirited contest with the Senate Government Affairs Committee, which wanted to create a new Advanced Civilian Technology Agency.

In addition, the 1988 trade act gave NIST control of a new program of regional centers to provide matching funding to assist small manufacturing companies adopt new technology and manufacturing techniques developed by federal agencies. This program was later expanded to create the Manufacturing Extension Partnership, a nearly $100 million-a-year program which, among other things, operates regional manufacturing technology centers to offer hands-on technical advice to smaller industrial companies.

The 1990 Defense Authorization Act created a National Critical Technologies Panel whose mandate was submission of biennial reports to the president and Congress through the year 2000 identifying technologies deemed "essential for the long-term national security and economic prosperity of the United States." When the Bush administration dragged its feet in implementing these studies, the Democratic-controlled Congress did an "end run," passing legislation creating the Critical Technologies Institute as a federally funded research center operated by a private contractor (the Rand Corporation).

The American Technology Preeminence Act of 1991 extended and increased the funding of NIST's programs, created a National Quality Council, and instructed the executive branch to identify the kinds of R&D efforts needed to close any significant gaps between the U.S. technology base and its major trading partners. The High Performance Computing Act, passed in the same year with the full support of the Bush administration, provided multi-year funding for the development of supercomputers and the creation of a high-speed national network linking their users around the country.

A more defined outline of a rudimentary science and technology policy as an adjunct to domestic and international economic policies slowly began to coalesce during the latter half of the Bush administration. A self-initiated thaw occurred in the Bush administration's public denunciation of governmental outlays for assisting in the development of commercial technology. A widely circulated statement (attributed at various times to different CEA officials) had come to symbolize the Bush administration's industrial philosophy: "It does not matter whether the United States makes semiconductor chips or potato chips as long as markets decide." At least two senior officials, the head of DARPA and a deputy secretary of commerce, had been fired by the White House because they crossed the line of acceptable advocacy and action.

Important sources of the administration's new flexibility on this subject were the increasingly vociferous entreaties from the business community and the influence of D. Alan Bromley, assistant to President Bush for science and technology policy and a Yale University physicist. Dr. Bromley apparently convinced some of his key White House colleagues of the economic rationale of basic research and its differentiation from later phases of research in commercial product development. The 1990 annual report of the Council of Economic Advisers acknowledged the economic theory that at early stages of R&D, the social rate of return usually exceeds the private rate of return. (A major reason for this is that competing companies quickly cash in on important new technological breakthroughs). The policy implication is that society as a whole benefits if the federal government encourages private investment in basic scientific research to reach levels higher than they would otherwise be in a completely free market environment.

Parts of the Bush administration now proclaimed their belief that the federal government could make a cost-effective contribution to competitiveness above and beyond macroeconomic policy "by investing in basic research, by contributing to the development of generic, pre-competitive technologies, by improving the transfer of federally funded technology to the private sector, and by catalyzing cooperation among industry, academia, and government."[10] The White House's Office of Science and Technology Policy would soon boast of a series of initiatives taken in technology policy: increased budget requests for basic research funding, especially by the National Science Foundation; establishment of the Council on Competitiveness;[11] appointment of a presidential Council of Advisers on Science and Technology; and the presence of an "upgraded," more activist Federal Coordinating Council for Science, Engineering, and Technology (FCCSET).

The seven standing committees of FCCSET coordinated the independent technical research programs of no less than 21 different federal departments and agencies, each of whom was independently proceeding on its own research agenda. Much of Council's coordination came in the form of a "crosscut" tactic of identifying programs in advanced technological research that would be of interest to several agencies, recommending budget increases for the agencies that would be actively involved in these programs, and developing interagency coordinating structures to manage the new projects. To the extent FCCSET technology programs were included in the Bush administration's federal budget, the senior White House Staff (especially the powerful Office of Management and Budget director, Richard Darman) considered them to be preemptive concessions to congressional Democrats rather than a genuine administration embrace of science and technology policy.[12]

THE CLINTON UPGRADE MEETS BUDGET RESTRAINTS

William Clinton was the first president to express enthusiasm for and commitment to a science and technology policy aimed at promoting U.S. competitiveness. As a candidate, he argued that the need to improve the development and commercialization of new technologies was "critical" to the goals of regaining industrial leadership for the United States and ensuring long-term prosperity.[13] His inauguration had important evolutionary but not revolutionary effects on the development of programs in support of this policy. When only a few weeks old, the Clinton-Gore administration released a 36-page industrial technology initiative (the term "industrial policy" never appeared) based on the explicit premise that the country needed to recognize that government can play a key role helping private firms develop and profit from innovations. Among the many specific proposals offered was an increase by 1998 of nearly $9 billion, a 31 percent increase, in annual government funding of commercial and dual-use technology R&D.

Separately, both the executive and legislative branches began dealing with "conversion" policy, a post–cold war effort to encourage the transition by defense contractors and the federal laboratories to civilian production and research, respectively. This program included direct financial assistance to affected companies and indirect measures, for example, relaxing legal restrictions on the transfer to commercial sources of technology originally generated for military purposes.

The Clinton administration's enthusiasm for advancing science and technology led to an organizational upgrade of FCCSET and other high-level interagency scientific groups. The National Science and Technology Council (NSTC) was established by executive order in 1993. Chaired by the president, its main objective was to "establish clear national goals for Federal science and technology investments and to ensure that . . . programs are developed and implemented to effectively contribute to those national goals."[14] The NSTC, once described as a "virtual agency," seeks to assure a maximum information exchange on science and technology issues and goals among 23 presidential advisers and heads of departments and agencies. Senior agency officials prepare presidential decision directives and participate in the NSTC's five standing committees and approximately 60 working groups.[15]

The NSTC has not yet come close to achieving the status of the National

Economic Council or the National Security Council, mainly because enhancement of science and technology policy has not become a genuinely top-priority item with President Clinton. Nevertheless, the Advanced Technology Program's budget increased from $68 million in fiscal year 1993 to $218 million in fiscal 1997. The National Science Foundation's budget grew from $2.7 billion in fiscal 1993 to $3.4 billion in 1997.[16] In addition, the Clinton administration convinced Congress to continue co-funding such industry-specific projects as the Partnership for a New Generation of Vehicles (to reduce emissions, increase fuel efficiency, and improve manufacturing techniques) and networking technologies for the "next generation Internet."

EPILOGUE

Overtaken by the extraordinarily good performance of the U.S. economy, the great debate in Washington over international competitiveness and enhanced science and technology policies did a quick fade in the late 1990s. American industry had largely downsized and restructured itself in response to intense competitive pressures from Japan and elsewhere. Silicon Valley became a metaphor for U.S. technological innovation and dominance of the fast-growing information technology sector. American companies in the services sector were world-class competitors in such growth fields as financial services, data transmission, retailing, and entertainment. Pessimists declaring the need for more government support of high-technology companies were in short supply.

The net benefits of an expanded science and technology policy still have not been proven empirically and unambiguously. We do not know how much technological progress made possible by federal funding would still have been achieved if only private seed money had been available. In short, advocacy of expanded U.S. government financial support for a more competitive U.S. industrial sector is based on assumptions, not empirical data. Supporters still advocate an active role for the U.S. government in science and technology policy in the belief that more of a good thing is a good thing. Opponents remain adamant that the government should not waste taxpayers' money doing something that is properly left to the private sector.

NOTES

1. For a detailed examination of the economic and methodological ambiguities in assessing competitiveness, see the author's "Does the United States Have an International Competitiveness Problem?" in *National Competitiveness in a Global Economy*, David P. Rapkin and William P. Avery, eds. (Boulder, Colo.: Lynne Rienner Publishers, 1997).

2. Reproduced in *Powernomics—Economics and Strategy after the Cold War*, Clyde V. Prestowitz, Jr., Ronald A. Morse, and Alan Tonelson, eds. (Lanham, Md.: Madison Books, 1991), pp. 129, 134.

3. Linda R. Cohen and Roger G. Noll, *The Technology Pork Barrel* (Washington, D.C.: Brookings Institution, 1991), p. 2.

4. See, for example, Wendy Schacht, "U.S. Industrial R&D: Trends and Analysis," Congressional Research Service report dated January 17, 1996, p. 1.

5. Report of the President's Commission on Industrial Competitiveness, *Global Competition—The New Reality* (Washington, D.C.: U.S. Government Printing Office, 1985), pp. 1, 5.

6. National Science Board, "The Competitive Strength of U.S. Industrial Science and Technology: Strategic Issues," Washington, D.C., 1992, p. ii.

7. Competitiveness Policy Council, "Building a Competitive America," First Annual Report, 1 March 1992, pp. 1, 32.

8. Data sources: *Wall Street Journal*, 1 July 1992, p. A1; and the Lexis/Nexis database of congressional bills.

9. Technically, the first significant statute goes back to 1980, when the Stevenson-Wydler Act sought to promote the development and diffusion of industrial technologies through such means as the creation of Centers for Industrial Technology and provision of incentives for federal laboratories to work more closely with industry.

10. Executive Office of the President, Office of Science and Technology Policy, "Science and Technology," 1992, pp. 103–104.

11. The Council on Competitiveness, which should not be confused with the privately operated organization of the same name, was led by Vice President Dan Quayle; in 1992, angry congressional Democrats stripped the council of staff funding on the grounds that its contributions to increased competitiveness consisted of little more than dilution of existing environmental, worker safety, and health regulations on behalf of petitioning industrial corporations.

12. David M. Hart, "Managing Technology Policy at the White House," in *Investing in Innovation, Creating a Research and Innovation Policy that Works*, Lewis M. Branscomb and James H. Keller, eds. (Cambridge, Mass.: The MIT Press, 1998), p. 443.

13. "Technology: The Engine of Economic Growth," Clinton-Gore Campaign press release dated 21 September 1992, p. 1.

14. "Executive Summary of 1995 Strategic Plans," National Science and Technology Council web site: www.whitehouse.gov/WH/EOP/OSTP/NSTC/html/.

15. Given the pressure to reduce the federal budget deficit, the top implicit goal of the NSTC has been to settle interagency disagreements over R&D spending before they reached the final OMB budgetary review (see Hart, "Managing Technology Policy at the White House," p. 446).

16. Data supplied to the author by the ATP and NSF.

12 The Non-Making of International Economic Policy: The Process in Paralysis, 1996–20??

> The whole free-trade thing turned out to be for the big companies, not the little guy.
>
> —Ricardo Granado

> It was the best of times, it was the worst of times.
>
> —Charles Dickens

The two dominant themes of U.S. international economic policy in the 50 years after World War II were leadership and promotion of a growing global economy relatively unencumbered by government-imposed barriers. Inertia was the dominant theme in the last half of the 1990s. Whereas previous chapters have described a stream of decisions and actions associated with an activist U.S. policy, this chapter analyzes the uncharacteristic inaction that marked the 1995–1999 period. The inter-branch model of decision-making suffered gridlock. A new strain of multidimensional opposition to any movement towards a more integrated world economy became a factor in nudging governmental activism into a state of hibernation. No assumption about what was "good" policy was safe from revisionist thinking. No longer was there such a thing as a non-controversial international economic legislative proposal that could be enacted amicably and quickly.

It is too early to know whether the massive cracks that recently appeared in the status quo represent a momentary blip while traditional thinking regroups or whether the cracks signal the start of another major turning point in how the United States relates to the world economy. In either case, a study of policy-making is incomplete to the extent that it does not discuss the confluence of unprecedented factors responsible for what the U.S. government has *not* done in recent years to promote global economic "progress" as the term has been defined since the Reciprocal Trade Agreements Act was passed in 1934.

Major feuds caused by bureaucratic politics were virtually nonexistent in the Clinton administration's international economic decision-making efforts during the late 1990s. Congress did not pro-actively try to restore a protectionist stance. An analysis of U.S. international economic policymaking during this period parallels the Sherlock Holmes case that turned on his observation that a dog did not bark. This chapter discusses failures of the legislative and executive branches to take actions that in earlier years would have been done with relatively little controversy. It identifies new issues, new private sector actors, and new political alliances, and it explains how and why they effectively silenced parts of the international economic policy decision-making process. (The exception that proves the rule was the Treasury Department's extensive behind-the-scenes orchestration of International Monetary Fund [IMF] lending policies in Asia and Russia.)

THE CHANGED WORKING ENVIRONMENT FOR U.S. INTERNATIONAL ECONOMIC POLICYMAKERS

The most important change since the mid-1990s in the U.S. international economic policymaking process is the coalescence of new issues and new actors that brought vigorous opposition to long-standing, basic assumptions and a near halt to decisions to further enhance global economic cooperation. A seamless web of miscalculations and domestic and external economic and political changes is responsible for altering—to a still undetermined extent—the contours of the political base of U.S. international economic policy. The altered political equation has not produced a u-turn in U.S. policy back to protectionism or isolationism, but it did induce a legislative gridlock that impeded traditional policymaking. There was no ignoring the demands by citizens groups to be given a full-time seat at the policymaking table alongside government officials and executives of big business.

The New Issues

In the largest sense, the halt in policy momentum is the byproduct of a rapid-to-develop, worldwide backlash against globalization. The latter is an umbrella term for the dramatic increase in recent decades in integration among the goods and capital markets of national economies, due in part to the progressive relaxation by governments of barriers to the international flow of goods, services, and capital. For most Americans, the criticism of globalization erupted at a strange time. Reliance on the market mechanism was spreading around the world as the drawbacks of both planned economies and extensive industrial policy became painfully clear throughout Latin America, Asia, and Eastern Europe.

Emphasis on market forces was a major factor in the unusually long period of sustained, non-inflationary growth in the American economy that raised the overall standard of living and created tremendous financial wealth thanks to a booming stock market.

Even stranger was the political phenomenon that saw people and groups at opposite ends of the American political spectrum united in their antipathy to the alleged vices of globalization. Political liberals argued that reductions in trade barriers were causing less-skilled workers in the labor force to disproportionately bear the brunt of lost jobs and reduced wages and benefits. Political conservatives saw IMF programs as unwise bail-outs of inept governments and reckless investors. A new breed of economic nationalists warned that globalization threatened the ability of the United States to control its own destiny and bestowed too much power on faceless, unelected heads of international economic organizations. American human rights groups and foreign policy hard-liners jointly urged increased use of economic sanctions against China and other countries to protest what they deemed to be unacceptable foreign behavior. Environmentalists saw policies to maximize economic growth and minimize trade barriers as leading to irreparable harm to the earth's resources (see Chapter 6).

Liberal trade advocates lacked passion. They were quiet relative to the zealously vocal anti-globalization faction. The center did not hold.

A closer look at the American economy reveals data showing that an overwhelming percentage of income gains since the 1980s has accrued to people already in the upper income brackets, with workers in the bottom quintile experiencing little or no increases in real wages. If fringe benefits are ignored, the statistical result is greater income inequality. Those who feel left out of the new American prosperity criticize the domestic and international economic order for seeking to protect owners of capital far more than workers. The move to freer trade is seen as enriching only the already affluent and hurting vulnerable, relatively unskilled labor by shifting their manufacturing jobs abroad or causing their salaries to decline in order for their companies to compete better against imports of goods from low-wage countries. An official of the AFL-CIO summarized the case for the so-called economically disenfranchised by arguing that existing policies mainly were benefiting the corporate elite.

> Our current trade policy is lopsided: it protects copyrights, but not workers' rights. It takes care of international investors, but not the environment. We are opening markets abroad in financial services and agriculture, but we are not taking care of displaced workers at home. Let's get our priorities straight before launching yet another round of the wrong kind of trade liberalization.[1]

The ability of interest groups to force government officials in the United States and elsewhere into an agonizing reappraisal of globalization has been enhanced by the end of the cold war. Generating prosperity throughout the world through additional trade flows and providing loan packages to countries facing financial and social instability were long used as basic tools to contain the spread of Soviet influence. The loss of the "cold war card" deprives the administration of using the national security imperative to enlist congressional support for international economic policy initiatives to help friendly countries. Members of Congress are less willing to ask constituents to accept economic sacrifices for the good of the world order when there is no world communist menace to fight. Putting American interests first is back in style.

A considerable body of economic research casts doubt on the assertion that "globalization" is largely to blame for stagnant salaries among less educated and skilled American workers.[2] Nevertheless, interest groups sympathetic to American industrial workers remain unyielding in their demand for a new direction in trade policy. They denounce the almost 70-year-old U.S. government effort to enhance global economic efficiency by negotiating the progressive liberalization of trade barriers on a reciprocal basis. Their neo-protectionist campaign has the potential to alter a decision-making process that since 1934 has supported the more-trade-is-better guideline to U.S. trade policy.

The sudden influx of important new lobbyists was an inevitable outgrowth of the enlargement of the definition of trade relations. International trade negotiations gradually moved beyond traditional focus on the reduction of barriers imposed at the border to overtly discourage imports, and they steadily intruded into what previously had been considered off-limits internal matters. In the 1990s, officials were routinely discussing what kinds of multilateral regulations ought to be imposed on government procurement procedures; environmental, health, and safety standards; and competition policy (mainly antitrust enforcement) to limit the adverse effects of these government activities on the flow of international commerce.

Trade policymaking in the United States and elsewhere has been permanently complicated by expansion of the trade agenda to include two important *social* issues: environmental protection and enforcement of labor standards. The relatively simple question of whether to reduce international trade barriers for the purpose of more efficiently utilizing the world's limited resources suddenly expanded into an unaccustomed social context thanks to demands made by a new mix of influential interest groups throughout the world. This process paralleled the earlier, successful efforts of interest groups to force a rethinking of foreign aid to include protection of the environment and natural resources as part of an effort to promote "sustainable development." Advocates of measures to protect the environment and to protect workers' rights (safe working conditions, the right to organize unions, minimum wages, and strict limits on child labor) realized that international trade is an appropriate vehicle to promote their causes. Opponents of further reductions in U.S. trade barriers have demanded tangible progress in both of these social causes as a means of postponing the implementation, or at least diluting the impact, of new trade liberalization agreements.

Environmental and workers' rights concerns made their first big impact on trade negotiations in the U.S. talks with Mexico that led to the North American

Free Trade Agreement (NAFTA). This pact is an important cause of the globalization backlash in the United States. As one U.S. trade official privately noted, events associated with the creation of NAFTA "poisoned the well." Pro-NAFTA forces grossly oversold the short-term benefits of bilateral free trade in a marketing blitz designed to secure what was then an unsure congressional approval. In addition, several members of both parties in the House of Representatives were angered because many of the administration's promises of special rewards for their voting in favor of NAFTA were never delivered.[3] "We got nothing but broken promises out of NAFTA," said Esteban Torres (D., CA), a leader of the Hispanic Caucus. "I don't think anybody in the caucus appreciated the smoke-and-mirrors pitch President Clinton made to us."[4]

Many U.S. labor unions remain adamantly opposed to NAFTA because of fears of "runaway" plants. Anecdotal evidence exists of threats by management to assembly-line workers that they must not unionize or that they must accept the wages and working conditions offered them or else production will be shifted to Mexico. Furthermore, opponents of freer trade are angry because they believe that American companies have broken most of their promises to create new export jobs as the result of free trade with Mexico.[5] There is widespread consensus that NAFTA's side agreement on environmental protection lacks the enforcement teeth to effectively prevent further air, water, and land pollution from increased industrial production on the other side of the border with Mexico. Consensus also exists that the labor side agreement lacks the enforcement machinery to guarantee protection of workers' rights in Mexico. None of the original opponents of the NAFTA proposal changed their minds one iota after it went into effect. The whole experience has reinforced their concerns that reductions in trade barriers overwhelmingly enrich corporations and hurt the environment and the relatively less skilled American workers producing labor-intensive goods that can be made more cheaply elsewhere.

Congress is a critically important piece of the mosaic of the new political landscape of U.S. international economic policymaking in the late 1990s. A number of factors prevented a majority, especially in the House of Representatives, from voting in favor of legislation to keep U.S. international economic policy responsive to unfolding contingencies. First, one must go well back in time (perhaps to the nineteenth century) to find the same degree of visceral dislike exhibited by so many members of the majority party toward the president. Even without NAFTA-induced inter-branch strains, many Republican members of Congress would have been in no mood to disregard an unusually intense partisanship and enact President Clinton's legislative program. To some degree, the problem was bipartisan. A journalist argued that Mr. Clinton had a problem with both parties in his second term since the "Republicans fear him and loathe him, and the Democrats resent him as the cause of their being in the minority."[6]

The 1994 elections had produced a resounding victory for the Republicans, who took control of both houses of Congress for the first time in 40 years. Newt

Gingrich, the new speaker of the House, convinced most of his fellow Republican House members of two things. First, they had been given a mandate by the voters to enact basic changes in domestic American political values as embodied in the "Contract with America," and second, they had a limited amount of time to take advantage of momentum and get the job done.

Many of the newly elected Republican members arrived in Washington not predisposed to promoting more international economic interdependence—an attitude that was shared by many returning Democrats. A large number of the Republican freshman class were more grounded in small-town, rural, and religious political interests than in foreign affairs.[7] Many had never traveled abroad and reportedly did not even own passports when elected. The most parochial of them embraced isolationism. Others were populists who were suspicious of big business. Some were on the same wavelength as the religious right and would not vote against its platform, which had begun to overlap trade relations (discussed below). One theory argues that this may not be a transitory phenomenon: perennially light voter turnout may be magnifying on a cumulative basis the influence of strongly motivated single-issue advocates and making a larger number of Democratic and Republican members of Congress more ideological and less pragmatic.

Another element in the new political equation blocking decisions to implement international economic policy actions in the late 1990s was the unprecedented storm of criticism, from both the left and right, directed at the IMF for its questionable efforts to assist Asian countries and Russia after they were pummeled by global financial "contagion."

The New Actors

One cohort of new actors was the new congressional Republicans just discussed. The other important new cohort of actors contributing to the paradigm of policymaking inertia was the alliance of disparate interest groups campaigning against what they saw as the injurious effects of an accelerating global spread of capitalism. Previously, interest group lobbying on issues of U.S. international economic policy had been dominated by companies and workers with an immediate economic stake in the flow of imports, exports, foreign direct investment, and economic assistance. Beginning in the 1990s, however, many groups on the liberal pole of the U.S. political spectrum abandoned their traditional suspicion of nationalism in favor of an economic policy agenda aimed at preserving American jobs, pressuring other countries to adopt U.S. health and environmental standards, and raising foreign workers' rights and incomes toward American standards. Simultaneously, a number of groups on the traditionally free market–oriented right-wing underwent their own reversal of international economic ideology. They now saw the free flow of trade and capital across national borders as part of a process undermining U.S. sovereignty and social stability. One can look at the web sites of the AFL-CIO, Friends of the Earth, the arch-conservative Republicans for the National Interest, or the Pat Buchanan presidential campaign and find identical positions on the same group of contemporary international economic issues.[8]

The swift rise in the activism and influence of non-governmental organizations (NGOs) whose core agenda lay outside the realm of trade policy was a particularly important part of the new policymaking environment. NGOs are a subset of civil society, which can be defined as a collectivity of individuals who have joined together in non-governmental groups to promote laws, values, and institutions of common concern. NGOs are comprised of "citizen activists" representing non-commercial, non-establishment causes like human rights, environmental protection, worker rights, humanitarian relief, consumer interests, animal rights, and preservation of national cultural values.

Reflecting the global nature of these issues, NGOs have spread far beyond the democratic, industrial countries where they first flourished. They have flexed their muscles and intervened in areas of political and economic policies that previously were controlled entirely by the state. The question facing national governments, international organizations, and multinational corporations is not whether to include the growing numbers of NGOs in their deliberations and activities. The question is *how* to incorporate them into the international system in a manner most compatible with their strengths and weaknesses, and their capacity to disrupt as well as to create.[9] On the one hand, NGOs pursue noble-sounding, not-for-profit causes, and they seek to stop government officials from taking decisions behind closed doors with scant regard to public opinion. On the other hand, NGOs are special interest groups defending a particular viewpoint that they have declared to be in the public interest. They want to get their own way with little or no compromise. "The best of them, the ablest and most passionate, often suffer most from tunnel vision, judging every public act by how it affects their particular interest."[10] Ironically, NGOs, like the multinational corporations and international investors they abhor, are institutional manifestations of globalization in that their actions have the effect of compromising national sovereignty and local control.[11]

Anti–free trade, anti–free international capital movement elements in civil society became leading actors in the international economic policymaking process mainly because of three factors. One was the NAFTA review process's formally integrating social issues into the traditional trade debate previously dominated by the question of free trade versus protectionism. Another was the spread of financial crises in the emerging markets that caused even the staunchest believers to have doubts about unregulated international markets.

The uncommonly quick impact of NGOs on congressional international economic decision-making is also attributable to their quick mastery of another 1990s phenomenon: the revolution in information technology and telecommunications. The spread of the Internet to all corners of the planet is a tool of incalculable value for allowing civil society to form powerful multinational alliances and to loosen the historical power of governments to collect and disseminate policy-related information. "Instantaneous access to information and the ability to put it to use multiplies the number of players who matter and reduces the number who command great authority."[12] For the first time in history, warnings, calls for action, and solicitations for allies can be quickly and cheaply transmitted to people around the world who otherwise would never hear of, or pay attention to, international economic policy proposals.[13] However, another inherent feature of the Internet is the absolute lack of control over the sources and content of either web sites or messages posted in news groups. Absolutely no criteria have been established (or are in the offing) to assure accuracy, fairness, or responsibility as in the case of traditional media. Sensationalism and apocalyptic worst-case scenarios are regularly used by interest groups to attract readers in an ocean of clutter on the Internet.[14]

The new wave of international civil society trying to influence international economic relations is overwhelmingly opposed to what it perceives as the prohibitively costly byproducts of globalization. To them, the trend to a more integrated, market-based global economy is associated with the effort to maximize domestic economic growth with little or no regard for the damage inflicted in the form of displaced workers and a more polluted environment. The process of globalization is seen as conferring too much power on multinational corporations and international economic organizations while denuding national and local governments of authority to protect the health and welfare of their citizens.

Global Trade Watch is a branch of Public Citizen, an ostensibly pro-consumer group founded by Ralph Nader. It epitomizes recent efforts by NGOs to stop U.S. international economic initiatives in their tracks. Unfailingly anti–free trade (an anti-consumer position) and anti–multinational corporation, Global Trade Watch has been one of the most effective NGOs in organizing domestic and international coalitions to voice opposition to almost every international economic policy initiative proposed by the Clinton administration. Beginning in the mid-1990s, the group actively opposed all moves to lower U.S. trade barriers lest any American jobs be lost to increased imports. Hence, they argued against NAFTA, fast-track extension, the proposed Trans-Atlantic Economic Partnership with the European Union, proposed legislation to lower trade barriers on goods from African countries, and legislation that would lower barriers on textile and apparel products from Caribbean countries (to give them market access parity with Mexico). Additionally, the World Trade Organization (WTO) in general and its dispute settlement mechanism in particular have been portrayed as being injurious to U.S. interests and sovereignty. Global Trade Watch condemns any international economic actions by governments that might directly or indirectly assist large manufacturing or banking companies. Hence it urged defeat of both additional funding for the IMF and the proposed multilateral investment treaty.[15]

Despite a limited budget and membership base, the organization in 1999 could claim a higher correlation between the international economic program it advocates and actual public policy than could larger, longer-established pro-business groups.

Groups advocating religious values were the last of the advocacy groups who emerged in the late 1990s as activists trying to advance their larger agenda through international economic policy. As discussed below, the so-called religious right convinced their friends in Congress to add anti-abortion language to the legislation approving a U.S. financial contribution to the IMF. Religion and trade policy were united in the Freedom from Religious Persecution Act that passed the House but died in the Senate. The bill, inspired by reports of persecutions of Christian minorities in several countries, for the first time pitted groups like the Christian Coalition and the National Association of Evangelicals against big U.S. exporting companies. The proposed statute's most controversial provision mandated automatic imposition of economic sanctions against any country (China, for example) that the U.S. State Department determined was conducting or condoning religious persecution. Proponents argued that U.S. foreign policy could no longer ignore this issue. Opponents contended that economic sanctions would hurt American foreign policy and export competitiveness while doing little or nothing to end the persecution.

THE NEW PARADIGM OF POLICY PARALYSIS

The successful conclusion of the Uruguay Round of multilateral trade negotiations, implementation of the NAFTA, and agreement on timetables to achieve free trade in the Western Hemisphere and in the Asia-Pacific region—all of which largely were due to U.S. leadership—made the mid-1990s a time of extraordinary progress in pursuit of a freer global trading system. In retrospect, it was a high-water mark immediately followed by a rapidly spreading backlash in the United States against any further trade liberalization and the free flow of international capital. In most cases, legislation was bottled up by a combination of right- and left-wing opposition that had different dislikes but similar goals.

Neither the relentless vehemence of opposition by interest groups to proposed policy initiatives nor the strange bedfellows coalitions conducting the negative lobbying campaigns were foreseen. The "old order" was caught off guard. The IMF had become the internationally recognized 911 number to call when "emerging market" countries faced financial crises and social strains as the result of falling exchange rates and massive capital flight. Nevertheless, the Congress for many months refused to approve the executive branch's earlier commitment to contribute to the increase in the IMF's financial resources that had been approved by its member countries.

Equally paradoxical was the Congress's refusal to act on the administration's request to renew once again the expired fast-track trade negotiating authority. One of the basic tenets of political economy is that proposals to reduce trade barriers are significantly more palatable to a nation's legislative branch during a period of rapid domestic economic growth and low unemployment than they are during recession and growing unemployment. The extraordinarily good U.S. economic performance during the Clinton administration was inconsistent with failure to secure renewal of the legislative authority that had become indispensable for negotiating comprehensive reductions in trade barriers. Opponents of fast-track renewal did not openly advocate reimposition of a prohibitively high U.S. tariff wall, but they did look unfavorably at any further negotiated reductions in trade barriers. An additional anomaly was that the combination of a widespread support for fast-track renewal by the American business community and a Republican-controlled Congress suggested easy passage of the renewal legislation. Failure to get such a bill passed in this seemingly favorable environment suggested the obsolescence of another basic tenet of political economy.

Neither the request for additional IMF funding nor the fast-track request represented a policy innovation. They were, at most, new wine in old bottles. In both cases, the administration was merely seeking to extend established practices. As balance of payments problems intensified in magnitude in the wake of increases in the value and volume of international transactions, the resources of the fund had been increased numerous times since the late 1950s. Fast-track negotiating authority was created (on a temporary basis) by the 1974 trade act and subsequently renewed. Neither had previously inspired a prolonged controversy or legislative delay.

A relatively innocuous legislative proposal was offered to provide limited incentives to encourage long-stagnant African economies to reduce government interference and rely more on market forces. Improbably, the bill stalled when left-wing and right-wing groups joined forces to portray it as imposing unacceptable harm on the American economy and devastating harm on Africa.

A fourth example of the new paradigm of inaction, also unexpected, was the collapse of efforts to conclude the Multilateral Agreement on Investment. Only a few people were even aware of the onset of these negotiations, which were not intended to go much beyond codifying on a multilateral basis the guidelines of hundreds of existing bilateral investment treaties.

For better or worse, the widely embraced "Washington consensus" that optimal economic policy emphasizes market forces, deregulation, privatization, reduced government spending, moderate tax rates, and liberal trade policies came under an intensifying attack by private groups for failing to provide the greatest good for the greatest number. A new generation of lobbying bitterly attacked the global spread of capitalism as having forced an excessive transfer of power from governments to corporations whose mounting profits enriched only the elite circle of shareholders and executives.

THE DECISIONS NOT TO MAKE DECISIONS

The paradigm of policy paralysis is empirically demonstrated in the details of five case studies of policymaking gridlock. Four involved pending legislation in the Congress and one dealt with ongoing multilateral negotiations.

Congress Turns Its Back on Mexico

The first significant manifestation of the new mood in Congress regarding international economic relations occurred in January 1995, when the Clinton administration sought congressional approval of a large U.S.-backed loan guarantee for Mexico that was aimed at braking the free-fall of the Mexican peso. A loss in confidence in the Mexican economy at the end of 1994 sent capital flowing out of the country, threatening to deplete reserves and again putting into question Mexico's ability to repay its foreign debts. The financial crisis threatened to create political and social instability that the neighboring United States could not ignore. Nevertheless, the legislative branch showed itself to be in no mood for what many members viewed as a bail-out of unsound Mexican economic practices and irresponsible foreign lending. Congressional opposition to approving a loan guarantee was actively encouraged by anti-NAFTA lobbyists that wished to make another anti-Mexico statement.

The administration had thought the time-honored call to duty to support the president in a time of crisis would be persuasive. It was not. Congress rejected with impunity the calls for U.S. leadership, the defense of U.S. national security interests, and related goals. The Cold War was over. The new majority in Congress had a domestic agenda.... Foreign aid, bailouts, and other forms of support for developing countries had little resonance in the Capital.[16]

The result was the administration's hurried resort to the Treasury Department's Exchange Stabilization Fund to provide emergency funds to Mexico. This action infuriated many members of Congress and led to legislation imposing temporary restraints on the executive branch's use of the stabilization fund.

Fast-Track Authority Goes off the Rails

The "cooperative" variant of the inter-branch model faced a major dilemma in 1974. The administration was explaining that the upcoming Tokyo Round of multilateral trade negotiations would have to be the first to tackle the relatively complex subject of non-tariff barriers (NTBs). Previous multilateral negotiations had reduced tariffs to the point that increased governmental resort to NTBs had made them the dominant form of trade restriction. However, the prospect of delegating authority to the executive branch to liberalize NTBs caused major discomfort on Capitol Hill. Whereas delegating authority to the administration to negotiate and implement tariff reductions of specific amounts required relatively simple legislation, reducing NTBs largely meant modifying existing legislation dealing with such matters as health and safety standards. The Nixon administration's request for virtual carte blanche authority to change any existing domestic statute in order to enact NTB trade agreements went well beyond the limits of congressional tolerance (especially in the atmosphere of Watergate). A large majority of legislators felt that enabling the president to modify a broad range of existing laws constituted not only a reversal of the constitutional roles of the two branches but also an abrogation of Congress's legislative responsibilities.[17] Thus was born the fast-track compromise. This term referred to the extraordinary new statutory language that modified standard legislative procedures by requiring Congress to take a simple up-or-down vote (no amendments) within a fixed period of time on trade agreements specifically concluded under this negotiating authority. Fast track subsequently was renewed four times, the last three of which were associated with negotiating the multilateral Uruguay Round agreement and creating free trade areas with Canada and Mexico. When the fast-track negotiating authority expired in early 1994, only perfunctory efforts were made to renew it since no major new trade negotiations were scheduled, and the trade community was focusing on efforts to implement the many provisions of the just-concluded NAFTA and Uruguay Round agreements.

Serious efforts on both ends of Pennsylvania Avenue were made in 1997 and 1998 to enact legislation renewing fast track. These efforts were glaring failures. Nothing seemed to go right for supporters of fast track. Because of a distinct lack of support in the House, what would have been a sure vote against renewal was canceled in 1997. One year later, a renewal bill was defeated in the House by a vote of 243 to 180.[18] The several issues and actors contributing to this legislative stalemate reappear in the other case studies of policy paralysis that follow.

The backlash to globalization and the relatively esoteric nature of the subject deprived the fast-track issue of enthusiastic support from the general public. Still licking their wounds from their failure to defeat implementation of the free trade agreement with Mexico, a number of unions made defeat of fast track their top trade legislation priority. Their natural alliance with the environmental lobby against lower barriers and increased international trade was easily reconstituted. For the bill to pass, effective lobbying efforts conveying a sense of urgency were needed from the White House and business groups. Neither delivered. Although he declared fast-track renewal a top legislative priority, President Clinton "barely lifted a finger to push it through Congress."[19] The Clinton administration respected the AFL-CIO's strong opposition to renewal because it was grateful to organized labor's ability to deliver campaign contributions and votes to the Democratic party. With Vice President Al Gore positioning himself to run for president in the 2000 elections, the administration was not about to turn its back on its labor allies, especially since House minority leader and unofficial presidential candidate Richard Gephardt was publicly against fast-track renewal. Business groups did lobby for renewal[20] but with an intensity suggesting that priorities of top executives lay elsewhere. This would be understandable inasmuch as industry and agriculture did not stand to reap any major short-term benefits; only a free trade agreement with Chile, a small market, was planned at the time.

Process and tactics were not exclusively responsible for killing the presumably good chances for restoring the fast-track provision in 1997 and 1998. A fundamental ideological disagreement on the course of U.S. trade policy was also present, one that could not be resolved in the prevailing political atmosphere. It existed in the form of irreconcilable differences over the inclusion of labor and environmental standards in negotiations conducted under fast track. Free trade advocates believed that if multilateral trade negotiations included detailed formulas for universal labor and environmental standards, the world trading system would soon be impaired by the spread of protectionist barriers disguised as countries' efforts to enforce their domestic environmental and labor laws.

Most unions and environmental, development, and human rights NGOs resolutely refused to support fast-track renewal without strong labor and environmental provisions—not NAFTA-like unenforceable side agreements. This position reflected both a direct concern for these issues and a strong desire to either prevent outright the revival of fast-track authority or at least scale back its potential impact. Although raising world standards to protect workers and the environment is a desirable goal from a social policy perspective, protectionists understand the implications for international trade and investment. Compliance with more vigorous environmental and species-protection standards would inevitably lead to more U.S. import barriers and occasional outright bans on offending foreign-produced goods. Reducing global disparities in wages and benefits would raise production costs in most countries, especially low-wage LDCs, and make their goods less competitive with U.S.-made goods.

The fast-track bills approved by the Senate Finance and House Ways and Means committees would have effectively required trade agreements negotiated under fast-track authority to contain only provisions reducing trade barriers and trade distortions. Hence, provisions related to environmental and labor standards would be acceptable only to the extent they ensured that labor, environment, health, and safety regulations were not employed as disguised trade barriers and that existing standards were not waived by a country as a means of enhancing its ability to export or attract foreign direct investment. An effort to significantly modify this language in either direction would have alienated a large number of House members. Both sides preferred no fast-track legislation to ''bad'' legislation. Without stronger labor and environmental provisions, most Democrats would not have voted to restore fast track and thereby anger labor and environmental activists. If stronger standards had been inserted, most Republicans and many free trade Democrats would have voted against the bill. Impasse was perpetuated because neither side wanted, or needed, to compromise.

Encouraging Market-Based Economic Policy in Africa

Sub-Saharan African countries account for a very high proportion of the world's poorest and most poorly managed economies. Exclusive of oil, imports from these countries account for well under 1 percent of total U.S. imports.

Foreign direct investment in these countries by American multinationals is negligible. In an effort to reverse these negative trends, members of Congress's bipartisan Africa Trade and Investment Caucus and later the Clinton administration proposed a series of policy initiatives. Ultimately, they were designed to alter the foreign aid–oriented U.S. economic relationship that had always existed with that continent—with very limited success.

The market-based strategy embodied in the proposed Africa Growth and Opportunity Act, originally introduced by members of Congress in 1997, became a lightning rod to severe criticism for a proposal that probably would have attracted little attention and opposition if introduced just a few years earlier. The proposed legislation boiled down to giving the president authority to do a number of things: offer greater market access for African goods through lower tariffs, earmark government funds and guarantees to support U.S. private sector investment in Africa, forgive government-to-government debt, increase bilateral foreign aid, and establish a negotiating framework at the ministerial level to improve the trade and investment climate in Africa. The proposed legislation stipulated that in order to be eligible to participate in these programs, an African country would have to be certified by the U.S. government that it ''has established, or is making continual progress toward establishing, a market-based economy.'' The bill was supported in Congress by a broad coalition that ranged from liberal Democrats to the then–Speaker of the House, Newt Gingrich. However, an unlikely coalition of opponents succeeded in persuading a majority of the Senate not to join the House in passing it.

Part of the opposition to the proposed bill came from historically protectionist sources. The U.S. apparel industry and unions opposed any phase-out of import barriers on the basis of potential job losses, despite the fact that the U.S. International Trade Commission foresaw such minor increases in imports of African-made apparel as the direct result of reduced tariffs that it estimated less than 700 American jobs would be lost.[21] The larger, more strident opposition came from intellectuals to the left of center who might otherwise have been expected to support efforts to promote economic growth in Africa. The most visible attack on the bill came from self-styled consumer advocate Ralph Nader and from Randall Robinson, president of an organization called TransAfrica. In an op-ed piece, they warned of ''ominous'' effects and ''harsh new conditions'' that would compromise the sovereignty of African countries. ''We must not replace European colonialism . . . with a new colonialism of servitude to external corporate interests,'' they wrote.[22]

Criticism leveled by the Global Trade Watch group was so extreme that an objective analysis suggests that some of it did not have a basis in fact. The Africa Growth and Opportunity Act, as written in 1998, was characterized as ''NAFTA for Africa'' and condemned as ''lethal medicine'' for the region's economic problems. Global Trade Watch claimed that the bill's real driving force was a coalition of scheming U.S. oil and manufacturing corporations. The group said that it and its NGO allies opposed the bill on grounds that it would undermine "African interests in sovereign, equitable development in order to promote U.S. corporate control of African economics and natural resources."[23] African countries were pictured as being forced to accept imposition of harsh IMF-style budget cuts and to privatize public assets at fire-sale prices, and as being vulnerable to a disruptive onslaught of incoming foreign direct investment. There is no public record of political leaders of African countries echoing these concerns. A Global Trade Watch web site lists 35 African-based NGOs as opposing the bill, but not a single government agency.[24]

The Delay in Replenishing the IMF

In September of 1997 the IMF's Executive Board approved the eighth increase in the capital subscription, or quota, that member countries pay into the fund to give it currency balances to lend. Heavy lending commitments to "emerging market" countries had reduced uncommitted reserves to the point that a weighted majority of member countries agreed that a quota enlargement was urgently needed to provide adequate financial resources to cope with future financial crises. The U.S. share of the approved quota increase, along with its share of funding for a new supplemental lending facility (the New Arrangements to Borrow), came to just under $18 billion. The Clinton administration and the manufacturing, financial, and agricultural sectors of American business vociferously pressed for the expansion of the IMF's resources. They viewed it as being necessary to prevent outbreak of a serious global recession that would severely hurt American foreign policy goals, exports, and bank balance sheets. In early 1998, the Senate approved the bill by an overwhelming majority.

A major reason for urgency in replenishing the fund was escalating requests for loans beginning in the second half of 1997 as the global financial crisis swept across Asia, Russia, and then Brazil. The Fund's response to this extraordinary crisis was the catalyst for an outbreak of controversy that, for the first time, created a clear and present threat that Congress would reject an IMF appropriations bill requested by the administration. A suddenly familiar scenario had materialized: opposition from liberal Democrats and conservative Republicans created a pincers movement in the House of Representatives that put proponents of the U.S. contribution on the defensive and therefore put the entire IMF replenishment at risk.

The first legislative roadblock to approval of the U.S. share of additional currency balances for the fund was the decision of the then–speaker of the House, Newt Gingrich, to amend the legislation authorizing (among other things) the transfer of $3.5 billion for the U.S. share of the newly approved fund lending facility, the New Arrangements to Borrow. Gingrich added a non-germane provision banning U.S. funds going directly or indirectly to any family planning groups whose activities included performing or advocating abortions in other countries. This was an effort to placate demands from the religious right that the Republican party be more responsive to their social policy goals. The

Clinton administration responded with a firm promise to veto any bill containing the anti-abortion provisions.

Groups representing labor and environmental interests used the replenishment debate to voice their opposition to the fund's existing policies and to demand basic changes in its operating procedures as the condition for expanding its financial assets. The AFL-CIO argued that the market-oriented economic philosophy of the IMF imposed austerity on workers and ignored workers' rights. Environmental groups condemned IMF loans for "paving the way for further resource-exploitive growth" by ignoring the social and economic value of environmental resources, encouraging borrowing countries to attract more foreign direct investment by lowering antipollution standards, and forcing cutbacks in government spending.[25]

Economic arguments from across the political spectrum opposed increasing the IMF lending resources as a means of curbing the damage allegedly inflicted by misguided and overly secretive IMF lending practices. Criticism of the fund increased geometrically after the inevitable happened. When responding to an Asian financial crisis not caused by the traditional combination of inflation, large national budget deficits, spiraling trade deficits, and so on, the IMF still deemed it appropriate to impose its standard lending criteria despite widespread criticism that they are too inflexible and restrictive. The fund's standard of "conditionality" emphasizes domestic austerity measures, such as tight monetary and fiscal policies and currency depreciation. Repeatedly forcing borrowing countries to endure recession instead of encouraging faster growth aimed at promoting investor confidence and expanding their capacity to produce goods for export had cost the IMF support from the growth-oriented economic school of thought that included economists at the World Bank, the fund's sister institution. Given the absence of an instruction manual for dealing with the lightning-quick spread of economic malaise across previously healthy Asian economies, the mathematical probability of the IMF's making policy mistakes in at least some of these countries was 100 percent. The result was the assertion made across the political spectrum that its misguided programs and overly intrusive demands had turned what was originally a difficult situation in Asia into a near depression that harmed social and political stability. The implication was that countries facing balance-of-payments problems might be better off *not* applying for loans from the fund. The House majority Leader in 1998, Dick Armey, voiced his opposition to the replenishment bill by declaring that the IMF "has the Midas touch in reverse—virtually every country it tried to help has become worse off from the experience."[26]

The IMF's alleged "bail-outs" of Asian countries also reinforced dissatisfaction in what might be called the "right-wing" school of economic thought. They viewed fund lending practices as having escalated beyond the mission originally agreed to in the 1940s of helping countries with short-term liquidity problems keep their exchange rates stable. Now the IMF regularly was providing emergency lending to what were deemed irresponsible governments and private corporations. The "moral hazard" argument claims that large IMF rescue packages have undermined good domestic economic policies and prudent lending practices. Government economic policymakers and commercial bank loan officers allegedly have come to believe that they can take excessive risks because they will not have to suffer the full consequences of their mistakes. If irresponsible risk-taking causes an economic crisis, the IMF presumably would lend generously to any country "too big to fail." The immediate implication of this argument is that the IMF is a cause of international financial instability, not a cure. Three senior members of the American financial establishment attracted a lot of attention when they concluded that the IMF was "ineffective, unnecessary, and obsolete" and should be abolished.[27]

In the end, the impasse was broken by use of the back-door maneuver of incorporating the $18 billion IMF funding package in an omnibus appropriations bill that Congress hurriedly passed in October 1998. Passage of the bill was a far better option for legislators than the alternatives: staying in Washington instead of going home for campaigning in the final weeks before the election or forcing another politically unpopular shutdown of the federal government.

MAI Day

In the spring of 1995, negotiators representing the industrialized countries that comprise the Organization for Economic Cooperation and Development (OECD) quietly commenced efforts to draft the text of what was to be the Multilateral Agreement on Investment (MAI). Few serious technical obstacles confronted the negotiators. No major innovations were envisioned. A multilateral agreement would simply build on the principles contained in more than 1,600 bilateral investment treaties and several non-binding multilateral codes already in existence. Larger industrialized countries like the United States had already phased out most of their formal controls on inward foreign direct investment. The task at hand was mainly creating a comprehensive legal framework that would encourage further reductions of obstacles to foreign direct investment, prevent discriminatory treatment by governments of foreign-controlled companies, and provide a better mechanism for resolving disputes between these companies and host governments.

The official explanation of the need for an MAI was that it was "a logical step" to consolidate and complete existing agreements. The "bilateral approach is less than ideal in a rapidly integrating world economy and bilateral investment agreements do not exist between many of the OECD countries."[28] The OECD countries, which represent upwards of 85 percent of all foreign direct investment flows, hoped to produce an agreement to which non-member governments would be invited to join. The ultimate goal was the belated creation of an international regime for foreign direct investment comparable to the trade rules embedded in the General Agreement on Tariffs and Trade (GATT).

Three years after they started, the negotiations were suspended indefinitely in hopes that the OECD governments could regroup. One reason for the shutdown of talks was that the United States and others would not accept the demands by several countries, including the European Union and Canada, that they be allowed to exempt large sectors of their industries (e.g., companies engaged in cultural pursuits) from terms of the agreement.

The larger reason for the breakdown of the MAI negotiations was a contentious campaign against it that was waged globally by NGOs through the Internet, letter-writing, newspaper advertisements, and even street protests. The coalition of development, environment, human rights, labor, and consumer groups opposing the MAI included the AFL-CIO, Oxfam, the Sierra Club, Amnesty International, the Third World Network, the Western Governors' Association, the Council of Canadians (whose web site included a logo claiming that the MAI "could crush Canada"), and Public Citizen's Global Trade Watch. A search engine entry for "Multilateral Agreement on Investment" in early 1999 produced citations for 4,100 web postings. The stridency and relentlessness of private sector opposition in North America and Western Europe eventually unnerved the negotiators and magnified the lingering substantive disagreements among the OECD governments to such an extent that progress in the talks ground to a halt. The proposed treaty was so demonized that the negotiations became a highly sensitive political issue that could not continue to be debated behind closed doors. The potential power of an electronically networked global civil society to help stop a seemingly mundane multilateral negotiation in its tracks provides an example of the society-centered theory of decision-making theory discussed in Chapter 7.

The substance (a tilt toward the interests of private investors) and procedure (secret negotiations among a handful of rich countries) associated with the MAI represented everything about globalization that angered and frightened the NGOs opposing the proposed text. They claimed it would give corporations the "sovereign power to govern countries" and "radically limit" pursuit of social, economic, and environmental justice.[29] A detailed case against the agreement was made in a "Joint NGO Statement" posted on the Internet that eventually was "signed" by more than 600 groups in more than 70 countries. It claimed that the MAI as written was "explicitly designed to make it easier for investors to move capital, including production facilities, from one country to another, despite evidence that increased capital mobility disproportionately benefits multinational corporations at the expense of most of the world's peoples."[30] The working text of the MAI in 1998 was hardly perfect and negotiating in secret was not an absolute necessity. Depending on one's beliefs, it can be argued that the NGO opponents performed a valuable service in protecting global society from some seriously flawed provisions that tilted far too much in the direction of protecting investors' rights and ignoring their responsibilities to society at large. One of the most criticized provisions in the working text suggested that a foreign-controlled company could demand compensation from the host government for a wide range of reasons including "a lost opportunity to profit from a planned investment.'' Opponents argued that this language could be interpreted as barring enforcement of national and local environmental, health, safety, and workers' rights laws and regulations that did impede, or could impede, a foreign-controlled corporation's right to make a profit. Public Citizen warned of ''an international commercial treaty empowering corporations and investors to sue governments directly for cash compensation in retaliation for almost any government policy or action that undermines profits.''[31] In the end, the OECD countries opted to suspend negotiations rather than just rewrite the most contentious provisions.

THE OUTLOOK

Traditional patterns of U.S. decision-making, at least temporarily, have been distorted by the burst of sentiment among interest groups on both ends of the political spectrum that U.S. international trade and financial policies no longer should be guided by the dictum that free markets are good and government controls are bad. The seemingly endless eruption of international financial crises during the 1990s has undermined the decades-old U.S. consensus on the desirability of pursuing further liberalization of the international economic order. Traditional policies are being attacked by a philosophy that believes a system of unregulated markets can and does career dangerously out of control. This belief leads to the call for the free market to be reined in on a global basis because it allegedly is ''prone to crises and even depressions, and does not necessarily allow the majority of its participants to share in the gains from economic growth and technological progress. Globalization is a way of forgetting all this. . . . It is capitalism in denial.''[32]

The future might bring a steady growth in public disenchantment with the pro-liberal trade, pro-globalization positions currently embraced by the mainstream in both U.S. political parties. It is equally possible that some of the shrill rhetoric and often simplistic solutions proposed by self-declared populists will recede if official policy ''humanizes'' globalization by successfully addressing the major weaknesses and inequities of the global economic order.

In the meantime, U.S. policymakers cannot stop efforts by an influential network of NGOs to push the decision-making process in a direction different from where they wish to go. The ability of the United States to continue its leadership role in creating a more market-based global economic order—assuming most people still believe this to be desirable—cannot be taken as a given. As long as the U.S. executive branch is without fast-track negotiating authority, it is highly unlikely that other countries will seriously discuss additional trade liberalization with the United States in the proposed millennium round of multilateral trade negotiations or implementation of free trade areas in the Asia-Pacific and Western Hemisphere regions.

The communications revolution is linking like-minded people around the globe with unprecedented ease. A globalized force is evolving that can more forcefully demand government accountability and augment the limitations of individual national governments in solving problems common to mankind. At the same time, however, transnational activist groups have the potential to intensify "political and social fragmentation by enabling more and more identities and interests scattered around the globe to coalesce and thrive."[33] Both the positive and negative aspects of the new private sector activism have potentially profound implications for the U.S. international economic policymaking process in the twenty-first century.

NOTES

1. Congressional testimony of Thea Lee on 9 July 1997 to the House Committee on International Relations, downloaded from the AFL-CIO web site: www.aflcio.org/stop-fasttrack/.

2. See for example, Gary Burtless, Robert Lawrence, Robert Litan, and Robert Shapiro, *Globaphobia—Confronting Fears about Open Trade* (Washington, D.C.: The Brookings Institution, 1998).

3. See, for example, the report by the Public Citizen group posted on the Internet at www.citizen.org/pctrade/trick.html/.

4. As quoted in *New York Times*, 11 November 1997, p. A6.

5. See, for example, Jack Beatty, "Nasty NAFTA," at the *Atlantic Monthly* web site: www.theatlantic.com/.

6. Owen Ullmann, "America's New Four-Letter Word," *International Economy* (July–August 1998): 62.

7. Edmund B. Rice, as quoted in the *New York Times*, 2 September 1998, p. A13.

8. The sites can be found at www.aflcio.org/; foe.org/; rni.org; and theamerican-cause.org/. The same basic arguments can be found on the sites of Public Citizen's Global Trade Watch at www.citizen.org/.

9. P. J. Simmons, "Learning to Live with NGOs," *Foreign Policy* (Fall 1998): 83-84.

10. Jessica T. Matthews, "Power Shift," *Foreign Affairs* (January–February 1997): 64.

11. Stephen J. Kobrin, "The MAI and the Clash of Globalizations," *Foreign Policy* (Fall 1998): 99

12. Matthews, "Power Shift," p. 51.

13. Software programs allow visitors to interest group web sites to sign their names to policy statements and to sign on as affiliates of the cause. Other programs provide texts of "grassroots letters" that can be downloaded and mailed in volume.

14. See, for example, a description of the allegedly unscrupulous attack on the proposed U.S. ratification of the Convention on Biodiversity in P.J. Simmons, "Learning to Live with NGOs," p. 82.

15. For details, see the web site at: www.citizen.tradewatch.org/.

16. Riordan Roett, "The Mexican Devaluation and the U.S. Response: Potomac Politics, 1995-Style," in *The Mexican Peso Crisis—International Perspectives*, Riordan Roett, ed. (Boulder, Colo.: Lynne Rienner Publishers, 1996), p. 40.

17. Vladimir Preglj, "Fast Track Implementation of Trade Agreements: History, Pro-

cedure, and Other Options,'' Congressional Research Service report dated 23 September 1997, p. 3.

18. One political school of thought held that with the outcome known in advance, Speaker of the House Newt Gingrich held the vote only to please business interests and to spotlight the division between Democrats who advocated freer trade and those bowing to organized labor's opposition to fast-track renewal.

19. Bruce Stokes, ''An Erratic Hand at the Helm,'' *National Journal*, 16 January 1999, p. 119.

20. See, for example, the web site of America Leads on Trade at www.fasttrack.org/.

21. Data source: results of an investigation of the International Trade Commission of September 1997, as cited in Chailendu K. Pegues, ''The Africa Trade Bill—Bringing Africa into the Global Economy,'' report of the Progressive Policy Institute, March 1998, p. 3.

22. The text of this op-ed piece is posted on the Internet at: www.citizen.org/public_citizen/pctrade/africa/rrrn.htm/.

23. Public Citizen web site at: citizen.org/pctrade/africa/stopthe.htm/.

24. Available at www.citizen.org/pctrade/africa/35.htm/.

25. ''IMF Bailouts: How Do They Impact on the Environment?'' downloaded from the Friends of the Earth web site at www.foe.org/ga/infenv.html/.

26. Downloaded from the Internet at www.freedom.house.gov/library/imf/expansion.asp/.

27. George Shultz, William Simon, and Walter Wriston, ''Who Needs the IMF,'' *Wall Street Journal*, 3 February 1998, p. A22.

28. Downloaded from the OECD web site at www.oecd.org/publications/Pol_brief/9702_pol.htm#1/.

29. As quoted in Kobrin, ''The MAI and the Clash of Globalizations,'' p. 98.

30. The statement can be found at: www.citizen.org/pctrade/MAI/Sign-ons/mai600ngo.htm/.

31. Global Trade Watch web site at: www.citizen.org/pctrade/mai/maievery/htm/.

32. Mark Weisbrot, ''Globalization for Whom?'' downloaded from the Internet at www.preamble.org/Globalization.html/.

33. Matthews, ''Power Shift,'' p. 52.

Part V

Prescription

13 A Critique of Existing Organization

[W]hile organization isn't everything, disorganization isn't anything.
—Senator Daniel Patrick Moynihan

Foreign economic policy in the United States is shaped not systematically, but almost by accident. It is a least common denominator, worked out, as some have so aptly put it, by a kind of guerrilla warfare among the Departments of State, Treasury, Agriculture, the Federal Reserve Board, and a whole host of other Executive Branch agencies.
—former Senator Lloyd Bentsen

The society of the United States is hopelessly pluralistic. Reflecting this situation, the strengths and weaknesses of American society and government are inherent in the international economic policymaking process. In a democracy with a population whose interests are so diverse, there is a degree of virtue and logic in providing each of several constituencies a designated pipeline to the decision-making process. The downside is a large, shifting, and overlapping organization. Despite this untidiness, the process often works efficiently, blending contrasting views into a consensus that serves the national interest reasonably well and attracts widespread support. But when the system is working poorly, policy usually is delayed, deficient, or both.

PROBLEMS INHERENT AND INEVITABLE

At the onset, it should be noted that it is natural for one's perception that organization is either excellent or inept to be linked to one's opinions of the policy substance that has been produced. If one is pleased with substance, he or she usually would not have a need or impulse to criticize the arrangements under which decisions were formulated and actions implemented. Nevertheless, an objective observer should be able to distinguish between good policy output and flawed process. Since this book is not intended to pass any judgments on substance, the critique that follows focuses strictly on organization and process.

An inherent problem with all organizational questions is the virtual impossibility of determining whether certain kinds of governmental organization have predictable effects on the nature and quality of decisions and actions subsequently taken. Bad organization will hinder, but not necessarily shatter, an operation run by good people determined to work together for the common good. Conversely, excellent organization can help but can seldom overcome excess parochialism or weakness in the caliber of available personnel.

A balanced evaluation of the international economic policymaking organization of the United States should include, along with praise and criticism, a recognition of the inevitable. Certain forces are inherent in the process and cannot be dismissed. The overriding fact of the U.S. penchant for pluralism has already been alluded to. A second inescapable factor is that the breadth of international economic policies requires full consideration be given to the four components of the subject: domestic economic policy, domestic politics, international economics, and foreign policy. Only then can conflicting priorities be reconciled ''reasonably'' well. No reconciliation process can fully finesse the disconnect resulting from politics being local and economics becoming global in scope.

The existence of at least two sides to the story in every major international economic issue is a third constant that complicates the decision-making process. Policy dilemmas tend to be dominated by shades of gray rather than being clearly divided between black and white absolutes. A political decision to undemocratize the policymaking process by reducing the number of legitimate viewpoints and interests currently participating would permit an extensive reduction of bureaucratic boxes on the organizational chart. The resulting centralization of authority would facilitate swifter, more unequivocal decisions. However, such an approach (which is unlikely to be tried any time soon) runs the risk of dogmatic and biased policy that serves the interests of only a relatively few people. The increasing role of Congress and civil society in this area and the sophistication with which business, labor, environmental, consumer, and foreign viewpoints are presented in Washington suggest that participation in international economic policy debate is more likely to expand than to contract.

The leadership role of the United States in world affairs is a fourth inherent factor affecting organization. The end of the cold war notwithstanding, it is unrealistic to assume that the reality of being the world's lone superpower can be ignored when formulating international economic policies. For the United States, these policies will almost never be based strictly on internal or regional interests as is frequently the case in other countries. Given the limited controversy at home or abroad about the important political and military roles that can only be played by the United States in shaping the new world order, a uniquely heavy weighting must be given to strategic concerns. Hence, a streamlining of international economic policy organization that marginalizes the national security bureaucracy and its concerns would be inconsistent with the apparent destiny of the United States to play a major global role for the foreseeable future.

The inevitability of a cumbersome and uneasy partnership between the executive and legislative branches is yet another unavoidable variable shaping the international economic policymaking process. It can be fine-tuned at the margins, but short of amending the Constitution, this relationship will remain inconsistent with a textbook version of a streamlined, fast-moving organization. Harmonious inter-branch relations become even more problematic if both houses of Congress are controlled by one political party, the majority of whom dislikes an incumbent president of the opposite party.

A final inherent reality affecting the nature and output of organization in this policy area is the inevitable presence of the cult of personality syndrome, especially in the U.S. executive branch. More than in any other democracy, a large number of high-ranking political appointees (as opposed to senior civil servants) derive their power and influence more from their strength of character, ambition, and relationship with the president than their titles and agency affiliations. The presidential system in this country uniquely bestows appointive power on a more flexible basis than in parliamentary democracies (for example, cabinet members need not be members of Congress) and on a deeper basis (no other head of government in a democracy can make political appointees as far down as the equivalent of the deputy assistant secretary rank). The net result is to give the president the potential to load the senior policymaking ranks with officials of similar ideological persuasion, thereby introducing a formidable intellectual bias into even the most rationally designed executive branch.

WHAT'S RIGHT WITH THE SYSTEM

The U.S. international economic policymaking process easily passes the test of minimum acceptability and competence. It is neither a disaster nor a threat to the Republic. A number of positive things can be found in the organizational structure. For the most part, the international economic policymaking process is "rational." In *most* cases, decisions are reached only after: relevant data are collected and analyzed; a variety of opinions are solicited from different agencies and, as appropriate, from congressional and private sector interests; and the relative advantages and disadvantages of several policy options are calculated. On occasion, the system has shown itself quite capable of generating innovative ideas. Impetuous decision-making rarely happens. When a firm deadline is unavoidable, the process usually responds on time.

The lack of structure in the system works against consistent and coherent policy. However, at times organizational, jurisdictional, and coordination flexibility can be a strength. The inevitabilities of new presidents being inaugurated and the recurring organizational tinkering that seems to be part of the American psyche result in perpetual modifications, many of which are improvements. The resulting organizational change can compensate for perceived weaknesses, prepare for newly emerging issues, or adjust to a president's individual style. Although good may be discarded with the bad, no one need despair that all organizational problems are necessarily immutable or beyond the purview of the organizational study that periodically springs up.

The system frequently has demonstrated reasonable ability to adapt to new or special circumstances. The latter have ranged from the need for closer executive-legislative branch consultations on reducing non-tariff trade barriers, to the initiation of measures to contain global financial "contagion."

The U.S. international economic policymaking organization on occasion has astutely coordinated viewpoints in an effort to reach an acceptable trade-off between domestic and international priorities. There is a fairly well-ingrained appreciation of the need in principle to provide an airing of the views of all agencies with a direct interest in a matter under discussion. Bureaucrats at all levels may disdain the advice and goals of others, but very few would question their legitimacy as part of the policy formulation process. It is this very diversity of interests and needs that has served to produce balanced, albeit least-common-denominator, policy more frequently than extreme actions.

A final strength of the organization is the caliber and diverse expertise of its personnel. The civil service of the United States may not receive the domestic prestige accorded its counterparts in some other nations, but it still has attracted, on the whole, a very capable group of bright, dedicated, professional people. The sheer size and diversity of the international economic policy establishment has also fostered a broad range of knowledge and analytic abilities on almost every aspect of the subject.

WHAT'S WRONG WITH THE SYSTEM

The ideal organization may not be achievable, but the status quo is unacceptable for policymaking at the crucial nexus between the United States' domestic economic performance and its external relations. Changes are necessary to assure the maximum degree of coherence, consistency, and complementarity among policy sectors. The right kind of reorganization could also raise the overall quality level of policy substance.

The international economic policymaking process cannot be radically reduced in size, but it can be made to operate more effectively. The current system is too disjointed. In too many issue areas, responsibilities are too widely disseminated. High-level coordination procedures change significantly from administration to administration. When the U.S. executive branch deals with complex policy sectors like foreign trade and assistance to less developed countries (LDCs), it tends to look at individual issues in isolation rather than as parts of an integrated whole that should be examined in a comprehensive manner. Existing organization does not give sufficient attention to the importance of making sure interrelated policies in different sectors (e.g., trade and LDC debt problems) are consistent with one another. The tendency to formulate policies in a less than comprehensive fashion is perpetuated because a systematic reform of the system would create bureaucratic winners and losers as lines of authority are redrawn. The international economic policymaking process reflects the central dilemma of governmental bureaucracies throughout the world: preservation and expansion of power and prestige are too often given higher priorities than producing policies of optimal substance.

Above and beyond executive branch decision-making problems, the existing organization and procedures of the legislative branch present an additional set of complications and institutional shortcomings. Furthermore, the mutual need of the Congress and the administration to accommodate each other's authority, needs, and sensitivities has created a byzantine and ad hoc arrangement in international economic policy. It is vexing enough to have caused more than one frustrated observer to suggest changing the U.S. Constitution to straighten things out.

Organizational reforms have not stopped criticism of the methods by which the United States makes trade policy.[1] A 1984 report by the Senate Committee on Governmental Affairs found four main shortcomings in the decision-making system that persist to this day:

(1) it does not focus national and Presidential attention on trade; (2) it divides trade leadership, leaving our government without a strong trade advocate and hindering the development of coherent, strategic trade policy; (3) it is a management nightmare requiring principal trade policy officials to spend a significant portion of their time on coordination rather than on the design and implementation of effective trade policy; and (4) it does not adequately support improvements in U.S. competitiveness.[2]

This report on the proposed Trade Reorganization Act of 1983 went on to list no fewer than 14 specific organizational weaknesses that had been alluded to in the testimonies presented during hearings held on a bill that sought (unsuccessfully) to create a unified trade department:[3]

Uncertain focus

Uncertain power

Limited influence

Inadequate leadership

Unclear responsibility

Weak, incoherent policy

Policy vacuums

Turf battles

Inefficiency

Duplication

Dual hierarchy

Lack of accountability

Personnel turnover

Reactive rather than strategic policy

A good case can be made that these perceived shortcomings still characterize the policymaking process at the millennium.

Another point of departure for evaluating the deficiencies of the U.S. international economic policymaking process is the four broad criteria of organizational excellence offered in the 1975 Report of the Commission on the Organization of the Government for the Conduct of Foreign Policy, more commonly known as the Murphy Commission:

- Foster a consistent general framework for policymaking responsive to, and integrated with, vital considerations of domestic and foreign policy.

- Permit and even encourage a broad sharing of authority and responsibility for the formulation of policy, while preventing narrow and isolated views from becoming dominant.

- Encourage greater foresight in perceiving, analyzing, and attacking problems at an early stage.

- Provide adequate assurance that, once the president or cabinet members make decisions, they are followed up and implemented at the working level in the spirit intended.[4]

Except for the fourth criterion, existing organization does not measure up very well. U.S. international economic policymaking comes up short on the Murphy Commission's recommendations of an effective, consistent framework for integrating the components of international economic policy and a broad, clearly delineated distribution of authority. The system has been capricious in distributing authority and responsibility. Turf battles occur with excessive frequency. Jurisdictional authority constantly changes, but the overlap factor is constant.

There appears to be no method to predict how the system will (or will not) handle any given economic issue. A quick, responsive, and creative policy or program is more a matter of luck than design. Policymaking is hindered by the need to delay substantive decisions on all new international economic issues until procedural guidelines first have been thrashed out by bureaucratic units scrambling for control. The result is an uncertain, cumbersome procedure in which inordinate amounts of time and energy are too often expended in intra–executive branch debates about departmental leadership and interagency coordination before negotiations with foreign governments even begin. At least two Office of the U.S. Trade Representative (USTR) officials told the author over the years that they often found interagency negotiations to be more taxing and vicious than those with foreign governments. The question of who is to chair an interagency working group can tie the bureaucracy in knots for weeks.

The decision-making process is arbitrary and imprecise. Only in those relatively few cases where bureaucratic turf has long been clearly delineated—multilateral trade negotiations and international monetary relations, for example—is a fixed pattern of command and control predetermined. In most cases, leadership roles are fought for, bartered, shared, or assigned by the president—sometimes with no apparent rhyme or reason. Bureaucratic infighting and fragmentation are too common for the system to be considered an example of management excellence. Whereas there is no shortage of views introduced in most policy deliberations, there is no permanent, built-in mechanism to force a decision short of an openly impatient president, legislative deadline, or an exploding economic crisis. Nor is there anything inherent in the system that favors bold and innovative decisions over a least-common-denominator bureaucratic compromise.

The fleeting interest and leadership displayed by presidents in international economic policy spawns a standing invitation to cutthroat competition among line departments and agencies for domination in the decision-making process. Power and influence more often than not are the outgrowths of a survival of the fittest struggle in the cabinet. Power and influence tend to be associated more with the personalities of key officials and their relationships with the president than manifestation of their institutional affiliation.

No effective senior-level coordinating mechanism is possible without either the president's active participation or the leadership of a strong presidential surrogate, such as George Shultz in the 1972–1973 period. The impact of the Council on International Economic Policy (CIEP), the White House coordinating mechanism established in 1970, was barely visible on major problems in international trade, finance, and resource-transfer policies, where primary jurisdiction was claimed by State and/or Treasury. The CIEP was able to realize its potential as a White House coordinator and planner only on new issues where bureaucratic jurisdiction had not been demarcated (for example, foreign direct investment in the United States), on issues where jurisdiction became so contentious that all participants agreed to negotiate on neutral territory (for example, policies towards expropriation actions by foreign governments), and on issues of no great importance to any individual agency. The principal factor in the atrophying of the CIEP and its termination in mid-1977 was the prolonged absence of presidential attention to it.

The ephemeral nature of agency authority has been clearly visible since the 1960s in the dramatic ups and downs in the impact of the USTR. The heads of this office have had very different skills in playing the Washington game and different political connections. In the early years of the Nixon administration, the job all but disappeared from the bureaucratic map because of White House indifference both to the person it had nominated as USTR and to his office. By the end of 1985, the ascendancy of the James Baker–led Economic Policy Council had eclipsed the authority of even a USTR as aggressive and competent as Clayton Yeutter.

The Office of the USTR still is lacking a mandate that permanently makes it the dominant entity in trade policy formulation. Three years after the 1980 reorganization that was supposed to elevate and solidify the USTR's leadership role in trade policy, the Reagan administration sought to implement another reorganization that would have folded the USTR into the Commerce Department. In many respects this was a case study of how not to reorganize. Widespread public opposition, based in part on the business sector's lack of confidence in that department's ability to successfully manage U.S. trade policy formulation, squelched the idea. However, the USTR office was left in the position of being an "unfinished" operation. It is a negotiator with little say over many U.S. government economic actions directly affecting the trading partners with whom it must negotiate. The USTR's effectiveness has also been hampered by the fact that while trade flows and issues have expanded rapidly, the office's already small staff (many Washington law firms are larger) has not been expanded since the 1980s.

The current mandate of the USTR epitomizes the illogical, artificial bifurcation of the current U.S. trade policy organization in which policy formulation authority is separated from program administration. It has little jurisdiction over enforcement of trade statutes dealing with imports, management of import and export programs, and oversight over agricultural trade policies.[5] Four other bureaucracies share responsibilities for the administration and enforcement of statutes regulating imports and relief from import competition: Agriculture (import quotas administered under the Agricultural Adjustment Act); the Commerce Department (the antidumping and countervailing duty statutes and adjustment assistance for companies); the Labor Department (adjustment assistance to workers); and the International Trade Commission (investigations of alleged injury from fair and unfair competition and Section 337 investigations of alleged intellectual property rights infringements). The USTR has titular authority at best over export promotion and control programs because operational authority lies elsewhere, mostly in the Commerce Department. These two entities repeatedly quarrel over jurisdiction in enforcing the numerous trade agreements made with other countries.

The procedural inconsistencies of the most visible sector of international economic policymaking—trade—were vividly demonstrated in early spring 1981, while the Reagan cabinet debated the wisdom of securing reductions in the imports of Japanese cars. As described in the press, the State Department and the Office of the USTR fought over the lead role in bilateral negotiations with Japan concerning possible "voluntary" export restraints. In the same week that Secretary of State Alexander Haig was telling a congressional panel that he was the "general manager" of U.S. foreign policy, he reportedly tried to seize leadership of the automobile negotiations during talks with a surprised and confused Japanese Foreign Minister. A spokesman for the USTR quickly announced that it was their understanding that "any negotiations on trade would be led by the U.S. Trade Representative."[6] The Japanese mission presumably went home uncertain of exactly what was the U.S. position on import policy and with whom they were supposed to negotiate.

The automobile talks were not the only occasion on which preparations for bilateral trade negotiations with Japan stirred up a hornet's nest of bureaucratic rivalries. Duplicative preparatory meetings became the order of the day on at least two other occasions. To lay the groundwork for President Reagan's January 1985 meeting with Japanese Prime Minister Nakasone, a duplicative series of interagency meetings were held. The reason was bureaucratic efforts to protect turf, not substantive need. In December 1984, Commerce Secretary Baldrige convened a meeting of the Cabinet Council on Commerce and Trade; the USTR convened a meeting of the Trade Policy Committee; and the State Department (which had overall responsibility for backstopping the Reagan-Nakasone meeting) convened its own planning session.[7] No agency could forgo the urge to chair a preparatory interagency meeting despite redundancy and crowded personal schedules.

In a similar vein, murky jurisdictional authority led to a tripolar interagency meeting response to the 1986 Japanese government announcement that it intended to provide financial relief (i.e., subsidies) to small exporters adversely affected by the appreciation in the exchange rate of the yen. U.S. officials, anxious to see a quick diminution of Japan's enormous trade surplus, were furious at the prospect of any Japanese effort to thwart the anticipated trade adjustment effects of a stronger yen. Meetings were convened by the Economic Policy Council, the Commerce-chaired trade relations strike force, and USTR's Trade Policy Staff Committee. All discussed the same subject: the nature of the administration's response to the proposed subsidies.

The propensity for disarray in international economic policymaking presents an added dilemma to American business and labor. Receiving conflicting information from different departments concerning U.S. international economic policies has been a commonplace occurrence. Even in the best of times, relations between government and business officials can be less than cordial. This is in keeping with the adversarial tone of U.S. business-government relations in general. Mutual suspicion and a government physically and spiritually distant from industry have produced in Washington the least pro-business culture of any major industrial country government. For their part, most executives of large American corporations have little use for government officials until they run into problems and need Washington's assistance.

The system also has proven itself consistently inadequate in meeting the third Murphy Commission standard: presenting policymakers with advanced warnings about and preemptive strategies for potential future problems. U.S. international economic policy has mostly been defensive or reactive. For sure, one cause of this situation is the limited accuracy of economic forecasting, but the size and impact of policy research and planning efforts remain inadequate. Former Secretary of State Henry Kissinger's remark that planning is usually a "sop to administrative theory" unfortunately is still a good characterization of the prevailing gulf between U.S. policymakers and analysts in international economic relations. The result is minimal staff expertise in assessing the competitive strengths and weaknesses of American high-tech industries and insufficient capability in monitoring competitive trends in foreign countries, especially Japan.

The costs of the resulting knowledge vacuum can be seen in the cases of severe import competition from Japanese semiconductors and flat-panel display screens. In both instances, the U.S. government was dealing with deeply rooted domestic industrial problems. However, in responses that arguably were too little and too late, it was forced to use the antidumping statute, a less than optimal option. By raising the prices of critical components imported from Japan, the U.S. government caused American-made computers to become less price competitive without significantly increasing domestic production of either memory chips or flat-panel displays. Had the government and business sectors been talking earlier, a more constructive strategy might have been developed.

The "great grain robbery" pulled off by Soviet officials in 1972 and the soybean export control episodes (discussed in Chapter 8) demonstrated that the system is fully capable of being totally surprised and of grossly misconstruing an unfolding situation. Even when staff analysts can foresee a problem, the policymaking system still might not function properly. The energy problem had become clear in the minds of technical experts in the early 1970s, but senior policymakers exhibited no sense of urgency until the Arab oil embargo was suddenly imposed on the United States in the fall of 1973. A 1980 study by the General Accounting Office (GAO) on the formulation of U.S. international energy policy concluded that it was essentially "an ad hoc process." The GAO found no evidence of "policy analyses designed either to develop an overall integrated set of international energy policies or to assess whether existing policies comprise an integrated whole."[8]

The organizational structure also has performed inadequately in the final stage of the policy process: evaluation. The executive branch is devoid of any bureaucratic actor whose major assignment is to critically review policies in place, and to do so with a dispassionate point of view devoid of self-interest in the findings.[9] Change in presidential administrations is the most likely event triggering the initiation of a full-scale review and reevaluation of what are good, bad, and obsolete policies. Otherwise, once in place, most policies linger until political and economic pressures literally force policymakers into revising them.

In sum, the organizational process by which U.S. international economic policy is made suffers from the following deficiencies:

• Decision-making has suffered from underutilization of the president's unique leadership and integrating perspective.

• Much of official Washington still views international economic policy not as a unique blend of policy concerns, but as something to be subordinated either to domestic economic policy management or to foreign policy/national security objectives.

- Organizational arrangements, at least at the senior level, are excessively ephemeral. In some periods they work well, sometimes just adequately, and at still other times they work poorly.
- The coordination process at senior levels has been extensive if measured in terms of the number of interagency working groups. Qualitatively, it has suffered from excessive ''ad hockery'' and inconsistency. There is no provision for a neutral figure with no policy ax to grind whose job it is to assure the right officials are assembled at the right time and make timely decisions.
- Authority too often is arbitrarily seized by the toughest bureaucrats.
- The bureaucracy remains too intellectually removed from the business community to fully understand what makes it tick and exactly what kinds of pressures it faces in the global marketplace.

THE REQUIREMENTS OF AN OPTIMAL U.S. POLICYMAKING SYSTEM

A perfect system for the formulation and conduct of international economic policy that would appeal to all future presidents and congressional leaders is beyond the grasp of mortals. Senior officials have different goals and organizational preferences. A sense of pragmatism has therefore guided selection of the concrete prescriptions for improving the policymaking structure presented in the next chapter. These proposals build largely on the existing system, with only limited changes involved. Even so, they will not be able to bridge the wide variety of views on organizational theory and on the exact function of international economic policy. To some, they will be too radical; to others, too modest. It is even unlikely that everyone will agree with the underlying assumptions that follow as to what conceptual criteria constitute an optimal system.

Creation of policymaking excellence begins at the very top. The president must openly demonstrate interest, leadership, and presence. The U.S. government is geared to function effectively by responding to his articulation of policy direction. It needs his unique ability to make decisions on difficult matters and on issues that cut across bureaucratic boundaries. Not even the best-constructed organizational and procedural model will hold up over time without the commitment of the president to use it and support it. Hence, the first specific prerequisite of an optimal system is increased presidential involvement.

The search for organizational excellence should be guided by both the old axiom that ''knowledge is power'' and the new axiom that in the new world order, economic power is what really counts. The system must appreciate that international economic policy is a unique balancing act that needs to reconcile the many inherent tensions and competing priorities between internal and external, and economic and political objectives. This perspective reduces the likelihood of an "excessive" tilt to either foreign or domestic economic policy priorities. Moreover, organizational process should never lose sight of how one sector of international economic policy can affect another, most notably the impact of exchange rates on trade performance.

In terms of more specific procedural requirements, an optimal organization both understands current international economic developments and spends at least a little time thinking about the future. It considers the consequences of emerging trends rather than just reacting after the fact. A good organization assembles and collates data on global macroeconomic trends, international competitiveness indicators in key industries and technologies, and on trade and international financial flows necessary to keep policymakers properly informed. Analysts need to distill these data into cogent reports and present them to senior policymakers well before problems escalate into crises.

A first-rate system articulates all options and forces decisions on a quick, well-organized, and responsive basis. It successfully walks the tightrope so as to avoid two extremes: sudden, unnecessary variations in policy, and an inability to respond to changing political-economic realities. It does not stifle dissent. It eloquently enunciates decisions and forcefully implements them. An optimal organization would not easily succumb to the blandishments of special interest groups at the expense of the overall public welfare or of essential U.S. responsibilities in world affairs.

An optimal organization must serve the president well. Whenever a presidential decision is necessary, the president should be provided with complete and objective information. All interested agencies should feel that they were given an opportunity to have their own conclusions and recommendations included in the memoranda forwarded to the Oval Office. By assuring that the president is exposed to all relevant arguments and counterarguments in an international economic policy issue, the system will foster confidence among cabinet members that all have roughly equal access to the chief executive, either in person or by memorandum.

One of the more important aspects of an optimal organizational process is to clearly establish a hierarchy of responsibility for policy formulation and for program management. Specifically, a line of command needs to be established and adhered to, whereby an appropriate department or agency has primary responsibility, while others have subordinate jurisdiction. Duplication of efforts should be minimized. Assignment of responsibilities should be made sufficiently clear that bureaucratic in-fighting is minimized and the public's understanding of who is in charge is maximized.

The combination of clearly established lines of command and guaranteed access to the policymaking process for all relevant bureaucratic viewpoints would minimize the propensity for defeated viewpoints to try to undo, embarrass, or reverse official policy once it has been implemented. In an optimal system, bureaucratic actors direct their institutional energies primarily at seeking policy excellence rather than simply jockeying for position against one another in an ongoing bureaucratic rat race. Energy expended in negotiations should be directed mainly to those outside the administration, not within it.

Still another requirement is a system that operates with a full appreciation of the soundness of cooperating and communicating with the key players outside of the executive branch. Good communication at early stages of policymaking usually increases mutual understanding of goals and motivations between the official sector (the executive branch and Congress) and the private sector (business, labor, and civil society) for whom the majority of international economic policy is conducted.

A simplified, but comprehensive, system of coordination is another sine qua non of an optimal policymaking system. A coordination system operating as an "honest broker" is needed to ensure that the administration communicates effectively within itself and speaks with a unified voice to the outside. The White House-level coordinator of international economic policy should have no policymaking jurisdiction of its own. This mechanism should guarantee that the views of all relevant branches of the executive branch, key members of Congress, and the private sector have been factored into the policy formulation debate and, as necessary, brought to the attention of the president. Another important task of the coordinator is to provide a fair system of appeal and arbitration when controversy is severe. In fulfillment of these responsibilities, the senior coordination group and its director must have the president's endorsement and active participation, provide a fixed and recognizable forum for debate, assure that decisions meet established deadlines, and resist domination by parochial interests. At the same time, the head of the senior coordinating group must avoid visions of grandeur and respect the ultimate jurisdiction of the line, or operating, departments and agencies.

A final trait of an optimal system is avoidance of great concentration of power in any individual institution. The models of a strong White House or a single dominant department risk a relatively closed policymaking process where diversified participation is not welcomed. In contrast, moderately decentralized authority is most conducive to encouraging a competitive marketplace of ideas drawing on a broad participation of viewpoints and specialized knowledge. It also can adapt relatively well to the complexities of congressional authority and organization.

NOTES

1. For two excellent examples of criticism, see the statement of Harald Malmgren before the Senate Committee on Banking, Housing and Urban Affairs, in *International Economic Policy Act of 1975, Hearings*, 94th Congress, 1st session, p. 91: "Widespread confusion exists as to who is responsible for what. Both policy and daily decisions seem to be aimed in several different directions simultaneously. . . . [T]he fact is that there is no coherent, overall foreign economic policy." See also C. Fred Bergsten, ibid., p. 11: "There now exist no procedures which can even begin to resolve the issues."

2. Senate Committee on Governmental Affairs, *Report [on the] Trade Reorganization Act of 1983*, 3 April 1984 (Washington, D.C.: U.S. Government Printing Office, 1984), p. 5.

3. Ibid., pp. 5–7.

4. *[Report of the] Commission on the Organization of the Government for the Conduct of Foreign Policy* (Washington, D.C.: U.S. Government Printing Office, 1975), pp. 57–58.

5. The USTR is in charge of investigating and responding to complaints filed under the Section 301 provision by American companies alleging discriminatory foreign trade practices.

6. "Haig Taking Charge of Talks with Japan on Auto Import Curb," *Washington Post*, 25 March 1981, p. A1.

7. Not-for-attribution interviews with USTR and State Department officials, May and August 1986.

8. U.S. General Accounting Office, "Formulation of U.S. International Energy Policies," mimeographed, 1980, p. 13.

9. The OMB occasionally assumes this role, though it tends to approach problems and investigations from the point of view of restraining government spending. The independent International Trade Commission has done a good job assessing trade issues. The GAO, a relatively obscure part of the legislative branch, has objectively evaluated executive branch policies and programs from an outsider's vantage point. However, its efforts at international economic analysis have been relatively few and usually have not involved sophisticated economic inquiry.

14 Proposals for Organizational and Procedural Changes

> [T]here is nothing more difficult to carry out nor more doubtful of success . . . than to initiate a new order of things. For the reformer has enemies in all those who profit by the old order and only lukewarm defenders in all those who would profit by the new order.
>
> —Niccolò Machiavelli

> Every new truth which has ever been propounded has, for a time, caused mischief; it has produced discomfort, and often unhappiness . . . sometimes merely by the disruption of old and cherished association of thoughts. It is only after a certain interval . . . that its good effects preponderate; and the preponderance continues to increase, until at length, the truth causes nothing but good. But, at the outset there is always harm. . . . Men are made uneasy; they flinch. . . . [O]ld interests and old beliefs have been destroyed before new ones are created.
>
> —Henry Thomas Buckle

The detailed discussions in previous chapters of the nature of international economic policy and of the operational dynamics of the policymaking process suggest the need for improvements in the organization by which the United States formulates and conducts such policies. The proposals that follow are designed to be consistent with the ratiocination that preceded them. They are also designed to represent the most likely means of producing an excellent policymaking system. They are not the last word in organizational improvements, but no other changes present themselves as sure bets to produce better results.

A critical caveat must be emphasized: the reforms proposed below are a necessary but not sufficient force for improving the policymaking process. Another precondition is an increased commitment at the top levels of government to giving international economic policy a high priority commensurate with the degree to which global economic forces affect domestic economic performance and relations with other countries. Yet another necessary complement to good organization is capable people who will manage the restructured bureaucracy in a non-parochial, far-sighted manner. How the new institutions and procedures are administered can assure—or frustrate—organizational reforms. In the final analysis, U.S. international economic policymaking, like executive branch organization in general, will reflect the policy goals and management style embraced by the president. His (or her) preferences, and not an elaborate organizational chart, will dictate how the real lines of decision-making flow.

GUIDELINES FOR RECOMMENDING CHANGE

The proposals for organizational change that follow adhere to six important intellectual guidelines. The first is the need to *objectively* measure what is needed against what currently exists. No consideration was given to using procedural shifts to enhance one bureaucratic perspective or constituency at the expense of another. International economic policy's extraordinary need to judiciously reconcile its four components must be respected. Recommendations for organizational change therefore ought not favor domestic over external, nor economic over political, priorities.

Another guideline is that change for the sake of change should be avoided. Efforts at reorganization can and should be built around existing institutions, at least in part because this approach would tend to encourage real world acceptance of an academic's proposals. No matter how good the latter may be, they are of minimal utility if they are not transformed from abstractions into reality.

Third, it is necessary to acknowledge that reorganization of the executive branch is only one part of the equation. The autonomy of the president in the making of U.S. international economic policy is limited at best. The desirability of changes in congressional procedures cannot be dismissed, nor can the need to assure that an executive branch reorganization is as compatible as possible with preferences of members of Congress and the existing jurisdictions of their committees. Without a responsive Congress, excellent policy proposals of a more efficient executive branch decision-making process might be bottled up in a recalcitrant legislative branch. Some of the organizational changes in the executive branch suggested below will require congressional approval to be implemented.

The next guideline is *not* to equate federal government organization with that of private purveyors of goods and services. The former is not in business to make a profit. It should not exist to extol a particular priority or promote a single constituency. Government policymakers justify themselves by producing carefully thought out, well-balanced initiatives that provide the maximum good for the maximum number of people.

Fifth, reorganization proposals cannot be offered in isolation. New institutions and procedures need to be compatible with one another and with continuing organization to assure smoothly functioning linkage.

The final guideline is the need to reject flawed concepts that would lead reorganization efforts down the wrong path. First, the quest for organizational panaceas must be dismissed. The worst shortcomings and excesses of the policymaking process can, and should, be reformed. Yet international economic policymaking can never be perfectly sound and smooth. Executive branch structure in general and international economic policy organization in particular reflect the values, conflicts and competing forces inherent in the ultra-pluralistic American society. The ideal of a neatly symmetrical, frictionless organizational structure is an illusion. Some degree of discord is a desirable feature of the policymaking process in a complex subject like international economic relations where a number of legitimate needs and interests perpetually compete with each another.

Proposals for reorganization should avoid a wholehearted embrace of one of the two alluring but "skewed" models of government that ostensibly would simplify their task. One model is that of the strong White House, where overlapping jurisdictions and imprecision in lines of command in cabinet departments and agencies would be minimized. Responsibility for all major decisions would be delegated to a handful of senior presidential assistants. In this scenario, the U.S. international economic policymaking apparatus would resemble the 1969–1974 Nixon-Kissinger National Security Council (NSC) system that was responsible for developing all major foreign policy strategy. Alternatively, comprehensive leadership of international economic policy could be bestowed upon a super-strong department, presumably State or Treasury. Once again, this model is dangerously simplistic. Whereas apparent bureaucratic tidiness would result from the adopting of either model, there are counterarguments that suggest that such ostensible neatness would come at too high a cost. In the White House model, heavily concentrated power likely would produce an administrative logjam (unless a huge bureaucracy is quickly assembled) and a feeling of alienation in the bureaucracy. In the single dominant departmental model, cabinet dissension and biased international economic policy favoring either domestic interests or foreign policy objectives is the likely outcome.

The reorganization proposals that are presented below reject the idea that a combined trade and industry department should be created. In a subject area with few absolute boundaries of logic, this approach is admittedly somewhat inconsistent with this book's recurring theme of strong links existing between domestic and external economic policies. Despite the link between American industrial strength and U.S. trade relations, it would still be preferable to have two "friendly adversaries" in the cabinet. One bureaucratic actor should have a trade relations orientation while the other should be concerned primarily with internal productivity gains and technological progress. Ideally, the two departments would utilize their relatively distinct identity, expertise, and mission to produce a creative tension that could wisely reconcile the conflicts inherent in seeking the best possible balance between inward versus outward priorities and between the free market versus government intervention. An effort to combine both industrial concerns and trade policy into a single new department is most likely to result in an unwieldy bureaucracy. It would be hard to avoid intradepartmental struggles to establish which of two priorities—good trade relations or enhanced domestic industrial performance—should dominate. Less likely to occur is the timely generation of effective, balanced, and consistent internal and external economic policy substance.

Creating two new departments would not significantly complicate the reorganization of the executive branch. If a trade department is created, establishment of an industry and technology department would be a natural follow-up measure to deal with what would be a decimated Department of Commerce.

The best time by far to begin the approval process for creating the two new departments would be during a presidential transition before cabinet members have been installed and while the successful candidate's electoral mandate is still fresh in everyone's mind. Even if this window of opportunity is taken, an administration will need to exhibit articulate reasoning, tenacity, and steadfast commitment to obtain congressional approval of the two new cabinet departments recommended in the next section.

The proposals for changes in existing organization and procedures that follow are divided into two categories. The first includes structural changes designed to alter the locus of decision-making by changing the means by which different perspectives and recommendations are introduced, evaluated, and selected. The second category deals with more narrowly focused procedure. It consists of relatively modest proposals to make the policy machinery operate more effectively and to provide better support to policymakers.

STRUCTURAL CHANGES

Establishment of a Department of International Commercial Policy—Or Its Equivalent

The dilemmas facing U.S. trade policy are becoming more complex even as the economic stakes are rising. Although good organization is not a guarantee of good substance, the shortcomings of the existing U.S. trade decision-making system will be progressively less able to keep pace with growing challenges in this sector. At the onset of the millennium, the U.S. trade policymaking organization reflects historical considerations more than it does administrative soundness or common sense. The resources that the U.S. government devotes to the formulation and conduct of trade policy are more commensurate with a secondary national concern than a booming $2 trillion–plus "business" generated annually in the United States by exports, imports, and two-way foreign direct investment capital flows.

The trade policy debate continues to move well beyond the traditional issues of whether to impose import barriers at the border to minimize disruption to domestic production and jobs and how to promote exports. Trade officials now discuss purely internal economic practices, like competition policy, and "social" issues such as environmental protection and international labor standards. A powerful trade department with comprehensive authority and broad vision is needed to deal with the expanding agenda and to lead an interagency response to the current backlash against globalization.

The increases in the impact of the external sector on the American economy and on foreign policy suggest that a stronger cabinet voice is needed to formulate and advocate a more coherent, forceful trade strategy. The existing departments cannot adequately perform this role because their institutional culture focuses on narrow slices of the total policy pie, and they are predisposed to serve narrow constituencies. The Office of the U.S. Trade Representative (USTR) is impaired in providing a dominant voice on the totality of U.S. trade relations because it lacks the jurisdiction, staff, and prestige of a cabinet department. A fully empowered trade department would be the most efficient means to develop a constructive, forward-looking consensus on the objectives and priorities of U.S. trade policy and the tactics to achieve them. A strong trade department, unlike existing entities, would be in a position to argue effectively against another round of White House/Treasury indifference to the competitive implications of an overvalued exchange rate for the dollar. It would have the necessary resources to manage interagency consultations seeking to integrate environmental and worker rights issues into U.S. trade policy. Such a department also would allow for more than the mere two or three USTR officials assigned in recent years to work exclusively and full-time on Japan, arguably the United States' most important trading partner, as well as the single largest source of its trade deficit.

A compelling intellectual argument can be made for consolidating the bifurcated trade policymaking process created by the 1980 reorganization that gave more policymaking authority to the USTR and more program management authority to the Department of Commerce. The results of this reorganization make sense only when viewed as a convenient compromise between a number of senators who wanted to establish a new trade department and a Carter administration reluctant to go beyond minor, cosmetic organizational changes. No compelling organizational logic suggests itself in the arbitrary separation that currently exists between the trade policy formulation function in USTR and the program administration function that is mostly located in the Commerce Department. The current "two-headed" arrangement is better than the even more scattered, disjointed, and duplicative responsibilities in the trade policy organization that preceded it. Nevertheless, the results of the 1980 reorganization resemble something designed by a committee. The administrative integration process is far from complete. The status quo is sustained not by the popularity of current organization, but by fear of the unknown and the perceived cachet of USTR's unique organizational status as an operational unit within the Executive Office of the President.

A Department of International Commercial Policy[1] should be created as the comprehensive, undisputed focal point for the management of U.S. international trade and investment policies. The new department would have lead responsibility for: (1) multilateral, regional, and bilateral trade liberalization negotiations and general trade consultations; (2) operation of major export and import programs; (3) enforcement of trade agreements; and (4) foreign direct investment issues. It would chair all senior and mid-level interagency meetings on trade and international investment policies.

A Department of International Commercial Policy (DICP) would be, after the president, the voice that most matters in virtually all important facets of U.S. foreign trade and investment relations. It would be the intellectual core of the government's thinking in these areas, the clearly designated trade negotiator on behalf of the president, and the sole source of "definitive" executive branch policy statements to the public, Congress, domestic business, and foreign governments and corporations.

A centralized trade department is the best vehicle for developing sound strategy and assuring maximum consistency between policy goals and program administration. It would diminish (not eliminate) the abilities of clever lobbyists and foreign governments to exploit the existing decentralized system by looking for friendly agencies and applying divide-and-conquer tactics. A unified trade department would sharply reduce the unproductive efforts and ugly backstabbing long associated with internal bureaucratic struggles for trade policy dominance. The reason for centralizing trade policy responsibility in a single department is not the guarantee of quick and dramatic improvements in the quality of trade policy or in the arithmetic of the very large, long-lived U.S. trade deficit. The chief rationale is the far better odds that improved, more consistent, and more expeditious trade policy will follow in the wake of its relatively inexpensive creation. A DICP could be implemented easily and cheaply. It mainly involves merging the Office of the USTR with selected sections of the Commerce Department.

A properly constituted DICP needs to have primary jurisdiction over all trade issues that significantly affect U.S. export and import performance and U.S. relations with other countries. To assure adequate authority, a number of functions would need to be transferred from existing departments and agencies. First and foremost, the proposed DICP would consist of the USTR's leadership role in all World Trade Organization (WTO) deliberations and all negotiations seeking to reduce trade barriers on goods and services. The new department also would head the U.S. negotiating team in discussions of international agreements involving civil aviation, maritime and fisheries, and telecommunications. The lead trade policy department should have clear leadership in administering the generalized system of tariff preferences extended to less developed countries

(LDCs), and it should lead the U.S. delegation in all special bilateral trade groups (e.g., the Joint Committee on Commerce and Trade established with China). Domestic political sensitivities, however, would seem to mitigate against any efforts to formally transfer primacy in agricultural trade policy from the Department of Agriculture to a new trade department.

The consolidation of export policy jurisdiction makes it logical that the Export-Import Bank and the Overseas Private Investment Corporation (whose insurance and financing programs reduce the economic risks faced by American companies investing in less developed countries) report to the secretary of international commercial policy. The new trade department should be in charge of the U.S. Foreign and Commercial Service, currently a part of the Department of Commerce. The president's Export Council also should be moved from Commerce to the DICP. In addition, the DICP would absorb the USTR's authority to conduct so-called Section 301 investigations of accusations of foreign trade practices that discriminate against U.S. commerce. The trade department should head the U.S. delegation in periodic meetings of the 33 countries adhering to the Wassenaar Arrangement, an agreement to promote common approaches to export controls on conventional arms and sensitive dual-use goods and technologies.

The proposed DICP would appear to be the most appropriate site for the politically sensitive task of investigating private sector complaints of two unfair foreign trade practices—dumping (foreign sales in the United States at less than fair value) and official subsidies of exports. The Commerce Department has attracted heated criticism from liberal trade advocates and from foreign governments and corporations that its investigations to determine the validity of complaints of unfair foreign trade practices are heavily biased in favor of domestic interests. Those who prefer a hard-line approach in such matters would look favorably at keeping these investigations in an agency with a mainly domestic constituency. Many advocates of more impartial investigations would prefer assigning this function to the independent International Trade Commission (ITC), which generally has enjoyed a good reputation for objectivity and technical competence in the investigations assigned to it by other trade legislation. A strong argument for assigning this investigating function to the proposed DICP is that this would increase continuity when the U.S. government pursues ''out-of-court'' settlements of apparent unfair foreign trade practices. The Commerce Department has often negotiated with foreign officials to either have export prices raised or the volume of exports reduced in return for not being hit with antidumping duties (e.g. the Russian steel agreement). On occasion, Commerce has convinced foreign governments (as in the case of Airbus) to reduce official subsidies to avoid imposition of U.S. countervailing duties. These are delicate negotiations and absolutely should be conducted by the new trade department no matter which agency conducts the investigations.

The proposed DICP unequivocally should have primary jurisdiction on policy matters relating to outward and inward foreign direct investment. U.S. trade has become inextricably linked with the overseas operations of multinational companies, both U.S.- and foreign-owned. The principal responsibilities here are negotiating multilateral and bilateral investment treaties, overseeing the U.S. position in WTO discussions of trade-related investment measures, and chairing the interagency committee that reviews the national security implications of foreign acquisitions of American companies. Trade and direct investment are the two principal vehicles for corporations to sell their goods and services to foreign consumers. A technical link results from the fact that a very significant proportion of U.S. exports of manufactured goods takes the form of intracorporate transfers where arm's-length sales directly to unaffiliated foreign buyers are not involved. On the import side, the large volume of foreign direct investment in this country has altered the composition and level of U.S. imports, just as exports of some goods have been increased, while others have been displaced, by the proliferation of overseas production facilities by U.S. companies.

DICP leadership would not apply to negotiations asking other countries to join the United States in imposing economic sanctions to punish the allegedly unacceptable political behavior of states like Iraq and Libya. Sanctions involve national security policy more than trade and should be led by the State Department. Nor would the new trade department need to absorb Commerce's responsibilities for reviewing thousands of applications annually for licenses to export sensitive dual-use technology. Having primary responsibility for processing such applications is a labor-intensive, national security-related task that is *not* a natural fit for a newly created international trade department. Arguably, the expertise involved in administering export controls is more about the potential military capabilities of various goods than about trade relations. Hence, a credible argument can be made that this responsibility would best be assigned to the industry and technology department proposed below, leaving the DICP to be part of the interagency export control review process.

There are a number of things that the DICP would not and should not be. First, it would *not* be a department of international economic policy; it would have primary jurisdiction in only two sectors—trade and investment. The new department would *not* singlehandedly dictate substance or monopolize the policymaking process. Instead, it would be a clearly designated first among equals. It would *not* operate as an island unto itself. Instead, it would be the unambiguous head of an ongoing interagency process where specialized inputs would still be regularly received on behalf of all the appropriate constituencies of trade policy: industry, labor, agriculture, foreign policy, balance of payments and financial concerns, consumers, the environment, and so on.

Other viewpoints must continue to be factored into the decision-making process. On agriculture trade issues, the expertise and domestic political connections of the Agriculture Department will always assure it of a lead role. On trade issues involving the LDCs, agencies having development policy responsibilities must have input. The national security apparatus unavoidably must be an integral part of export control and sanctions determinations. The department would not be intellectually co-opted by trade policy ideologues because it cannot escape the checks and balances inherent in a diverse executive branch and an activist Congress. The DICP would not be susceptible to monolithic thinking. The objective of creating a unified trade department is a relatively modest proposal to rationalize the decision-making process, not make radical changes in power or policy substance.

The United States is unique among industrialized countries in not having a single ministry charged with the overall direction of trade policy. There are three possible explanations that immediately present themselves. The first is that this country knows something (or does something) that nobody else does. If so, it is a very well-kept secret. The advantages of a single designated spokesman for trade policy when dealing with persons and institutions outside the executive branch are obvious. Dismissing this answer, we come next to the possibility that the U.S. internal situation is so extraordinary that a trade ministry is wholly inconsistent with reality. While one can argue that the more powerful models of such a ministry (for example, Japan's MITI) are inappropriate to the tenor of U.S. government-domestic business relations, the concept of a trade ministry is not irrefutably at odds with the U.S. experience. This leaves a third explanation: U.S. international trade and investment policy organization has grown piecemeal, influenced by historical circumstances and the chance presence of strong personalities in the executive branch and Congress. Existing organization is accepted mainly because "that's the way it always has been done."

No matter how many assurances are made that a trade department would not come close to possessing dictatorial powers, opposition to such an entity will persist. However, the most serious obstacle to its creation is the absence of strong, vociferous proponents capable of generating enough political muscle that they displace the inertia of organizational status quo. There are several reasons for limited enthusiasm and for opposition. Many of those who wish to influence policy prefer a decentralized system in order to maximize their chances of finding a sympathetic ear in at least one agency for the pleas of their special interests. Some observers think a trade department would move U.S. policy too far to the extremes of free trade or protectionism. Others have a lingering fondness for the supposed "special relationship" between the president and the USTR. This attitude seems misplaced in view of the overwhelming tendency for the person serving as the USTR *not* to be a White House insider and the increasing propensity for the Office of USTR to be just another advocate rather than a dispassionate, senior-level policy coordinator. Some think that the Congress would be reluctant to terminate its special relationship with the USTR. This feeling is inconsistent with the fact that an angry Congress could exercise as much leverage over a newly created cabinet department as it does over the White House–based USTR.

Although the creation of a full-fledged DICP is the first-best option, the constraints imposed by political reality in Washington suggest that it would be useful to offer a more modest, second-best proposal. This would involve a mini-reform that would simply expand the operational authority of the existing Office of the USTR. Such an expansion would have to be sufficiently modest to keep the size of USTR small enough to remain compatible with the relatively small scale of units within the Executive Office of the President.[2] An upgraded USTR could incorporate some but not all of the additional authority proposed above. A half-way reorganization would have the advantage of avoiding a potentially extended and divisive debate in Washington's "power-centric" culture about the advisability of congressional passage of legislation authorizing a new cabinet department of trade. It would have the distinct disadvantage of allowing continuation of an excessive, random decentralization of authority in trade policy.

One reorganization configuration is emphatically *not* being suggested: folding the USTR into an expanded Department of Commerce. It is a department with an undistinguished past, a perceived bias toward domestic industrial interests, and more than its share of internal organization problems stemming in part from its heterogeneous composition. The Reagan administration's ill-fated effort in 1983 to move in this direction inspired overwhelming opposition both inside and outside government.

The structure of the new department would be concentrated in four major bureaus. One would be headed by the deputy secretary for trade negotiations and would replicate the core functions of the current Office of the USTR. It would coordinate the development of all foreign trade and investment policy negotiating positions and lead the U.S. delegation in multilateral trade forums (the WTO, OECD, UN, etc.), in negotiations of regional free trade areas in the Western Hemisphere and Asia-Pacific, and in bilateral trade matters involving trade agreements, resolution of disagreements, market opening efforts, protection of U.S. trade rights, and so on. It would also have the lead role in administering the private sector liaison function (mainly the trade advisory committees). The staff of this bureau would be created by transferring a select group of specialists currently working in the Commerce Department's International Trade Administration and the offices within USTR dealing with geographic regions and functional issues (the WTO, agriculture, industry, services, foreign direct investment, the environment, transportation and telecommunications, intellectual property rights, and natural resources).

Two bureaus would deal with import and export "operations," respectively. One would handle general export policy and export promotion programs. It would consist of four major divisions. The first would consist of Commerce's advisory, advocacy, overseas trade show, and database services provided to exporters and would-be exporters, mostly small and medium-sized companies. The second major division of the bureau would be the 1,200-plus persons comprising the U.S. Foreign and Commercial Service. This corps provides commercial attaches to major embassies and consulates as well as most of the staff for the nearly 100 Export Assistance Centers operating in U.S. cities. The third and fourth divisions would consist of the Export-Import Bank and the Overseas Private Investment Corporation operating as semiautonomous financing and guarantee agencies. In addition, this bureau would maintain a small office to articulate the department's positions on export controls and sanctions in inter-agency deliberations. If and when the DICP was given an operational role in administering export controls, an additional bureau would need to be created, one totally separate from the export promotion bureau.

The import programs bureau would handle all import restraint programs. It would conduct investigations into allegations of foreign dumping and subsi-dies—*if* these responsibilities are placed under the DICP's jurisdiction. This bureau would participate in multilateral negotiations discussing universal guide-lines for conducting investigations of antidumping and subsidies allegations, and as appropriate, it would negotiate settlements with foreign interests in specific cases of U.S. government investigations of these unfair trade practices.

The import and export bureaus would each have separate offices to monitor and enforce foreign compliance with the many trade agreements signed by the United States with other countries and trade blocs. These understandings involve both promises of overseas market opening efforts to assist U.S. exports and promises to forgo unfair trade practices when exporting to the United States. It is sometimes necessary to file a complaint in the WTO or to threaten retaliation against foreign violators who refuse to modify a discriminatory action that is the harming U.S. exports. The DICP should lead considerations of these very sensitive decisions. Both the Commerce Department and USTR personnel cur-rently assigned to compliance supervision would be assigned to the DICP in order to put an end to the current duplication of these efforts and the jurisdic-tional jealousies between these two agencies.

The fourth bureau would centralize analytical, research, and policy planning capabilities. The small staff in the Commerce Department's International Trade Administration doing international trade and investment analysis would be com-bined with USTR's small economic analysis staff to create this operation. In addition, the bureau could contain a small secretariat for major interagency trade coordinating committees, and liaison officers for Congress, the private sector, and state and local governments.

A limited number of professionals in the new trade department should consist of persons brought in on a temporary duty basis (perhaps one to two years) from other departments; their numbers presumably would rise during major trade negotiations. The twin objectives would be to broaden the DICP's horizons and to instill enhanced trade policy skills in civil servants who would return to trade-related positions in their regular agencies.

Creation of a Department of Industry and Technology

The establishment of a Department of International Commercial Policy (or its equivalent) would provide an excellent opportunity to redefine and sharpen the mission and identity of the Department of Commerce. Rather than sustaining a department with a jumble of unrelated domestic functions if most or all of its major trade policy functions were removed, Commerce should be reconstituted as a slimmed-down Department of Industry and Technology (DIT). It would be the executive branch's focal point for introducing the interests of manufacturing and service industries into relevant interagency deliberations. The second major function of the proposed department would be extension of official technical, financial, and administrative support for encouraging the private sector to accelerate its productivity growth and to increase its research in science and basic technology.

The new department proposed here would assume many of the existing Commerce Department responsibilities. First, it should operate a bureau of industrial affairs built around a staff of experts on the economics of and business conditions in all major U.S. manufacturing and service sectors. This expertise would be used to backstop executive branch decisions on foreign trade, taxation (e.g., research and development credits), environmental regulations, and so on, as well as to prepare research reports such as the *U.S. Industrial Outlook*.

This bureau should include an office of international competitive assessment that would specialize in monitoring overseas business trends and innovations potentially affecting the ability of American manufacturers and service companies to compete in the global economy. It would seek to identify major breakthroughs in science, technology, and manufacturing processes in other countries and to assess the impact of foreign government policies and business practices on the relative competitiveness of American goods and services. If the bureaucracy can maintain an early warning system through good communication with industry, it will occasionally be able to suggest policy options to the White House before industries are severely injured by imports. This would be advantageous because, as suggested in previous chapters, U.S. trade officials have often been forced to respond without adequate time to formulate an economically constructive program to reinvigorate a domestic industry suffering import-induced injury. The absence of advanced warning that an industry is seriously lagging behind its foreign competitors usually leaves policymakers with only the two extreme options of trade barriers or doing little or nothing to assist the industry to reinvent itself.

The proposed DIT should assume the Commerce Department's responsibilities for enforcing export controls and approving export license requests. The bureaucratic "culture" of the new department would be divided between protecting American technology and promoting exports. Consequently, it would likely take a more balanced approach to export control decisions than a more unequivocally export promotion-oriented department like the proposed DICP.

Another major bureau in the new department would incorporate the various technology-related responsibilities currently found in the Commerce Department's Technology Administration. One is an office of technology policy that works with the private sector to formulate and advocate policies supportive of developing new technologies and expanding the application of technology. The most important component of this bureau would be the more than 3,000 scientists and technicians and $750 million budget of the National Institute of Standards and Technology (NIST). Established by Congress, this agency is charged with assisting American industry to develop technology to improve product quality, modernize the manufacturing process, ensure product reliability, and so on. The NIST administers the Advanced Technology Program that provides matching funds for companies to encourage research into high-risk projects that otherwise might not be funded. Funding is provided at the pre–product development stage in hope of expediting the commercialization of potentially high-impact scientific discoveries and the refinement of manufacturing technologies. This bureau would logically manage the administration's high-priority civilian science and technology funding projects, such as information "superhighways" and the Partnership for a New Generation of Vehicles in the Clinton years. It would also disburse government contributions to privately run research consortia such as Sematech. Another responsibility would be to assume the Commerce Department's duties in selecting recipients of the prestigious Malcolm Baldrige National Quality Awards to industry. Finally, this bureau would inherit management of the National Technical Information Service, which disseminates documents published in the United States and elsewhere that deal with technical, scientific, and engineering topics.

Government experts and the private sector scientific community should study the relative merits of placing the National Science Foundation (NSF) within the proposed DIT as a semiautonomous agency. The close relationship between basic science and the development of new technologies suggests a natural intellectual partnership that logically belongs in the same cabinet department. However, absent assurances that the foundation's shift could be accomplished without jeopardizing its reputation of professionalism and independence, the NSF's incorporation into a Department of Industry and Technology would best be postponed.

The technology promotion goals of the DIT would be consistent with a key recommendation in the 1985 report of the President's Commission on Industrial Competitiveness. It suggested creation of a science and technology department to elevate the perceived importance of these two issues, to "transform the current fragmented formulation of policies for science and technology into one that would be far more effective in meeting long-term national goals," and to "improve the effectiveness with which Government, industry and academia interact in the process of building our Nation's science and technology base."[3]

The DIT proposed here is *not* intended to be a springboard for large increases in federal spending or greater government involvement in the private sector. Nor is it based on the premise that any bureaucracy within the Washington Beltway could ever be more important in assuring industrial strength than managerial and production excellence in the private sector. The proposed DIT is designed to be a useful but limited catalyst in pursuit of the higher standard of living that would come with faster growth in U.S. productivity and a more rapid pace of technological innovation. The proposed department is intended to enhance market forces, not to distort or smother them. No positions in the new department should be appropriate for out-of-work economic planners who formerly toiled in the Kremlin. A federal government dispenser of science and technology support funds absolutely must be kept sufficiently insulated from the political process that it never becomes a giant "pork barrel" handing out funds on the basis of the connections and lobbying talents of applicants rather than the pure technical merits of their high-tech funding proposals. The DIT's mandate to underwrite science and technology policy needs a clear, detailed statement of mission and an ongoing evaluation of its performance by reviewers outside of the government with distinguished credentials in science, technology, engineering, manufacturing, or research.

A number of the Commerce Department's current functions not directly germane to the proposed DIT should be transferred elsewhere. For example, the Bureau of the Census should be moved out, perhaps to an expanded Bureau of Labor Statistics in the Labor Department. Existing oceanographic, atmospheric, and weather forecasting duties should be shifted either to the Department of the Interior or the Environmental Protection Agency.

International Economic Policy Coordination in the White House

A high-level economic policy coordinating group has repeatedly proven its value. It should become a permanent, albeit non-statutorily based, fixture in the White House organizational structure. Future coordinating groups will likely continue being renamed by successive administrations, but still perform the same essential task of managing domestic and international economic policy decision-making at the highest level. It is important that they respect the distinctive role of international economic policy and its widening overlap with both domestic policy management and national security objectives. An excellent way to accomplish this is to retain the innovation of the Clinton administration's National Economic Council (NEC) and have its deputy director for international economics hold the same position in the National Security Council (NSC). In this way the president can have a single international economic affairs adviser whose two hats and dual perspectives maximize continuity and minimize bureaucratic jealousies between the White House economics and national security staffs.

The nonpartisan person selected for this position should have a demonstrated understanding of both internal and external economic policies and real-world business conditions. He/she must have easy access to, and the confidence of, the president. At the same time, however, this assistant must be trusted and respected by cabinet members in order to minimize palace politics and divisive end runs to the president. Good working relationships with the cabinet begin with the assistant's willingness to keep a low public profile and resist becoming an open advocate of specific courses of action, in other words avoiding the excesses of "Potomac fever." The assistant to the president for international economic policy should choose his or her small staff of perhaps eight to twelve experienced professionals (also jointly serving the NEC and the NSC) on the basis of knowledge and good interpersonal skills. No one should serve in this capacity for more than four years as a means of discouraging the development of vested interests and personal agendas. The only expense incurred in creating this expanded council would be the salaries of its few staff members, and the net cost could be reduced to zero simply by cutting an equivalent number of positions in other parts of the Executive Office of the President.

The first and foremost purpose of White House–level efforts to coordinate international economic policy is to assure that all viewpoints have been fully factored into a carefully considered, expedited cabinet decision or recommendation to the president. The White House economics coordinator also needs to ensure that the president and the cabinet are fully briefed on the external economic consequences of proposed domestic economic and social policy initiatives, as well as on the economic implications of proposed national security policy initiatives.

The proper role of White House staff is to assure that no gamesmanship is played to bias the policymaking process (such as by neglecting to invite every appropriate agency to all interagency deliberations or failing to promptly provide some agencies with all relevant paperwork). The presidential assistant for international economic policy and his/her staff must provide the president with independent evaluations, free of constituency bias, of policy options under review. Their other major roles are to assure that senior interagency deliberations on international economic policy operate smoothly and fairly and to assure that cabinet advice on international economic policies reaches the president in a prompt manner through established channels. They should be in charge of the scheduling of White House meetings, preparation of agendas, dissemination of position papers, and management of paper flow into and out of the Oval Office. White House coordinators should excel in assuring that feedback on presidential decisions reaches line agencies in a manner that maximizes the likelihood of complete compliance. The staff of the White House economics council also should be a source of new ideas in policy direction and should convene interagency meetings to do occasional long-term planning. The international economics staff of the NEC and NSC, like previous White House coordinators, should be deferential, but not subservient, to line agencies. Their charge is to walk the fine line between minimizing bureaucratic inertia and parochialism, on the one hand, and respecting the proper leadership and know-how of the line departments, on the other hand.

The senior White House economics council (whatever its name) is the optimal locale for respecting the fact that international economic policy is the concentric circle linking national security and the domestic economy. Viewing international economic policy simply as a subset of foreign policy or of domestic economic policy tends to create unbalanced, second-best policy. The best means of preventing this is a White House coordinating mechanism with regular presidential involvement that formally recognizes the degree to which international economic policy is the critical nexus between domestic economic prosperity and successful foreign policy, not a "stepchild" of domestic economic or national security policies.

The economics council should have as broad a mandate as possible in the area of international economic policy. However, it is unlikely that any future White House economic policy coordinating group will displace the domination of the Treasury Department in formulating and conducting international monetary and financial policies. If and when a trade department is created, its secretary should chair cabinet-level trade policy coordination meetings that would continue to meet under the auspices of the White House.

The Congress and Executive-Legislative Relations

Recommending organizational change in the legislative branch is problematical because of the jealousy with which members of Congress guard existing prerogatives. Outsiders offering congressional reorganization plans tend to rush in where angels fear to tread. An elected legislature is a fundamentally different kind of institution than an executive branch, and it will never strive to conform to some kind of organizational ideal. Indeed, the U.S. Congress was not designed to be a slick, high-speed decision-maker.

The immediate prospects for the implementation of restructured congressional committee jurisdiction in international economic policy to coincide with executive branch reorganization must be categorized as very bleak. Nevertheless, given the importance to the U.S. national interest of being able to react promptly to changing international economic situations, the sensitivities of committee chairpersons do not nullify the desirability of suggesting rationalization of committee jurisdiction. The heavy and growing work load encompassing the several sectors of international economic policy suggests an outside chance that agreement could be struck on a equitable reapportionment of authority that satisfies key members in both houses at the same time it streamlines the committee hearings process. Ideally, there should be a reorganization of committee responsibilities that would seek to reduce overlapping jurisdictions in international economic relations and seek to reallocate responsibilities in a way that parallels the recommended creation of two new executive departments dealing with foreign trade and industry/technology.

A second-best solution could be found in the enhancement of useful procedural changes already employed by the leadership in the Senate and House. Whenever feasible, joint hearings should be held by subcommittees in two or more committees with overlapping jurisdictions (trade relations with Japan, foreign direct investment, and so on). Congress should consider creation of a nonpartisan International Commercial Policy Steering Group in both houses that would be composed of members of relevant committees. The primary function of the two groups would be that of traffic controller, determining which specific issues should be referred to which committees in an effort to minimize the procedural slowdown associated with duplications of hearings and with markups of proposed legislation by more than one committee. The steering groups would be most active when Congress was considering major trade legislation. The precedent for this proposal is the process managed by former House Majority Leader Jim Wright when H.R. 4800 was being drafted in the summer of 1986 (see Chapter 5).

Along with a rationalized committee system, a high priority for procedural change in Congress is the assurance of a forceful, mutually respectful, and focused dialogue with the administration. The Founding Fathers deliberately did not try to construct a friction-free relationship between the executive and legislative branches. A modicum of inter-branch contentiousness is both inevitable and desirable, just as limited intra–executive branch adversarial tensions tend to keep everyone involved a little more alert and articulate. Still, respect by key officials in one branch about the rights and prerogatives of the other branch generates the goodwill that can make inter-branch relations work relatively smoothly.

Prior consultations concerning evolving administration trade policies and negotiating positions do more than inform and flatter Congress. They can also serve to accommodate extreme congressional dissatisfaction, curb criticism and delaying tactics on the floors of the House and Senate, and reduce the likelihood of an unexpected congressional rejection of supporting laws or treaties. The harmony that characterized passage of the Trade Act of 1974 even in the midst of the Watergate controversy is proof of how well the two branches can work together. A similar experience occurred in the drafting of the Trade Agreements Act of 1979. If senior administration officials are sensitive to Capitol Hill sentiments, especially with respect to import policy, Congress will not be brushed off as it was in the 1984–1985 period. The Reagan administration dangerously incited congressional anger when it first refused to alter trade and exchange rate policies and then opposed passage of new trade legislation.

Creation of the proposed DICP and the DIT would enable the executive branch to make clearer to Congress (and everyone else) where specific responsibilities and jurisdictions are assigned. Although legislative and oversight hearings are useful and informative, there is something to be said for periodic closed-door, informal communications between the two branches. This would provide relief from the inevitable role posturing required by both sides when they are in the public spotlight.

The presence of members of Congress and their senior staff as observers in U.S. delegations to major international trade negotiations has been an excellent vehicle for allowing the legislative branch to be in on the take-off as well as the landing of trade agreements. This process should become a permanent fixture in U.S. trade relations.

Congress should severely cut back the number and length of annual reports on international economic relations required of executive branch agencies. In return, the White House economic policy coordinating group should submit a comprehensive international economic policy report on an annual basis. It would be sent to all committees with major jurisdiction. Oversight hearings on the report could be held on a combined committee basis in both houses. Explaining policies and analyzing major economic trends would impose the discipline on executive policymakers of rethinking their strategies while subjecting them to congressional and public review.

Congress should move toward two- to three-year authorizations and appropriations for the two capital-intensive parts of international economic policy: foreign assistance and the Export-Import Bank. In return for a relatively small loss in congressional control, programs that are a relatively small part of the overall federal budget could be planned on a longer-term basis.

ISSUE-SPECIFIC PROCEDURAL CHANGES

A number of more narrowly focused procedural reforms are needed. In a more limited way, they would strengthen the U.S. international economic policymaking process and from time to time enhance the quality, consistency, and clarity of policy substance.

Retaining Key Personnel

The U.S. government is still lagging in efforts to retain its most productive personnel. This should be corrected. Higher salaries and annual financial bonuses for especially meritorious performances are needed. A career corps of trade negotiators should be established to maximize the talent and institutional memory of the proposed new trade department. Highly rated members of this group should receive material incentives to remain in government service. A major objective of the new corps should be to discourage the ''revolving door'' system, whereby negotiators leave USTR and become consultants and lobbyists for the same foreign governments and corporations with whom they had negotiated on behalf of the U.S. government.

Updating U.S. Embassy Staffing

The allocation of staff in most U.S. embassies does not reflect either the end of the cold war or the increased role of economics in foreign policy and national security. Fewer political and military officers and more specialists in economics and export promotion would make embassies better able to meet the present and future needs of the United States. The national interest cannot be best served when 42 professionals are dealing with political and military matters in the U.S. embassy in Brazil, the largest economy by far in Latin America, and only six Americans are doing commercial work.[4]

Government–Private Sector Relations

Better communication between government and business, labor, farmers, consumers, and non-governmental organizations (NGOs) could be fostered in four ways:

- The DICP, State Department, and the international bureaus of the major domestic-oriented economic policy departments should establish a liaison office to act as a clearly designated contact for business people with questions or problems.

- The same agencies (plus the Environmental Protection Agency) should assign one or two mid-level officers to serve as liaison with NGOs. Their job would be to listen to the ideas of these groups and keep them informed of government activities affecting their interests. These officials also should monitor NGO publications and web sites and prepare clarifications or corrections as necessary.

- Semiannual government briefings on international economic policy matters should be held with private sector groups and NGOs on a regional basis in the Northeast, South, Midwest, and Far West. These briefings would be conducted by senior-level personnel of the departments concerned with international economic affairs.

- The now extremely limited personnel exchange program between the private sector and the federal government should be expanded in the area of international economic policy. Care must be taken to assure that objectives are carefully thought through, good positions made available, and career benefits accrue to government officials who have a one to two-year tour of duty in the private sector, and vice versa. A more extensive use of ''borrowed'' businesspersons by the domestic and overseas branches of the U.S. and Foreign Commercial Service would seem an especially good place to maximize communications between official export promotion efforts and private sector expertise.

Strengthening the International Trade Commission

Although relatively unknown ''outside the Beltway,'' the International Trade Commission (ITC) is an independent, bipartisan fact-finding and advisory agency whose principal ongoing function is determining whether American companies are being injured by imports (see Chapter 3). The ITC's impact on U.S. trade relations is significant enough that greater efforts are needed to assure that the six sitting commissioners are nominated and confirmed more on the basis of professional competence and less on the basis of political connections and Capitol Hill experience. As discussed above, a public discussion should be conducted about the relative merits of the commission's jurisdiction being expanded to include investigations into the existence of foreign dumping and foreign government subsidization of exports. This authority would be a logical addition to its existing responsibility for what are known as Section 337 investigations, a third category of unfair foreign trade practices usually involving allegations of patent and trademark violations.

The professional staffs of three of the ITC's offices—Economics, Industries, and Tariff Affairs and Trade Agreements—should be enlarged to enable them to increase their output of analytical studies. Their published research on the whole has a reputation for objectivity, technical merit, and thoroughness. These merits are directly related to an atmosphere of relative objectivity found in an independent governmental agency with no policy responsibilities to exercise and no specific constituency to represent. The capabilities of the commission's economists and business specialists are a major untapped resource that should play an important role in the needed enhancement of the U.S. government's knowledge of such key trade issues as U.S. international competitiveness on an industry-by-industry basis, the economic impact on American industries of other countries' industrial and trade policies, the effects of specific U.S. import barriers, and the anticipated effects of international trade agreements nearing completion. The ITC also is an ideal agency to prepare evaluations of existing international trade and investment policies.

Research, Analysis, and Policy Evaluation

Improvements in the information-gathering and analysis functions can contribute to better policies by assuring that policymakers get relevant data quickly and in the forms desired. The White House economic policy coordinating council is in the best position to oversee an executive branch–wide international economic research, analysis, and policy evaluation function that is responsive to the current needs of policymakers but also is able to look ahead in the effort to discern emerging trends and formulate new policy strategies. More attention should be given to longer-term strategic thinking because far too much of policymakers' time and energy has been devoted to extinguishing unexpected fires requiring immediate attention.

Coordinating Development Policies

U.S. economic policies toward less developed countries and countries in economic transition continue to proliferate without any integrating strategy. Bilateral and multilateral foreign programs have grown in number. Large-scale private capital flows into and out of the so-called emerging markets have given rise to global financial contagion, arguably the most serious international economic problem of the late 1990s. Many LDCs have become major actors in the international trading system. Nevertheless, there is scant effort to coordinate the numerous North-South economic policies conducted by various U.S. departments and agencies. This shortcoming could best be corrected by an informal coordinating group convened by the aforementioned White House economic policy council. The current disjointed nature of U.S. policymaking in this sector increases the likelihood of ineffectiveness and inconsistency in U.S. economic relations with the countries of the South.

The job of the Agency for International Development (AID) is to disburse development grants to those countries that both need them and have domestic policies in place that are compatible with promoting economic growth. Foreign policy objectives should be distant considerations in making these disbursements. AID therefore should remain independent and not be incorporated into the Department of State.

Department of State Incentives

Opportunities for advancement to the Foreign Service's top echelons—career ministers and ambassadors to major countries—should be as open to economics specialists as they are to political officers, traditionally the State Department's power elite. While this notion of equality technically exists, the department's culture does not always ensure that it is practiced. Ideally, the culture of the State Department should be irrevocably reprogrammed in order to respect the increased importance of economic factors in determining the global role of the United States. Without this appreciation, State risks further diminution of its influence in the international economic policymaking process because it is often perceived as being interested only in improving political relations with other countries.

POSTSCRIPT

International economic policy must be intellectually liberated from the shadows of foreign policy and domestic economic policy management. It is a policy area that can never escape its mixed heritage of economics and politics, but it is one that can and must demand respect for its distinctiveness. The process by which it is made should be custom-fitted to accommodate its unique nature and its growing importance. As the saying goes, all politics is local. But economics is increasingly global. International economic relations overlap both phenomena.

Americans and the world can ill-afford to allow the U.S. government's international economic policy machinery to grow obsolete while operating at half-speed. This policy should be made not by roving gangs of freelance operators, but by people who appreciate the seamless web of domestic and external economics and politics that international economic policy has become. There is no guarantee that any reorganization, even one that exactly replicates the recommendations in this chapter, would improve policy. But guarantees are not a precondition to addressing obvious weaknesses. Better organization and procedures can provide a greater probability of achieving the best and most consistent policy possible.

In an interview conducted during preparation of the first edition of this book, a Senate Finance Committee professional staff member recounted his frustrations in trying to determine firsthand what the international economic policies of the United States were, how they were being made, and by what means the executive branch agencies were coordinating their efforts. The quest for understanding was a complete bust. Contradictions and equivocations were the norm in his meetings, not specifics about policy substance and process. The policymaking process is not as disorganized today. However, it is still not good enough to dismiss completely the analogy made by this staff member to sum up his procession of unproductive interviews. He likened it to peeling off the leaves of a large artichoke and finding no heart. At the core, he said, "nothing was there."

The adoption of the new organization and procedures advocated in this book would help to assure that the international economic policymaking process of the United States displays heart, as well as a brain and a backbone.

NOTES

1. Although the term "Department of International Trade and Investment" is often used, I strongly prefer the "Department of International Commercial Policy." This is primarily because the former's acronym, DITI, rhymes with MITI. It suggests at least a partial effort to create a U.S. version of Japan's Ministry of International Trade and Industry. This is not my intention because a powerful and lavishly funded trade and industry department is neither compatible with American tradition nor needed.

2. Some have advocated the middle-ground creation of a U.S. international trade *agency*. This would be mainly a symbolic change and not something advocated here.

3. "Global Competition—The New Reality, Report of the President's Commission on Industrial Competitiveness," vol. I (Washington, D.C.: U.S. Government Printing Office, 1985), p. 22.

4. Data source: Transcript of remarks by the then–Under Secretary of Commerce, Jeffrey Garten, to the Institute for International Economics, 13 October 1995.

Index

About the Author

STEPHEN D. COHEN is Professor of International Relations at the American University's School of International Service in Washington, D.C., where he specializes in international trade and financial policies. Prior to joining the faculty in 1975, he served as a senior staff member for the White House–Congressional Commission on the Organization of the Government for the Conduct of Foreign Policy. Previously he had been an international economist at the U.S. Treasury Department and served as the Chief Economist at the U.S.-Japan Trade Council from 1969 to 1973. He was a Visiting Fulbright Scholar at the London School of Economics for the 1981–1982 academic year. Among Dr. Cohen's books are *International Monetary Reform, 1964–69: The Political Dimension* (Praeger, 1970); *Cowboys and Samurai: Why the United States Is Losing the Industrial Battle and Why It Matters* (1991); *Fundamentals of U.S. Foreign Trade Policy: Economics, Politics, Laws, and Issues* (1996, with Joel R. Paul and Robert A. Blecker); and *An Ocean Apart: Explaining Three Decades of U.S.-Japanese Trade Frictions* (Praeger, 1998).

ISBN 0-275-96503-1

9 780275 965044

90000>

EAN